Linguistic Human Rights

O
H
A
O'
/

Linguistic Human Rights
Overcoming Linguistic Discrimination

Edited by
Tove Skutnabb-Kangas
Robert Phillipson

in collaboration with
Mart Rannut

Mouton de Gruyter
Berlin · New York 1995

Mouton de Gruyter (formerly Mouton, The Hague)
is a Division of Walter de Gruyter & Co., Berlin.

This work originally appeared as volume 67 of the series
Contributions to the Sociology of Language.

∞ Printed on acid-free paper which falls within the guidelines of
the ANSI to ensure permanence and durability

Library of Congress Cataloging-in-Publication Data

Linguistic human rights : overcoming linguistic discrimination /
   edited by Tove Skutnabb-Kangas, Robert Phillipson, in
   collaboration with Mart Rannut.
       p.   cm.
   An appendix includes extracts from selected UN and
regional documents covering linguistic human rights, proposals for such, and resolutions on language rights.
   Includes bibliographical references and index.
   ISBN 3-11-014878-1
   1. Linguistic minorities — Government policy. 2. Language policy. 3. Human rights. 4. Language and education. I. Skutnabb-Kangas, Tove. II. Phillipson, Robert.
III. Rannut, Mart, 1959 —   .
P119.315.L55   1995
306.4'49 — dc20   95-11298
                                         CIP

Die Deutsche Bibliothek — Cataloging-in-Publication Data

Linguistic human rights : overcoming linguistic discrimination /
ed. by Tove Skutnabb-Kangas ; Robert Phillipson in collab.
with Mart Rannut. — Berlin ; New York : Mouton de Gruyter,
1995
   ISBN 3-11-014878-1
NE: Skutnabb-Kangas, Tove [Hrsg.]

Contents

Introduction

Robert Phillipson — Mart Rannut —
Tove Skutnabb-Kangas[1]

The papers in this volume serve to establish the contours and scope of the concept of *Linguistic Human Rights (LHRs)* through theoretically oriented papers and descriptions of experience in a number of countries. The book brings together *language* and *human rights*, topics which are seldom merged, and politically sensitive and inextricably interwoven with power structures. The book represents an effort to create conceptual clarity and to map out an area which is hitherto relatively uncharted. LHRs are still not a coherently defined topic, despite work in international law, the social sciences and humanities, all of which are represented in this volume. The need for multidisciplinary clarification is urgent in view of the obvious importance of language as a means of social control, and abundant evidence that language is often a factor in the mediation of social injustice. As many of the papers show, it is common for people to be deprived of their linguistic human rights. The rapid growth of language professionals in applied linguistics, minority education, language planning, and the sociology of language means that much more attention is being paid in the contemporary world to devising structures which respect the multilingual reality in our midst. Human rights have become a major concern of the international community and governments worldwide. The role of language in ensuring a greater observance of human rights needs to be addressed. The challenge to lawyers, politicians and language professionals is to see how a human rights perspective can support efforts to promote linguistic justice.

What are linguistic human rights and why are they important? Why are linguistic human rights needed for all?

Linguistic rights should be considered basic human rights. Linguistic majorities, speakers of a dominant language, usually enjoy all those linguistic human rights which can be seen as fundamental, regardless of how they are defined. Most linguistic minorities in the world do not enjoy these rights. It is only a few hundred of the world's 6–7,000 languages that have any kind of official status, and it is only speakers of official languages who enjoy *all* linguistic human rights.

Observing LHRs implies at an *individual* level that everyone can identify positively with their mother tongue, and have that identification respected by others, irrespective of whether their mother tongue is a minority language or a majority language. It means the right to learn the mother tongue, including at least basic education through the medium of the mother tongue, and the right to use it in many of the (official) contexts exemplified below. It means the right to learn at least one of the official languages in one's country of residence. It should therefore be normal that teachers are bilingual. Restrictions on these rights may be considered an infringement of fundamental LHRs.

Observing LHRs implies at a *collective* level the right of minority groups to exist (i. e. the right to be "different" — see Hettne 1987 and Miles 1989). It implies the right to enjoy and develop their language and the right for minorities to establish and maintain schools and other training and educational institutions, with control of curricula and teaching in their own languages. It also involves guarantees of representation in the political affairs of the state, and the granting of autonomy to administer matters internal to the groups, at least in the fields of culture, education, religion, information, and social affairs, with the financial means, through taxation or grants, to fulfil these functions (see UN Human Rights Fact Sheet 18, Minority Rights; Alfredsson 1991, and Leontiev, this volume). Restrictions on these rights may also be considered an infringement of fundamental LHRs.

The principle underlying the concept of universal human rights is that individuals and groups, irrespective of where they live, are entitled to norms which no state can be justified in restricting or violating. But not all human rights are a question of the death penalty, torture, or arbitrary imprisonment. Often individuals and groups are treated unjustly and suppressed by means of language. People who are deprived of LHRs may thereby be prevented from enjoying other human rights, including fair political representation, a fair trial, access to education, access to information and freedom of speech, and maintenance of their cultural heritage. There is therefore a need to formulate, codify and implement minimal standards for the enjoyment of LHRs. These should be an integral part of international and national law.

Applied linguists, teachers and other language professionals who are involved in the task of creating optimal conditions for the learning and use of languages have a special responsibility to see in what ways an awareness of the multiple dimensions of LHRs can be harnessed to this task. This may involve unmasking the false arguments used by educational administrators (Cummins, this volume), educational language planning for multilingual societies at the state and local authority levels (Leontiev, this volume) or at school level (Gibbons et al, this volume).

Who has and who does not have linguistic human rights? Why do minorities not have linguistic human rights?

Despite the good intentions of drafters of covenants, from the United Nations Charter onwards, and the ratification of them by member states, there are still major social inequalities where linguistic injustice appears to be a relevant factor. Many of the papers in this anthology document this.

Since the groups who do not enjoy full linguistic human rights today — regardless of how these are defined — are mostly minorities, minority rights overlap substantially with linguistic rights.

According to Alfredsson, of the UN Center for Human Rights in Geneva (1991, in a survey article on minority rights, their formulation and implementation), it is governments who should be blamed for their reluctance to set standards for the treatment of minorities or to guarantee them the kind of special protection that the position of minorities requires.

Because of the structure of international organisations, which represent states, the predicament of many groups, such as the Armenians, Basques, Berbers, Kurds, Roma, Tamils and West-Irians, has gone largely unnoticed (Alfredsson 1991: 34), and to some extent been excluded from access to the human rights system. It is a serious weakness that the complaints procedures under international law, for instance to various UN bodies, do not apply collectively, but are restricted to submissions from individuals.

When we affirm categorically that *all* individuals and groups should enjoy universal LHRs, this claim needs to be seen in the light of the political reality of unequal access to power. Most linguistic majorities seem reluctant to grant "their" minorities rights, especially linguistic and cultural rights, because they would rather see their minorities assimilated (see Grin, this volume, on the "tolerability" of the majority group). But this antagonism towards linguistic minorities is based on false premises, and in particular on *two myths*, that monolingualism is desirable for economic growth, and that minority rights are a threat to the nation state.

The myth that monolingualism is desirable for economic growth

In many nation states the (uneven) distribution of power and resources is partly along linguistic and ethnic lines, with majority groups taking a larger share than their numbers would justify. A comparison between states with different linguistic policies shows a certain correlation between poverty and multilingualism: "monolingual" (Western) states tend to be richer than multilingual non-Western states. This has been interpreted, by those who think that the correlation represents a causal relationship, as meaning that multilingual states should strive towards monolingualism if they want to improve their economies — monolingualism makes operations (industry, education, information, etc) more efficient. This inevitably involves the assimilation of minorities, i. e. no rights for minority languages, and support for activities and education in the majority language for minorities. In fact the relationship between multilingualism and poverty is *not* a causal one, as Joshua Fishman has shown in a thorough study of some 120 states (1989). Besides, monolingualism in a multilingual state is uneconomical and violates LHRs (see e.g. Pattanayak 1988).

National unity and territorial integrity — the myth that minority rights are a threat to the nation state

Linguistic and cultural rights are central for maintaining and reproducing a minority group *as a distinct group*. Thus the exercise of linguistic and cultural rights by minorities is often seen by majorities as preventing the minorities from assimilating into what majorities call the "mainstream" society. Many dominant groups see the mere existence of (unassimilated) minorities as a threat to the (nation) state. According to the conventional nation state ideology, the ideal state is homogenous, consists of one nation/ethnic group only, and has one language. Fostering diversity is necessarily seen as a threat to the political unity and territorial integrity of a state: at some point, so the argument goes, the minorities will themselves start striving towards this "natural", ideal political organisation, a nation state of their own. Granting linguistic and cultural rights will lead to quests for autonomy and independence (first culturally, then economically and politically), and in the end to the disintegration of the nation state. It is also in this light that we need to see the fairly absolute refusal to grant im/migrants any linguistic and cultural rights which might support them in developing into new national minorities.

The disintegration of Yugoslavia is attributable to many factors, but one significant element in the build-up to the wars of 1990–92 was the refusal of Belgrade/Serbia/centralising forces to accept the cultural demands of minorities such as the Slovenes and the Kosova Albanians (Klopčič 1992). The same pattern occurred vis-à-vis the Serbian minority in Croatia.

The Yugoslav catastrophe confirms that "internal suppression of minority issues does not work; assimilation has been attempted and it inevitably fails. Minorities do not simply disappear; they may appear dormant for a while, but history tells us that they stay on the map. Nationalism and the drive to preserve identities are strong forces and they apply in equal measure to nation-states and to minorities" (Alfredsson 1991: 39).

"National experience teaches us that the recognition of and respect for special minority rights are viable alternatives to oppression and neglect", Alfredsson continues. Some states have of course accepted the validity of demands for LHRs from (some) ethnic minority groups, mostly in cases where this step is not regarded as posing a threat to the integrity of the state (small groups, non-territorial groups, groups which have not voiced secessionist demands, etc, see for instance Kāretu on the Māori in New Zealand and Magga on the Sámi in Norway, in this volume), or where NOT granting rights might lead to secession (e.g. rights to French in Canada). Some traditional national minorities also have or are starting to acquire linguistic rights. But the overall impression is still one of many states wanting to be *seen* as doing something rather than in fact committing themselves fully. This is reflected in how the rights have been formulated in universal or European covenants, with a combination of on the one hand "legitimate" flexibility and on the other many escape clauses which often substantially undermine the rights.

The gulf between the good intentions expressed in preambles of international or regional documents and the de facto dearth of LHRs can thus be understood as symptomatic of the tension between on the one hand a genuine wish on the part of the (nation) state to secure (or give the impression of securing) human rights to minorities, and on the other hand the (nation) state believing that granting human rights, especially linguistic and cultural human rights, to minorities, is decisive for reproducing these minorities as minorities, which may lead to the disintegration of the state. It is not very likely that any state would voluntarily work towards its own fragmentation.

Since many states "have problems" with their own minorities, i. e. do not treat them in a way consistent with all minority and general rights in human rights treaties, they are often reluctant to criticize other states' treatment of *their* minorities. It is possible, Hettne claims (1987: 85), that many nation states, with motives connected to both domestic and foreign policies in fact support an escalation of ethnic conflict up to a certain level — and this includes violation of the basic LHRs of minorities.

Minorities cannot, on the other hand, "take" rights themselves, just by proclaiming them. The rights need validation from the state where the minorities live. This can only be a achieved in a negotiation process, where minorities are almost inevitably the weaker party. The alternative, when negotiation fails, is for a minority community to hope that other states will recognize their viability. Slovenia achieved this, as did Croatia and later Bosnia, but without war being prevented. The Yugoslav fragmentation process showed clearly that the international community is extremely unsure how such disputes should be handled. Language is of course only one dimension in such conflict, but not one that can be ignored. It is imperative to take into account the relative power and status of speakers of languages ("symmetry", as Grin calls it, this volume). There is an urgent need for a clarification of how (speakers of) threatened languages can be supported (see Annamalai 1993) without this being perceived as undermining the position of the majority group or the integrity of the state.

What happens if people do not get linguistic human rights? Language and ethnic conflict

"Interethnic cooperation and solidarity" between groups with different languages, "peaceful coexistence", is "at least as common and persistent as interethnic conflicts", according to Rodolfo Stavenhagen (1990: 39). But when conflict occurs, *language* is in many situations one of several factors *separating* the parties. In other conflicts, the parties *share a language* but differ on other counts. Bosnians shared a language with Serbs and Croats, but this did not prevent war. Thus there is no necessary *correlational relationship* between conflict and differences of language.

But when difference of language coincides with conflict, does language play a *causal* role?

In the first place, differences of language can*not* in most contexts be said to "cause" war or even inter-ethnic conflict. "If and when ethnic hostility or rivalry occurs, there is generally a specific historical reason for it that relates to *political struggles over resources and power*" is Stavenhagen's assessment (1990: 39). However, even if

> ... the economic factor is seldom absent in ethnic conflict, it does *not* usually constitute any kind of triggering factor. Existential problems in a deeper sense are involved. The hatred that an ethnic group can develop against another group probably has less to do with competition per se and more with the risk of having to give up something of oneself, one's identity, in the struggle... It is therefore more a question of survival in a cultural rather than a material sense ... The horror of ethnocide is a more basic impulse than the struggle to reap economic benefits at the expense of another group, ...

Björn Hettne claims (1987: 66–67). "To sum up, the problem is not that ethnic groups are different, but rather *the problem arises when they are no longer allowed to be different*, i. e. when they subjectively experience a threat to their own identity, a risk of ethnocide. This is a fundamental cause behind the politicising of ethnic identity" (Hettne 1987: 67).

Without supporting crude forms of primordialism or instrumentalism (see below), we see *lack* of linguistic rights as one of the causal factors in certain conflicts, and linguistic affiliation as a rightful mobilizing factor in conflicts with multiple causes where power and resources are unevenly distributed along linguistic and ethnic lines.

Language is for most ethnic groups one of the most important cultural core values (Smolicz 1979, and this volume). A threat to an ethnic group's language is thus a threat to the cultural and linguistic survival of the group. Lack of linguistic rights often prevents a group from achieving educational, economic and political equality with other groups. Injustice caused by *failure to respect linguistic human rights* is thus in several ways one of the important factors which can contribute to inter-ethnic conflict − and often does.

This means that we see language-related issues as potential causes of conflict *only* in situations where groups lack linguistic rights *and/or* political/economic rights, and where the unequal distribution of political and/or economic power follows linguistic and ethnic lines. Granting linguistic rights to minorities reduces conflict potential, rather than creating it.

In the ongoing work for LHRs a number of conceptual issues need clarification. The papers in the first section of the book pursue central issues in LHRs, but some of the key concepts and distinctions which are to a large extent problematic in most work on human rights will be presented here.

Some important problems and distinctions in analysing, formulating and implementing linguistic human rights

Are there hierarchies of languages, language rights, and implementation?

In international law, human rights are regarded as indivisible and presupposing each other, so that in principle there can be no hierarchy of human rights: they are implicitly equal. The only "absolute" right which the state ought not to constrain in any way is the right to life (though use of the death penalty in the majority of the countries in the world shows that not even this right is inalienable — see Shelton 1987 for a short history of current moves to make it so). In practice it seems that a three-tier system has emerged in the UN Human Rights Committee's work on clarifying the scope of rights: there is a top layer of "hard core" rights which do not admit any derogation (the right to life, prohibition of torture and slavery, and freedom of religion), the bottom layer permits restrictions in the enjoyment of certain rights in specific cases (e.g. in relation to the rights of freedom of movement, of association and to peaceful assembly). The rest presumably fall into an intermediate category (see Centre for Human Rights publication HR/PUB/91/6, 20). But where do language rights come in? Are there also hierarchies of languages, language rights, and of beneficiaries of language rights?

Hierarchies of languages: primordialism or instrumentalism?

While we acknowledge the great importance of languages to their speakers, especially the importance of a mother tongue, we want to distance ourselves from uncritical primordialism and anthropomorphism in our conceptualisation of (the importance of) languages, and from harsh instrumentalism. Primordialists in general see the mother tongue as something that one "inherits" with one's mother's milk (in the sense of not having *chosen* to learn it). It is ascribed not acquired, almost in the same sense as skin colour. A crude form of primordialism would also conceptualise language in an anthropomorphic, "biologized" way, as an organism with a life of its own, more or less despite the speakers. Some languages can then be labelled as more logical, rich, beautiful or developed than others, and then hierarchized on the basis of "their" presumed characteristics. Views of this kind do not have any basis in reality: all natural languages are complex, logical systems, capable of developing and expressing everything, provided that enough resources can be used for their cultivation. There is thus no basis for the hierarchization of languages (except in terms of the more "technical" results of unequal resources accorded to them earlier). In an overstated version this view can be (and has been) used to support hierarchizations of people under the cover of hierarchization of languages, ethnoses (ethnic groups) and cultures, which can lead to genocide.

In contrast to primordialism, instrumentalists see language as acquired and manipulable, something that an individual or group can take on and off more or less at will. According to instrumentalists, emphasis on language by an ethnic group serves to mobilise the group for the purpose of economic/political or other benefits. In this mobilisation the (elites in the) group use all the characteristics of the group which are effective as mobilising factors, including language. In this view of things, language in itself is of no special importance, it only has an instrumental value. It can also be used to divert people's attention away from the "real" problems (which are seen as economic and political).

The importance of these distinctions for LHRs relates to hierarchies of languages (the idea of which can be supported with a crude form of primordialism and anthropomorphism) and the role of language in ethnic conflict (where harsh instrumentalism does not recognise the genuine feelings of deep attachment to mother tongues but sees the expression of these feelings as proof of successful manipulation by elites). We regard the *sources* of linguistic identification as primordial, but the *manifestations* as contextual. Identification with a mother tongue, the need to develop the language, and related concerns are equally important for speakers of *all* languages, regardless of number of speakers, citizenship, etc. Thus languages cannot be hierarchized for purposes of assessing their speakers' need of LHRs.

Hierarchies of language rights: rights to mother tongues, second languages, foreign languages

Language learning generally follows a chronological sequence. The language of the *close community and primary, ethnolinguistic identity*, the **mother tongue**, is learned first. The next comes a language of *national integration*, a **second language** for linguistic minorities, a **second variety** (in the sociolinguistic sense of particular registers) for linguistic majorities, and finally languages of *"wider communication"* beyond the confines of the state, i. e. **foreign languages** (Ngalasso 1990: 17). In the case of those whose mother tongue happens to be a standard variety of an internationally dominant language, these three types will be conflated to a single language, so that the learner adds different registers rather than different languages. Granted that languages are often learned sequentially, one might postulate that rights in relation to these languages represent a hierarchy from most important to least important. As a result, being prevented from enjoying LHRs can be seen as graver in relation to languages learned earlier in one's socialisation, and might have more serious consequences for the individual's development, access to education and access to other human rights. This hierarchization of rights might implicitly serve to hierarchize the languages too, the mother tongue being the most important.

Hierarchies of implementation of language rights

Both the existence of LHRs and, especially, the degree to which they are implemented in practice, are inextricably interwoven with the question of the collective political status of each linguistic group — are they autochthonous or indigenous, national majorities or minorities, territorial or non-territorial, or (recent) immigrants? As the goal of human rights is to maintain and protect humane values, they recognize the right to identity as a cultural characteristic of both minorities and majorities. The right to self-determination is a basic principle in international law, aimed at recognizing the right of peoples (not only states) to determine their own political, economic and cultural destiny, possibly within their own sovereign state, and hence avoid being assimilated. There are no specific instruments of international law that specify how the right to self-determination should be implemented, but the principle has been recognized as universally valid since the nineteenth century and was widely used in the period of decolonization. States have been reluctant to apply the principle, as the experience of the Eritreans, Kurds, Namibians and Palestinians, among others, shows.

The right of *peoples* to self-determination dovetails with the implementation of LHRs. In the contemporary world, several minority groups (like the Catalans and Basques) are involved in comprehensive linguistic normalization processes within a framework of autonomy, one of the forms that self-determination can take. For autonomy, whatever it is labelled (self-government, self-management, home rule, etc), the essential element is that a central government is willing to share and delegate power, so as to respect local wishes and needs. This is stipulated in the UN Declaration on Indigenous Rights (see Appendix), the model for which is the Danish home rule legislation for Greenland, by which responsibility for education, land and housing, economic affairs, etc is passed on, whereas foreign affairs, defence and monetary affairs remain the business of the central (Danish) government. The European Charter for Regional and Minority Languages extends the principle of autonomy to non-territorial minorities (see Skutnabb-Kangas — Phillipson, this volume), but leaves it up to the state to decide which minorities the rights should apply to.

Another set of problems relates to the role of foreign powers in connection with the implementation of LHRs. As the relevant implementation principles are largely implicit, any accusation that a state is not observing LHRs principles can be construed as interference in the affairs of a sovereign state. Equally, because of the vagueness of LHRs criteria, a state may use or misuse them in order to pursue its own political goals. This happened when Russia accused the Baltic states of human rights abuses in the early 1990s, in particular of depriving Russian-speakers of LHRs (see Rannut's paper, this volume). The UN investigated these complaints and played a key role in attempting to prevent such inter-state confrontations from escalating. In such contexts, where LHRs have a high profile, action is needed at the highest international level.

Are linguistic human rights individual rights or collective rights or both? Is there a contradiction? Who are the beneficiaries of collective LHRs?

One of the long-standing unresolved human rights issues is whether they relate to the individual or to the group. Linguistic human rights can be regarded as having *both* dimensions, one primarily *individual*, another primarily *collective*. The first involves *continuity* from one generation to the next over time. It is therefore a linguistic human right to acquire the

cultural heritage of preceding generations, initially in primary socialization in the family and close community. The second involves *cooperation*
between individuals, binding together a group, a people, a population of
a country, through sharing the languages and cultures of all.

The first element involves the right to a native language (or languages;
there may be more than one), the right to learn it, the right to have it
developed in formal schooling through being taught through the medium
of it, and the right to use it. By its nature this right is personal and
individual. It therefore is inherent in everyone, even those who leave their
community of origin and migrate or flee to another country or community. The *developmental,* diachronic learning aspect of this right relates
particularly (but not only) to the child, whereas the right to use a native
language concerns everybody, regardless of age.

The second element is *contemporary,* synchronic, and focusses more
on humans as social beings. It grants everyone the right to participate in
the riches provided by the social environment, through learning the
official language(s) of the environment, locally, regionally and nationally.
This part involves the right to be taught and to learn the official lan-
guage(s) of the country. This also implies the right to learn those *varieties*
of the language(s) of the environment that enable everyone to participate
fully in the cultural, economic and political processes of the country. This
right is a *collective* right (even if the learning itself still happens in
individuals).

As Hamel's paper on the rights of Amerindian indigenous peoples
shows, the evidence is that a system of *individual* rights has not proved
adequate to provide support for such threatened peoples. Although autonomy can be both territorial (an area) and personal (for instance the
Sámi in Norway can run for and vote in elections for the Sámi Parliament
wherever they live), autonomy is also "by its very nature a *collective*
right. It is the collective entity which claims the right, enjoys it and
through its membership determines the form and structure of its administration. Similarly the group would lay claim to, and complain about
violations of, the right to autonomy at the inter-governmental level."
(Alfredsson 1991: 28). Many of the papers in this book probe into the
collective/individual dichotomy. But broadly speaking, *collective and individual LHRs presuppose and complement each other and are in no way
alternatives to each other.*

But if LHRs are seen as having collective beneficiaries too, these
collectivities have to be defined. The question of the definition of concepts
like *nations, peoples, indigenous peoples/minorities, tribals, national (eth-*

nic) minorities, (ethnic) groups, im/migrant minorities/groups has been one of the most tricky ones in the social sciences and international law. Despite many attempts (see e.g. Capotorti 1979; Andrýsek 1989), there is, for instance, still no commonly accepted definition of a *minority* for human rights purposes (see Skutnabb-Kangas — Phillipson, this volume).

"Ethnic" is notoriously difficult to define too. During the fairly long period in the social sciences when many researchers proclaimed that ethnicity was dead or at least dying, ethnicity was often seen by these "evolutionists" as a characteristic that only minorities possessed. Majorities were devoid of ethnicity. Ethnicity was seen as a somewhat primitive, traditional category which would disappear with modernization or socialism, with more functional categories like class or occupational group or more overarching identities like de-ethnicized national identities replacing it. Primordialist claims about ethnicity fulfilling deeply felt needs which neither the state nor other forms of organisation could satisfy seem to have been more realistic, judging by the upsurge of revitalisation movements.

Most *indigenous peoples* do not accept a minority label, whereas many *immigrant* groups strive towards being accepted as minorities. *Tribe* is by many seen as a negatively loaded term ("nations are tribes with an army, languages are dialects with an army"; "why are several million Zulus a tribe while 240,000 Icelanders are a nation?") whereas India's *"scheduled tribes"* are mostly included among *indigenous peoples*. *National minorities* (and *minority languages*) are difficult to define too, and it seems more than likely that both the European Commission of Human Rights and the European Court of Human Rights will have to determine the scope of these notions in relation to new European instruments on minorities and regional or minority languages. This also includes several terms used in the definitions themselves. Is around 400 years of use of a language enough, for instance, for the language to deserve the epithet "traditionally used"? In that case both Romani and Yiddish should be treated as those non-territorial languages that the European Charter for Regional of Minority Languages should apply to, in most European countries — but we suspect that most countries have not included them when ratifying the Charter.

Usually nations and peoples enjoy many more LHRs than national (ethnic) minorities, who in turn often have more rights than indigenous peoples/minorities and tribals. Those who are only (ethnic) groups usually have few LHRs, and im/migrant minorities/groups (and refugees) have almost none. Of course tourists could be even worse off, but that is generally a temporary, self-imposed inconvenience.

Khubchandani (this volume) also demonstrates that the reality of shifting linguistic identities in plural societies means that the concept *language* is itself inherently problematical. As a result, legal measures to enact and implement linguistic human rights can also pose new problems. A Unesco report of an international symposium on language rights in Pécs (1992) therefore sees concept clarification as vital for work on LHRs.

Beneficiary — duty-holder

There can be no beneficiary of a right unless there is a duty-holder. Traditionally, it was individual citizens who were entitled to enjoy human rights. As the history of the evolution of human rights shows, early formulations in the American and French declarations of the 18th century were those of the citizen of a state. Modern human rights do not presuppose a given status in the society like the property qualification which political rights depended on in most Western societies in the 19th century, or like the rights which excluded individuals on the basis of their gender or marital status.

It is the state which has the duty to create conditions in which individuals can enjoy their rights and to ensure/guarantee their enjoyment. Legislation is normative in the sense that its task is to promote the development of communities and individuals, resolve conflicts and protect interests, including human rights.

But it is not only the state that has duties. Many paragraphs of language rights or minority rights include formulations stating that these rights "should not be to the detriment of the official languages and the need to learn them" (this example is from the Preamble of the European Charter for Regional or Minority Languages). If, for instance, citizenship presupposes fulfilment of certain official language knowledge requirements, it is the duty of a citizen to know the official language (to some extent). The state then must make arrangements for this to be possible (which requires the allocation of resources to teacher training, curriculum development, etc), and its citizens are assumed to be willing to profit from such an arrangement, i. e. they have duties once the state shows evidence of performing *its* duties.

If the citizen in a multilingual state (i. e. virtually all states, including those that make up the European Community) is accorded a *right* to learn three or more languages, she or he may also have a *duty* to learn them — a point made by Leontiev in his paper.

One of the weaknesses of most covenants is that the nature of the duties that the rights presuppose is left unclear, as well as the specific obligations of the duty-holder. These obligations may be clarified by litigation.

Can the courts clarify the scope and interpretation of linguistic human rights? From non-discrimination to affirmative action

As the Universal Declaration of Human Rights states: "It is essential, if man is not to be compelled to have recourse, as a last resort, to rebellion against tyranny and oppression, that human rights should be protected by the rule of law."

To ensure enforcement of the law, the citizen may need recourse to the courts. In some countries, international covenants that the state has ratified become part of national law, meaning that litigation is in principle possible in the same way as if a litigant is seeking enforcement of a national law (see Turi's paper for examples of court cases in France and Canada). Litigation may play a significant role in clarifying the scope of LHRs.

One of the important issues that needs clarification through litigation is how far a state can be forced to take positive action on behalf of a minority language speaker. Since most international legally-binding treaties and covenants which mention language (e.g. Article 27 of the UN International Covenant on Civil and Political Rights, 1966) are formulated in a *negative* way, as non-discrimination prescriptions, court interpretations on whether any kind of affirmative action is needed in order for the right to be effective are of extreme importance. The prohibition of discrimination is not achieved by according "equal" rights to all. The right to a fair trial, for instance, may require interpretation, i. e. a special right for the members of the minority group. What minorities in fact need is affirmative action, probably over a prolonged period. Such "special rights" do not represent a privilege but merely a means to ensure equality of treatment.

If a child belonging to a minority "shall not be denied the right, in community with other members of his or her group ... to use his or her own language" (The UN Convention on the Rights of the Child, 1989, Art. 30), it would be important to clarify by litigation whether the state has to ensure this by taking *positive* measures. The European Court of Human Rights has so decreed in a comparable case (the Marckx case of 1979, as reported in Alston 1991: 5). An *affirmative obligation* on the part of the state could thus mean, for instance, that the state has the obligation to organise day care, pre-schools and schools so that minority children are not denied the right to use their languages, i. e. their languages should be the media of instruction.

It is also important to mention the European Court of Human Rights, to which the individual (from one of the relevant European countries) can address a claim. The court has pronounced on a wide range of human rights issues and at least two cases on language rights issues have been referred to it recently. Appeal to the UN Human Rights Committee is restricted to submissions by governments.

Time to include linguistic human rights in international law

The history of human rights shows that the concept of human rights is not static. It is constantly evolving in response to changed perceptions of how humans have their fundamental freedoms restricted, and the challenge to the international community to counteract injustice. The more recent UN covenants (for instance the Universal Declaration of the Rights of the Child of 1989) include clauses which aim more at implementation, at affirmative action (e.g. governments pledge themselves to "respect and ensure" the observance of the designated rights — see Alston 1991).

In many international fora, the UN, the ILO, the Council of Europe and the CSCE (the Helsinki process), there is considerable activity aimed at granting more rights to minorities and their languages, through developing various new conventions and recommendations. In these endeavours the following aspects are of central relevance:

WHICH GROUPS ARE SUCH RIGHTS TO APPLY TO, i. e. how will minorities be defined? Will immigrant minorities be covered or not? Immigrant minorities are mostly excluded in the definitions of who the rights are applicable to, and the only opportunity provided for some of them to become included under definitions in existing or draft multilateral agreements clauses is the Council of Europe's Commission for Democracy through Law, in its latest draft European Convention for the Protection of Minorities, Art. 2 (see the Appendix).

WHAT RIGHTS WILL BE COVERED? In the light of discussions at seminars under the auspices of Unesco about a Universal Declaration of LHRs, it appears that the most difficult question is the right to learn the mother tongue fully, and the right to teaching through the medium of the mother tongue. This is something majorities take for granted for themselves, but most of them are not willing to grant this to minorities. By contrast, most majorities are only too willing to approve of measures which grant minorities the right to learn the majority language, because these rights are seen as promoting the assimilation of minorities.

TO WHAT EXTENT WILL THE BASIC REQUIREMENTS that one should expect of a covenant of LHRs BE RESPECTED? The following points may be relevant:

— The rights have to be formulated explicitly, in a sufficiently specific and detailed way, so that difficulties of interpretation are minimized (see e.g. the critique of the European Charter, which has *not* been formulated in this way, in Skutnabb-Kangas — Phillipson in this volume).
— The rights have to be legally binding, not merely recommendations, and they must be incorporated into national law.
— The convention must specify whose duty it is to guarantee observance of the rights.
— The convention must specify whose financial responsibility it is to ensure implementation of the rights (also in situations where political changes imply territorial reorganisation).
— Both individuals and groups (as well as states) must have access to the complaints procedure, and must have the right to give evidence; the grounds for court decisions must be made public.

We would *not* wish to suggest that *linguistic rights* are anything *new*. They have long been explicitly legislated for in national constitutions and international covenants, and struggled for in political fora on all continents (as is clear from the historical account in our own article in this volume). Several principles in international law (including the right to identity, to a name — see Jernudd's article — and nationality) already dovetail with language rights and have been given expression in various covenants.

What *is* relatively new is the attempt to clarify *what should be regarded as inalienable, fundamental linguistic human rights*, to codify them and seek to promote them as a means to achieve greater social justice. Now is the time to include positive linguistic human rights fully in international law. Hopefully the contributions to this book can further this and assist in the struggle against the violation of linguistic human rights worldwide.

The section introductions summarize each paper and highlight key matters raised in them.

Notes

1. Many of the contributions to this book were initially papers given at the 9th AILA World Congress of Applied Linguistics held in Thessaloniki in April 1990. Others were given at a symposium on linguistic human rights in Tallinn, Estonia in October 1991, organized by Mart Rannut on behalf of the Estonian Language Board, the purpose of which was to collate worldwide experience in this area (see the Tallinn Declaration in the Appendix). The book has been edited in collaboration with Mart Rannut in that he has been involved in many of its phases, as well as having written the introduction with the two editors. Others whom we should like to record our thanks to are two anonymous reviewers and Mike Long.

Serhat and Gulda are Kurds from the Turkish part of Kurdistan who live in Denmark. They have just had their first child, Mizgin (which means "good tidings") and want to visit Turkey to show the grandchild to their parents. They need Mizgin's name to be added to their passports. The Turkish Embassy refuses to record the Kurdish name. Mizgin is over 3 years old before the Embassy agrees to do this, as a result of pressure from the Danish Helsinki Committee — and the grandparents have missed the first three years of the grandson's life, because Kurdish names are not allowed in Turkey. This is a question of linguistic human rights.

Johan Mathis Mikkelsen Gávppi, a Sámi from the Norwegian part of Sámiland, starts school as the only Sámi child in the school, at the age of seven. He only speaks and understands Sámi, and the teacher only speaks and understands Norwegian. The first Norwegian sentences his classmates teach him (when he is supposed to say the Lord's Prayer) are a crude obscenity about Our Father. *He* gets punished. He left school illiterate (see Skutnabb-Kangas — Phillipson 1989, chapter 10). This is a question of linguistic human rights.

A young Finnish immigrant in Sweden is hospitalized in Stockholm. He is in acute pain at night, despite being heavily drugged. He tries, tired and desperate, to explain his pain to the nurses but nobody understands Finnish. He jumps from a fifth floor window and dies. This is a question of linguistic human rights.

A school class in Guovdageaidnu/Kautokeino, a municipality with 90 percent Sámi speakers, wanted to organise a bazaar and wrote in Sámi to the police for permission. Their letter was returned with a note that it should be written in Norwegian, and their teacher was accused of using the pupils for her/his own political purposes. When the decision was questioned in Parliament, the Minister of Justice said that the police had followed the rules correctly (reported by Magga in the Danish daily paper *Information* on 12 October 1992). This is a question of linguistic human rights.

The electrical company Philips has officially forbidden employees at their factory in Denmark to speak anything but Danish on the premises (1990). Turkish women who do not know much Danish cannot talk to each other at all. When asked on TV about whether Philips guests from other countries were also asked to speak Danish on the premises, the director said that English of course was a completely different matter. This is a question of linguistic human rights.

A Sámi woman working on an oil tanker writes a letter to her mother in Norwegian — she has never learned how to write in her native language. The mother who does not know much Norwegian has to ask a neighbour to translate the letter, and her reply. They can communicate orally in Sámi, but transatlantic phone calls are expensive (see Magga's article in *Information* 12 October 1992). In one of the richest countries in the world, with officially a 100 per cent literacy rate, neither the mother nor the daughter have learned how to write their own language. This is a question of linguistic human rights.

A Kurdish mother in Diyarbakir visits her son in prison. The guard says that they have to speak Turkish to each other. The mother does not know any Turkish. This is a question of linguistic human rights.

"In Kenya, English became much more than a language: it was *the* language, and all the others had to bow before it in deference. Thus one of the most humiliating experiences was to be caught speaking Gikuyu in the vicinity of the school. The culprit was given corporal punishment — three to five strokes of the cane on bare buttocks — or was made to carry a metal plate around the neck with the inscription: I AM STUPID or I AM A DONKEY." (Ngũgĩ 1985: 112). This is a question of linguistic human rights.

Refugees in Denmark (and many other countries) with university degrees who read and write Arabic/Farsi/Tamil etc, are considered "illiterate" and have to be "alphabetized". This is a question of linguistic human rights.

According to a survey of medical doctors practising in Tallinn, Estonia in 1991/1992 undertaken by EMOR Ltd., doctors failed to understand the complaint in Estonian "I have a singing feeling in my ears" 50% of the time, and "a stinging, smarting pain" 45% of the time. When an Estonian patient referred to the "navel", 10% of the doctors thought it was the forehead, a shoulder blade or hip. 59% were unable to instruct the patient in Estonian how to take medicine on an empty stomach. This is a question of linguistic human rights.

In Kozmodemyansk, in the republic of Mari, Russia, there is a secondary school where all the schoolgoers are Maris except for just two Russians and one Bashkir. The language of instruction after the first five grades of primary school is Russian exclusively, and not Mari, the official language. This is a question of linguistic human rights.

In the Komi-Permian district of Russia, where the indigenous people make up more than 60% of the population, the language of education and administration is Russian. No translation is provided. This is a question of linguistic human rights.

Have you, dear reader, always been able to do the following in your mother tongue:
— address your teachers in school?
— deal with the tax office?
— answer a query from a police constable on the street?
— explain a medical problem to a nurse or doctor?
— write to a national newspaper?
— watch the local and national news on television?
— ask a question at a political meeting?
All these listed points and the boxed examples are a question of linguistic human rights.

I THE SCOPE OF LINGUISTIC HUMAN RIGHTS

Section introduction

FRANÇOIS GRIN's paper **Combining immigrant and autochthonous language rights: a territorial approach to multilingualism** probes into the criteria which should guide the allocation of language rights in a polity. His basic premises are that diversity is desirable, that all language groups should be accorded language rights, and that the allocation of rights to minority groups is in fact in the interest of all groups. (These are beliefs that are probably shared by all the contributors to this volume.) Grin's theoretical model addresses the question of rights for immigrant as well as all autochthonous groups, the need to take into account the relative power and status of languages (*"symmetry"*), the complicated issue of minorities being geographically interwoven (*"inclusion"*), and the dynamics of migration in the contemporary world. He discusses the relative merits of rights based on individuality and rights based on territoriality.

He also addresses the political reality of the antagonism of dominant groups to minorities, the reluctance to grant them rights. He wants to put in guarantees which make the granting of rights to minorities "tolerable" to majorities. The *"tolerability"* of minority rights is achieved by guaranteeing that people who form the linguistic majority in a state always get service in their own language, regardless of whether they "qualify" for it numerically in a certain area or not. His principles of territorial multilingualism (which demonstrate that it is false to equate territorialism with unilingualism) operate with a three-tier system of political power, at the state, provincial and local/municipal level.

While representing an explicit and innovative attempt to theorize so that all possible trilingual realities are envisaged, his paper draws on detailed familiarity with the Swiss and Canadian contexts (and warns against seeing these in too simplistic and rosy terms). It is an important contribution towards clarification of how threatened languages can be supported without this being perceived as undermining the position of the majority group or the integrity of the state.

However, as Grin himself points out, his concerns are theoretical (which does not mean that they are not eminently practical) and his model has not been empirically verified. It has to be expanded, in order to cope with more than 3 languages. In many local areas in most metropoles in the world there is not only one immigrant language that would qualify but several, unless the numbers needed for *"qualifying" for language rights* are set extremely high. In Stockholm, Sweden, for instance, 9 languages (as of December 1993) would "qualify" as official languages according to Grin's model, if the "qualifications" were, for instance, to follow the model from Finland referred to by Grin. This decrees that if the Swedish- or Finnish-speaking minority represents 8% of the population, or consists of at least 3,000 people in a given local authority, the authority is officially bilingual.

JOSHUA FISHMAN's paper **On the limits of ethnolinguistic democracy** probes into the reality behind official endorsements of multilingualism, exemplified by European Community (since November 1993 the European Union) pronouncements, to see what constraints there are on the use of languages in intra-state, sub-state and inter-state communication. Just as political democracy restricts individual rights, ethnolinguistic democracy can be constrained by factors of complexity and cost, and by "proportionality" or the results of functional differentiation (e.g. de facto "working languages" in international organizations). There are inconsistencies ("double standards") in government policy: the same state can frequently show a resistance to according linguistic rights to minorities within the state ("small" languages are not granted the same rights as the dominant official, "big" languages), whereas the same states, if they represent internationally "small" languages (such as Dutch or Danish) in an organization such as the EC, demand for themselves the same rights as the "big" languages, English and French. Hitherto such parity between languages has largely been granted in the EC. What policies will emerge, when the EC is expanded, is an open question, but limitations on language use are likely to be in conflict with officially declared approval of multilingualism and to constrain democratic participation.

Fishman shows that *ethnolinguistic democracy* is a far cry from *ethnolinguistic equality*. It is the smallest languages which are obliged to protest most vociferously about their lack of linguistic rights. A top-down democratic structure effectively marginalizes ethnolinguistic minority groups and forces them to re-linguify and re-ethnify. Fishman makes a passionate plea for members of the dominant group to understand and feel what language death involves (echoing Smolicz, this volume) and to oppose abuse of power as effectively domestically as they apparently do at the inter-state level.

ALEXEI LEONTIEV's paper **Linguistic human rights and educational policy in Russia** contains a concise presentation of the linguistic complexity of

Russia and current efforts to implement and plan an educational policy which respects linguistic human rights. Leontiev contributes to the clarification of the nature of LHRs, and specifically how they are the province of the *person*, the *ethnos* (and how these two interact), and the *state*. The latter has executive, regulative and stimulatory functions, and should aim to provide genuine support for each language and culture. In education this means creating conditions where several languages can be learned, the number and choice of these depending on whether the mother tongue is the state official language, a minority language, the sole language of inter-ethnic communication or one of several of these, and whether a choice of foreign languages is offered. With Russia in a phase of transition, and Russian playing a different role (cf Rannut's paper), the problems of implementing a policy which is essentially equitable are considerable.

Leontiev also stresses that *linguistic rights and linguistic duties presuppose each other*. The *state* has the *duty* to make the learning of three or more languages feasible, and must follow a principle of "parity" in curriculum organization for each language. The *individual* also has the linguistic *duty* to learn the mother tongue, an official or inter-ethnic language, and a foreign language within the educational system. Leontiev's solution is provocatively simple — and addresses several of the key questions discussed in the book. Instead of it being the state or the local authority that decides which languages are to function as media for teaching (the preferred solution in, e.g., the European Charter on Regional and Minority Languages — see Appendix), each ethnos has the right to organize schools or classes, through the medium of its own language, within the state educational system, in regions where this ethnos can guarantee the necessary numbers of students. It is the minority, not the state, which has the right to determine how such modifying terms as "sufficient numbers" should be interpreted (see Skutnabb-Kangas — Phillipson, this volume). Thus ethnolinguistic vitality can over-rule a reluctant state power.

TOVE SKUTNABB-KANGAS and ROBERT PHILLIPSON's paper on **Linguistic human rights, past and present** begins with a short historical review of linguistic rights over the past two centuries. The "universal" and major regional human rights covenants elaborated in recent decades are then assessed, to see how far their provisions ensure the promotion of minority languages in education. It transpires that they do not in fact do so, and that litigation to ensure equality of treatment for speakers of minority languages in the education system so far has been unlikely to succeed. This is the position in international law, and under most national legal systems, despite many constitutional clauses which are supposed to guarantee enjoyment of cultural rights and to counteract discrimination.

Covenants which have been recently passed or are in draft form are analysed, and current work on devising a *Universal Declaration of Linguistic Human Rights* is described. The problem of specifying and defining what *is* a linguistic human right is exemplified with reference to a proposal that the learning of foreign languages should be considered a human right. Various types of language right are identified, and considered in relation to various types of language learning need for the individual and the group. The article closes with brief consideration of the reasons why dominant groups seem to be so insensitive to the hierarchisation of languages that is a feature of contemporary society, and what structures and ideologies contribute to the operation of *linguicism*, which to some extent has taken over from racism as a way of maintaining and legitimating structures of inequality.

JOSEPH TURI's paper **Typology of language legislation** comes from the field of comparative linguistic law. It describes the contribution of the *legal* profession to the *regulation of linguistic conflicts*, and draws particularly on the extensive Canadian experience (primarily that of Québec). Legislation is put into a broader context, as it has a *historical* dimension — rights have been acquired as a result of struggle for their recognition. It also has what Turi refers to as a *"futuristic"* dimension, in that the law regulates how society is to be ordered from the date on which laws take effect.

The comparative dimension involves the study, by lawyers, sociologists, linguists and others, of how different legal systems enshrine language rights. The article has interesting examples of how freedom of speech has been understood in courts in Canada and France. In passing, Turi also makes a challenging comparison between norms in law and norms in language.

The article presents a wide range of useful definitions and distinctions (e.g. between *official* and *non-official* uses of language). These are not drawn from some idealized notion of how LHRs might best be formulated but rather from the actual experience of the formulation of language law in Quebec (Turi has also personally made a study of constitutional stipulations on language worldwide, involving the analysis of how different legal systems enunciate linguistic rights). He distinguishes the right to "*a*" language from the right to "*the*" language. The right to "a" language means the use of *a specific designated language* in particular (official or non-official) domains. An example could be the right of a French-speaking child in Ottawa ("non-French" area) to be educated through the medium of French but not, e.g., through the medium of Ukrainian, because French has been designated, specifically selected, while Ukrainian has not. The right to "*the*" language relates to the right to use *any language*, e.g. the right of any child, including both the French-speaking child and the Ukrainian-speaking child, to use her/his *mother tongue* (whatever it may be) as the medium of education, as opposed to a foreign or second language.

One key issue in formulating linguistic human rights is what rights should be rights that everybody has, i. e. rights to "the" language, rights that speakers of *any* language have; and which rights should be granted only to speakers of designated languages, i. e. what should be the rights of "a" language. The tendency so far seems to have been that majority language speakers have seen their languages as "designated" for all rights, and have been reluctant to accord minorities rights to "the" language.

The first type of language rights are such "fundamental" human rights that the state cannot be justified in constraining them, whereas the second type can be so constrained.

BJÖRN JERNUDD's paper **Personal names and human rights** takes up one particular aspect of linguistic rights, namely what freedom or rights individuals have to name themselves and their offspring as they wish. Names are a key marker of the social identity of an individual (*unique personal identity*) and ethnic allegiance (*group identity*). Does the state though have the right to restrict personal naming freedom? Jernudd presents a wide range of evidence from Asia and Europe which demonstrates the significance and universality of the issues.

Throughout history many aboriginal and colonized people have been forced to adopt the names of the invader. Some still bear these names. Jernudd also refers to the practice of *women* adopting their *husband's* name when they marry. (In so doing it is of course not their "own" name they are dropping, but their father's).

Jernudd's paper shows that even if there is broad social support for a given naming policy (Singapore, Hong Kong, Sweden), one which evolves to meet changing societal needs, the issues are not straightforward. He draws parallels between the constraints that characterize interactive conversational behaviour and those that may legitimately impell a state to engage in such language engineering. Naming practices which imply a departure from dialectal forms need sensitive implementation, but no violation of human rights may be involved in the relevant limitations on individual freedom. By contrast, repressive laws aimed at depriving an ethnic group of their distinctiveness (Indonesia, Romania, Turkey) are clearly a human rights violation, and Jernudd suggests that human rights declarations should refer to naming practices (which many of them do, see the Appendix) and specifically guard against the state curbing *the individual expression of group identity* in this way (which such declarations seldom do).

Combining immigrant and autochthonous language rights: a territorial approach to multilingualism

François Grin[1]

Immigrant and autochthonous language rights: making the necessary link

Much of the literature dealing with language rights consists of case studies, with more or less emphasis on the rights granted (or denied) to a dominated speech community under some language policy. This is illustrated by countless articles and books on autochthonous minorities, and evidenced by recent edited volumes on language planning such as Maurais (1987) or Weinstein (1990). Of a growing number of publications on immigrant communities in Western countries, few focus on language rights (see for example Steiner-Khamsi 1989; Marta 1991), and fewer still consider autochthonous and immigrant language rights simultaneously, except in settings where the distinction between "immigrant" and "autochthonous" is not as sharp as in Europe (Marshall 1986).

The same holds true, by and large, of contributions that aim at developing a general, theoretical perspective on language rights (see for example Verdoodt 1985). Ever since Kloss (1971) brought up the question of immigrant language rights in a pioneering paper, the relationship between those and autochthonous minority language rights has not been examined in detail, even in international charters, covenants and declarations in favour of extended language rights. In recent papers, both types of rights are considered, but the focus is alternately put on immigrant and autochthonous language rights (Guy 1989; Skutnabb-Kangas − Phillipson 1989). The well-documented case of Quebec includes some theoretical contributions in which the balancing of conflicting language rights is mentioned, but politics have tended to blur the issue (see for example Plourde 1988). More technical considerations on language legislation (Turi 1989 and this volume; De Witte 1989) provide tools for a rigorous characterization of language rights, but do not discuss the relationship between autochthonous minority and immigrant language rights.

Nevertheless, the relationship between language rights that are usually considered separately is bound to require considerable attention from language planners in years to come, because the objective occurrence of multilingualism within national borders, as well as general awareness of the fact, have recently increased and will probably continue to do so. There are two main reasons for this evolution.

First, there has been a resurgence in the sense of pride of a number of traditional minority communities (Foster 1980; Fishman 1989). In the Western capitalist world, this interest can be traced back to cultural changes in the sixties: the relevance of the dominant societal model was questioned in North America and in Western Europe, arousing interest for "alternative" lifestyles in various ways. Among the alternatives, traditional cultures, which appeared by and large to be removed from capitalist mass-consumption society, reappeared at the forefront in spite of the reactionary traits often associated with some of them (for a discussion of somewhat different interpretations of the alternative character of ethnicity in Western Europe, see Williams 1980). The sixties' concern with alternative lifestyles did not create the renewed vitality of traditional cultures; however, it gave them a new seal of legitimacy in the perceptions of broad segments of majority opinion. Some of the central tenets made popular in the sixties gradually acquired a widely accepted theoretical background; for example, the monolithic homogeneity of societies has by and large ceased to be taken as a proof of "modernity": human societies are increasingly perceived as deeply complex organizations, in which a variety of values and codes − which includes languages − may complement each other.

In formerly Eastern block countries, the revival of minority languages and cultures can also be seen as a backlash. In this case, however, the dominant model against which minority languages and cultures have been vying is political more than socio-economic (Grin 1991a). The demise of communist regimes in Eastern Europe and in the USSR afforded the possibility for numerous groups to reassert their cultural identity. This evolution is taking place precisely at a time when some relevant theoretical counterparts of the sixties' revolution in the West are coming to fruition. While adjusting to a free-market system, Eastern Europe can accommodate some of the needs of minority communities by drawing on new perceptions in the West, namely the idea that the coexistence of a number of different languages and cultural values, far from denoting backwardness, appropriately reflects the objective complexity of human society.

Second, the spread, extent and direction of migration flows is one of the striking characteristics of the latter part of the 20th century (Massey 1981; Salt 1989).[2] Consider for example migrants in North America. 19th century settlers were, for the most part, seeking refuge from material (or sometimes political and religious) hardship in their country of origin; they were prepared not only to adapt to their new surroundings, but also to relinquish most cultural and linguistic ties with the country they had left. The causal links involved are complex and still hotly debated. Kloss (1977: 283), notes that

> the non-English ethnic groups in the United States were anglicized not because of nationality laws which were unfavourable to their languages but in spite of nationality laws relatively favourable to them [...] the manifold opportunities which [American] society offered were so attractive that the descendants of the 'aliens' sooner or later voluntarily integrated themselves into this society.

Marshall (1986: 14), however, writes that "the period from 1850 to 1920 saw many states [in the U. S.] institute statutes that effectively blocked the non-English speaker from participation in public education, voting and other civic activities" (see also Hernández-Chávez 1988 and this volume).

Though also driven from the country of origin by hardship, as well as hopes of brighter prospects elsewhere, modern migration flows appear less likely to result in the fading of allophone communities. In the case of the Spanish-origin population in the United States, this may be heavily dependant on a steady inflow of immigrants (Veltman 1983, 1988), and be enhanced by unprecedented demographic concentrations which maintain functioning language communities (Solé 1990). We may also venture the hypothesis that quicker travel, as well as cheaper and more efficient telecommunications, make it easier to maintain direct or indirect ties with the country of origin and the associated cultures and languages. Technological change helps to resist assimilation, whether deliberately or not. It follows that present-day migrants are more likely, on average, to claim a right to maintain the language and culture of their native country in their new surroundings. This gives rise to a new category of minorities, who ground their legitimacy not in a historical connection with the piece of land on which they happen to live, but in a non-territorial right to the maintenance of cultural and linguistic identity.

The combination of these factors generates new patterns of multilingualism, and increases their incidence: instead of being separated by political boundaries, autochthonous and immigrant languages will increasingly be united by them. This, in turn, increases the need for a perspective on the simultaneous allocation of autochthonous and immigrant language rights.

From policy to implementation choices

Prior to devising a system that would generate an appropriate allocation of language rights, as well as ensure an efficient and equitable link between the geographical spread of languages on the one hand, and of language rights on the other hand, some priorities of a political nature must be set. Assuming some measure of agreement is reached in favour of extending language rights, it is still not indifferent to know why planners make this choice.

The case for granting language rights to relatively powerless immigrant and autochthonous minorities usually rests on one of two arguments, namely, fairness or variety. This paper is concerned with variety. The hypothesis made here is that language rights may be granted not because it is presumably more fair or generous to the speech communities that would benefit from them, but because linguistic diversity sustained by a broad range of language rights will benefit all of society, including the majority language group. Proving this point is not the subject matter of this paper, and there is no use for yet another restatement of the case for diversity (see for example Fishman 1989: 568–576 for an overview), but it is always worth recalling that all languages, no matter how few their speakers, can equally well contribute to variety (Camartin 1989). In addition, stressing variety rather than fairness as the main rationale for extending language rights can prove useful for three main reasons: first, this skirts thorny moral and political issues of legitimacy; second, we will see that what would be a dilemma if fairness were the main goal ceases to be one when variety is the guiding principle; third, it is presumably easier to win over reluctant members of majority opinion to the cause of linguistic human rights by stressing increases in their own welfare rather than in the welfare of other speech communities.

Once motivations are by and large agreed upon, serious problems of implementation remain. The extent and nature of language rights given to speakers of different languages is one of the most important problems faced when designing language policy (Abou 1989). When addressing the issue, language planners usually draw on two well-known concepts, namely, the personality principle and the territorial principle. The former states that language rights attach to individuals, irrespective of their geographical position, much in the same way as more traditional human rights. The latter traditionally means that each language should correspond to a specific area, in order to ensure the latter's linguistic homogeneity; the language rights enjoyed by individuals are then conditional on their geographical position. The two principles are frequently contrasted, either because they appear to rest on conflicting priorities, or because they may result in diverging, or even opposing, policy recommendations. However, they can also be viewed as the natural counterpart of each other. Essentially, the territorial principle rationalizes limits to personal language rights, because it provides criteria by which to decide where certain language rights will be granted, and where they will not; the personality principle helps to link language rights to other human rights, and to define the extent and nature of language rights granted in a given territory. The personality principle is generally regarded as offering better safeguards to individuals, whose language rights are not subject to geographical restrictions, while the territorial principle is usually seen as a better protection for collective rights, because it is considered more conducive to the maintenance of linguistically homogeneous settings in which a group's language and culture can thrive (see Turi 1990, for a detailed discussion).

In this paper, I have chosen to focus on the territorial principle, and to evaluate its ability to mesh with the requirements of new and more complex patterns of multilingualism. This emphasis in no way implies that other principles are not equally worthy of attention; however, my choice has been guided by a number of reasons.

First, let us remember that, in so far as language policy is designed and implemented by an authority that has power over a given polity, all language policies have a geographical extent, leading to a *de facto* territorialization of all language rights. The territorial principle will therefore remain a necessary concept and, at least, a general frame within which other principles can be applied.

Second, calls for the introduction of the territorial principle in countries that have hitherto applied the personality principle are much more frequently heard than appeals for moves in the opposite direction. For example, lingering constitutional problems connected with specifically linguistic issues are slowly altering Canada's approach to language questions; voices are now often heard suggesting that Canada adopt the

"Swiss principle", or "model", by which authors usually mean the territorial principle (Hilton 1990; see Trent 1991, for a discussion).[3]

Finally, this paper reflects the conviction that, contrary to standard interpretations (from Kloss 1971, to Mar-Molinero — Stevenson 1991), the territorial principle does not necessarily promote unilingualism or produce what some have branded as "linguistic apartheid". Hence the title of this paper: I believe that the territorial principle can be turned into a modern and flexible instrument, accommodating multilingualism just as well as unilingualism. In order to demonstrate this point, the following sections propose alterations to the classical version of the territorial principle, and develop the concept of *territorial multilingualism*.

Before we move on to a presentation of territorial multilingualism, it is necessary to clarify the substance of the territorial principle itself. Indeed, it is open to a wide range of interpretations, and its legal effects can be more or less precise, binding, homogeneous, and extensive. Language legislations based on the territorial principle have extremely varying implications for the school system, the judiciary, or the provision of services by administrations; they may or may not regulate the use of language in business, and may do so in more or less detail. For our purposes, we shall assume that the territorial principle serves (as it frequently, but not always does) to decide which language(s) will be made official, and in which language(s) residents will be able to receive service from, and communicate with authorities.

Shortcomings of the territorial principle

Switzerland is often described as having successfully dealt with its multilingualism precisely because it has applied the territorial principle; however, the latter cannot be seen as a panacea.[4] Traditional implementations of the territorial principle do not embody a ready answer to three important questions, which can be summarized by the words asymmetry, inclusion and dynamics.

Asymmetry

Within nation-states, the territorial principle often rests on a purely arithmetic approach to the respective positions of the languages in contact. The basic pattern is one where each area is strictly monolingual (the "area" can actually be an entire nation-state). Typically, a limited number of districts are designated as bilingual (or multilingual, if more than two languages are used). The main problem then is the choice of criteria for assigning a given geographical area to one language (or set of languages) or another. The standard solution is to grant language rights to minorities if they represent a sufficient percentage of the resident population, or if they reach a certain absolute number of speakers. In short, language rights are granted exclusively on the basis of demographic data, as if *other* characteristics were either not relevant, or present to an equivalent or *symmetrical* degree in the two speech communities.

The provision of language rights to the Swedish-speaking community in Finland offers a classical example of this type of arrangement, and apparently meets with remarkable success and approval (Jansson 1985). However, this probably reflects the fact that both languages are in fairly symmetrical positions of power and influence, in spite of the numerical difference between the two groups. The assumption of symmetry is simply not tenable in other situations, such as Canada and Switzerland.

Rossinelli (1989) considers the latter case in his thorough discussion of the legal status, interpretation and implementation of the territoriality principle in Switzerland in general, and in the particular case of the eastern Canton of Grischun (Graubünden), where the languages in contact are German, Romansch and Italian. When population numbers are low, a local Romansch majority can quickly become a local minority, in addition to being a minority at the national level, with serious consequences.[5] This situation arises when a few German-speaking couples retire in the municipality, and a few young Romansch-speaking families leave in order to seek more rewarding employment in a major town or city (all of which are located outside of Romansch-speaking areas).[6] The same also applies, with a time-lag of a few decades, in the case of cross-cultural marriages: children are, as a rule, much more likely to be educated in German rather than Romansch, even if the family goes on living in a Romansch community, just because the Romansch-speaking spouse is always bilingual, whereas the German-speaking one is not. Given the disparity in numbers, small-scale demolinguistic changes have a powerful effect in undermining the position of Romansch, while similar changes in the opposite direction would have no effect whatsoever on the dominant position of German (Cathomas 1988; Rossinelli 1989; Furer 1991).

In several rulings, the Swiss Supreme Court has progressively clarified its stand regarding officially bilingual communities, or communities where a degree of *de facto* bilingualism is present (Switzerland 1989).[7] One jurisprudential principle that has emerged as a result is the 30% level required for members of a minority language group to be entitled to education and services in their language (compare this to Finland, where 13 minority children in a local authority is enough to entitle to education in the minority language). Although this would, at first glance, look like a provision favouring minorities, it may well backfire — and usually does in the case of the Romansch-speaking community — precisely because it makes the formalistic (and inaccurate) assumption of symmetry between language groups. Romansch is not just a *minority* language (in static terms); it is also a *threatened* language (in dynamic terms) because German is gaining influence. As a result, the rule put forth by the Supreme Court works against the declining group, and in favour of the expanding one.

The distinction between "minority language" and "threatened language" must be built into the territorial principle — or, for that matter, into *any* theoretical or practical consideration about language planning — if it is to protect minorities efficiently. Treating on an equal footing languages in unequal positions is tantamount to giving the stronger language an edge to increase its influence and spread. Except in rare cases where some degree of symmetry may realistically be assumed (presumably, Swedish and Finnish in Finland), the respective positions of languages in contact are different. This raises a complex issue, namely, how to measure the extent to which a language is threatened, whether in absolute or in relative terms. I have elsewhere (Grin 1992) suggested using the existence of *asymmetric diglossia* as an indicator.[8] Whether this or another criterion is applied, minority language survival requires an asymmetric policy that will help reduce the power of the larger language group — or groups. The excuse of promoting multilingualism is not acceptable, because the latter is likely to be of a subtractive type, detrimental to the survival of the threatened language. In other words, the protection and promotion of threatened languages would lead us to grant unequal language rights to different speech communities; more precisely, the preservation of linguistic diversity may imply that the language rights of some groups, whether autochthonous or immigrant, have to be curtailed.[9]

Inclusion

Let us for a moment put aside the problem of the unequal weight of language groups, and focus on their spatial distribution. Language groups are often interlocked in patterns that are topographically discernable only by using highly detailed maps (see Williams — Ambrose 1988), and one frequently encounters minorities within minorities. This can often be observed in cases of serious conflict, as crises in Yugoslavia or Georgia amply illustrate. For analytical purposes, let us make a distinction between two types of situations: (i) the minority-within-the-minority speaks the national majority language (as with Quebec anglophones or Serbs in Croatia — when it was part of Yugoslavia); and (ii) the minority-within-the-minority speaks another language altogether (for example the Montagnais in Northeastern Quebec, or the Ossetians in Northern Georgia — in the days of the Soviet Union). The second case is similar to that of first-level minorities, whose particular needs have been discussed in the preceding paragraph. We shall therefore focus on the first case, which will be referred to as that of an *included* minority, who will be assumed to speak a non-threatened language.[10]

Let us consider the case of anglophones in the Montreal metropolitan area. Under the present system, the protection of French as a minority *and* a threatened language in Canada (or, perhaps more to the point, in North America) results in restrictions on the use of English in the province of Quebec, including in local communities where speakers of English are a majority. This has created much outrage, and loud demands for the repealing of all or part of the language act, in particular section 58 pertaining to the language of commercial signs (see Quebec 1977). French in North America certainly faces an uphill battle for survival, because of the generally dominant position of English. It follows that the Québécois can hardly afford to relax existing regulations. However, the protection of French as a minority language could probably be achieved at a lower psychological cost to the anglophone community, by granting the latter territorially limited rights to a broader use of English.

In more general terms, granting adequate linguistic rights to included minorities calls for territorialization and a high degree of decentralization along with the devolution of significant law-making and spending power to local authorities. Ideally, several tiers of government should be created, each with its clearly defined set of attributions. The (essentially) three-tier Swiss system, for example, is made up of communes, cantons and the Confederation, each having its own set of tasks.[11] Selecting official languages independently at every tier — possibly allowing for bi-or multilingualism at each of them — will generate an overall distribution of language rights more closely matching the geographical distribution of language groups.

Of course, relatively significant included minorities can always be found by considering ever smaller geographical units. However, few countries have really exhausted the flexibility potential of decentralization combined with territoriality. The conclusion reached at the end of the preceding section was that in many cases, the territorial principle should be implemented in an asymmetric fashion (which implies a centralized perspective on territoriality); the conclusion reached now is that there are also situations in which a decentralized implementation is necessary. This confirms that general rules of language policy must often be qualified prior to implementation in a real-world context.

Dynamics

The preceding paragraphs have shown that assigning a geographical area to one or the other language (or set of languages) is complex enough when demolinguistic data are fairly stable, and when the languages in contact can be considered autochthonous. However, migration flows will make such situations less frequent. Newcomers may have citizenship of the same nation-state, but yet speak a different language; they may also come from another continent, and have no deep-rooted historical, cultural, linguistic or other connections with any part of the host country. A different degree of legitimacy would probably attach to different categories of migrants, in their own eyes or in those of the people among which they settle. As pointed out earlier, I do not intend to discuss the issue of legitimacy. However, experience suggests that the emotional link between language and territory is a strong one, and that autochthonous populations are not inclined to consider non-national languages and cultures as having a legitimate claim to recognition anywhere but in the latter's area of historical distribution. Racism towards non-European immigrants in Western European countries, or incidents associated with "ethnic boundary contacts" (Calvet 1987; Dormon 1981) are ample testimony to the fact that multiculturalism is not a matter of course. This suggests that the granting of language rights to immigrant communities requires careful planning.

Our starting point (the value of variety) warrants the provision of language rights to immigrants who wish to retain their language and culture, not to mention the fact that forcing adaptation upon them is arguably neither practically feasible, nor financially sensible. The territorial allocation of official languages must adapt accordingly, and adaptability must be built into the territorial arrangement. At the same time, care must be taken to avoid a racist backlash in majority opinion. Members of the autochthonous majority are more likely to be scared if the influx of outsiders is suddenly reflected in nation-wide language rights for speakers of foreign languages. Such fears will probably be assuaged if geographical limitations are built into the system. There again, territorialization along with the establishment of a multi-tier system can be used as a means to smooth the passage from a linguistically homogeneous to a multilingual society.

Principles of territorial multilingualism

Let us now see how territoriality can be amended in order to meet the concerns expressed earlier. In this section, I will only outline the territorial multilingualism model; a detailed presentation can be found in Grin (1991b). The reader should bear in mind that what follows is not a readily implementable system (in particular, it assumes more readiness from majority opinion to grant immigrant language rights than can usually be observed), and that a number of related issues, such as costs, are not discussed here. Rather, this section provides a theoretical exploration into a class of solutions to the complex status planning problems described in the preceding sections.

Let us consider a polity where a balance of rights must be granted to speakers of three languages. Three main assumptions are made:

Assumption 1. There are three language groups: A (autochthonous majority language); B (minority language spoken by immigrants; B is a majority language in the immigrants' country of origin); C (autochthonous, threatened minority language, whose geographical spread has been declining for several decades).

Assumption 2. There are three levels of government, or *tiers*: national, provincial, and local (or municipal), each with clearly defined tasks, or *areas of jurisdiction*. Typical tasks or areas of jurisdiction are the social security system, education, roads, defence, justice, etc.

Assumption 3. Each level of government has control over the language used in its areas of jurisdiction. Jurisdictions are allocated between government tiers in such a way that each tier has roughly equivalent influence on language use in the overall provision of services to the public.

The polity being split up in a number p of *provinces*, each subdivided in a number m of *municipalities*, a considerable number of cases could be observed. For example, municipalities may have a majority of residents speaking language A, B or C. Let us suppose that minorities may qualify for services in their language. As a result, each community may harbour one or two *qualifying minorities*.[12] Each municipality may belong to one of twelve demolinguistic categories. Let each of them be denoted by one, two or three letters, the first representing the local majority language, and the others representing the languages of qualifying minorities, if any:

A	B	C
A, B	B, A	C, A
A, C	B, C	C, B
A, B, C	B, A, C	C, A, B

The *p* provinces may also encompass similar demolinguistic variety. Since each municipality belongs to a province, we may well find a municipality where a majority of residents speaks A, with a qualifying minority of speakers of B, even though this municipality belongs to a province where the threatened minority language C has survived well enough to represent a majority, although there may be a qualifying A-speaking minority at the provincial level. In principle, no less than 144 (12 ^{2}) demolinguistic situations are possible. These demolinguistic situations will be called *configurations*, and each municipality belongs to one configuration. Not all of them are of equal relevance. For example, immigration into European countries may have resulted in the emergence of "A,B", "B,A" or even "B" municipalities; however, the existence of "B,A" or "B" provinces is probably a much rarer occurrence, with the possible exception of Baltic states that have experienced massive Russian-speaking immigration over the last fifty years (see Magga, this volume, for different configurations featuring language C).

Our earlier discussion points to the need for highly diversified arrangements, in order for the geographical distribution of language rights to match that of speech communities as closely as possible. We have seen that keeping a close correspondence may provide ways to deal with two of the three problems discussed above, under the headings *inclusion* and *dynamics*. Let us, however, start out with a perfectly *symmetrical* approach to language rights. Each configuration will therefore have its own combination of official languages, which is expressed as a set of three elements. These combinations are generated by very simple rules. The first element in the set is the official language(s) of the local authorities: it is the language of the local linguistic majority, plus the language of the local qualifying minority, if any; the second element in the set is the official language of the provincial authorities: it is the language of the provincial majority, plus the language of the qualifying minority at the provincial level, if any. The third element in the set is the language used, in a specific configuration, by services under national jurisdiction. We shall assume that national authorities provide services in any of the languages otherwise used in the configuration, whether by local or by provincial authorities.

Under this system, official j-unilingualism can occur only in configurations that have a j-language majority with no qualifying minority either at the municipal or at the provincial level. With three languages present, only three out of the 144 configurations would provide monolingual surroundings. All other configurations (almost 98%) would be officially bi-or trilingual. Consider for example a municipality where a majority of residents speaks A, but where there is a qualifying B-language minority. The languages of local authorities will then be A and B. Suppose this municipality belongs to a province where the majority of the population speaks A, but there is a C-language qualifying minority at the provincial level. The languages used by provincial authorities will then be A and C. In the basic version of territorial multilingualism, this configuration will be characterized by the set of official languages {A,B (local); A,C (provincial); A,B,C (national)}. This amply demonstrates that a territorial allocation of language rights is not synonymous with unilingualism or linguistic apartheid; it also shows how a very simple set of rules can generate a complicated arrangement. The latter, however, is simpler than it seems. First, only a few of the 144 configurations would occur in a real-world situation: assuming a three-tier government structure in Western European countries, most of the population would be found in provinces where the majority of the population speaks A — with or without B-or C-language qualifying minorities. Second, under the hypothesis that a qualifying minority enjoys the same language rights as the majority, many configurations have identical sets of official languages.[13]

This system, however, requires some amendments, because (i) it does not provide adequate protection for the threatened language C, and (ii) some sections of the A-speaking majority opinion may be antagonized by it. It is therefore necessary to depart from the symmetrical distribution of language rights.

Minority language protection

As shown in the preceding section, an asymmetry must be introduced in order to ensure the survival of language C. The creation of unilingual C-language areas may be indispensable to overall diversity. In such areas, the traditional meaning of territoriality is to be maintained, so that the main or unique language of all tiers of public service there would be C, regardless of the presence of A- or B-speaking residents — exceptions being made, of course, for the linguistic consequences of traditional human rights. Planning measures should be taken to promote a language environment in which the need to use a language other than C is no greater than the need to speak a language other than A in the primarily A-speaking areas elsewhere in the country. At the same time, immigration should not be discouraged, in order to avoid turning traditional C-speaking regions into ghettoes; however, conditions must be created for non-speakers of C moving into such regions to have a strong incentive to learn C.[14]

The geographical extent of regions in which C would be the only official language used by authorities, and the only language in which public services would be provided, cannot be drawn at will. Ideally, it should meet two requirements, namely *range* and *historical relevance*. The criterion of historical relevance may not offer means to avoid conflict; however, it is difficult to ignore, and it is implicitly referred to by the European Charter on Regional or Minority Languages (section 1, a and b; see Appendix). The range criterion allows for the fact that long-term language survival is highly sensitive to the possibility to conduct a wide range of activities in the language in question. In our case, the boundaries of official language regions should be defined so that there is at least one C-language urban environment, offering at least one institution of higher learning in the language, etc. This, unfortunately, may be next to impossible to achieve in many minority contexts, because there is no large town or city where natural and spontaneous minority language use is of any consequence; there may then be no choice but to be content with language regions satisfying historical relevance but not range. Conditions under which this can be sufficient in the long run is another question discussed elsewhere (Grin 1992).

Tolerability of immigrant language rights

Let us now focus on the balance between the three languages in other parts of the national territory.[15] The basic version of territorial multilingualism may have insufficient *tolerability*, in particular to speakers of A, because some local authorities would not be using A any more.[16] Therefore, it is probably wise to introduce another asymmetry, namely, to require that local (or, for that matter, provincial) authorities *outside of the all-C districts* be able to function in language A and provide services in it. This would affect only a few of the configurations (those where speakers of B are a majority at the local and/or provincial level, without any qualifying minority), and would not entail a loss of official status for B.

Once this asymmetry is introduced, territorialized multilingualism still fosters linguistic diversity, because immigrant language rights are present in all municipalities and in all provinces where immigrants represent a minority large enough to qualify. In addition, national authorities use B alongside the traditional autochthonous languages wherever speakers of B represent a qualifying minority at the local or at the provincial level. These rights far exceed those granted under what is at present, to my knowledge, the most advanced piece of legislation on the matter, namely, Canada's *Law on Canadian Multilingualism* (Canada 1988). However, the asymmetry introduced now (that is, the fact that type B municipalities or provinces would offer bilingual services, just like type AB and type BA ones, whereas type A municipalities or provinces are not required to function in language B), ensures that there will be no government tier where authorities would not provide services in language A; besides, all municipalities or provinces where the majority speaks A but no other language group qualifies would retain official unilingualism, and use only A.

Under steady B-language immigration, this asymmetric version of territorial multilingualism also ensures that the institutional position of language B *progressively* achieves parity with language A. As speakers of B settle in areas from which they were hitherto absent, they become qualifying minorities at the local and provincial level, and the resident population displays increasing linguistic diversity. At the same time, the official language set of the configurations in which they live will also move towards more multilingualism, but the process will be smoothed by the joint use of decentralization and territorialization, and give majority opinion more time to adjust to the evolution in the respective status of the languages spoken in the polity. This may significantly increase tolerability, and thereby create firmer grounds on which to build immigrant language rights.[17]

Conclusion

Extensions to the territorial principle appear to have significant potential for dealing with complex patterns of multilingualism, and defining a simultaneous allocation of language rights that are usually considered separately. By departing from the rigid interpretation of the territorial principle and introducing variety-enhancing and tolerability-enhancing asymmetries, we can generate forms of territoriality that have nothing to do with linguistic segregation, and can actually smooth the progressive evolution of societies towards more wide-spread multilingualism. Territorial multilingualism allows for the fact that the link between language and territory is a complex, and often emotional issue to be handled with care. In addition, it uses decentralization, which remains, by and large, one of the best safeguards of democracy.

However, the territorial multilingualism model presented here is only a blueprint, which has served to chart little-explored options. A number of points deserve closer consideration, and only a few will be mentioned here.

First, the allocation of tasks between government tiers becomes a language-planning issue. While certain tasks can be assigned to one or the other tier without much hesitation, some key domains, such as transport or education, raise trickier problems. Simulating the territorial multilingualism model in several real-world cases, such as Quebec or the Republic of Russia, would be a useful exercise in order to identify such problems precisely.

Second, particular attention must be devoted to the way in which education fits into the general model. Since territorial multilingualism aims at maintaining diversity, mother tongue medium education in various languages should be provided *in so far as it serves this goal*. This unquestionably applies to C-language education up to and including university level. Mother tongue medium education in language B should also be available with a view to enable speakers of B to become fully functional in it, and therefore contribute to linguistic diversity; this, however, does not necessarily require a full range of B-language university courses, which interested individuals, having been prepared to do so by B-language medium education throughout pre-university schooling, can presumably take at universities in a B-language country.

Third, more precise and elaborate versions of the model can be developed. I wish to make two main suggestions. The first is to develop a more formal approach, in which the choice of official languages at every government tier would be explicitly modelled; I have referred to the rational choice model by Pool (1991a), but consistency with the stated or unstated hypotheses of territorial multilingualism may require that some of Pool's assumptions be replaced by others. Second, the robustness of territorialized multilingualism remains to be checked theoretically, in order to assess whether its apparent virtues also manifest themselves if the choice of the rule for defining qualifying levels is left up to each local and provincial authority, or if another decision rule is applied when selecting language(s) used by national authorities.

Finally, territorial multilingualism must be part of a broader perspective on language planning. Regulation of languages in official use should be designed in relation with observed patterns of language use in other domains of everyday life such as business and commerce; an integrated approach is necessary for language planning to succeed in fostering viable linguistic diversity.

Notes

1. National Science Foundation, Switzerland. This paper was written during a visiting fellowship at the Center for the Humanities of the University of Washington, Seattle. Additional financial support from the Holderbank Foundation (Switzerland) is gratefully acknowledged. An earlier version of this paper has been presented at the Symposium on Linguistic Human Rights, Tallinn, Estonia, October 13–16, 1991. The author wishes to thank Tove Skutnabb-Kangas, Robert Phillipson and Jonathan Pool for helpful suggestions and comments.
2. See also "IMR at 25 – Reflections on a Quarter Century of International Migration Research and Orientations for Future Research" (Editors' foreword to the *International Migration Review*, 23: 393–402).
3. *A contrario*, when some Irish language activists brand territoriality as *passé*, I am led to suspect that such a disclaimer is a rationalization for the dramatic failure of the essentially non-territorial Irish language policy, more than a strongly buttressed scientific argument.
4. A complete overhaul of Swiss language policy had to be undertaken because the territorial principle, *as it has been applied up to the present time*, has failed to maintain an adequate environment for the most threatened of the four autochthonous language communities (Camartin 1985; Rossinelli 1989; Switzerland 1989).
5. The territorial principle is implemented in two different ways in Switzerland. Contrary to tradition and jurisprudence in the rest of the country, the Canton of Grischun has devolved the choice of the official language to local authorities. According to 1981 census figures, Romansch-speakers represent less than 1% of the national population, and some 22% of the Canton's population (Switzerland 1989).
6. 40% of Romansch-speakers live outside of the Romansch-language areas, enjoying no maintenance programs of facilities.
7. Important Supreme Court rulings about the language of education are *Association de l'école française* (1965), *Derungs* (1976) and *Brunner* (1982). They explicitly refer to the territorial principle, and turn out to have negative consequences for linguistic minorities.
8. When a minority language is excluded from certain domains, while the associated majority language can be used in all and is excluded from none, there is asymmetric

diglossia. Examples of such a relationship throughout Europe abound, such as Occitan and French, Irish and English, etc.

9. If fairness instead of diversity were the main goal of language planners, it would be considerably more difficult to decide how and why arbitration between conflicting language rights should be made.

10. A number of languages, such as Kurdish or Kabyle, are spoken by migrant communities in Western Europe, but are not majority languages in the nation-states from which speakers originate. This problem is not examined in this paper which, for all practical purposes, suggests that it is akin to the situation of threatened languages spoken by indigenous minorities (see Skutnabb-Kangas and Bucak, this volume).

11. For example, Swiss communes take care of some cultural and recreational activities, cantons manage the school system, and the federal government is in charge of what social insurance there is.

12. Pool (1991) has suggested a procedure generating an "efficient and fair" language policy for selecting official languages. The first adjective means that such a policy would have the lowest cost among all proposed policies; the second that the net cost of the policy would be spread among language groups on the basis of relative demographic size. Introducing numerical values as inputs in Pool's model yields efficiency thresholds for making languages official; such thresholds can be expressed as percentages of the total resident population. Pool's "language regime" is one method among those that could be used to define the *qualifying minorities* mentioned here.

13. It makes no difference whether a municipality has an A-speaking majority with a qualifying B-speaking minority or the reverse, since the languages used by the municipality will then be A and B in both cases.

14. A whole spectrum of measures can be suggested, ranging from the purely promotion-oriented approach presently used in Wales, to more demanding regulations under which a certain level of proficiency in language C would be required in order for newcomers to be eligible for certain benefits or authorizations, such as buying property in the C-language area.

15. This geographical area would then cover the entire national territory *minus* provinces and local communities where only C is used by all authorities.

16. A priori, configurations generating the set of official languages {B ; A,B ; A,B}, or even {B ; B ; B} are conceivable.

17. Formally, the model introduces two additional assumptions, namely, that qualifying levels are defined in absolute numbers of speakers (as is, for example, the case in Finland for eligibility to mother tongue education in Swedish), and that the absolute size of any speech community in any configuration may not decrease, although its relative size may. This ensures that B achieves institutional parity with A by degrees, and that the institutional position of A nowhere becomes second to that of B. The number of steps, and therefore the smoothness of the process, can be increased by allowing different official language arrangements across jurisdictions (as defined in assumption 3) within each tier (see Grin 1991b). The territorial implementation of the rule for granting language rights ensures that this evolution will never have landslide proportions that might antagonize majority opinion.

On the limits of ethnolinguistic democracy[1]

Joshua A. Fishman

The principle of ethnolinguistic democracy

The various fargoing political and economic realignments that have recently swept over Europe, both Western and Eastern, make it necessary for all who have previously advocated ethnolinguistic democracy to try to rethink the practicality and the advisability of this ideal. The growing prospects and problems of democratization in Eastern and Southern Europe and the increasing integration of the European (Economic) Community often lend a particular urgency to either broadening or restricting the principle of ethnolinguistic democracy and simultaneously raise cogent questions as to the justifiability of its invocation in one context or another. Clearly, the extent to which this principle has been examined and implemented in Western and West-Central Europe has very definite implications for its examination and implementation elsewhere. Accordingly, I will base my comments, below, on Western and West-Central European examples; I do so, however, only as a matter of metaphorical parsimony. The issues, as well as the dimensions, that I will discuss and posit also have, I firmly believe, rather general and even worldwide relevance.

What exactly is the principle of ethnolinguistic democracy?

On December 11, 1990, the European Community's Parliament adopted the "principle of complete multilingualism" with respect to its own operations. This resolution goes beyond any previous policy or resolution of the European Community (hereafter: EC) in that it posits this principle to be "consistent with the respect which is owed to the dignity of all languages which reflect and express the cultures of the different peoples who make up the EC" (Argemi 1991). Admittedly, this resolution was adopted due to Catalan pressure (as evidenced by 100, 000 signatures delivered to the President of the EC's European Parliament in 1987, in

support of granting Catalan some sort of official standing in the EC
organization's operations), but its adoption three years later was justified
on grounds going far beyond the Catalan position, namely as being
appropriate in order that the "people of Europe do not regard European
institutions as being out of touch with and foreign to them"...but, rather,
that they "look upon them as important elements playing a part in the
daily life of the citizens" (Argemi 1991).

The implications of this position go far beyond the EC organization
alone, and even far beyond language use in official institutions. Presumably, the cultures of the peoples that make up Europe should be even
more basically enabled and assured of their right to *conduct their intra-
cultural affairs in their own languages*, since such enablement must precede
and provide the foundation for any rights or enablements to use their
languages in inter-cultural affairs, such as those of the EC. The latter
without the former would merely be a dishonest display, a Potemkin
village built over a festering wound, just as the former without the latter
is an affront to that "respect which is owed to the dignity of all ...
cultures". In addition, it should be noted, the resolution is couched within
a principle (the principle of "complete multilingualism") that posits the
view that all parties to a particular sphere of of joint interaction should
be able to engage in that interaction in their own language and that
appropriate provisions for bi-directional communication must flow from
that principle rather than dictate or limit its feasibility. Both the intra-
cultural and the inter-cultural assumptions mentioned above, taken together, constitute the principle of complete ethnolinguistic democracy.

Note, however, that at the same time as the European Parliament's
new resolution was adopted (a resolution that was fully in agreement, by
the way, with its previous resolutions in recent years), it did not grant
Catalan official status within EC operations. In essence, in operational
organizational terms, the resolution merely served to encourage Catalans
to continue exploring some sort of recognized status. Short of the full
official status now recognized for nine languages, there is also possibly
the status of "working language" insofar as relations between the Autonomous Catalan Community and the EC are concerned. The principle of
ethnolinguistic democracy does not require that all languages be declared
equally important and equally privileged in all functions, i. e., at some
point in the total interaction matrix that is imaginable between them,
some consideration of proportionality between them may still be appealed
to and implemented. Therefore, while acknowledging the principle of
ethnolinguistic democracy, the European Parliament also recognized that

within its own operations (and, implicitly, within any complex multilingual framework) some notion of limits must also exist, very much as notions of limits have existed in all theories of political democracy and individual rights from the very earliest times.

Just where and when the the limits of democratic rights should be drawn, be they linguistic or more general, can well be viewed as a dilemma within the democratic ethos itself. Limits can be set in self-serving ways and those who wield greater power are particularly likely to have a disproportionate say in the establishment of such limits. Establishments are more likely to limit others than to limit themselves, and, therefore, to appeal to or to implement any notion of limits primarily for the preservation and furtherance of their own power, rather than to permit others to have access to power by engaging in power-sharing.

In this last connection, the dilemma faced by the European Parliament is actually a global one. Languages are not merely innocent means of communication. They stand for or symbolize peoples, i. e., ethnocultures, and it is not obviously apparent to what extent administrative or econotechnical structures (cities, regions, states, international organizations) can, in practice, actually recognize, empower and/or assist them all. Languages may very well all be equally valid and precious markers of cultural belonging, behavior and identity, while nevertheless being far from equally valuable or viable as vehicles of either intergroup or econotechnical communication. Whether, where, when and how to draw the line between the two, i. e., between ethnolinguistic democracy, on the one hand, and ethnolinguistic equality, on the other hand, is often a matter frought with tension, guilt and outright conflict as well.

The principle of ethnolinguistic democracy at the suprastate level

Suprastate organizations, we must bear in mind, are originally and basically the creatures of states. As such, these organizations are rarely, if ever, strong enough to impose their own will on the strongest of their own creators. Thus, when the EC came into being, it quite understandably designated the official state languages of all of its creators as its official languages. As the EC has expanded, over the years, it has correspondingly expanded the number of its official languages. Thus far this has been feasible, but it has already become difficult (not to say expensive). After all, 72 different translation skills are called for in order to handle nine different but theoretically equal languages in all possible directions (although, admittedly, a few of these directions are seldom if ever called for in practice, whereas others are so common as to virtually represent the norms; see Haselhuber 1991). Indeed, the Language Service has become one of the EC's largest administrative budgetary items. However, a more parsimonious approach, e.g., the adoption of a subset of one or more "administrative" super-languages for the public operation of the European Parliament, has thus far proved to be absolutely impossible. Obviously, French, German, Italian and Spanish — but particularly French — cannot bring themselves to recognize English for what it has generally become, namely, primus inter pares. To do so would be viewed and experienced as an act of relative demotion for the others, even though their customary functions and perquisites, both at home and throughout the world, would in all probability remain unchanged. An administrative "Big Brother" (or even "Big Quintuplets") for the EC would smack of "internal colonialism" and that would be the kiss of death for the EC per se, particularly since French still retains disproportionate prominence in conjunction with the EC operations in Brussels (as distinct from the European Parliament's operations in Strassburg).

The UN, however, from the very outset, unabashedly differentiated between a small subset of "working languages" (English and French) and a somewhat larger cluster of "official languages" (English, French, Russian, Chinese and Spanish). All other languages received no official standing or recognition whatsoever. More recently, the UN added Arabic to its short list of "working languages" and whereas the Secretariat continues to use English and French alone, various other UN bodies use various other "working languages" as well. Thus the "working languages" are a subset of the "official languages" and both clusters taken together are no more than half a dozen and quite Eurocentric in nature. Its worldwide purview obviously led the UN away from any attempt at formulating a principle of "complete multilingualism" from the very outset, just as its super-power origins led it from the very outset to make distinctions between the super-powers (with their permanent seats and veto-power in the Security Council) and the lesser powers.

By contrast, the EC, with a much smaller membership, also has integrative responsibilities even in the social and cultural realms, responsibilities that the UN does not even contemplate. These integrative responsibilities heighten authenticity sensitivities and these sensitivities render any linguistic distinctions (such as "administrative" or "working" vs. "official") apparently impossible for the immediate future. Thus far, the

EC must follow the "equal in principle" approach vis-a-vis all of its *state* languages, even though it is quite clear that these languages are by no means equal insofar as their European and worldwide inter-state functions and utility are concerned (Haarmann 1991). The states insist on considering the EC organization as one in which they are completely equal in principle and, accordingly, one in which the state languages too are completely equal and equally indispensable for all symbolic EC purposes. While it is generally true that all adopted EC decisions become binding as national laws in each member-state and that, therefore, they must be authoritatively translated into all the official languages of the member states, the internal operation of the EC organization per se is paying a very heavy price for this particular intra-state function, a price which its own bureaucrats attempt to escape from "unofficially" for internal and closed EC operations, but for which there is no public "official"relief.

What will this principle of "complete multilingualism" mean when the EC is further expanded, as now seems absolutely predictable, given that Austria, Sweden and Finland is certainly assured of membership, with membership for Norway almost equally certain? Membership for Hungary and Czechoslovakia (or separately for Bohemia-Moravia and Slovakia) is also already under discussion. If the six new official languages of these additional states (six new languages and not seven, because the state language of Austria is already represented in the EC) are also to be treated as equal in principle with the current nine, that would result in 210 directions of translation between 15 languages. if all other European states are ultimately admitted, even barring separate membership for the subdivisions of the former Yugoslavia and USSR, the application of the unlimited principle of "complete multilingualism" would result in fully 420 directions of translation for the official communications between 21 members in the EC. If the Soviet subdivisions too are admitted, 600 directions of translation would obtain between 25 official state languages! Clearly, some theory of limits must be invoked, perhaps via a distinction between administrative ("working") and official languages, even when equally sovereign states are involved in inter-state or supra-state activities (Leitner 1991). But it is very difficult for sovereign states to agree to limit themselves, and even more difficult to do so once their organization has been established precisely on the principle of ethnolinguistic equality.

The principle, of ethnolinguistic democracy at the sub-state level

The Council of Europe, on the other hand, has a much more varied and inclusive membership than the current EC. Furthermore, unlike the EC the Council of Europe has no legal standing within its own member states. As a result, it should come as no surprise that it not only uses only English and French as its official and working languages, but that within the limits of its 23 member states there are fully 85 non-state languages (counting only those whose speakers are of pre-World War II autochtonous vintage; Verdoodt 1991). Given a number this large, it should also come as no surprise that these sub-state languages and their ethnocultural communities are differentially recognized (or ignored) and differentially treated (or maltreated) by their corresponding state authorities. Màny Catalans — their own language being more prestigeful within the Autonomous Catalan Community than is the language of the Spanish state — may be less than fully satisfied by their less than fully autonomous status within Spain (not to mention their less than fully equal status within the EC organization). But their lot would be considered quite a fortunate one by the Catalans in France and, indeed, by the Occitans, Bretons and Basques in France, not to mention the Frisians in the Netherlands, the Ladins and Friulians in Italy, and a large number of quasi-recognized and entirely unrecognized regional ethnolinguistic concentrations throughout the member countries of the Council of Europe.

By and large, many members of the autochtonous sub-state ethnolinguistic communities in Western Europe (not to mention other, less democratically-oriented parts of the world), do not believe that the principle of ethnolinguistic democracy is being applied to them even vis-a-vis their *intra*-communal lives, let alone the principle of complete multilingualism or complete equality of languages. These languages are very often not recognized even for educational, media, judicial, legislative or other public services, even in their very own areas of concentration, insofar as the state authorities and state funding are concerned. Indeed, many of these ethnolinguistic communities are already in such weakened circumstances that very carefully pinpointed and informed efforts are required in order to salvage even the intimate family-home-neighborhood foundations of their intergenerational mother-tongue continuity (Fishman 1991). Barring such informed efforts at reversing language shift — efforts which are difficult to plan precisely because they must focus on the elusive processes of informal /private intra-familial and intra-communal life during the early childhood years prior to and pari-passu with elementary education — even the genuinely "good intentioned" acts of supporting some instructional, publication and/or media efforts in threatened languages predictably bear little intergenerational fruit. Obviously the states are even more reluctant to apply the principle of ethnolinguistic democracy *below* (or within) the level of the state than they are to set aside the principle of ethnolinguistic equality above the level of the state.

States manifest concern about the possibility of disruptive ethnic unrest, on the one hand, and pyramiding costs, on the other hand, should the principle of ethnolinguistic democracy be recognized to any significant degree below the level of the state, in addition, states often shed crocodile tears as to the lamentable corpus characteristics of those of their sub-state varieties that claim language (i. e., not merely dialect) status, characteristics which presumably always make these sub-state languages patently unsuitable for school, media or public administration use. The Netherlands is very certain that Nederlands is as good a language as English for the operation of the EC, but it is not sure that Frisian is as good a language as Nederlands for the operation of local public services in Friesland. In other words, states are not slow to apply to languages lower in the pecking order than the state-languages per se, the very same notions of limits that the state languages are so unwilling to apply to themselves vis-à-vis the EC organization's operations.

There is a double standard here, the concept of limits being vociferously put off in one context (the "manageable" inter-state case) and prematurely applied in the other (the "obviously unmanageable" intra-state case). And, as always, the implementation of a double standard leads to self-confirming hypotheses, i. e., it results in perpetrating cumulatively increasing harm to the statuses and the corpuses of the sub-state languages involved, without offering them the benefits of the same kind of corpus planning in which the state languages themselves engage in order "to be intertranslatable with English". Friulian does become less and less suitable to be the language of public institutions the longer it is denied this function and the corpus planning it would require. The above sorry picture — certainly sorry insofar as providing "the respect which is owed to the dignity of all languages which reflect and express the cultures of the different peoples who make up the EC" (to once more use the EC's wording) — does not even include the indigenous minorities outside of Western/Central Europe, not to mention the immigrant languages of this continent. The latter, the immigrant languages, are truly low-men on the ethnolinguistic democracy totem-pole. They benefit neither from primum mobile nor from ideologies that tend to contribute to the conservation or democratization of cultural resources at the intra-state level.

Sociolinguistic repertoires in search of ethnolinguistic democracy

It is clear that many autochtonous European ethnocultural minorities (even Western European ones) do not as yet approximate what the Catalans of Spain may well have to settle for in the EC organization, namely, some overt sign of respect for and acknowledgement of the mother tongues that represent and express their ethnocultural identities (even though these signs may fall short of officialization). What way out of their dilemmas should and could an enlightened language policy attempt? Quite obviously, the principle of ethnolinguistic democracy will come up against different objective limits at the levels of individuals, of peoples (or cultures), of regions and of states. At the lowest or smallest ethnolinguistic levels, the problems of critical mass must come into play very early (as they often do even with the delivery of postal, medical and other vital social services that are provided by recognized regional or central authorities). Mail and medical services too are not always delivered to the door in the smallest and furthest outlying points. But setting such considerations aside, as involving an obvious and too often utilized excuse for official inaction, there is yet another consideration to keep in mind, namely, the status of the particular local/regional languages when viewed in a larger, more inclusive perspective.

In Northern Italy, German, French or even Slovenian can more easily be acknowledged for authoritative regional social services — even if they are not always so acknowledged — than can Valdostian, Friulian or Ladin which are often co-present in roughly the same areas. Speakers of the former require no more than a one language supplement in order to function both at a broader regional as well as at the national level. Those starting with German, e.g., need add only Italian as a second language, an addition which usually occurs at or before the elementary school level. However, those starting out with a variety of Friulian, need not only to add Italian and French or German, but these Friulian speakers cannot even take Friulian for granted in most localized social services. Obviously, local/regional languages themselves vary greatly in total size, status and support possibilities, both from within and from without the particular states in which they find themselves.

The smaller the total speech community, combining both those members within and those without the boundaries of any given state, the more serious are the problems of fostering even its intergenerational mother tongue continuity., let alone its use for out-of-home functions The more pressing, therefore, are the reasons why various other, larger languages must be resorted to among the mother tongue speakers of the smallest languages, in order to enable these speakers to participate effectively at regional, state and supra-state levels. The larger the total speech community, the more likely its language is to be a state language somewhere. Therefore, even if another state language as well as supra-state language will need to be learned (e.g., among German speakers in Northern Italy), the mother tongue itself still possesses the corpus and status resources necessary for variegated modern functioning. Only the speakers of unquestioned international "super languages" can *pretend* to be totally effective in modern life while remaining monolingual. Thus, clearly, those who start off *weakest* are required to protest the *most vigorously* at three levels, in order to (a) secure ethnolinguistic democracy in intra-communal affairs, (b) engage in the minimally adequate corpus planning required by local government and new media, and (c) attain access to national and international roles in their intergroup lives. The price they have to pay is a considerable one, not because it is difficult for individuals to learn several languages, but because it is difficult for societies to maintain several languages simultaneously, particularly when these languages differ greatly in functionality and when the width of the linguistic repertoire characterizing a speech community is demonstrably inversely related to its econotechnical autonomy and its sociocultural self-regulation.

The dilemmas of the smallest mother tongues, namely those that are "non-governmental" everywhere that they are spoken

Sub-state mother tongues, particularly mother tongues that are non-governmental everywhere that they are spoken, are obviously often viewed as "multi-problem languages", whether in Western Europe or elsewhere (Mackey 1991), even though their problems are far from self-inflicted but derive from their less than sympathetic neighbors. Unfortunately for the future of ethnolinguistic democracy, these very languages constitute the vast majority of the world's languages and they pertain to approximately a quarter of the world's population. These languages most commonly lack even any effective legal conventions to either protect or assist them. Most of them have no written functions or very meager ones, and, therefore, no standard orthographies or grammars to bridge their dialect differences. They lack budgets for audio-visual media and, even if such exist, their media programs cannot compete, either in number or in quality, with those of their surrounding "Big Brothers". At present they have very little econotechnical value. Above all, they may even lack sufficient demographic concentration in the very districts in which they are autochtonous, i. e., "sufficient" in order to make intergenerational mother-tongue continuity the effortless and normal experience that it is for speakers of the state languages.

Others are always looking over the shoulders of sub-state languages, particularly when we consider those that are sub-state languages everywhere, in order to decide if they are "worth the time and effort" required in order to keep them going. Worst of all, this literally "existential" question is often answered for them by outsiders. Ethnolinguistic democracy, or (again in the words of the Parliament of the EC) the principle of "respect owed to the dignity of all languages which reflect and express the cultures of ... different peoples", requires that insiders make this decision under unpressured circumstances and with equitable access to the general budget for local cultural efforts and social services. The smallest sub-state languages will always entail additional burdens and call for additional dedication on the part of their speakers, but decisions concerning the futures of these languages should therefore be made by those most likely also to value the integrative blessings of such languages as well, blessings in the form of relatively undislocated ethnocultural identities, belongingnesses, and intergenerational ethnolinguistic continuities.

When all is said and done, the question of the limits of ethnolinguistic democracy usually raises its head first for those who are speakers of the smallest sub-state languages, the ones that are sub-state everywhere that they are spoken. Furthermore, the subdivisability of both human ethnocultural identity and ethnolinguistic expression is fairly infinite, corresponding to the gradients of intensity of human interaction under the influence of various economic, geographic and historical circumstances. Even relatively small written languages often subsume several different spoken varieties and the speech communities utilizing these varieties can, under certain circumstances, each strike out on their own, developing their own written standards, stressing their own distinctive authenticity and, possibly, even their own political aspirations. In principle, this process never runs its course, not even in the light of the uniformizing effects of modern mass-markets and mass-media. Further subdivisions are always possible, though perhaps less probable, even where shared political and econotechnical institutions and experiences exist. The overarching resources and powers of the state seemingly reach their integrative limits much earlier than do the multiple identity capacities of humankind.

We are, all of us, simultaneously, identified as individuals, as family members, as neighborhood residents, as members of communities that may involve a considerable variety of religious, occupational and political sub-networks, as regional participants, as state citizens and, more recently, as supra-state participants as well. We often feel little conflict between such multiple roles and identities, but should such conflict arise, any of the smaller identities can become not only contrastively available but even salient as well, and their linguistic counterparts can, sometimes rather quickly, become part and parcel of new and mobilizable language and ethnicity linkages that had previously been quiescent or even nonfunctional.

Conclusion: resolving tensions between broader and narrower identities

Smaller ethnocultural and ethnolinguistic units are obviously under pressure to re-ethnify and relinguify in the direction of the more powerful reward-systems that surround them. It is the fear of just such potentially dislocative re-ethnification and relinguification that keeps the member states of the EC from overtly adopting just one, two or three overarching languages of administration. However, this same type of fear characterizes the sub-state languages vis-à-vis the state languages. Indeed, in some regions there are sub-regional ethnolinguistic aggregates that experience this same fear vis-à-vis the regional languages that surround them, albeit the latter themselves are also minority languages within their respective states. Thus, just as some Nederlands speakers fear being relinguified and re-ethnified by English, so some Frisians fear relinguification and re-ethnification by Nederlands, and, startlingly enough, some Stellingwerfsk speakers fear being relinguified and re-ethnified by the Frisians that surround and outnumber them.

Nevertheless, the co-occurrence of both broader and narrower identities and loyalties are not only often possible but inevitable, and the further down one goes in the scale of ethnolinguistic and ethnocultural identity, the more (rather than the less) such co-occurrences of part-identities are encountered. "Down there", in the deepest reaches of small ethnocultural identity, the notion of limits quite frequently seems more flexible, more expandable and more multiply-rewarding than such identity seems from above. More Frisians also consider themselves Netherlanders than main-line Netherlanders suspect. Of course, the view from above *has to be* a different one than the view from below. Indeed, the obvious advantages of multiple identities, when conceived of most generally, are often very apparent to mainstream individuals, although they may not as frequently conceptualize these identities along ethnolinguistic lines. That is precisely why the limits of ethnolinguistic democracy should never be defined from the top alone. Rather, these must be significantly defined from the bottom as well. Certainly, the smaller members of the EC would appreciate being consulted before any subset of administrative super-languages is selected by the super-powers among them. Similarly, all EC members must learn to consult the sub-state speech communities within themselves if fairness in ethnolinguistic affairs is ever to be more than a null set.

It is unfortunately true that very few people (including most of their own speakers) care about the impending demise of small languages. Modern language consciousness is a byproduct of the nationalist response to the widespread social change attributable to urbanization and indus-trialization. Accordingly, this consciousness is not evenly distributed throughout the world and is very seldom applied to "other people's little languages", not even by the most enlightened co-participants in intercul-tural processes. Very few people pause to consider what it is that is lost when a language is lost, particularly if it is someone else's language. But what is lost when a language is lost, especially in the short run, is the sociocultural integration of the generations, the cohesiveness, naturalness and quiet creativity, the secure sense of identity, even without politicized consciousness of identity, the sense of collective worth of a community and of a people, the particular value of being "*X*ians in *X*ish", rather than "*X*ians in Yish" or Yians in Yish, even when the conveniences of daily living are "greener in the other field". The loss of the above characteristics exacts a price via elevated levels of alienation, via injury to both corporeal and mental health in two or more generations, via a vastly increased incidence of social dislocation manifested as civil and criminal offenses, and via elevated public costs in order to overcome or contain such dislocations (many of which have come to constitute the warp and woof of much of modern life). Finally, what is lost is the cultural creativity (in song, story, theater, myth, dance and artifacts and in the representational arts) that ultimately enriches not only the immediate vicinity in the original language but also the total human experience in a myriad of translations. The loss of all of the foregoing is survivable, but, in many ways, the result of such loss amounts to a seriously lowered quality of life, including the very meaning of life itself. It is the particular gift of the most threatened languages and cultures to makes us all more aware of this issue, but it is the peculiar responsibility of the largest and most secure languages to respond constructively and magnanimously to this universal problem in human cultural-ecology.

The EC organization needed the prodding and the protests of the Catalans in order to expand its previous concept of "complete multilingualism". Those who care for small languages and identities (e.g., Stauf 1991) and who treasure the intimate ethnocultural patrimonies that these languages index, symbolize and implement, those who willingly accept the extra stimulation and enrichment — and burdens and tensions — that multiple memberships entail, they deserve all of the assistance that a generous theory of limits can provide so that, to quote the European Parliament for the last time "the people of Europe [and of the world at large — JAF] will not regard ... [their] institutions as being out of touch with and foreign to them" ... but rather "look upon them as important elements playing a part in the daily life of its citizens". On the other hand, if limits and accommodations *are* sometimes necessary in applying this declaration at the sub-state level, then it should be remembered, such limits may well be equally or even more necessary at the supra-state level. The arbitrariness of power must be opposed, in the ethnolinguistic arena, just as it must be opposed in the political and economic realms of which the EC is apparently more aware.

Notes

1. This is a revised version of a paper originally presented at a celebration honoring the 700th anniversary of the Swiss Confederation, Disentis, August 1991, at the Symposium on Linguistic Human Rights, Tallinn (Estonia), October, 1991, and at the Tenth Annual Conference on Language and Communication, New York, December, 1991, i.e. before the separation of Czechoslovakia, Yugoslavia and the Soviet Union into constituent independent states. I am indebted to many members of the audience at all of the above meetings and, most particularly, to Tove Skutnabb-Kangas, Robert Phillipson and Humphrey Tonkin for their helpful comments which have enabled me to substantially improve my original presentations.

Linguistic human rights and educational policy in Russia

Alexei A. Leontiev

Russia: the ethnolinguistic map

Educational policy needs to address three main issues when converting linguistic human rights into practice:

a) the choice of the language of instruction,
b) teaching non-mother tongues, and
c) teaching the mother tongue.

To understand the real complexity of these problems in the former Soviet Union in general, and in the Russian Federation in particular, we need a brief sketch of Russia's ethnolinguistic map.

Genetically, the languages of Russia belong to different language families: Indo-European, Uralian, Altaic, Abkhaz-Adygh, Nakh, Daghestanian, Chukchi-Kamchatkian, Eskimo-Aleutian, plus some isolated languages. Beside the Slavic languages there are such Indo-European languages in Russia as Yiddish, Romani, Ossetian, Armenian, German and Greek. Assessing the precise number of languages in the Federation is fraught with definitional problems. The official number of ethnoses in the Russian Federation is 123. Most of the languages are not mutually comprehensible.

Officially, most national republics — members of the Russian Federation — have decreed that the language of the relevant nation or ethnos is the official, state language of the republic, mostly along with Russian. Under the terms of the most recent law ("On languages of the peoples of the RSFSR"), Russian is the state language of Russia in toto.

Functionally, there is substantial variation among the languages of Russia. For instance, 23 languages are used in Russia as the media of instruction, 66 languages are taught as subjects. The entire former Soviet Union had TV programmes in 49 languages and radio programmes in 71, books published in 70, magazines in 44, newspapers in 56, theatre in

45. The functional status of the languages, i. e. their full set of social functions, varies from languages with a maximal range (from world communication to family communication in Russian) to those with a minimal range (communication within the family and with neighbours in the same village only, for instance in minor languages of Daghestan). As a result there has been a massive spread of diglossia and multiglossia.

Diglossia is typical of all regions of the Russian Federation, but its extent varies. The most widespread type of diglossia is "minor language + Russian", but not the reverse. Only 3.5% of Russians are bilingual, whereas 70% of Chuvashians are.

Inter-ethnic communication is accomplished in more than 20 languages. It is often erroneously thought that Russian is the only language of inter-ethnic communication, but in reality the official language for links between the republics need not be identical with the actual language of inter-ethnic communication. In Daghestan, for instance, there are 4 common languages (Russian, Azerbaydzhanian, Avar and Kumyk) and 7 contact languages (Lak, Dargin, Lezgin, Tabasaran, Tsakhur, Chechen and Georgian).

There are approximately 58,000 (monolingual) Russian-medium *schools*, in which Russian is taught as a mother tongue subject. There are 4,300 "bilingual" schools, which in Russia means schools for non-Russians from one ethnic group, with Russian as the medium of instruction and their own language taught as a subject. There are 1,500 "mixed" schools, with a multiethnic population, but also with Russian as the medium of education and the different mother tongues taught as subjects. And finally, there are some 6,200 "monolingual" schools with other languages as media of instruction (and the same languages as mother tongue subjects) — these schools also teach Russian as L2.

Against this background it is highly desirable to elaborate a practical educational policy which enshrines linguistic human rights. The outline of such a policy is described below, but first I shall consider some basic concepts and notions, beginning with the notion of linguistic human rights.

Linguistic human rights: theoretical idea or practical tool?

In most official or semi-official documents, the notion of linguistic human rights seems to be purely theoretical. For instance, in FIPLV's draft declaration (quoted — and also criticized — in Skutnabb-Kangas —

Phillipson, this volume) of August 1991, there are such formulations as "Everyone has the right of expression in any language." I gravely doubt whether such formulations can serve as a principle or basis for practical language policy. Let us contrast them with equivalent formulations in some official texts elaborated in the then USSR at the same time, for example point 4 of the "Declaration of human rights and freedoms" adopted by the USSR Peoples' Deputies Congress in September 1991: "To every person is guaranteed the right to use the mother tongue, to education in the mother tongue, and the protection and growth of the national culture...". Another example is the draft of the law "On languages of the peoples of the RSFSR", for approval by the Supreme Soviet of the Russian Federation. It includes such notions as the "linguistic sovereignty of peoples and of the individual", "guarantees of the protection of the languages", "social, economic and juridical defence of languages by the State", and, of course, linguistic human rights, but in a somewhat different variant, the "linguistic rights of peoples and of a person".

In my view, linguistic human rights have *three* subjects: a) the person; b) the ethnos; c) the state. We therefore have three corresponding types of sovereignty: a) the sovereignty of a single human being or of the individual; b) the sovereignty of an ethnos; c) the sovereignty of the authorities at the State or local level.

Thus the Tatar Republic is not juridically identical with Tatars, even those living in this republic. Members of each ethnos living in Tataria have the *same* rights, but these rights have to be distinguished from the rights of the Tatarian authorities.

All the problems of the development of the national culture or of the national language, including the teaching of this language in schools and its use as a medium of education in schools, have to do with the sovereignty of an ethnos. This sovereignty is made manifest in different forms, such as People's Congresses, and the activities of various cultural societies. It is not connected to the frontiers of republics or other state (administrative) units: the sovereignty of the Kurdish, Armenian, Assyrian people applies to all Kurds, Armenians and Assyrians wherever they live — assuming, of course, that they recognize this sovereignty themselves. In solving language or culture problems, this kind of sovereignty has priority, rather than the sovereignty of authorities. In practice this means that if Estonians living in the region of Pskov intend to open Estonian schools or to teach Estonian in schools which Estonian children attend, the authorities of this region have *no right* to put obstacles in their way and are *obliged* to open such schools (which assumes adequate financial support).

The state, or local, authorities have in general three main functions in the area of language and culture policy:

a) an *executive* function, in carrying out the decisions of an ethnos within the limits of its sovereignty;
b) a *regulative* function: the State has, for instance, the right to declare some language(s) the state or official language(s) and to decide that all official occasions and meetings are to be organized in an official language (this is thus the case in the law "On the Uzbek SSR state language");
c) a *stimulatory* function, the indirect regulation of the development of languages and cultures (thus the "Uzbek SSR provides for the teaching of the state language of the republic, free of charge, to citizens not knowing the Uzbek language", paragraph 4 of the law just referred to).

It is generally the second function, regulation, which dominates. Stimulation is often erroneously regarded as relating only to the language which has given its name to the relevant republic (Yakut in Saha-Yakutia, Ingush in Ingushetia), but all other ethnoses have equal rights to the "main" ethnoses, and the republican authorities should stimulate their cultural and linguistic development to the same degree.

A vital issue is the relationship between an individual and the relevant ethnos. In the first place, every person has the right to identify with any ethnic group, irrespective of her/his mother tongue, nationality (parental or the individual's), confession, etc. In this sense, individual rights override those of the ethnos. Secondly, every stipulation of LHR in the field of language education must cover two aspects, the rights of the individual and the rights of the ethnos.

There should not be any legislation covering the relationship between the individual and the authorities, other than the right of the individual to speak her/his own language in any state institution, for instance in court, and linguistic demands that the State may require of people working in its offices.

Each language and national culture has an equal right to support and stimulation by the State. All languages and all national cultures are axiologically and juridically equal. However, some minorities are effectively unable to survive demographically, culturally and linguistically. In such cases, the State *must* ensure real linguistic and cultural development.

State and other authorities must defend such languages socially, financially and juridically (see also Grin, this volume, about threatened languages).

It is only when LHRs are understood in such a non-trivial sense that the notion of LHR can serve as a guiding principle for a valid linguistic policy in education.

Some linguistic proposals for an educational policy

1a) Every ethnos has the right to offer the broadest possible range of teaching of its language in schools, irrespective of what the medium of instruction is in these schools.

1b) Every individual who identifies with this ethnos and considers its language to be her/his mother tongue has the right to learn this and any other language (including languages not used for inter-ethnic communication in this region), if this language is taught in schools or if there are appropriate self-instructional materials.

1c) These rights are guaranteed through
   — the publication of textbooks and other teaching materials,
   — teacher training in this language.
1d) These rights are constrained by
   — whether the languages exist in a written form,
   — the actual numbers of pupils intending to learn the language, overall and in particular towns or regions,
   — the number of copies of textbooks, including self-instructional ones, and the number of trained teachers.

2a) Every ethnos has the right to organize schools or classes with instruction through the medium of its own language in regions where this ethnos can guarantee the necessary numbers of students.

2b) Every individual who identifies with the ethnos or speaks its language has the right to be taught through the medium of this language when such teaching is available in the relevant town or region.

2c) These rights are guaranteed through
   — the publication of textbooks and other teaching materials,
   — teacher training in this language.

2d) These rights are constrained by
- the appropriacy of learning particular subjects in this language, depending on the availability of scientific literature and the elaboration of terminology, etc.,
- the actual number of pupils intending to enter the school or class with this language of instruction,
- the provision of textbooks and other teaching materials and trained teachers for the process of education in this language.

If there are children who wish to be taught in the relevant language but an inadequate number for classes or even groups, teaching through the medium of this language may, if the pupils or their parents agree, be substituted for by extensive teaching of the language and its culture (literature, ethnic history, etc.).

Linguistic rights and linguistic duties

The authorities must guarantee the teaching of:
- all mother tongues used in the relevant region,
- the state/official language(s) of the republic,
- Russian as the official language of the Russian Federation,
- the most widely used languages of inter-ethnic communication in the region, if not already covered,
- at least one foreign language.

State or local authorities have no right to impose the teaching of all subjects in a given language unless such a policy corresponds to the wishes of the relevant ethnos. In other words, nobody should force students to be educated in a particular language. Choice of the language of instruction depends entirely on the wishes of an ethnos and the individuals who belong to it.

There must, however, be some linguistic "duties", not only rights, for the individual.

Firstly, the mother tongue must be a compulsory subject in the school. Of course choice of the mother tongue is a personal matter. Nobody has the right to force Bashkirs, for instance, to learn Bashkir as their mother tongue if the real language of communication in the family is Tatarian or Russian. But whatever it is, the mother tongue must be taught.

The *second compulsory language is an official language or the language of inter-ethnic communication.* In some regions, this issue does not arise, for instance in purely Russian ones. In others there are three possible situations:

a) mother tongue (not Russian) + Russian as official language;
b) mother tongue (Russian) + another language as (non-official) language of inter-ethnic communication;
c) mother tongue + one or two official languages of the republic.

In all such situations, the second obligatory language should be taught. Naturally it is not every language of inter-ethnic communication that must be taught compulsorily: this is required only if instruction through the medium of the mother tongue ends after merely two/four/seven years, and the language of inter-ethnic communication becomes the medium of instruction.

The *third compulsory language* to be taught is a *foreign* one. Every student in every school has the right to learn at least one foreign language and is obliged to learn it. The school is obliged to organize the teaching of at least one foreign language. Choice of foreign language(s) is problematical, reflecting the needs and wishes of students and their parents, local traditions, availability, etc.

The educational authorities of each region have the duty to teach all these languages. In "Russian" schools situated in regions where a different language is the dominant one, this dominant language must be taught. The obligation on the student is to learn only *one* language in addition to her/his mother tongue and the foreign language. If four or five languages are offered, the student must choose from them, and any additional languages are optional.

Let us demonstrate these principles in a specific situation. In Ossetia there are many Ingushes. In Ingush schools, where such exist, Ingush children must compulsorily learn the Ingush language, either Ossetian or Russian (from which they have a legal right to choose), and a foreign language.

The principle of parity

This principle seems to be very important too. It runs as follows: the total number of school hours dedicated to every mother tongue must be identical, at any rate in the same republic or region, for examples Chuvash as the mother tongue in Chuvash schools and Russian in Russian schools in the Chuvash republic. The same principle holds in relation to the teaching of the second obligatory languages, foreign languages, and other optional languages.

There is a discrepancy between the duties and rights of students, including Russian students, in national republics or in non-Russian speaking regions, and the duties and rights of Russian-speaking students in purely Russian regions. These have to learn only two languages — Russian and a foreign language — meaning that the modest proportion of bilinguals in Russian-speaking regions is perpetuated. For the time being there is no clear resolution of this problem, but in future the introduction, perhaps on an optional basis, of at least one non-Russian language other than a foreign language is highly desirable. Another way to avoid "monolingual stupidity" (see Skutnabb-Kangas — Phillipson, this volume), is the compulsory learning of a second foreign language.

The situation in Russia seems to be more complicated than is the case in any other European country. In principle, however, the education of any student, including Russians, should result in the learning of at least two languages beside the mother tongue.

Who will pursue this policy?

The former autonomous republics have sovereign responsibility for their educational policy. Hence the only way to implement the principles outlined above in educational practice is to explain that all the rights and duties in this area are mutual — Tatars in the Ulianovsk region will be in the same position as Russians in Tataria, and vice versa. In any case, the Russian Ministry of Education has the right to suggest these, or other, principles to local educational authorities. To discuss them, to direct their implementation, and to coordinate their application in varying sociolinguistic situations, a special Council of Experts in linguistic educational policy is to be set up at the RF Ministry of Education. It includes leading specialists in the teaching of mother tongues, second and foreign languages, in socio- and psycholinguistics, etc.

At least the principles described above seem to be reasonable enough...

Linguistic human rights, past and present

Tove Skutnabb-Kangas — Robert Phillipson

Introduction

We will provisionally regard linguistic human rights in relation to the *mother tongue(s)*[1] as consisting of the right to identify with it/them, and to education and public services through the medium of it/them. Mother tongues are here defined as "the language(s) one has learned first and identifies with" (see Skutnabb-Kangas 1984a, chapter 2). In relation to *other languages* we will regard linguistic human rights as consisting of the right to learn an official language in the country of residence, in its standard form.

It is extremely common, in virtually all parts of the world, for people to be deprived of such basic linguistic human rights. The speakers of most minority languages are discriminated against on the grounds of language (see note 2 for definitions of minorities). Some groups are not allowed to identify with their mother tongues (e.g. Kurds in Turkey, see Skutnabb-Kangas — Bucak, this volume). Speakers of more than 6000 languages are not entitled to education, nor to the administration of justice or public services through the medium of their mother tongue. This is true of most *indigenous* minorities and almost universally of *migrant/immigrant* and *refugee* minorities. By contrast, some well established *"national"* or *"regional"* minorities (e.g. in Belgium, Canada, Finland, India, Switzerland, and, until recently, the Soviet Union and Yugoslavia) are empowered to exercise most or at least some of their linguistic human rights (see Appendix and e.g. Annamalai 1986a, 1986b; McRae 1983, 1986).

Ethnolinguistic minority children, indigenous and immigrant, often attend pre-schools and schools where no teachers understand their language and where it is not used, either as a subject or as a medium of education. The school has been and still is the key instrument, on all continents, for imposing assimilation (forced inclusion) into both the dominant language and the dominant culture (see e.g. Cahn — Hearne 1969; Jordan 1988; Wong Fillmore 1991; there are also hundreds of novels and collections of short stories in many languages describing this). As much analysis shows, much of the recent focus on multiculturalism in education has in fact excluded multilingualism (e.g. Clyne 1986, 1991; Cummins — Danesi 1990; Mullard 1984; Pattanayak 1988, 1992; Skutnabb-Kangas 1990a, b; Smolicz 1979; de Vreede 1991) and thus excluded and separated language from culture. Linguistic human rights can thus well be violated within a purportedly multicultural framework.

While this is generally the somewhat grim reality for minority groups at the present day, many of them are energetically pressing for recognition of their rights (including rights for *sign language users,* see Appendix). Substantial efforts are currently under way in many supranational fora to produce declarations, conventions and charters which can promote respect for the rights of minority language speakers. This paper will report on and analyse these, but begins by surveying some aspects of the history of linguistic human rights. A framework is presented for analysing the extent to which constitutional texts in national and international law provide support for minority languages, especially in education. We also describe current moves towards drafting covenants to protect linguistic human rights. The issue of what is and what is not a linguistic human right is exemplified in relation to the learning of foreign languages. Finally we suggest that depriving individuals or groups of linguistic human rights reflects a sophisticated contemporary form of racism, namely linguicism.

A historical overview of linguistic rights

We shall now briefly assess the historical development of linguistic rights for minorities, especially educational rights. The narrowing of focus from linguistic human rights in general to educational linguistic human rights for minorities acknowledges the fact that linguistic rights are more urgently needed for minorities than for majorities, and that formal education, where it exists, plays a decisive role in the maintenance and development of languages — or in their demise. Many minority children are still punished for speaking their mother tongue, both physically (as Kurds in Turkey) and psychologically and economically (see Skutnabb-Kangas 1984a, chapter 12, Violence and minority education; Skutnabb-Kangas — Phillipson 1989a). In fact, formal education through the medium of majority languages has extremely often *forced* minority children to assimilate and change identity. We are reminded of the definition of genocide, where one of the acts counting as genocide is "forced transfer of children to another community or group" (which in such Criminal Codes as Portugal's "shall be punishable by imprisonment for 10 to 25 years" (Art. 189d), UN 1991 May, 145). This transfer can, of course, be either physical or psychological or both.

Prior to this century international law was restricted to the Law of Nations, i. e. relations between nation states (on this highly controversial concept, see e.g. Riggs 1985, 1986; Stavenhagen 1990). No state had any legal right to be concerned about the internal affairs of another sovereign state. The charters of human rights formulated after the American and French Revolutions are forerunners of the post-1945 conventions on human rights, but they made no claim to universal validity and could in no sense be regarded as part of international law. These charters did not contain clauses on the rights of minorities, and they certainly did not guarantee minorities any linguistic rights (for America, see Hernández-Chávez, in this volume; for France, see Brunot 1967).

"The principles of international law" were invoked at the Berlin Conference of 1884–1885 in order to condemn slavery (the primary purpose of the conference being to share Africa out between the European imperialist powers and impose colonialism on African peoples). The League of Nations implemented the first international human rights treaty, the Slavery Convention, in 1926.

Human Rights universal declarations have progressed through various phases.[3] The *first generation* related to personal freedoms, civil and political rights. These were extended in the decolonisation phase from the rights of individuals to the right of oppressed peoples to self-determination. The *second generation* related to economic, social and cultural rights. The *third generation* covers "solidarity" rights (peace, development, an unspoilt environment). Even if specific covenants focus on particular sets of rights, an underlying principle is that all human rights essentially form a coherent whole and presuppose each other (Alfredsson 1991; Stavenhagen 1990).

Human rights are currently being linked to North-South "aid" and the worldwide promotion of "democracy". Their observance is being required as a precondition for aid or investment, and for membership of the Council of Europe, where ironically a higher standard of minority protection is being required of Eastern European states than exists in many existing member states (Skutnabb-Kangas 1993b). At root there is considerable conceptual confusion and fuzziness in the way "democracy" and "human rights" are understood, marketed and used as a lever vis-a-vis governments in Eastern Europe (Tomaševski 1993a) and "developing" countries (Tomaševski 1993b). The role of the United Nations and its various organs in the promotion and monitoring of human rights (Eide in particular on minority rights) is comprehensively reviewed in Alston 1992.

The formulation of linguistic human rights in international legal texts can be regarded as falling roughly into *5 periods*, reflecting differences in the scope of the rights (state level, bilateral, regional/multilateral, international) and the interest in specific rights for linguistic (as opposed to other) minorities, individuals as opposed to groups, and, of course, fluctuations in the extent to which rights were granted. We will briefly characterise the periods, provide a few examples from each, and summarize implications for future work.

The FIRST PHASE is pre-1815. Language rights were not covered in any international treaty, other than in *bilateral agreements*. Rights concerning minorities were primarily to be found in agreements covering *religious but not linguistic minorities* (Capotorti 1979).

The notion of imposing a single language on all the groups living within the borders of the state was first proposed as an instrument of government policy in Spain in the late fifteenth century, the time when the expansive modern European states began to take shape (Illich 1981). The dominant language was seen as a means of securing conformity internally and expansion externally (on language policy in Mexico from this period on, see Heath 1972). A monolingual doctrine and adherence to the principle of "one state, one nation, one language" have been exported worldwide. In colonial empires, the promotion of the language of the colonizer generally resulted in local languages being deprived of most rights.

In France less than half the population had French as their mother tongue at the time of the French Revolution (Calvet 1974), but civil liberties were extended to all through the exclusive medium of French. In both Britain and France the structural favouring of the dominant language was accompanied by an ideology of *glorification* of this language and vilification of marginalised languages, which were *stigmatised* as "dialects" or "patois" of limited value and potential. Such beliefs about the languages of others can be traced back at least to the Greek categorization of the world as consisting of the Greeks themselves and of Barbarians, the term originally meaning speakers of meaningless noises, a non-language.[4]

The SECOND period begins with the Final Act of the Congress of Vienna 1815. It was "the first important *international* instrument to contain

clauses safeguarding *national minorities*, and not only religious minorities"
(Capotorti 1979: 2). Most national minorities are simultaneously linguistic
minorities. The Congress concluded the age of Napoleonic expansion and
was signed by seven European major powers. Poles in Poznan were
granted the right to use Polish for official business, jointly with German.
However, most nineteenth century multilateral treaties, which involved a
large number of European powers, accorded no rights to linguistic minorities.

During the 19th century, several national constitutions and some
multilateral instruments safeguarded national linguistic minorities.

An early example of the recognition of linguistic rights in a national
constitution is the Austrian Constitutional Law of 1867, which contrasts
strongly with the monolingualism which other powers were attempting
to impose at the same time. Article 19 states that

> All the ethnic minorities of the States shall enjoy the same rights
> and, in particular, have an absolute right to maintain and develop
> their nationality and their language. All the languages used in the
> provinces are recognized by the State as having equal rights with
> regard to education, administration and public life. In provinces
> inhabited by several ethnic groups, the public educational institu-
> tions shall be organized in such a way as to enable all the ethnic
> groups to acquire the education they need in their own language,
> without being obliged to learn another language of the province.
> (quoted in Capotorti 1979; 3).

During the THIRD period, between the two World Wars, the Peace Treaties
and *major multilateral and international conventions* worked out under
the auspices of the League of Nations contained clauses protecting minorities, and many *national constitutions* stipulated the rights of linguistic
minorities.

The Peace Treaties that concluded the First World War attempted to
safeguard the rights of linguistic minorities in central and eastern Europe
(roughly 20% of the population of the 13 countries affected). A substantial number of international instruments emanated from the Paris treaties
(listed in the League of Nations Official Journal, special supplement no.
73 of June 13th 1929), embracing multinational agreements and the
national constitutions of many European states (essentially those in the
Baltic and south-east and central Europe). The essential points are summarized on page 47:

As regards the use of the minority language, States which have signed the treaties have undertaken to place no restriction in the way of the free use by any national of the country of any language, in private intercourse, in commerce, in religion, in the Press or in publications of any kind, or at public meetings. Those states have also agreed to grant adequate facilities to enable their nationals whose mother tongue is not the official language to use their own language, either orally or in writing, before the Courts. They have further agreed, in towns and districts where a considerable proportion of nationals of the country whose mother tongue is not the official language of the country are resident, to make provision for adequate facilities for ensuring that, in the primary schools (the Czechoslovak Treaty refers to 'instruction' in general), instruction shall be given to the children of such nationals through the medium of their own language, it being understood that this provision does not prevent the teaching of the official language being made obligatory in those schools.

Such rights were supposed to prevail in countries like Hungary, Rumania and Yugoslavia (for an analysis of the fragility of the states which were formed in Europe post 1919, and similarities between these states and post-colonial African states, see Davidson 1992). Similar principles guided the treaties relating to Turkey and the minorities within its territory. Britain, France and the United States were signatories to the minorities' treaties, but did *not* offer equivalent rights to their own minority group citizens.

The treaties provided for the right of complaint to the League of Nations (which had a Minorities Secretariat), and the International Court of Justice. This right of appeal proved to be of limited value: whereas 204 complaints were filed in 1930–31, only 4 were in 1938–39 (Boudoin — Masse 1973: 19).

Very few, if any, countries were willing to press for minority protection at the highest international level. Latvia (1922), Lithuania (1925) and Poland (1932, 1933, 1934) proposed universal protection within the framework of the League of Nations, but the Supreme Council rejected all the drafts (Andrýsek 1989: 20). A token gesture was made in a League of Nations' Assembly recommendation in 1922:

The Committee expresses the hope that the States which are not bound by any legal obligations to the League with respect to minorities will nevertheless observe in the treatment of their own racial, religious or linguistic minorities at least as high a standard of justice and toleration as is required by any of the Treaties and by the regular action of the Council. (from Protection of Linguistic, Racial or Religious Minorities by the League of Nations, 2nd edition, Document C.8.M.5 I. B.1, Minorities, Geneva, 1931, quoted in Andrýsek 1989: 20).

The FOURTH period, from 1945 to the 1970s, saw a wish on the part of the victors of the Second World War to prevent the abuses against human rights perpetrated by fascist regimes. Within the framework of the United Nations a major effort to legislate internationally for the protection of human rights was undertaken. "Universal" declarations have been elaborated and codified, with the aim of establishing minimal conditions necessary for a just and humane social order. The primary goal of all declarations of human rights, whether national or international, has been to protect the individual against arbitrary or unjust treatment.

However, the thrust of promoting the full gamut of human rights resulted in the *relative neglect of the protection of minorities*, with the exception of broad formulations outlawing discrimination. It was thought that human rights instruments in general provided enough protection for *everybody* and that specific rights for minorities were thus unnecessary. There was therefore, relatively speaking, a lack of attention to minority rights during this phase. This is admitted by the UN itself too. The recent *Human Rights Fact Sheet on Minorities* (No 18, March 1992: 1) states that

the setting of standards which would create additional rights and make special arrangements for persons belonging to minorities and for the minorities as *groups* — although a stated goal of the United Nations for more than 40 years — has made slow progress.

The United Nations Charter does not mention minorities at all.

A draft treaty for the protection of minorities submitted by Hungary to the 1946 Peace Conference in London was not accepted. Proposals to include a provision on minorities in the Universal Declaration of Human Rights did not succeed. (*Human Rights Fact Sheet* 18, 1992: 3–4).

The FIFTH period saw a *renewed interest in the rights of minorities*, including linguistic rights, and work began on the formulation of several multilateral declarations. This new focus of interest can be seen in the

Capotorti report (commissioned by the UN in 1971 and published in 1979), a major survey of juridical and conceptual aspects of the protection of minorities. Information on how minorities are treated de jure and de facto was solicited for the report from governments worldwide. Capotorti proposed, among other matters, the drafting of a declaration on the rights of members of minority groups.

The overall pattern in the phases above also reflects the extent to which linguistic human rights are explicitly proclaimed in different instruments. The *strongest* degree of protection for some minorities is discernible in the types of texts which were the first to guarantee linguistic rights to minorities, namely in *national constitutions* and relevant legislation. There is *less support* in the *multilateral* but still geographically restricted human rights instruments (e.g. "European" or "African" instruments, mostly covering one continent or parts thereof), and *still less* in *"universal"* ones. The more general human rights instruments usually mention language only in passing. Language rights are often somewhat more specifically elaborated in instruments which are restricted to certain themes or apply to numerically small groups only, such as instruments relating to education or genocide, or to minorities or indigenous peoples.

We shall look later in more depth into a variety of UN universal covenants, and here merely make some provisional generalisations about linguistic human rights in the UN framework thus far.

1. It is recognized (for instance in the Capotorti report) that most minorities, not least linguistic ones, are in need of much more substantial protection. Some of the very recent recognition given to linguistic rights in declarations of intent or other texts with no legal force is laudable (e.g. *UN Human Rights Fact Sheet* 18 (1992: 4) on Minorities:

> Only when minorities are able to use their own languages, run their own schools ... can they begin to achieve the status which majorities take for granted.

2. The coverage of educational linguistic human rights in existing international instruments reflects the relative neglect of minority rights during the 30-year period after the Second World War.[5]

3. Language has not figured prominently as a concern.[6] It has been thought until very recently that the cultural characteristics of minorities, including language, were adequately covered by general references to "ethnic, religious and linguistic minorities".

4. Immigrant minorities were deliberately excluded from consideration in the Capotorti Report, hence from the main thrust of UN efforts to end discrimination against minorities. Migrant workers, refugees, stateless persons and other non-nationals are still "not true minorities" (*UN Human Rights Fact Sheet* 18, 1992: 9).

The analysis of international covenants covering linguistic rights, especially in education

Our earlier study of a range of relevant international covenants and national constitutions (Skutnabb-Kangas — Phillipson 1986a, 1989a), drawing on distinctions made by Kloss (1971, 1977) and Cobarrubias (1983), attempted to gauge to what extent these legal measures provide support for dominated languages. To do so, a grid on which some of the important dimensions of language rights can be captured was devised. The first dimension used, and represented in our grid on the vertical axis, is *degree of overtness*, on which one can mark the extent to which laws or covenants are explicit in relation to the rights of minority languages in education. The second dimension, represented on the horizontal axis, is *degree of promotion*, on which the extent to which a language is *prohibited, tolerated or actively promoted* can be plotted (see Figure 1). We see both dimensions as continua.

The promotion continuum starts with *prohibition* of a language, the goal of which is clearly to force the linguistic minority group to assimilate to the dominant language. It continues via *toleration* of the language, a situation where the language is not forbidden (explicitly or implicitly), to *non-discrimination prescription*, where discrimination of people on the basis of language is forbidden, either overtly (discrimination is made illegal in a way which is explicit enough not to cause difficulties of legal interpretation and/or where there may be sanctions of some kind) or covertly (as part of general legislation on countering discrimination). The next point on the continuum would be *permission* to use the minority language. At the other end of the continuum we have *promotion* of the minority language. This is obviously oriented toward maintaining it.

In the earlier study we plotted on to the grid a range of national constitutions: *Finland*, for both the *Sámi* (No 5 on the grid) and the *Swedish* (No 4) languages); the then *Yugoslavia* (No 3); *India* (No 6)); proposals for constitutional change: *English Language Amendments* to the *USA* Constitution (Huddleston No 1, Hayakawa No 2; see Marshall

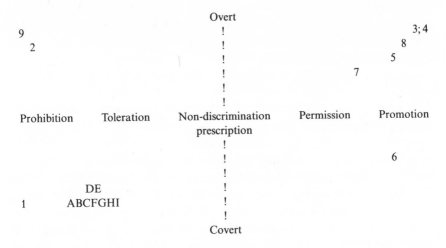

Numbers refer to countries, *letters* to covenants (see text)

1.   English Language Amendments to the USA Constitution, senator Huddleston
2.   as above, senator Hayakawa
3.   ex-Yugoslavia
4.   Finland, Swedish-speakers
5.   Finland, Sámi
6.   India
7.   The Freedom Charter of ANC and others, South Africa
8.   the Basque Normalization Law
9.   Kurds in Turkey

A: The Charter of the United Nations, 1945;
B: The Universal Declaration of Human Rights, 1948;
C: International Covenant on Economic, Social and Cultural Rights, 1966;
D: International Covenant on Civil and Political Rights, 1966;
E: The UN Convention on the Rights of the Child, 1989;
F: The Council of Europe Convention for The Protection of Human Rights and Fundamental Freedoms, 1950;
G.   The African Charter on Human and Peoples' Rights, 1981;
H.   American Declaration of the Rights and Duties of Man, 1948;
I.   American Convention on Human Rights „Pact of San Jose, Costa Rica", 1969.

Figure 1. Language rights in selected countries and covenants

1986: 36); *The Freedom Charter of the African National Congress (ANC) and others, South Africa* (No 7); the *Basque Normalization Law* (No 8). The paper on the Kurds in *Turkey* in this volume shows how Turkish legislation can be placed on the grid (No 9), and it would be possible to do the same for many of the other country studies in this volume. As stated above, many national constitutions provide more protection to minority languages in education than the international covenants. Conversely, none of the international covenants overtly prohibits the use of minority languages, as some national constitutions do.

We have also placed on the grid some of the results of our review of clauses on *language rights in education* (i. e. *not* the general clauses) in some international and European conventions and decrees (see figure 1). As can be seen from the grid, many national constitutions provide more protection to minority languages in education than the international covenants. Conversely, none of the international covenants overtly prohibits the use of minority languages, as some national constitutions do. The covenants are:

A: *The Charter of the United Nations*, 1945;
B: *The Universal Declaration of Human Rights*, 1948;
C: *International Covenant on Economic, Social and Cultural Rights*, 1966;
D: *International Covenant on Civil and Political: Rights*, 1966;
E: *The UN Convention on the Rights of the Child*, 1989;
F: *The Council of Europe Convention for The Protection of Human Rights and Fundamental Freedoms*, 1950.
G: *The African Charter on Human and Peoples' Rights*, 1981
H: *American Declaration of the Rights and Duties of Man*, 1948
I: *American Convention on Human Rights "Pact of San Jose, Costa Rica"*, 1969

Most of the articles referring to language in these texts are in the Appendix.

Example A. THE CHARTER OF THE UNITED NATIONS (1945) commits its member nations in its *general* articles to promoting

> universal respect for, and observance of, human rights and fundamental freedoms for all without distinction as to race, sex, language, or religion (paragraph 6.11, 55).

This can be understood as *overt non-discrimination prescription*. It has no specific article on *education* and thus nothing on language in education, implying only *covert toleration*.

The *general* articles in all the following covenants (B–I) can also be characterised as *overt non-discrimination prescription*. For instance, the UNIVERSAL DECLARATION OF HUMAN RIGHTS declares in paragraph 2:

> Everyone is entitled to all the rights and freedoms set forth in this Declaration, without distinction of any kind, such as race, colour, sex, language, religion, political or other opinion, national or social origin, property, birth or other status.

Example B. THE UNIVERSAL DECLARATION OF HUMAN RIGHTS (1948), in its paragraph on *education* (26), does not refer to language. The main thrust of the paragraph is to ensure free universal education. There are references to the "full development of the human personality" and the right of parents to "choose the kind of education that shall be given to their children". This can be considered *covert toleration*.

Example C. The INTERNATIONAL COVENANT ON ECONOMIC, SOCIAL AND CULTURAL RIGHTS, adopted in 1966 and in force since 1976, having mentioned language on a par with race, colour, sex, religion etc in its *general* article (2.2) again omits any reference to language in the *educational* article (13). There is an inconsistency here, because the covenant *does* explicitly refer to "racial, ethnic or religious groups" in the education article, though not "linguistic" ones. This also represents *covert toleration*.

> 13.(1) ... education shall enable all persons to participate effectively in a free society, promote understanding, tolerance and friendship among all nations and all racial, ethnic or religious groups, and further the activities of the United Nations for the maintenance of peace.

Example D. INTERNATIONAL COVENANT ON CIVIL AND POLITICAL RIGHTS (1966) does not have any *educational* clauses (i. e. there is *covert toleration*).

But Article 27 states:

> In those states in which ethnic, religious or linguistic minorities exist, persons belonging to such minorities shall not be denied the right, in community with other members of their group, to enjoy their own culture, to profess and practise their own religion, or to use their own language.

This represents *overt non-discrimination prescription*, tending towards permission, but does not include educational institutions.

This article has been one of the most important international articles for the protection of linguistic minorities, as both Capotorti (1979) and more recent UN reports (Eide 1990, 1991; Palley 1984) confirm. Both the UN Conventions on the Rights of the Child (1959 and 1989), and several Council of Europe and CSCE documents have approximately the same formulation.

Example E. The UN CONVENTION ON THE RIGHTS OF THE CHILD, 1989, stresses the maintenance of identity, including "nationality" and "name" (Art 7 and 8; see also Jernudd's article, this volume). It does not mention language in its general article on *education* (28; i. e. there is *covert toleration*), though it mentions

> development of respect for the child's parents, his or her own cultural identity, language and values (Art. 29.c),
> encourages "the mass media to have particular regard to the linguistic needs of the child who belongs to a minority group or who is indigenous" (Art. 17.d)
> and decrees that "due regard shall be paid to the desirability of continuity in a child's upbringing and to the child's ethnic, religious, cultural and linguistic background" (Art. 20.3)

— but only when a child is temporarily or permanently deprived of the family environment. The clause obviously does not refer to daily childcare or school. Article 30 is substantially the same as Art. 27 on minorities quoted above in Example D ("persons of indigenous origin" have been added, and "their" has been replaced by "his or her"). This *overt non-discrimination prescription* implicitly restricts use of the minority language to private minority community use. (This has been extended in the preamble of the European Charter for Regional or Minority Languages (see below), which, with reference to art. 27 (see D above) considers

> that the right to use a regional or minority language in private *and public* life is an inalienable right (our emphasis)).

In sum, the absence of any overt mention of language under the education clauses of these covenants is in contrast with the general clauses on non-discrimination, which relate to the exercise of all human rights. This means that the five UN conventions (A, B, C, D and E) have *general* provisions which are apparently an *overt non-discrimination prescription* (A, B, C) or even *overt permission*, mentioning language specifically (D, E). But the *education* clauses are no stronger than *covert assimilation-oriented toleration*. Minorities are allowed to use their languages in private, but not in schools. The same is also true of the following examples, from regional covenants.

Example F. THE COUNCIL OF EUROPE CONVENTION FOR THE PROTECTION OF HUMAN RIGHTS AND FUNDAMENTAL FREEDOMS, adopted in 1950 and in force since 1953, in its *education* section (first protocol, 2) represents *covert toleration* (see the European Court's interpretation in the Belgian linguistic case, below).

Example G. THE AFRICAN CHARTER ON HUMAN AND PEOPLES' RIGHTS, adopted in 1981, in force since 1986 and signed by 50 African States (as at 31 January 1990), also has a *general overt non-discrimination prescription* in its preamble and in Art. 2. The *education* clause (Art. 17.1) only confirms that "every individual shall have the right to education". Language is not mentioned, i. e. there is *covert toleration*. The Charter includes not only rights but also duties. This approach where rights are inseparable from duties, is "old" in Africa (and in the Americas — see example G — and Asia; the same Sanskrit word which means "right" also means "duty"), but the UN claims that it is "new in international instruments" (in its Introduction to The African Charter, UN 1990). One could, maybe, envisage that the promotion, protection, preservation and strengthening of everybody's mother tongue could come in under the duties of the State and the individual, since

> the promotion and protection of morals and traditional values recognized by the community shall be the duty of the State. (Art 17.3)

and since the individual has the duty

> to preserve the harmonious development of the family and to work for the cohesion and respect of the family; to respect his parents at all times ... (Art 29.1)

and "to preserve and strengthen positive African cultural values in his relations with other members of the society ..." (Art. 29.7).

Example H. AMERICAN DECLARATION OF THE RIGHTS AND DUTIES OF MAN, 1948 states, in addition to the usual *general* non-discrimination prescription (Art. II) and right to education (Art. XII, where language is not mentioned, i. e. there is *covert toleration*), in its Article on freedom of investigation, opinion, expression and dissemination (Art. IV) that this can be done "by any medium whatsoever". Likewise the article on the right to the benefits of culture (Art. XIII) stresses the right to

> participate in the benefits that result from intellectual progress, especially scientific discoveries,

something that may be difficult unless these results are available in a language one knows. Such formulations are common in many national constitutions (see UN 1991 May, HR/PUB/90/8) and in several of the international covenants.

It is also

the duty of every person to acquire at least an elementary education (Art. XXXI),

which again can be difficult if the child does not understand the language of instruction (see the Lau v. Nichols case below and Hernández-Chávez, this volume).

Example I. AMERICAN CONVENTION ON HUMAN RIGHTS "PACT OF SAN JOSE, COSTA RICA", adopted 1969, in force 1978, also has language in its *general* part (Art. 1.1) and does not have anything on *education* (i. e. *non-discrimination prescription* and *covert toleration*, respectively). It promises in its Art. 8.2.a on the right to a fair trial

the right of the accused to be assisted without charge by a translator or interpreter, if he does not understand or does not speak the language of the tribunal or court

(c.f. Magga and Kāretu, in this volume; this is also guaranteed for instance in the Covenant on Civil and Political Rights, Art. 14.2.a and f, Example D above, and, for children, in Art. 40.vi in the Convention on the Rights of the Child, Example E above). The Article on freedom of thought and expression (Art. 13.3) guarantees that this

may not be restricted by indirect methods or means" or "any other means tending to impede the communication and circulation of ideas and opinions.

Not understanding a language might be interpreted as this type of restriction.

The European, African and American conventions are thus similar to the UN conventions in being silent on languages in the education clauses. As we will see, some of the new (draft) declarations go further.

Litigation for language rights

That the rights are of limited value in supporting language maintenance via education can be seen from litigation in relation to similar rights. The Council of Europe Convention for the Protection of Human Rights and

Fundamental Freedoms (Example F above) declares in its first protocol, 2:

> No person shall be denied the right to education. In the exercise of any functions which it assumes in relation to education and to teaching, the State shall respect the right of parents to ensure such education and teaching in conformity with their own religious and philosophical convictions.

This has been interpreted by the European Court of Human Rights as only meaning that subjects have the right to avail themselves of the means of instruction available at a given time, and not to have any particular type of education established. Although the clause cited does not specify the language in which education must be conducted, in order that the right to education should be respected, the European Court observed that

> this right would be meaningless if it did not imply ... the right to be educated in the national language, or in one of the national languages, as the case may be. (Sieghart 1983: 249, reporting the "Belgian Linguistic Case").

This appears to give the state the right to decide what languages education should be offered in, hence which languages should be maintained and which should not, irrespective of minority wishes (and the European Charter for Regional or Minority Languages does not go further than this, because the state decides which languages the provisions should apply to, see below; for an alternative solution see Leontiev, in this volume). The European Court added that for the right to education to be effective,

> it is also necessary that the individual who is the beneficiary should have the possibility of drawing profit from the education received (Sieghart 1983: 249).

This is specified as meaning "the right to obtain ... official recognition of the studies ... completed", ie the right to credentials. It would be important to clarify by litigation whether this can be interpreted as meaning that a child does *not* have any right to *understand* the instruction, i. e. the language in which the education is given (which could also be seen as a prerequisite for "drawing profit from the education received").

The European Court ruling has affinities with the American Supreme Court case of **Lau** v. **Nichols**, in which students of Chinese ancestry claimed that the San Francisco Unified School District failed in its obligation to provide adequate education for them. The Supreme Court ruled that

> Under these state-imposed standards there is no equality of treatment merely by providing students with the same facilities, textbooks, teachers and curriculum; for students who do not understand English are effectively foreclosed from any meaningful education. (quoted in Center for Applied Linguistics 1977: 7).

The court's finding was that the school board failed in its obligation to provide the Chinese group with equality of benefits from education, and that this was in defiance of Title VI of the Civil Rights Act of 1964. The court avoided pronouncing on whether there was also an offence against the Equal Protection Clause of the 14th Amendment to the Constitution.

The significance of this and many similar court cases on bilingual education issues in the USA (see Hernández-Chávez 1988, 1990, this volume) and on issues of linguistic varieties and accents, for instance Black English or Hawai'ian English (see Labov 1972; Matsuda 1991; Sato 1991 and in press; Smitherman 1992) is that it is possible for individual rights, guaranteed by the state, to be enforced at the appropriate level. Indeed a review of legal aspects of bilingual education in the USA concludes that in that country "litigation has served, and will continue to serve, as a necessary strategy for educational reform" (Center for Applied Linguistics 1977: 40), though it is unlikely that there would be as optimistic a view of litigation substantially assisting minorities in the 1990's (see Sato 1991 and in press). Several cases have been brought on the enforcement of an "English Only" policy in the US (see summary in Crandall 1992), in particular on the right to ban the use of languages other than English at the workplace. The indications are that there is considerable confusion as to what constitutional rights to language are guaranteed, and that there is little understanding of bilingualism on the bench.

There are several dimensions to the issue of language rights in court. O'Barr (1982, 1990) is concerned with the question of legal access associated with the dialect, register, discourse and other sociolinguistic features of litigants and the legal system professionals. Is justice being done if a litigant is unable to function adequately in the type of language that characterizes law courts (c.f. Appendix, where several instruments require that the charge be delivered "in a language he understands" — apparently only males are charged). Are the individual's linguistic human rights being infringed if the discourse rules discriminate against certain litigants? These questions relate to access to the standard code and to specialized discourse, and to the role of the education system in equipping citizens to function in given ways. There can be no doubt that the individual is not receiving a fair hearing if court proceedings take place in a different language and interpreters are not provided. Here there is prima facie a violation of a human right (see Appendix; but see also Magga, this volume, about only getting fundamental rights by pleading helplesness), with language as the crucial factor. However, the situation with linguistic variation is not so clear. It is common for judges in criminal cases to be familiar with what they call underworld slang, but this does not guarantee that a litigant can communicate effectively in legal discourse. It would be important for the borders of linguistic human rights to be tested by more consideration of insights from forensic linguistics.

The litigation route may not be navigable in countries such as Great Britain, in the absence of relevant legislation, and where it would be difficult to build a case on a violation of a fundamental freedom. However, the new British Lord Chief Justice appointed in 1992 is on record as approving of the principle of the incorporation of relevant covenants into British law. Some countries, such as Norway, incorporate international covenants that the state ratifies into national legislation.

As the description of the Belgian Linguistic Case indicated, there is also the possibility for citizens of the European countries which are signatories to certain conventions to appeal to an international tribunal in order to enforce their human rights. Such petitions can only be heard once all remedies in the national courts have been exhausted. There are at least two Scandinavian cases pending, where linguistic rights are involved.[7]

In addition, UNESCO has had since 1978 a procedure for considering violations of human rights within UNESCO's field of competence. However, the procedure is confidential, a complainant does not have any opportunity of seeing, or commenting on, a respondent government's reply, and only the respondent government, and not the complainant, can appear before the UNESCO committee when it considers a complaint either as to admissibility or on the merits. UNESCO does not publish any details of complaints or action taken as a result (Sieghart 1983: 436). In view of our analysis of the education clauses of UN covenants, there appears to be a serious risk that complaints about linguistic assimilation policies would fail, as they probably would at the European Court of

Human Rights. (UNESCO is very active in accumulating and disseminating documentation on human rights, see UNESCO 1991, as is the UN through its Centre for Human Rights in Geneva).

We can end this survey of litigation and the legally binding international/universal declarations by concluding that *none of these are mother tongue maintenance-oriented.* None of them represents in their general clauses more than *overt non-discrimination prescription.* In fact, most of them in their educational clauses only require *covert toleration of minority mother tongues.*

Not even overt maintenance-oriented permission is enough for minority (or powerless majority) mother tongues to be maintained, developed and handed down from parents to children over several generations, which according to Fishman (1991) is the most vital link in the chain of reversing language shift. What they require is overt maintenance-oriented promotion (which necessarily includes the allocation of the economic means for supporting mother tongue medium schools[8] – one of the crucial deficiencies in UNESCO's own Convention against Discrimination in Education). No international covenants guarantee this to any minority groups, nor to any individuals (regardless of whether the individuals come from a linguistic minority or majority).

The existing international or "universal" declarations are therefore in no way adequate to provide support for dominated, threatened languages. The evidence unmistakably shows that while individuals and groups are supposed to enjoy "cultural" and "social" rights, linguistic human rights are neither guaranteed nor protected.

In order to avoid institutional discrimination, in education and elsewhere, against minority language children, there is a need for legislation which explicitly promotes minority languages within a maintenance-oriented framework. Most existing declarations tend to be too vague and conceptually confused, and both the right of redress and the economic prerequisites for using the rights have been deficient. In the next section we will report on some of the ongoing work to remedy this.

Ongoing international efforts to codify language rights for minorities

We shall now consider current efforts to codify language rights for minorities within the UN and UNESCO, the Council of Europe and the European Parliament (whose work in this field often merges) and the CSCE.

On the initiative of the *European Parliament*, the *"European Bureau for Lesser Used Languages"* was established in 1982 with the task of promoting the languages and cultures of autochthonous minority groups of the member countries of the European Community (which they estimate at close to 50 million of the 320 million citizens of the EC). Immigrant minorities are not a concern of the Bureau.

The *European Parliament* has passed two important resolutions on language rights, *Arfe* (1981) and *Kuijpers* (1987). The Arfe resolution of 16 October 1981 urged national and regional authorities to promote the use of minority languages in three main areas, education, mass communications, and public life and social affairs. Specifically in the domain of education, they are urged

- to promote and take steps to ensure that the teaching of regional languages and cultures is included in official curricula right through from nursery school to university;
- to provide, in response to needs expressed by the population, for teaching in schools of all levels and grades to be carried out in regional languages, with particular emphasis being placed on nursery school teaching so as to ensure that the child is able to speak its mother tongue;
- to allow teaching of the literature and history of the communities concerned to be included in all curricula. (excerpted from the resolution, reproduced in the bulletin of the European Bureau for Lesser Used Languages, *Contact*, 1, November 1983: 2).

The Arfe resolution was couched in terms of "urging" and "inviting" a course of action. It was followed by the Kuijpers resolution, adopted by the European Parliament in October 1987. It recommends that member states actively promote minority languages in education, local administration, and the mass media (*Contact*, 4/3, 1987—1988: 1). These two resolutions have been instrumental in paving the way for the *European Parliament* to consider a EROPEAN CHARTER FOR REGIONAL OR MINORITY LANGUAGES, which was finally approved by the Committee of Ministers on 22 June 1992. This is a comprehensive document on the use of language in education, public services, media, cultural, economic and social life (for the earlier forms, see Resolution 192, 1988, followed by CAHLR/DELA91.1, Strasbourg, 24 June 1991; for a description of its genesis, see Woehrling 1992; for the text, see the Appendix).

The preamble

- considers "that the right to use a regional or minority language in private and public life is an inalienable right",
- stresses "the value of interculturalism and multilingualism",
- and considers "that the protection and encouragement of regional or minority languages should not be to the detriment of the official languages and the need to learn them" but rather "an important contribution to the building of a Europe based on principles of democracy and cultural diversity within the framework of national sovereignty and territorial integrity.

Each state which ratifies the European Charter can specify which minority languages it wants to apply the Charter to (Art.3.1) (and the languages of migrants are explicitly excluded in the section on definitions, Art. 1a). A state can choose which paragraphs or subparagraphs it wants to apply (a minimum of 35 is required). The formulations include a range of modifications like "as far as possible", "relevant", "appropriate", "where necessary", "pupils who so wish in a number considered sufficient", "if the number of users of a regional or minority language justifies it", and a number of alternatives as in "to allow, encourage *or* provide teaching in *or* of the regional or minority language at all the appropriate stages of education" (our emphasis).

While the Charter demonstrates how difficult it is to write binding formulations which are sensitive to local conditions, it permits a reluctant state to meet the requirements in a minimalist way which it can legitimate by claiming that a provision was not "possible" or "appropriate", numbers were not "sufficient" or did not "justify" a provision, and that it "allowed" the minority to organise teaching of their language, at their own cost.

The *European Parliament* has also adopted a RESOLUTION ON THE USE OF LANGUAGES IN THE COMMUNITY (*Official Journal of the European Communities*, April 13 1984, no C 127/139). The resolution aims at strengthening the teaching of foreign languages throughout the community and improving the quality of teaching, translating and interpreting. It

1. Reaffirms the principle that all languages and the cultures which they express have an intrinsic value;
2. Reaffirms the right of each individual to express himself freely in his own language or in the language of his choice;
3. Stresses the importance of combating illiteracy;
4. Asks for all measures at Community and Member State level aimed at promoting the use of Community languages to be encouraged.

The resolution is formulated in general terms, which express *overt maintenance-oriented permission*. Logically this should apply to all minority languages. However it is the official state and European Community languages which were the main concern of the preparatory studies prior to the adoption of the resolution (just as it is speakers of these languages which are the beneficiaries of the LINGUA and ERASMUS programmes which permit European Community nationals to study abroad). A primary motive was to limit the dominance of English and to encourage multilingualism and parity between the official languages of the community (*European Parliament Working Document* 1 — 83/84/B; see also Fishman, this volume).

In the same Resolution the *European Parliament* also

> 10. Emphasizes once again the importance of the existing Directive on the education of the children of migrant workers; asks the Commission to use all the resources at its command to ensure that the Directive is applied in full and in all the Member States.

The Directive, referred to above (77/466/EEC of 25. 7. 77), is fraught with difficulties of interpretation and implementation (see the description of the origins of the Directive and discussion in Tosi 1984: 14; see also Reid — Reich 1992). It is unclear whether the EEC intends the directive as

> an embryonic "enriching" model for the promotion of EEC languages in the modern languages curricula of member states, or as a compensatory measure for the underprivileged.

and its effects will remain unclear until

> governments make a definite pronouncement on their interpretation and define their policies for its implementation" (Tosi 1984: 17).

The same uncertainty holds for the European Parliament Resolution in question, which does not clarify the Directive.

> According to the report presented on 3 January 1989 on the implementation of this Directive by the Member States ... the results are on the whole quite unsatisfactory as only the Federal Republic of Germany and especially the Netherlands[9] have made adequate provisions for the teaching of the languages and cultures of origin of the children of migrant workers. In other member States, this Directive was either ignored or given very little attention,

says the European Parliament's *Report drawn up on behalf of the Committee of Inquiry into RACISM and XENOPHOBIA* (A3 – 195/90, PE 141.205/FIN, 111). One of the Member States, Denmark (which in 1992 decided to make it optional for local authorities to offer the teaching of migrant children's mother tongues as subjects, in violation of the Directive), was instrumental in preventing the Committee from including more about migrant languages in education in the Report, according to Glyn Ford, the European Parliament official Rapporteur (at a hearing on the report on 2. 12. 1991 in Copenhagen and again 18. 6. 1993 at an Alternative Summit in Copenhagen).

The Racism and Xenophobia Report (see above) contains endless accounts of initiatives, plans, suggestions, resolutions etc on migrant rights with "no follow-up", "none of them ever saw the light of day", "never went beyond issue no 1", "nothing more was said or done", "has not been able to go further", "no further initiatives were taken", "did not take place" (all these just from a few pages, 104–107). (Racial discrimination against migrant workers was also a concern of the UN seminar on Political, historical, economic, social and cultural factors contributing to racism, racial discrimination and apartheid, organised in Geneva 10–14 December 1990 – see UN 1991 November). The many instances of non-compliance with the limited language rights of migrants thus seem to place the *implementation* of the Directive close to *covert prohibition*, despite the European Parliament Resolution's points 1–4 and 10 above.

While one should not underestimate the potential of the European Parliament (or the Council of Europe, see below) to influence member countries, the catch is that its resolutions are not legally binding on governments.

Another important international forum which is committed to the cause of human rights is the *Council of Europe*. One of its bodies, the European Commission for Democracy through Law, has drafted a *"Proposal for a European Convention for the Protection of Minorities"* (CDL 91 – 7, which is accompanied by a substantial Explanatory Report (CDL 91 – 8). The Convention stipulates that minorities, including linguistic minorities, shall have the right

to "respect, safeguard and development of their ethnical, religious, or linguistic identity" (Art. 3.2),
to "freely preserve, express and develop their cultural identity in all its aspects, free of any attempts at assimilation against their will" (Art. 6.1),

the individual has the right to "use his language freely, in public as well as in private" (Art. 7).

The Convention "does not permit any activity which is contrary to the fundamental principles ... of sovereignty, territorial integrity and political independence of States" (Art. 1.2).

Escape clauses figure prominently in the more detailed provisions for language, especially in education. Article 8 reads:

> Whenever a minority reaches a *substantial* percentage of the population of a region or of the total population, its members shall have the right, *as far as possible*, to speak and write in their own language to the political, administrative and judicial authorities of this region or, *where appropriate*, of the State. These authorities shall have a corresponding obligation. (our emphasis; compare this with the mandatory provisions already in force for speakers of Māori and Sámi, see the articles by Kāretu and Magga, in this volume; c.f. also Canada and Finland, see Turi and Grin, this volume).

Article 9 restricts the operation of educational language rights to members of large minority groups only:

> Whenever the condition of Article 8 are fulfilled, in State schools, obligatory schooling shall include, for pupils belonging to the minority, study of their mother tongue. *As far as possible*, all *or* part of the schooling shall be given in the mother tongue of pupils belonging to the minority. However, *should the State not be in a position to provide such schooling*, it must permit children to attend private schools. In such a case, the State shall have the right to prescribe that the official language or languages also be taught in such schools (our emphasis).

Even when the Council of Europe draft says nothing about the State's duty to maintain the private schools financially, the State has the right to prescribe that the official language is taught, whereas the minority of course does not have a corresponding right to prescribe that its own language is taught in state schools. The educational rights could be compared with those in Finland (with a combination of territoriality and personality principles, see Grin in this volume), where the presence of 13 children of obligatory school age in a local authority is enough to make it mandatory for the authority to have a school where the minority children's mother tongue, if Swedish or Finnish, is the medium of education during the first nine years of obligatory schooling (see e.g. CERI/ECALP/83.03, 15). Under Polish legislation in 1992, 7 kindergarten or primary school pupils or 14 post-primary pupils have the right to teaching through the medium of an ethnic minority language (*Council of Europe Education Newsletter* 3/1992, 28–29).

The Conference on Security and Cooperation in Europe (CSCE) became from the late 1980s a major forum for East-West links and for specifying what human rights should obtain in the member countries.[10] THE DOCUMENT OF THE COPENHAGEN MEETING OF THE CONFERENCE ON THE HUMAN DIMENSION OF THE CSCE (1990) states unambiguously that national minorities should have the right to maintain their ethnic, cultural, linguistic or religious identity, the right to seek voluntary and public assistance to do so in educational institutions, and should not be subjected to assimilation against their will (CSCE 1990a: 40; see the Appendix). Several later meetings (held in Paris, Moscow, Helsinki) have also made pronouncements on minorities, and, predictably, run into difficulties in defining them. As developments in ex-Yugoslavia and the former Soviet Union have shown, the need to strengthen international measures for conflict resolution and peace-keeping remains. Media coverage has tended to label such conflicts as "ethnic", which is very misleading as shorthand for conflicts which more fundamentally have to do with economic problems, lack of social justice, a political vacuum after the demise of "communist" regimes, a gulf between the state and groups which do not identify with it, and failure to grant equal rights to minorities (see e.g. Hettne 1987, 1990; Stavenhagen 1990; Davidson 1992).

The Copenhagen Document goes further than any of the international covenants presented earlier in specifying how national minorities should be protected. It represents a major step forward for the participating countries *if* "minority" is defined in the same way as in the Council of Europe draft proposal discussed above (see note 2), *if* it becomes legally binding, *if* there is a procedure for monitoring progress (which the European Charter for Minority or Regional Languages contains), *if* the individuals and communities concerned (the rights are explicitly invested in both, page 41) have effective legal recourse in the event of their rights not being respected *and if* the funds necessary for implementation are forthcoming. In relation to migrant workers the Document only reaffirms earlier international agreements, but expresses a

readiness to examine, at future CSCE meetings, the relevant aspects of the further promotion of the rights of migrant workers and their families" (page 36).

The *UN's* DECLARATION ON THE RIGHTS OF PERSONS BELONGING TO NATIONAL OR ETHNIC, RELIGIOUS AND LINGUISTIC MINORITIES was adopted by the General Assembly on 18 December 1992. It considers

> that the promotion and protection of the rights of persons belonging to national or ethnic, religious and linguistic minorities contribute to the political and social stability of States in which they live. (Preamble)

This contests the popular but mistaken belief that the existence of minorities is divisive for nation states, as do several of the (draft) instruments in their preambles.

Article 1.1 decrees that the states

> shall protect the existence and the national or ethnic, cultural, religious and linguistic identity of minorities within their respective territories, and shall encourage conditions for the promotion of that identity.

Art. 1.2 states that the states

> shall adopt appropriate legislative and other measures to achieve those ends.

The Declaration goes somewhat further than the important Article 27 above, in its Article 2.1, by replacing "shall not be denied" by "have the right" and by adding that these rights apply "in private and in public, freely and without any form of discrimination" and in Articles 4.1 and, especially, 4.2, which prompt the states to actively promote enjoyment of the rights:

> Persons belonging to national or ethnic, religious and linguistic minorities (hereinafter referred to as persons belonging to minorities) have the right to enjoy their own culture, to profess and practise their own religion, and to use their own language, in private and in public, freely and without interference or any form of discrimination. (Article 2.1)
> States shall take measures to create favourable conditions to enable persons belonging to minorities to express their characteristics and to develop their culture, language, religion, traditions and customs, except where specific practices are in violation of national and contrary to international standards. (Article 4.2).

Most of the articles use the formulation "shall" and have few let-out modifications or alternatives — except where linguistic rights in education

(Art. 4.3) are concerned. Here again, just as in the European Charter (see above), the alternatives permit a reluctant state to provide minimalist protection:

> 4.3. States *should* take *appropriate* measures so that, *wherever possible*, persons belonging to minorities have *adequate* opportunities to learn their mother tongue *or* to have instruction in their mother tongue. (our emphasis)

Clearly such a formulation raises many questions. What constitute "appopriate measures" or "adequate opportunities", and who is to decide what is "possible"? Does "instruction in" the mother tongue mean "through the medium of the mother tongue" or does it only mean instruction in the mother tongue as a subject?

The recent UN *Draft Universal Declaration on Indigenous Rights* (as contained in document E/CN.4/Sub.2/1988/25; quoted from First Revised Text, in *IWGIA Yearbook 1989*, 1990: 156–158) establishes as fundamental human rights that indigenous peoples have

> 9. The right to develop and promote their own languages, including an own literary language, and to use them for administrative, juridical, cultural and other purposes.
> 10. The right to all forms of education, including in particular the right of children to have access to education in their own languages, and to establish, structure, conduct and control their own educational systems and institutions.
> 23. The (collective) right to autonomy in matters relating to their own internal and local affairs, including education, information, culture, religion, health, housing, social welfare, traditional and other economic activities, land and resources administration and the environment, as well as internal taxation for financing these autonomous functions.

This is the only one of the (draft) declarations discussed here that clearly represents the *overt maintenance-oriented promotion of minority mother tongues*. It stands in striking contrast to the UN CONVENTION ON MIGRANT WORKERS AND THEIR FAMILIES, which accords minimal rights to the mother tongues and is *assimilation-oriented* (see Hasenau 1990).

In the final section of this article we shall discuss some of the structures and ideologies which lie behind the reluctance of states to accord such rights to minorities, but we shall first report on current work directed towards formulating specifically *linguistic* human rights for a universal declaration.

Towards the formulation of a universal declaration of linguistic human rights

The international community seems to appreciate, at least in principle (as expressed in Preambles), that the linguistic human rights of "indigenous peoples" and "national" or "regional" minorities should be promoted, possibly also those of migrants and refugees. This could indicate that there is appreciation of the need to draft at least a Universal Declaration of Linguistic Human Rights and later, possibly, a legally binding Charter or Covenant. The initial steps towards formulating such a Declaration have in fact already been taken. Researchers are confronted with a considerable challenge in clarifying the nature and scope of linguistic human rights.

At an international seminar on Human Rights and Cultural Rights held in October 1987 in Recife, Brazil, organised by AIMAV (the International Association for Cross-cultural Communication) and UNESCO, a Declaration of Recife was adopted. It ends as follows:

> Hence, conscious of the need to provide explicit legal guarantees for linguistic rights to individuals and groups by the appropriate bodies of the member states of the United Nations,
> *recommends* that steps be taken by the United Nations to adopt and implement a *universal declaration of linguistic rights* which would require a reformulation of national, regional, and international language policies.[11]

A preliminary Declaration ("Resolution on linguistic rights"/ "Resolução sobre direitos linguísticos)" was also adopted by the Seminar. It is based a provisional declaration first proposed by Tove Skutnabb-Kangas in 1983 (Skutnabb-Kangas 1984b). It is important to note that these points only list what type of rights should be linguistic human rights. The original 1983 formulation had "mother tongue" (defined by origin and internal identification — see Skutnabb-Kangas — Bucak, this volume) rather than "language (of his/her group)" in the first 3 points:

> 1. Every social group has the right to positively identify with one or more languages and to have such identification accepted and respected by others.[12]
> 2. Every child has the right to learn the language(s) of his/her group fully.[13]
> 3. Every person has the right to use the language(s) of his/her group in any official situation.

4. Every person has the right to learn fully at least one of the official languages in the country where s/he is resident, according to her/his own choice.[14]

There have been follow-up gatherings at UNESCO in Paris in 1989, Frankfurt 1990 and Pécs, Hungary in August 1991, organized by FIPLV, the Fédération Internationale des Professeurs de Langues Vivantes. A *FIPLV draft "Universal Declaration of Language Rights"* has been circulated to a substantial number of professional associations and researchers (see Appendix). As various responses to FIPLV drafts have shown, it is extremely difficult to reach agreement on the content or wording of such a document before a substantial number of issues have been clarified (see Leontiev's remarks on the draft, this volume). The issues were discussed at the Pécs workshop, including the compilation of a research agenda, after which a detailed report was produced and issued by UNESCO (see the report for UNESCO from the Pécs Workshop, rapporteur Tove Skutnabb-Kangas). The draft circulated by FIPLV after the Pécs workshop (and later refined within FIPLV, see FIPLV 1993) attempts comprehensive coverage of LHRs. It can, among other things, be criticized for

- ambiguity (mother tongue in Article 1, but a language which young persons or their family identify with in Article 6);
- ambivalence (official languages are to be taught, Article 7, but rights in relation to the mother tongue are unclear);
- impracticability and redundancy ("all persons have the right to learn languages of their own choosing").

Our feeling is that it is admirable that a language teachers' association has taken the initiative in highlighting the cause of LHRs, but that promulgating a declaration which is so manifestly inadequate is premature and ethically and professionally ill-considered. The professional platform of FIPLV is foreign language teaching; it is an association not so much of scholars as of teachers of foreign languages (*langues vivantes*, FIPLV is in translation the World Federation of Modern Language Associations). The issue of foreign language learning and linguistic rights is explored below.

The FIPLV document does not define the terms used. One of the points on the necessary research agenda is confusion in the use of terminology and concepts. These are often vague and imprecise, and the same concepts seem to be interpreted in widely divergent ways. There is a need to clarify such central concepts as *mother tongue, bilingual, official language, national language, learn a language fully, efficient communication,* etc. Most of these concepts can be defined in several different ways.[15] In any declaration the definitions used have to be stated, and reasons given for why these specific definitions have been chosen rather than others. There are definitions of some of the concepts used in some declarations — for example both the EUROPEAN CHARTER FOR REGIONAL OR MINORITY LANGUAGES and the *Proposal for a European Convention for the Protection of Minorities* (see above) define what they mean by "minority". The definitions used may have far-reaching implications. We shall use the CSCE COPENHAGEN DOCUMENT (see above) as an example.

All the rights in section IV (pages 40–42) apply to "persons belonging to national minorities", and "to belong to a national minority is a matter of a person's individual choice" (page 40), i. e. the same formulation as in the *Proposal for a European Convention for the Protection of Minorities.* The important question then is whether the state has to accept or confirm the existence of a national minority, before individuals can claim that they belong to one (see note 2). People who have come to a country as immigrants or refugees, and whose children may have been born in the new country and be its citizens, may feel ready to integrate. They may wish to change the status of their group from that of immigrants/refugees to that of a national ethnic minority group. The question then is whether they can claim that they belong to a national minority, and obtain all the rights accorded to a national minority, among them linguistic rights (for a case study of a state refusing this, see Skutnabb-Kangas 1991c). According to the definition of a minority used in the EUROPEAN CHARTER FOR REGIONAL OR MINORITY LANGUAGES it is *not* possible. If the definitions used in the *Proposal for a European Convention for the Protection of Minorities* and in the CSCE COPENHAGEN DOCUMENT, are *combined*, it *is* possible.

The scope of language rights — is learning foreign languages a human right?

Some researchers and organisations have voiced the view that the learning of foreign languages in school is a human right (e.g. Candelier 1990 in connection with the FIPLV proposed declaration, Gomes de Matos 1984). The mission of TESOL (Teachers Of English to Speakers of Other

Languages), according to its Presidents's message, *TESOL Matters*, June/ July 1993)

> is to strengthen the effective teaching and learning of English around the world while respecting individuals' language rights.

If such pronouncements are to be anything more than pious rhetoric or partisan lobbying by professional interest groups, the rights in question need to be specified and publicised so that individuals and groups know what they are. In this section we will consider whether there is a conflict of interest between the promotion of foreign languages as part of "internationalisation" on the one hand, and the need of minority languages to have support so as to ensure their survival and development on the other.

There are considerable pressures afoot in Europe at present to coordinate language policy (Coulmas 1991) and to ensure that all European children learn two foreign languages at school. A range of European Community programmes, including LINGUA, and indirectly ERASMUS, are designed to boost such a policy. The disagreement between Britain and its European partners (Britain has refused to agree on a policy of two foreign languages in schools) reflects a major difference in perception of the issues. The British insularly assume that the dominant position of English internationally is in their interest. Continental European countries wish to ensure that their children learn at least English and one other foreign language − French/German/Spanish/etc, i. e. they should learn the dominant languages of two neighbouring European countries. This reflects the wish of Europeans to provide a counterweight to the pervasive influence of English and to bolster the official languages of other European countries.

In fact many European educational systems already offer a wide choice of foreign languages. For instance, in Scandinavian state schooling it is possible, even for those not specialising in languages, to learn 3 − 4 foreign languages (unlike North America, or Australia − see Smolicz, this volume).

There is a significant difference, however, between the needs of speakers of dominated minority languages, in order to ensure that such languages are accorded basic justice and the chance to survive on the one hand, and the urge to promote European (or any other) unity through multilingualism for "international understanding" on the other (see Fishman, Grin and Turi, in this volume). It should undoubtedly be a human right to learn one's mother tongue, a right that speakers of the dominant language take for granted for themselves. The preamble to the EUROPEAN CHARTER FOR REGIONAL OR MINORITY LANGUAGES states that

> the right to use a regional or minority language in private and public life is an inalienable right.

There is also widespread agreement on an inalienable right to learn one of the official languages of the country of residence. Is it though, in the contemporary world, a human right to learn several languages in school (see Leontiev, this volume), and to choose which one(s) one wants to learn (as FIPLV advocates)?

One way of approaching ths issue would be to differentiate between *necessary* linguistic rights and *enrichment-oriented* linguistic rights. Necessary rights have to do with the learning and use of one's mother tongue, and the learning of a/the official language in the country of residence, i. e. they have to do with the learning and use of *mother tongues* and *second languages*. Enrichment-oriented rights are concerned with the right to learn and use *foreign languages*. We think that only the necessary rights should be considered inalienable, fundamental *linguistic* **HUMAN** *rights*. In our view the enrichment-oriented rights are important *LIN-GUISTIC rights* (in the sense that they relate to language), but not inalienable linguistic *human* rights.

We also appreciate that the terminology is far from ideal here. Also, there is a problem in that, as we indicated in our general introduction, human rights are generally regarded as being equal and not hierarchical. They do however evolve over time. Applied linguistic perceptions of which languages are more important than others (from L1 to L2 to Lx) in individual development are relevant and should inform debate about the nature of linguistic human rights.

When learning the languages guaranteed by "necessary rights" (the mother tongue and a second language) a child builds up a linguistic repertoire which is necessary for basic social and psychological survival and economic and political participation. These rights are necessary both to *prevent* **subtractive** language learning situations (where the mother tongue risks being forcibly replaced by official, majority languages or not being learned fully) and to *promote* **additive** language learning situations (where other languages are added to a person's linguistic repertoire, without any risk to mother tongues, which are allowed to develop fully; for these distinctions see Lambert 1975).

When learning languages guaranteed by "enrichment-oriented rights" (foreign languages), the mother tongue of the child is at no risk of being replaced or of not being learned fully. Here the child adds to her repertoire (which for a monolingual majority child consists of her mother tongue, which is an official language in the country) other languages which are not necessary for individual or group survival but can be important for personal and professional purposes and for international understanding. This is usually the situation for dominant majority language speakers, learning foreign (or even second) languages in school, regardless of how this learning is organised, in foreign language classes, in immersion programmes, in two-way programmes etc (for these, see Baetens Beardsmore 1990, 1993; Baetens Beardsmore – Kohls 1988; Baetens Beardsmore – Swain 1985; Cummins 1987; Cummins – Swain 1986; Dolson – Lindholm 1993; Duff 1991; Genesee 1985, 1987; Lambert – Tucker 1972; Lindholm 1992; Skutnabb-Kangas 1984a, 1990a, 1993a; Swain – Lapkin 1982; see also Swain – Lapkin – Rowen – Hart 1990 about minority children learning foreign languages).

If the two types of linguistic rights are merged, so that the right to mother tongues, to official languages and to foreign languages are treated as equivalent rights in a declaration, one risk that we fear is that the entire exercise may be seen as unrealistic, resulting in neither kind of rights being achieved. This would be unfortunate in relation to enrichment-oriented rights, which are laudable. It would be disastrous in relation to necessary linguistic rights for minorities.

Hence we think that an International Declaration should be formulated in a way which involves a maximalist position for minorities, so that they obtain those rights which majorities take for granted for themselves (the necessary rights above), and a minimalist position for majorities, so as to promote foreign language learning in a realistic way which does not have any restrictive effect on the necessary rights of minorities.

From racism to ethnicism and linguicism

In this final section we shall briefly consider what sorts of processes and ideologies it is that limit the enjoyment of LHRs and that tend to result in an unjust allocation of resources to speakers of different languages. Language appears to be playing an increasingly important role in the stratification of society. Earlier forms of biologically argued RACISM grouped together carefully chosen, purportedly biological "characteristics", visible (skin colour) or less visible (blood groups, skull form etc.), to function as defining criteria for "races". Various psychological "characteristics" were then linked with or attributed to the resulting "races". These were then hierarchized on the basis of an evaluation of "their" (first "alterable", later on "unalterable", "inherited") psychological characteristics. Some "races" were seen as fitter to rule than others. "Races" and "their" characteristics were thus socially constructed, the result of ascription and signification processes, and these ideological constructions were used to legitimate the unequal division of power and resources between the resulting "races". The ideology of biologically argued racism legitimated the control and exploitation by the "white" "race" of other "races" (Miles 1989).

When, for various reasons, biologically argued racism became untenable, it was necessary to find other criteria which could continue to legitimate the unequal division of power and resources. In most countries, biologically argued racism is in the process of being replaced by more sophisticated forms of racism, *ethnicism* (Mullard 1988) and *linguicism* (Skutnabb-Kangas 1988a). These use the ethnicities, cultures and languages of different groups as defining criteria and as the basis for hierarchization. It is no longer being claimed (at least not openly — except in populistic right wing anti-immigrant discourse) that certain "races" are fitter to rule than others. Now it is certain ethnic groups, cultures and languages which are claimed to be fitter to rule, expand, and be emulated by others. In a new social darwinist dress the argument is that the ethnoses, cultures and languages which are to survive and expand will do so because they are more adapted to modern technological life, to market economies and democratic forms of government, more developed or useful, or have more potential than others. The hegemony of the dominant group then ensures that the other ethnoses, cultures and languages are deprived of resources and a fair chance to survive. Central in this process are institutionally controllable measures such as education. Somehow it always turns out to be majority languages and cultures which are the fittest survivors. This empirical fact tends then to be used as proof of their being the fittest.

It is obvious that linguicism may also be a useful concept in analysing the role of language in schooling in relation to "monolingual" majorities. Similar processes of structurally favouring middle-class language and the "standard" code, and marginalising dialectal and sociolectal varieties, are at work in most national education systems, and still generate heated controversy, as seen in the recent debate on a "national" curriculum, with focus on the "national" language, in Britain and elsewhere.

While monolingualism (plus a selective learning of foreign languages in schools) is a central ideological pillar of the nation state, there is a similar hierarchisation internationally. English has become the dominant language in much scientific discourse, international politics and business, the media, etc. The progressive spread of this language internationally has implications nationally for the role assigned to English in education systems and for an increasing number of domestic functions (Phillipson 1992). If English is used as the medium of higher education (as it is in countries formerly under British colonial rule, and increasingly in Western countries such as Denmark), does this involve a downgrading and displacement of the national language? If proficiency in English is essential for success in the education system and the job market, does this mean that learning English is a human right in the contemporary world? (We suggest possible answers to such questions in the previous section, in our article on language rights in post-colonial Africa in this volume and in Haberland − Henriksen − Phillipson − Skutnabb-Kangas 1991).

Racism, ethnicism and *linguicism* are here defined as

> ideologies, structures and practices which are used to legitimate, effectuate and reproduce an unequal division of power and resources (both material and non-material) between groups which are defined on the basis of 'race', ethnicity/culture, or language" (Skutnabb-Kangas 1988a: 13).[16]

It is important to note that we define racism, ethnicism and linguicism as BOTH ideological and structural (cf. Miles 1989). Racism is *not* just a question of people being ill-willed, ignorant or misinformed. Ethnicism is *not only* people's attitudes or prejudices towards other individuals or groups. Linguicism is *not only* an information problem (that all languages are of equal worth, and if this is understood and respected, problems of discrimination will disappear or at least diminish). In addition to the ideological dimension, racism, ethnicism and linguicism all involve structures and practices which result in unequal access to power and resources. Thus even well-intentioned administrators (see Cummins, this volume) and bureaucrats (see our analyses of the draft conventions above) could, unintentionally, reinforce linguicist structures.

Ethnicism and linguicism socially construct the resources of powerless groups so that they become invisible or are seen as handicaps. In this way minority resources, among them their languages and cultures, become non-resources, hence cannot be converted to other resources or to positions of structural power. At the same time the resources of the dominant groups, among them their languages and cultures, are socially constructed so that they are seen as resources and can thus be converted into other resources or to positions of structural power.

Linguicism is a major factor in determining whether speakers of particular languages are allowed to enjoy their linguistic human rights. Lack of these rights, for instance their absence from school time-tables, makes minority languages invisible. Alternatively, minority languages are seen as handicaps which prevent minority children from acquiring the valued resource (= the majority language), so minority children should get rid of them in their own interest. At the same time, many minorities, especially children, are in fact prevented from fully acquiring majority resources, especially the majority languages, by disabling educational structures, when their instruction is organised through the medium of the majority languages in ways which contradict most scientific evidence (see Cummins, in this volume; Skutnabb-Kangas 1984a, 1990a; Skutnabb-Kangas — Cummins (eds) 1988).

Strategies through which racism is reproduced (see e.g. Preiswerk 1980) can be analysed in terms of images which the dominant majority groups create of themselves, of those whom they dominate, in this case minorities, and of the relationship between them. The first strategy is the *glorification* of the majority, its traditions, norms, life-styles, institutions, laws, level of development, culture — and language. The second involves a *stigmatisation* of the minorities, their traditions, norms, life-styles, institutions, laws, level of development, cultures — *and languages* (see Skutnabb-Kangas — Phillipson 1986b, 1989a and Phillipson 1992 for analysis of how illegitimate arguments are used to promote English worldwide).

The third strategy, false *rationalisations* of the relationship between majority and minority, always presents the majority favourably, as "doing good", with the minority as beneficiaries. The majorities "help", "support", "modernize", "civilize", "aid" and "integrate" the minorities — and work hard to accord them rights.

In view of the efforts of majorities, represented by state power, to "accord minorities linguistic rights", the relatively meagre results might suggest that the image created by different states of their own efforts to guarantee these rights needs further analysis. This is particularly so in education, where not even the newest, most progressive drafts of international charters guarantee minorities those most basic linguistic human rights which the majority populations take for granted for themselves. Linguicism may be at work...

Notes

1. Since it is possible to have at least two mother tongues, all the rights formulated should cover this eventuality. Hence any reference in the text to "mother tongue" should be read as "mother tongue or mother tongues". See Skutnabb-Kangas — Bucak, this volume, for details and definitions of mother tongue. See also Skutnabb-Kangas — Phillipson 1989b).

2. The definitions of both *minority* and different types of minorities (*indigenous, national, regional, territorial, immigrant* etc) are notoriously difficult (see e.g. Capotorti 1979; Andrýsek 1989; see also *UN Human Rights Fact Sheet* No 18, Minority Rights, 1992: 8–10). Most definitions use

   A. *Numbers* as a defining characteristics.

   B. *Dominance* is used in some but not others ("in an inferior and non-dominant position", Andrýsek 1989: 60; "in a non-dominant position", Capotorti 1979: 96).

   C. The group has to possess ethnic or religious or linguistic *traits, features or characteristics or cultural bonds and ties* which are (markedly) *different* from those of the rest of the population, according to most definitions.

   D. A will/wish (if only implicit) to *safeguard* or *preserve* or *strengthen* the patterns of life and behavior or culture or traditions or religion or language of the group is specifically mentioned in most definitions (e.g. Capotorti 1979: 96). Language is not included in all of them (e.g. not in Andrýsek's definition 1989: 60).

   E. Most definitions in charters and covenants require *nationality* in the state concerned as part of the definition, i. e. minorities are defined so as to give national or regional minorities more rights than to immigrants and refugees (who, by definition, are considered non-national and non-regional). In contrast, academic definitions for research purposes often make no mention of nationality as a criterion (cf. Riggs 1985: 155, 102).

   We use here the following definition of a minority for purposes of linguistic human rights:

   A group which is smaller in number than the rest of the population of a State, whose members have ethnical, religious or linguistic features different from those of the rest of the population, and are guided, if only implicitly, by the will to safeguard their culture, traditions, religion or language.

   Any group coming within the terms of this definition shall be treated as an ethnic, religious or linguistic minority.

   To belong to a minority shall be a matter of individual choice.

   The definition is based on our reformulation of the definition used by Council of Europe Commission for Democracy through Law (91) 7, Art. 2; see Appendix). We have in our definition omitted the requirement of citizenship ("who are nationals of that State"), because a forced change of citizenship to our mind cannot be required in order to be able to enjoy basic human rights. As long as many immigration states practice a fairly restrictive policy (for instance residence requirements which are more than 3–4 years, and/or linguistic requirements, often based on evaluations by non-linguists) in granting citizenship, it also seems to us that especially children may suffer unduly if they are only granted basic linguistic rights after upwards of 5 years in the new country.

   If an individual claims that she belongs to a national minority, and the State claims that there are no national minorities in that State (e.g. Kurds in Turkey or Finns in

Sweden), there is a conflict, and the State may refuse to grant the minority person/ group rights which it has accorded to granting to national minorities. In most definitions of minority, minority rights thus become conditional on the acceptance by the State of the existence of a minority in the first place, i. e. only exo-definitions (definitions by outsiders, not by the individual/group concerned) of minorities are accepted. According to our definition, minority status does NOT depend on the acceptance of the State, but is either "objectively" ("coming within the terms of this definition") or subjectively ("a matter of individual choice") verifiable. Many of the definitions of indigenous minorities have this combination of "objective" characteristics and self-identification (e.g. the definitions of Sámi for the purposes of voting rights to the Sámi Parliaments in Finland and Norway, see Magga, this volume). The trend seems to be towards self-identification only, for numerically small groups. Minority definitions can be compared to definitions of ethnic groups — see the discussions in Stavenhagen 1987; Skutnabb-Kangas 1987, 1991c; Riggs 1985.

3. Renteln reports that theorists of human rights have traditionally drawn on four sources: "(1) divine authority, (2) natural law, (3) intuition (that human rights are self-evident), and (4) ratification of international instruments", all of which criteria are suspect (Renteln 1988: 9). She advocates empirical validation of the existence of human rights in different cultures, and has undertaken a study of retribution (*lex talionis*, an eye for an eye) worldwide. Her claim is that "where it is possible to demonstrate acceptance of a moral principle or value by all cultures it will be feasible to erect human rights standards" (Renteln 1988: 30), and that, in the light of her study of retribution, this applies to genocide, summary execution and indiscriminate killing, the right to seek redress of grievance and proportionate punishment for those responsible.

4. Racism (which has from ancient times gone hand in hand with sexism) is clearly formulated as linguicism in the famous remark attributed by Diogenes Laertius to Socrates, who thanked fate for three things: "firstly, because I was born as a human being and not as an animal, secondly as a man and not a woman, and thirdly as a Greek and not a Barbarian".

5. Despite the General Assembly of the UN stating (resolution 532B (IV), 4 February 1952) that the prevention of discrimination and the protection of minorities were two of the most important branches of the work undertaken by the Commission on Human Rights and the Subcommission on Prevention of Discrimination and Protection of Minorities of the United Nations (Capotorti 1979: 28), the question of minorities was not dealt with in depth. The Subcommission's efforts between 1947 and 1954 to define the notion of minority and to specify measures "yielded no tangible results" (Capotorti 1979: 28). The Subcommission concentrated between 1955 and 1971 mainly on discrimination, and it was only after 1971 when the decision to undertake the Capotorti study was made that the question of minorities was included among the important subjects in the Subcommission's work.

6. In 1948 the UN General Assembly rejected a proposal ("... National minorities shall be guaranteed the right to use their native language and to possess their own national schools, libraries, museums and other cultural and educational institutions.") which the Soviet Union wished to have included in the Universal Declaration of Human Rights (Capotorti 1979: 27).

"Cultural" genocide was included in article III of the draft Convention on the Prevention and Punishment of the Crime of Genocide (E/794) but this article was not accepted. Language figured prominently in the proposed definition of cultural genocide:

(1) Prohibiting the use of the language of the group in daily intercourse or in schools, or the printing and circulation of publications in the language of the group (quoted from Capotorti 1979: 37).

7. Johan Mathis Mikkelsen Gávppi has sued the Norwegian State for not providing him with the basic education that he as a Norwegian citizen was entitled to. He spoke only Sámi when he started school and his teachers spoke only Norwegian (see Skutnabb-Kangas – Phillipson 1989a, chapter 11, for details of the court case). Kari Aro has accused Sweden of failing to follow the Nordic Cultural Convention in not offering education through the medium of Finnish to Finnish children in Sweden and breaking Swedish educational regulations in not negotiating with the Finnish minority parents about changes in the medium of education. Both have filed a complaint with the European Court of Human Rights in Strasbourg.

8. It is vital that minorities are entitled to education through the medium of their own languages, rather than in their own languages, i. e. merely studying them as a subject. Many studies show that when minority mother tongues are taught as subjects only, language shift generally ensues (e.g. Boyd 1985; Skutnabb-Kangas – Toukomaa 1976; Smolicz, this volume; Toukomaa – Skutnabb-Kangas 1977; see also Wong Fillmore 1991). Such teaching does not serve to maintain language proficiency at the same level as when the child started school, let alone develop it. Teaching a minority mother tongue for a few hours a week in a school where a majority language is the medium of education may be psychologically beneficial, but represents therapeutic and cosmetic support rather than a basis for language maintenance and development.

9. There are alternative views on the adequacy of these provisions in Germany and the Netherlands; see e.g. *Muttersprachlicher Unterricht in der Bundesrepublik Deutschland* 1985; Appel 1988; Appel – Muysken 1987; Reid – Reich 1992; Verhoeven 1991).

10. The 35 participating States at the first Helsinki meeting in 1975 were Albania, Austria, Belgium, Bulgaria, Canada, Cyprus, Czechoslovakia, Denmark, Finland, France, Germany, Greece, the Holy See, Hungary, Iceland, Ireland, Italy, Liechtenstein, Luxembourg, Malta, Monaco, the Netherlands, Norway, Poland, Portugal, Romania, San Marino, Spain, Sweden, Switzerland, Turkey, USSR, United Kingdom, USA and Yugoslavia. At the Helsinki meeting (July 1992) there were 51 states.

11. The seminar was organized by Francisco Gomes de Matos, who has campaigned energetically for linguistic rights, language learners' rights and peace education (see contributions to FIPLV Newsletter).

12. There are many studies of ethnic identity which try to clarify the relationship between internal and external identification and the verbal expression of these (endoethnonyms and exoethnonyms). There are also studies of the role of language in ethnic identification, language as a central cultural core value, and the verbal expression of linguistic identification (endolinguonyms and exolinguonyms). Having the right to both identify with a language and have that identification accepted and respected by others guarantees that the endolinguonym and the exolinguonym can merge. There are situations where insisting on the validity of one's endoethnonym and endolinguonym (for instance insisting that one identifies as a Kurd and a speaker of the Kurdish language in Turkey) can lead not only to the state insisting on the validity of an exoethnonym ("you are a mountain Turk") and an exolinguonym ("you speak a dialect of Turkish which has developed into an almost non-intelligible dialect because of the isolation in the mountains; the Kurdish language does not exist") but also to imprisonment and torture. Both rights are needed in order to counteract this type of situation.

13. This implies an inalienable right to education through the medium of of the mother tongue, at least during the first 6 years of primary education, and study of the mother tongue as a subject throughout the whole of schooling.
14. This implies studying the official language as a second language (as opposed to as a mother tongue), taught by bilingual teachers, throughout the whole of schooling.
15. For a demonstration aimed at clarifying some key concepts, see Skutnabb-Kangas — Bucak, in this volume, about the Kurdish language.
16. Many official definitions of racism, racial groups, etc, already recognize that *ethnicity* is involved and has partly replaced "race" (e.g. the British Race Relations Act 1976, Section 3. "Racial group" means a group of persons defined by reference to colour, race, nationality or ethnic or national origins ..." (UN 1991 May, 169), while *language* is not yet often mentioned.

Typology of language legislation

Joseph-G. Turi

Introduction

Major language legislation in the area of language policy is evidence, within certain political contexts, of contacts, conflicts and inequalities among languages used within the same territory. Objectively or apparently, these languages co-exist uneasily in a dominant-dominated relationship, thereby leading to a situation of linguistic majorities and minorities.

The fundamental goal of all language legislation is to resolve, in one way or another, the linguistic problems arising from those linguistic contacts, conflicts and inequalities, by legally determining and establishing the status and use of the languages in question. Preference is given to the protection, defence or promotion of one or several designated languages through legal language obligations and language rights drawn up to that end.

Canadian language legislation (the Official Languages Act) is an example of official legislation that applies language obligations and language rights to two designated languages, English and French.[1] Quebec's language legislation (the Charter of the French Language) is an example of exhaustive legislation that applies, in a different way, language obligations and language rights to French, to a few more or less designated languages and to other languages to the extent that they are not designated.[2]

Increasing legal intervention in language policy gave birth, or recognition, to a new legal science, comparative language law. Comparative language law is the study of language law throughout the world (as well as the language of law and the relation between law and language). To the extent that language, which is the main tool of the law, becomes both the object and the subject of law, language law becomes metajuridical law. To the extent that comparative language law recognizes and enshrines language rights, albeit sometimes rather timidly and implicitly, it becomes futuristic law which builds on historical roots. This in itself is remarkable, since the growing recognition or historical enshrinement, in time and space, of language rights promotes the cultural right to be different, which is a promise of creativity for individuals and families, as well as for societies, nations and the international community.

Types of language legislation

Language legislation is divided into two categories, depending on its *field of application*: legislation which deals with the *official* usage of languages and that which deals with their *non-official* usage. Needless to say, there are grey areas in this classification.

Language legislation can be divided into four categories, depending on its *function*; it can be **official, institutionalizing, standardizing or liberal**. Legislation that fulfills all these functions is *exhaustive* language legislation, while other language legislation is *non-exhaustive*.

Official language legislation is legislation intended to make one or more designated, or more or less identifiable, languages official in the domains of legislation, justice, public administration and education. Depending on the circumstances, one of two principles is applied: linguistic *territoriality* (basically, the obligation or right to use one or more designated languages within a given territory) or linguistic *personality* (basically, the obligation or the right to use one's own language or any language). As such, making one or more designated languages official does not necessarily or automatically entail major legal consequences.

The legal sense and scope of officializing a language depends on the effective legal treatment accorded to that language (for instance, when the law states that only official texts, or only certain official texts, are "authentic" so that they prevail, legally, over texts in one or more other languages — see Fishman, this volume, for consideration of European Community languages).

Institutionalizing language legislation is legislation which seeks to make one or more designated languages the normal, usual or common languages, in the unofficial domains of labour, communications, culture, commerce and business.

Standardizing language legislation is legislation designed to make one or more designated languages respect certain language standards in very specific and clearly defined domains, usually official or highly technical.

Liberal language legislation is legislation designed to enshrine legal recognition of language rights implicitly or explicitly, in one way or another. But language law, viewed objectively (as legal rules on language), make a distinction in language rights, which are subjective so that they belong to any person, between *the right to "a" language* (the right to use one or more designated languages in various domains, especially in official domains) and *the right to "the" language* (the right to use any language in various domains, particularly in unofficial domains). These language rights, based respectively on the principle of territoriality and the principle of personality, are both individual and collective. Moreover, if language rights are also collective rights, they can belong to artificial persons (e.g. corporations) as well as to natural persons. After all, a human being is not only an individual but also a "political animal", that is to say a person living in a variety of social organizations.

Comparative language law

Language legislation never obliges anyone to use one or more languages in absolute terms. The obligation stands only to the extent that a legal act of fact covered by language legislation is or must be accomplished. For example, the obligation to use one or more languages on product labels holds only if there is, in non-linguistic legislation, an obligation to put labels on products.

Moreover, it is the written form (the language as medium) and not the written linguistic content (the language as message) that is usually targeted by legal rules dealing explicitly with language. Both linguistic content and linguistic form can be the object of legislation that generally is not explicitly linguistic, such as the Quebec Civil Code, the Charter of Human Rights, or the Consumer Protection Act.

Generally speaking, linguistic terms and expressions or linguistic concepts (mother tongue, for instance) are the focus of language legislation only to the extent that they are formally understandable, intelligible, translatable, usable or identifiable, in one way or another, or have some meaning in a given language.[3]

For example, Section 58 of Quebec's Charter of the French Language states that, allowing for exceptions, public signs must be solely in French. Therefore, if a word is posted and it is understandable in French, it is legally a French word. In this case, the public sign is legal (for instance, "ouvert"). In other respects, if a word is posted and it is not understandable in French, it is not legally a French word only if it has some meaning in another specific language and it is translatable into French. In this case, the public sign is illegal (for instance, "open").

In principle, language legislation is aimed at the speakers of a language (as consumers or users) rather than at the language itself (as an integral part of the cultural heritage of a nation) unless that legislation is clearly a public policy law (a public policy law is any law comprising legal standards so fundamental and essential, individually and collectively, in the interests of the community, that they become imperative or prohibitive in absolute terms so that they cannot be avoided in any way).

Quebec's Court of Appeal in the **Miriam Case** (March 22, 1984), Quebec's High Court in the **Gagnon Case** (December 15, 1986) and the French courts, in a great many decisions, including the **Steiner Case** (Paris Court of Appeal, November 27, 1985), all confirm the essential points in the above.[4] Thus, anything that is linguistically "neutral" is not generally targeted by language legislation, as can be seen, among others, with Section 20 of the Quebec's Regulation respecting the language of commerce and business.[5]

While the presence of a language or the "quantity" of its usage can be the object of exhaustive language legislation, language "quality" or correct usage belongs to the realm of example and persuasion where language usage is unofficial, and to the schools and government where language usage is official.[6]

Legal rules in linguistic matters are less severe than grammatical rules. There are four fundamental reasons for this : firstly, the best laws are those that legislate the least, particularly in the unofficial usage of languages; secondly, language, as an individual and collective way of expression and communication, is an essential cultural phenomenon, in principle difficult to appropriate and define legally; thirdly, legal rules, like socio-linguistic rules, are only applied and applicable if they respect local custom and usage and the behaviour of reasonable people (who are not necessarily linguistic paragons) while grammatical rules are based on the teacher-pupil relationship; fourthly, on the other hand, as legal sanctions, criminal sanctions (fines or imprisonment) and civil sanctions (damages, partial or total illegality) are generally harsher than possible language sanctions (low marks, loss of social prestige or loss of clients), they are in the language field usually limited to low and symbolic fines or damages.

Jurists are therefore rather prudent when dealing with language policy, and rather reticent when interpreting language legislation exclusively as public policy law.

Since the legal sanctions of a public policy law are formidable (partial or total illegality, for instance), many jurists, especially Quebec's jurists, prefer not to think of language laws as being exclusively public policy laws, except when their legal context is clearly in favour of such an interpretation, as it could be in the official usage of languages.[7] True, the French *Cour de cassation* declared implicitly, in the **France Quick Case** (October 20, 1985) that French Language legislation was public policy law.[8] But that did not prevent the *Cour d'appel de Versailles*, in the **France Quick Case** (June 24, 1987) from considering terms such as "spaghettis" and "plum-pudding" to be, for all practical purposes, French terms, that is to say to be in keeping with such legislation, because they were "known to the general public".[9]

The fundamental goal of this legislation, then, is to protect both francophones and the French language. A francophone is anyone whose language of use is French, that is to say, from a legal point of view, any person who can speak and understand French, in an ordinary and relatively intelligible manner.[10]

In the **Macdonald Case** (May 1, 1986) and the **Ford Case** (December 15, 1988), the Supreme Court of Canada recognized and enshrined, for all intents and purposes, the distinction between the right to "a" language (principal right, foreseen as such in the Canadian Constitution, explicitly historical owing to the historic background of the country, in the domains of the official usage of languages) and the right to "the" language (accessory right, not explicitly foreseen as such in the Canadian Constitution, implicitly fundamental, in the domains of the unofficial usage of languages). The Court also recognized and enshrined the main differences between the official and the unofficial usage of languages.[11]

According to the Supreme Court of Canada, the right to "the" language is implicitly an integral part of the explicit fundamental right of freedom of speech. Moreover, in the **Irwin Toy Case** (April 27, 1989), the Supreme Court of Canada confirmed that artificial persons also held certain language rights, such as the implicit right to "the" language in the unofficial domain of commerce.[12]

A relatively complete study carried out for the United Nations in 1979, the Capotorti Report, indicates that, although the use of languages other than the official language(s) in the domains of official usage is restricted or forbidden in various parts of the world, the use of languages in the domains of unofficial usage is generally not restricted or forbidden.[13] We arrived at the same conclusion, in 1977, when we made an analysis of the constitutional clauses covering language of 147 States.[14]

It must be pointed out, however, that Turkey prohibits, in some cases, the use of some languages, languages other than the first official language of each country recognized by the Republic of Turkey.[15] The prohibitory measures contravene, **prima facie,** Section 27 of the International Covenant on Civil and Political Rights, of 1966, which recognizes to members of linguistic minorities the right to use their own language.[16]

Conclusion

The right to "the" language will become an effective fundamental right, like other fundamental rights, only to the extent that it is enshrined not simply in higher legal norms, but also in norms with mandatory provisions that identify as precisely as possible the holders and the beneficiaries of language rights and language obligations, as well as the legal sanctions that accompany them. Otherwise, the right to "the" language will be but a theoretical fundamental right, like several fundamental rights, proclaimed in norms with directive provisions that cover language rights but have no real corresponding sanctions and obligations.

While the law inhabits a grey zone, and the best legislation is that which says the least, especially regarding unofficial usage of languages, the right to "the" language (and therefore the right to be different) will only have meaning, legally speaking, if it is enshrined (above all for language minorities), in one way or another (particularly, in the official usage of languages), in norms with mandatory provisions, as the right to "a" language generally is.

As an historical right (that takes into account the historic background of each country), the right to "a" language deserves special treatment in certain political contexts, even if it is not in itself a fundamental right. As a fundamental right (right and freedom to which every person is entitled), the right to "the" language, even if it enshrines the dignity of all languages, cannot be considered an absolute right under all circumstances. A hierarchy exists that must take into account, in ways which are different but not legally discriminatory, the historical and fundamental linguistic imperative of the nations and individuals concerned, including the imperative of reestablishing a definite equality between several languages coexisting in a given political context.[17]

By ruling, in Section 89 for instance, that "Where this act does not require the use of the official language (French) exclusively, the official language and another language may be used together", Quebec's Charter of the French language recognizes and enshrines the right to "a" language and the right to "the" language, by creating an interesting hierarchical solution between them in the field of language policy.[18]

Notes

1. Official Languages Act, R. S. C., 1970, c. C-02. The Act was substantially amended in July 1988 (see Bill C-72, adopted by the Canadian Parliament on July 7, 1988, and assented to on July 28, 1988).
2. Charter of the French Language, R. S. Q., c. C-11. The Charter was rather extensively amended in December 1983 and in December 1988 (S. Q. 1983, c. 56; S. Q. 1988, c. 54). The Charter is popularly known as *Loi No 101* (Bill 101).
3. See below, note 18.
4. In the **Miriam Case**, Quebec's Court of Appeal, in an *obiter dictum* (something said by a judge while giving judgement that was not essential to the decision in the case and therefore creating no binding precedent in itself), concluded that Section 89 of Bill 101 (which, allowing for exceptions, permits the generalized use of both French and another language) and the Preamble of the Charter (where it says that the Act must be enforced in a "spirit of justice and open-mindedness") enshrined, for all practical purposes, the principle of linguistic freedom in Quebec (S. F. P C. v. Miriam, 1984, C. A., 104).

   In the **Gagnon Case**, Quebec's High Court recognized as French the apparently English term "office", used instead of the French word "réception", because it was an expression peculiar to Quebec, not forbidden by the law, and understood in Quebec (Charles Gagnon v. the Attorney General of Quebec, decision No 200-36-000035-86).

   In the **Steiner Case**, the *Cour d'appel de Paris*, in a decision rendered on November 27, 1985, confirmed the judgement handed down by the *Tribunal de Police de Paris* on December 1, 1984, recognizing as French the word "show", "because it is found in all good French dictionaries and is easily understood by all, as well as the word *showroom* since there is no French translation of the expression and it would be inquisitional and abusive to enforce the use of the term *hall* or *salle d'exposition*" (translation). See decision No 85-1233 of the *13ᵉ* Chambre des appels correctionnels, Section B, *Cour d'appel de Paris*, and judgement No 148-705 of the *Tribunal de Police de Paris*. (December 1, 1984).
5. Section 20 of the above-mentioned Regulation states that "Any inscription, any sign or poster, and any commercial advertising may be presented by pictographs, by figures, by any artificial combination of letters, syllables or figures, or by initials" (R. S. Q., c. C-11, r. 9).
6. Moreover, it should not be believed nor should the impression be given that language "quality" is a recent phenomenon or problem. The ancient Greeks spent much time quibbling over the benefits or detriments of "analogy" understood as an almost religious respect for the rules of grammar and of linguistic tradition and of "anomaly" seen as a synonym for linguistic freedom and creativity. Furthermore, the modern Greeks had the same discussions some years ago, in 1952, when they drafted their new Constitution. That is the reason why Section 107 of the Greek Constitution, of 1952, stated that "the official language of the country is the language in which the Constitution is written".

The Greek language could not be named, because the Greek language was not universally understood in the same way. Furthermore, that Section prohibited any attempt to corrupt the official language!

The same situation applies with the Swiss Constitution. Section 116 of that Constitution states that French, Italian and German are the official languages of the Swiss Confederation. But which German language, the German of Germany or of Switzerland? See Redard et al (ed.) 1981.

The problem of the understandability or intelligibility of a legal text is also important: the State of New York has made two consumer protection laws which enact that some contracts must be written in "understandable" or "plain" language (see Chapter 747, 1977, and Chapter 199, 1978, of the Statutes of New York State).

7. In the **Sutton Case** (February 23, 1983), and the **Miriam Case** (March 22, 1984), the Montreal Court of the Sessions of the Peace and Quebec's Court of Appeal respectively declared that in certain given situations, Quebec's language legislation only applies to francophones if they explicitly request to be served in French. It was thus concluded that francophones can renounce their language rights, which evidently suggests that the legislation in question is not deemed to be a public policy law (R. v. Sutton, 1983, C. S. P., 101; this decision was confirmed by the Quebec High Court in decision No 500-36-0000136-831, August 15, 1983. For the Miriam Case, see above, note 4).

8. In the **France Quick Case**, the *Cour d'appel de Paris*, in its decision of December 14, 1984, acquitted a firm accused of using the terms "giant", "big", "coffee-drink", "bigcheese", "fishburger", "hamburger", "cheeseburger", and "milkshake", on the grounds that the terms and expressions were either fanciful or understood by the French consumers (decision No 1327–84 of the *13e* Chambre des appels correctionnels, Section B). France's *Cour de cassation* quashed this judgement, arguing that French language legislation protected the French language rather than francophones, without entering into much detail (decision No 85–90–934 of the *Chambre criminelle de la Cour de cassation*).

9. The Versailles Court of Appeal was inspired in part by the decision of the *Cour de cassation* (see above, note 8) in its decision on the **France Quick Case** (decision No 69–87) of the *7e* Chambre de la Cour d'appel de Versailles).

10. See below, note 18.

11. **Macdonald v. City of Montreal**, (1986) 1 S. C. R. 460; **Ford v. Quebec** (1988) 2 S. C. R. 712. In the **Ford Case**, the Supreme Court of Canada declared that "Language is so intimately related to the form and content of expression that there cannot be true freedom of expression by means of language if one is prohibited from using the language of one's choice." (p. 748).

12. **The Attorney General of Quebec v. Irwin Toy Limited**, (1989) 1 S. C. R. 927. In this decision, the Supreme Court of Canada confirmed the thesis according to which freedom is a fundamental right held both by natural persons and artificial persons. The Court, however, concluded that the fundamental right of everyone "to life, liberty and security of the person" (as recognized in Section 7 of the Canadian Charter of Rights and Freedoms) could only be claimed by natural persons (p. 1004).

The Supreme Court also gave this definition of freedom of speech : "Indeed, freedom of expression ensures that we can convey our thoughts and feelings in non-violent ways without fear of censure" (p. 970). For the Court, freedom of speech means, in principle, any content (any message, including commercial messages) in any form (any medium, and therefore, any language), except violence.

13. Capotorti 1979 (see page 81, in particular). It must be pointed out that according to the Capotorti Report, however, not only the right to be different is a fundamental right, but also the right to be assimilated is of the kind of a fundamental right (p. 103).
14. See Turi 1977. Moreover, we should not forget that in the United States, 17 States (including California and Florida) passed language legislation enacting that English language is their official language in the official usage of languages.
    See also Skutnabb-Kangas and Phillipson 1989: 55–84.
15. Republic of Turkey, Law regarding publications in languages other than Turkish, Law No 2932 (October 22, 1983). This law was annulled on April 12, 1991 — see Skutnabb-Kangas — Bucak, this volume.
16. *Les Nations Unies et les droits de l'homme,* Nations Unies, New York, 1973. *La Charte internationale des droits de l'homme.*
    Nations Unies, New York, 1978. The International Covenant came into force on March 23, 1976.
17. See Turi 1989: 55–85.
18. As regards the non-discriminatory nature of certain provisions of Bill 101 (Section 35 of the Act requires that professionals have an appropriate knowledge of French language), see the Supreme Court of Canada decision in the **Forget Case** (The Attorney General of Quebec v. Nancy Forget, 1988, 2 S. C. R. 90). In this judgement, the Court declared that "The concept of language is not limited to the mother tongue but also includes the language of use or habitual communication ... there is no reason to adopt a narrow interpretation which does not take into account the possibility that the mother tongue and the language of use may differ." (p. 100).
    As regards the discriminatory nature of certain provisions of Bill 101 (Sections 58 and 69 of the Act, regarding the exclusive use of the French language for signs and posters and for firm names), see the Supreme Court of Canada decision in the **Ford Case** (see above, note No 11). In this judgement, the Court decided that the distinction based on "language of use", created by Section 58 of Bill 101, had the effect of "nullifying" the fundamental right "to express oneself in the language of one's choice" (p. 787).
    As regards Section 89 of Bill 101, see above, note 4.

Personal names and human rights

Björn H. Jernudd

The issue

Names[1] are intensely individual and mark identity both of the unique person and of the person as a member of a group.[2] The family chooses a name for a newborn. But society may impose constraints on the choice. Constraints inhere in social organization. A group's naming custom is one constraint. Other constraints arise in contemporary society from processes of economic, political and cultural unification and integration and from institutionalized state control over individuals. These processes separate a private sphere of speaking and conduct from a public one. The two spheres may coincide or be separate, for example, individuals may call each other by any name out of the hearing of others, but may be constrained to use certain names only in public, especially in writing.

In regard to the public use of names, the state may recommend and more or less vigorously enforce that people register their children with names of a particular form in a language or with names only in certain languages. For example, a name law promulgated in 1985 in Thailand makes it illegal to register a name that resembles the King's name or that has more than 10 consonants. People may be forbidden registration of names in their group's language. For example, the Chinese in Indonesia must adopt names that sound Indonesian and follow Indonesian language rules because the state prohibits use of any Chinese language, especially written Chinese characters.

Other circumstances than public regulation may constrain people's naming, e.g. when people migrate from countryside to town for work or migrate for whatever reason into a new language environment. For example, I allowed interlocutors to adjust Björn to John in Australia; or a friend of mine is known as George in Australia and not as Jiří. The practice of women being forced to give up their own names to take on their husbands' surnames at marriage by law in some countries is eroding as these societies change (cf. Adler 1978: 131–); but meanwhile this practice is regarded by many, not the least by women's rights movements, as conflicting with women's rights.

What is the relationship between the individually private and the collectively public management of names? When is regulation of naming a violation of human rights? When and why would people agree to public constraint on private naming?

Cases

I shall review several cases involving name change which exemplify how socially inclusive decisions may affect people's use of names.

Bulgaria

The Bulgarian Communist Party decided to abandon decrees to oppress Turkish names in Bulgaria on December 29, 1989, and gave Turkish-language minorities in Bulgaria the right to regain their Turkish names (Konstantinov et al. 1990: 7, 12). Turkish names had been oppressed because minorities who were ethnically and linguistically associated with Turkish identity and language and culturally associated with Islam had been oppressed at different periods during this century, most recently since the 1980's in the government's "Process of Rebirth", a program which offered to minority citizens of Bulgaria the opportunity to regain her/his original Bulgarian identity (Konstantinov et al. 1990: 8). Enforced name change was accompanied by other measures of official and unofficial oppression, which reportedly included condemnation of use of Turkish at all. The result was a mass exodus of minority ethnic Turks to Turkey. The superordinate problem was group conflict aided and abetted by state power through a rhetoric focussing on original identity (the reasons for this conflict and the succession of programs of identity management are not discussed here); the larger language issue was other Bulgarians' reaction to the possession and use of Turkish by members of the Turkish, Islamic and other minority groups. A Bulgarian citizen of Turkish ethnicity could not use his/her Turkish-marked name even in Bulgarian language discourse. Ethnically Turkish people were obliged to change Turkish-sounding names.[3]

Indonesia

There is a similar situation of oppression of an ethnolinguistic minority group in Indonesia. Very many Chinese in Indonesia have been made

stateless or are kept stateless as the intended result of Indonesian regulations (Thoolen 1987: 151–155). Chinese language books, papers, songs
and tape- recordings cannot be imported. The Chinese books and newspapers
cannot be published (although there exists one Government newspaper
partly in Chinese characters). The Chinese are allowed only to form clan
associations. There are no Chinese schools or Chinese-language schools.
The requirement of re- registration of foreigners serves to put pressure
on individuals of Chinese ancestry to take Indonesian names. According
to an article in *The Straits Times* (August 29, 1990) Mr. Kristoforus
Sindhunata, who represents a government-backed group to promote the
assimilation of ethnic Chinese, feels that

> ... efforts at assimilating ethnic Chinese should be made at the
> grassroots levels and in this regard, success could be seen particu-
> larly among the younger generation through mixed schooling and
> marriages. Indonesian authorities have encouraged the assimilation
> process through the single education system and by banning the
> public use of the Chinese language and characters. It has also
> encouraged ethnic Chinese to take on more Indonesia-sounding
> names and shed their Chinese names.

Adler (1978: 132) refers to the opposite practice in Hitler's Germany
where "one of the first acts of his government was to compel every male
Jew to carry the name of Isac and every Jewish woman to register the
name of Sarah."[4]

Japan

In Japan, a parent who was denied the right to register a child's name in
particular written characters contested this decision in court. The plaintiff
pleaded violation of his constitutional rights. Neustupný (1984) presents
the case as an example of violation of human rights.

This is the case. A Family Registration Law of 1947 stipulates that
for "names of children, common and easy (*jooyoo heii*) characters must
be used". A ministerial order defined these characters for the purpose of
registering names as the same as the set of 1850 Characters for General
Use, tooyoo kanji (supplementing the syllabic writing, kana) already
approved in 1946 and limited registration of names to characters included
in this set. The Mayor of the City of Chigasaki (Kanagawa Prefecture)
refused registration of two names in 1950 "on the grounds that the first
of the two characters used for each of the two names was not a Character

for General Use" (Neustupný 1984: 68). I reproduce in full the arguments involved in the appeal before the Tokyo High Court (Neustupný 1984):

1) Restrictions on name-giving violate basic human rights and in particular article 21 of the Constitution which guarantees freedom of expression. Hence, article 50 of the Family Registration Law is unconstitutional.

2) Even should this not be the case, the use of the General Use Characters stipulated in article 60 of the Enforcement Regulations issued by the Ministry of Justice is inappropriate. The preamble of the List of General Use Characters states explicitly that "since many legal and other problems are connected with the writing of proper names, the question will be considered separately". Hence, the List should not be used to specify the range of approved characters.

3) Naming of children is decided by parents and only "reported" (todokeru) to the City office. Since the names 瑛美 and 玖美 have been decided upon by the parents, any other reporting would be a case of "false reporting" and should be punishable under article 157 of the Penal Code.

The judges agreed that freedom was indeed restricted by the limitation on use of characters but that public welfare interests may justify such a limitation. The judges were of the opinion that since names are given for social use, "the use of rare and difficult names negatively affects the interests of others" (Neustupný 1984: 69). The judgement was rendered at a time in the development of modern Japanese society when promulgation of a limited list of approved characters for use in writing was an acceptable act of standardization. Neustupný observes that although the father lost his case before the High Court, the National Language Council released and had a List of Given Name Characters with an additional 92 characters accepted by the Ministry of Justice only a month thereafter.

Hong Kong

T'sou (1988) draws attention to the romanization of Chinese surnames in Hong Kong as an issue that needs resolution in view of what is likely to happen in naming practices after Hong Kong is integrated into the People's Republic of China in 1997.

Today in Hong Kong, romanization is based on Cantonese pronunciation. If the PRC policy of romanizing names according to their equivalent forms in Mandarin based on Mandarin pronunciation and pinyin romanization is also followed in the future in incorporated Hong Kong "more than three quarters of the population will need to have the names in their records changed" (T'sou 1988: 12–13, 17). T'sou identifies three difficulties, (a) violation of individual attachment to their "traditional romanized names"; (b) difficulties with individual identification because of "romanization according to a different and unfamiliar dialect"; and (c) difficulties with the legal basis for identification (e.g. for inheritance and criminal records purposes). T'sou foresees resistance if romanizing names according to only Mandarin pronunciation were to be required.

Singapore

In 1982, the Singaporean government began recommending that Chinese families in Singapore adjust to Mandarin pronunciation and Hanyu pinyin romanization of names. Those Chinese parents who now pronounce their names in Hokkien, Cantonese, Teochew or other Chinese dialects should register their children with the equivalent rendering of the family's name in Mandarin Chinese in Hanyu pinyin transliteration. Mandarin Chinese is designated as the language of the ethnic Chinese in Singapore and Hanyu pinyin has been designated as the standard transliteration system and reflects Mandarin Chinese pronunciation. There is a limited number of family names in Chinese and each of these family names is pronounced differently in different dialects. They are normally written with the same Chinese characters regardless of dialect. The Hanyu pinyin transliteration of a family name that is written in Chinese characters can be rendered on the basis of its corresponding Mandarin Chinese pronunciation. However, as is common practice in Singapore, when the family name is not written in Chinese characters, the corresponding Mandarin Chinese pronunciation cannot easily be determined and therefore neither can the accompanying Hanyu pinyin transliteration. The family's non-standard romanization of the name will normally but not uniquely identify the equivalent Mandarin pronunciation (and therefore standard transliteration) of the name.[5] For the individual's unique name, there is considerable variation. However, if characters are used to write an individual's unique name, the Mandarin Chinese pronunciation and transliteration are known regardless of the individual's dialect pronunciation of the name. For example, a person with the family name Teo is probably Hokkien and one with the family name Cheong is probably Cantonese. In Hanyu pinyin, both are Zhang [張]. The same name can also be spelt Chang, Cheung, Chong, Teoh, Thio, Tioe, Tiong, and Tiu, depending in the main on the dialect group.[6]

There is unease among the Chinese about having to give children Mandarin-based pinyin names. By giving up the dialect -based transliteration of the family name, the person may feel s/he is giving up continuity of kinship, a very serious matter for Chinese families. Also, individuals may understandably be upset when, as is known to happen, civil servants make difficulties over the rendering of a name when they register a child. The civil servant's behavior, and the regulation of registration of names, are closely related to, perhaps even a direct result of, the Speak Mandarin Campaign. The campaign was launched on September 7, 1979, by then Prime Minister Lee Kuan Yew. The government felt that the use of pinyin would go a long way in popularising the use of Mandarin. In conjunction with the campaign, the government in 1982 began persuading Chinese Singaporeans to register their children's names in Hanyu pinyin. The Ministry of Education also announced that all Chinese students from pre-primary up to pre-university classes would be known in school by their Mandarin names (in Hanyu pinyin when written) from 1982. Unlike the registration of names in birth certificates which was to be voluntary, adoption of pinyin names in school was obligatory. Pupils' names in school certificates are standardized to Mandarin Chinese. All Chinese pupils who take the Primary School Leaving Examination (PSLE) and General Certificate of Education (GCE) 0 and A level examinations have to use their Hanyu pinyin equivalent names with their registered (birth certificate) names in brackets when different. Those with names in Chinese characters will also have them included in the certificates.

In September 1984, opening the annual Speak Mandarin campaign month, then Prime Minister Lee Kuan Yew gave the figures for the types of names that were registered during a two year period in Chinese children's birth certificates (see figure 1).

Mr. Lee was reported (*The Straits Times* 22 Sept 1984) to have said the following:

> When parents registered their children's names between August 1982 and July 1984, 1/5 registered only their dialect names, a total rejection [of Hanyu Pinyin]. Over 1/3 registered their dialect names, with full pinyin in brackets, a concession to their identification with other Chinese of different dialects, a tentative and reluctant acceptance. Nearly 1/4 registered their surnames in dialect and their personal names in pinyin, a partial acceptance, i. e. they will not

	Pin	Dia	Bra	mix*
Aug to Dec 1982	18	21	44	17
Jan to Dec 1983	22	22	32	24
Jan to Jul 1984	21	18	35	26
Aug 82 to Jul 84	21	21	35	23

* Pin = entire name in full Hanyu pinyin; Dia = entire name in dialect; Bra = entire name in dialect with Hanyu pinyin in brackets; Mix = surname in dialect and name in Hanyu pinyin

Figure 1. Types of Chinese names in the birth certificates of Chinese children (% of total per period)

give up their total identification with their fathers' and grandfathers' dialect surnames but are prepared to concede an identification with Chinese of other dialects through using pinyin for their personal names. 1/5 did so in pinyin, a full acceptance.

He also noted that on another place in the birth certificate, over 1/3 of Chinese parents registered additional Western names for their children. 20 years earlier, in 1964, only 1/15 registered Christian personal names. The use of Christian names in the birth certificates for Chinese children was, in 1964, 7.6% of all registrations, and from August 1982 to July 1984, 35% of all registrations. Western influence, Mr. Lee inferred, has increased by 5 times. But he also noted that loyalties to dialect names are emotional and strong. This means, Mr. Lee was quoted to have said, that we have to accept that the home language will remain dialect for some time.

Three years later in August 1987, Mr. Lee again quoted figures to show that many Chinese Singaporeans still preferred to register their children's names in dialect.[7] Though displeased, he agreed that the dialect surnames held a great significance for Chinese Singaporeans.

In letters to the editor of *The Straits Times* (e.g. 7, 9 June, 24 July, 1982) quite unsurprisingly more people argue against the use of Hanyu pinyin for names than for it.[8] These are some examples of concerns. Because only pinyinized names should be used at school, problems of communication arose in schools, according to letters to *The Straits Times'* editor. Teo Geok Boey, a 6-year-old school girl, missed drinking her school milk. Her parents called her only by her dialect name. She did not recognise her Hanyu pinyin name, Zhang Yu Mei, on the milk carton at school. Another girl, Jenny Lim, was given a Chinese name by her school teacher who then used this Chinese name and not Jenny which her Catholic parents had given her. Another parent was unhappy that her son was addressed in his given Christian name in school because she preferred her child to be called by his dialect name. Perhaps some teachers are not sufficiently familiar with Hanyu pinyin to make reasonable decisions about what to call the children? There are teachers who struggle over pronunciation[9] and who find that they can not put faces to Hanyu pinyin names (*The Straits Times* 23 Feb 1986). Some Chinese teachers who had to convert their pupils' names to Hanyu pinyin experienced difficulties in the task for which they sought help from the Ministry of Education.

Some parents were not happy that the name tags and certificates which their children were issued at school did not bear the children's actual, official, names, i. e. the names in the children's birth certificates. One letter-writer considered his son's report card "useless" because it does not bear his son's registered name.

Sweden

Swedish name law builds on two principles, namely, that names are a public concern in that they distinguish and identify one individual in relation to another in society, and that the individual has a private right to her/his name because it is a unique identifier (SOU 1979: 25; Sandgren 1987; 355). Consequently, the Swedish government has been suggesting, since early this century, that individuals discard surnames of the type father's-first-name followed by -son which do not effectively distinguish and identify individuals and adopt unique surnames which then become the registered property of the individual (Person 1967). A name law upholds the individual's right to this unique surname and relates this right to children's names, spouse's name, name change, and so on.[10] For example, my father and uncle discarded the all too common Pettersson name which simply reflected son of Petter and invented Jernudd in response to this continuing government campaign to register unique family names in Sweden.[11] Their action was their voluntary adjustment.

Discussion

In what situations of adjustment of personal names are rights involved? We may claim in accord with work in the ethnography of speaking (from Goffman 1955 via Schegloff et al. 1977) that discourse situations in which one person, the Other, evaluates Self's utterance as inadequate are inherently unstable situations. We assume that self-adjustment (self-correction) is given preference in discourse by all people in all communication unless an exception has been specifically granted (such as for a teacher towards the student)[12]. If an exception has not been granted and if Other corrects Self, there is confrontation which may be overtly expressed unless mitigated or covertly suppressed.

It follows that if Other takes issue with Self's name, a unique identifier of Self[13], thus marking it as inadequate, then Other invites confrontation. There is potential conflict when Other demands or suggests a change of name by Self wholly or in part, or blocks registration of Self's chosen name. Other-initiated name change or refusal to register a name are impositions on Self, both by reason of violation of the discoursal preference given to Self for adjustment (correction) in communication, and by reason of identity of Self with a name. These impositions can be construed as violations of a human right.

My reasoning now implies that all language policy implementation is a violation of an individual's right unless the individual has ceded to Other the initiation of adjustment to which Self has a right.[14] Under what conditions will an individual do that?

Suggestions for adjustment that originate in State policies could perhaps be seen as mitigated by an implied public interest, an interest which includes Self together with all Others. Some aspects of the balance between Self's rights and collective rights are the individual's perception of the strength of community of interest, his or her own stake in the public interest, degree of knowledge about the relationship between policy and individual behavior and outcome, individuals' perception of compatibility of behavior in one aspect of life with other co-terminous aspects. These aspects all play a role in the unfolding of actual individual practices within the realm of the State.

Conclusion

State policy on language selection and language standardization (of character inventory, script, and transcription, and of morphology of name formation[15] may have consequences for naming and naming regulations, and naming may itself be regulated. In cases of people voluntarily complying with recommendations from the state, public debate of naming recommendations and experience with its implementation by state agencies and educational authorities will inevitably refer to problems of both principle and practice, but what is generally at issue here is not any human rights violation.

In a multilingual society, intensive state promotion of one variety over other ethnically marked varieties for a given ethnic group (such as of Mandarin over dialects for the ethnic Chinese in Singapore) may well have popular acceptance, yet the consequences of this repertoire adjustment may have been unforeseen and may engender conflicts of interest. Conflict in regard to naming consists in the clash between the linguistic form that the name already has (based in dialect) and the form that the standard variety would prescribe. Such conflict rests on identity of family with identity of form of name. It is reasonable to expect that unless the state seeks to circumvent the conflict by imposing adjustment, use will resolve it over time. Meanwhile, the conflict requires management by public information, discussion and flexibility of use, especially in schools and other public contexts of language use. Such conflict is potentially serious when a relatively homogeneous language community such as Cantonese-using Hong Kong becomes incorporated in China with Mandarin as the mandated public language to be required in registration of names.

The modernization process may paradoxically require a greater degree of distinctiveness of name forms when people come to participate in wider networks than the local rural one, as the Swedish case exemplifies. Since individual identity is enhanced by the individual's voluntary adjustment of name, within certain broad parameters of standard language form, people do not feel that rights are violated, rather, they gain a new right to a unique name.

The cases suggest that human rights are likely to be violated when the state intervenes in the relationship between individuals' names and group identity. Mandatory adjustment of name is a means to deny a group's existence *qua* group, as formerly with the Turks in Bulgaria, or to erode for significant numbers of individuals their ability to manifest their identity as members of a group, as with the Chinese in Indonesia. States wishing to forcibly assimilate visible ethnic groups require names to be changed. In a worst case, the state provides the new names and the individuals merely have to comply in use. Denial of name denies the identity, i. e. the particular existence of, the individual, and of all individuals who share characteristics of name. Name rights proclamations (cf. Alfredsson 1989 on indigenous peoples' rights, and Türk 1990 on minority rights) seem to aim at preventing rights violations along this dimension. Separate mention of name rights in rights proclamations is justified to prevent the state from threatening or denying individual expression of group identity.

Notes

1. I am grateful to Professor Edwin D. Lawson for his enthusiastic support of my interest in names. I gratefully acknowledge that I have made use of data from interviews and newspaper clippings that Ms. Tan Ai-lan gathered when she participated as a student in a language planning course that I conducted at the National University of Singapore. I am also grateful to Dr. Robert Stecker and Ms. Sharon Mann for making suggestions for improving the paper.

2. There are two fine bibliographies on names and naming, Smith 1965 and Lawson 1987. For networking and professional exchanges, Professor Edwin D. Lawson is easy to contact by e-mail per LAWSON
FREDONIA or LAWSON
SNYFREBA. BITNET.

3. Anthroponymic onomastic work is being done by members and associates of the Bulgarian Society for Regional Cultural Studies (Konstantinov et al. 1990) on the name behavior of the Pomaks in the region of Zlataritza. The Society intends to extend its studies to other minorities in Bulgaria. The field study investigates compromise behavior in anthroponymic realization, as a result of the oppression of Turkish (and Muslim) names.

4. Adler also points to the fate of the Spanish Jews in Catholic Spain of the 15th century. They had the choice of either being burnt at the stake–to save their souls–or to convert to Christianity and be baptised with Christian names.

5. The identification of the Mandarin form of the name is made a little easier by the fact that there exists only a limited number of family names among the Chinese. Dialects offer differentiation of names when Mandarin-based names reduce the inventory of available names radically.

6. The uniformisation of family names which is an outcome of the language policy to support Mandarin Chinese as the community language for the ethnic Chinese in Singapore clearly conflicts with the modern state's needs for unique identifiers of individuals in a standard format. Uniformisation may be allowed to win out because Singapore also issues identity cards with unique person numbers to all Singaporeans.

7. Mr. Lee pointed out (*The Straits Times* 17 Aug 1987) that only 12% of all Chinese babies born in January to June 1987 were registered with full pinyin names (including surnames), compared to 22% in 1983. But the number who insisted that their children retain surnames in dialect with personal names in pinyin had gone up to 50%.

8. Those who do not have a grievance or a problem do not have any reason to write to the paper.

9. This was confirmed in a small study undertaken for my language planning class at NUS in 1990/91 by Ms. Lee Chen.

10. The name law currently in force was promulgated in 1982 (SFS 1982: 1134) with a change in 1988 (SFS 1988: 261) and replaced the law of 1963 (SFS 1963: 521).

11. Of course, as a Swedish citizen I have a "personnummer" [personal number], too! My number is unique because the particular number as a whole refers to me only but it is not unique because it is constructed to reveal some civic facts about me. For example, the number tells how old I am, where I was born, my citizenship status. But isn't that a different matter? A numerical identification system takes the pressure off standardization of form of name in the state's system of record keeping.

12. Which constitutes this relationship!

13. I shall assume that the newborn are extensions of parents' Selves.

14. I suggest for consideration that the initiation of adjustment by Self is a so-called natural right.

15. Language standardization and uniformisation are typical of modern contemporary societies.

II COUNTRY STUDIES: TOWARDS EMPOWERMENT

Section introduction

EDUARDO HERNÁNDEZ-CHÁVEZ's paper **Language policy in the united states. A history of cultural genocide** reviews the history of language rights in the USA until the present day. The absence of explicit regulation on official language policy at the federal or constitutional level has not prevented a de facto thrust towards cultural and linguistic assimilation. The menu on the linguistic melting-pot has varied in different states in various historical periods, but the outcome, for both indigenous peoples (Native Americans) and colonised and immigrant groups, continental Europeans, Asians and Africans, has generally been a gradual transition to monolingualism in English.

Hernández-Chávez demonstrates how language rights have been systematically violated, and the motives for doing so, and usefully shows how the currrent mood of restricting language rights − the Official English movement in particular − is part of a general pattern of xenophobia, both at home and abroad. He also shows that the Civil Rights movement of the 1960s and 1970s, though not ostensibly concerned with language rights, was significant in permitting the enjoyment of increased language rights in various domains (education, courts, voting). Some court cases did not, however, succeed in asserting language rights, and when language rights were approved, the state was not endorsing fundamental linguistic rights. Support for languages other than English was rather a 'compensatory mechanism' serving to ease administrative burdens and the transition to English, and consequently assisted in acculturating ethnic minority groups.

JIM CUMMINS' paper **The discourse of disinformation: the debate on bilingual education and language rights in the United States** focusses on one particular aspect of the scene described by Hernández-Chávez. He draws a parallel between the discourse on bilingual education in the US and public discourse in the US on Latin American governments which might represent a threat to US interests. He demonstrates how the "enemy" is constructed in both cases and how the dominant group uses disinformation to achieve its goal of maintaining the status quo. The discourse on bilingual education is analysed in order to show how monolingually oriented Americans resist the empowerment that successful bilingual education represents. In academic and political discourse various successful programmes are misnamed, empirically documented success is misrepresented and ignored, in addition to which there are logical inconsistencies in the position of its opponents. The importance of the paper lies in the unpicking or "deconstruction" of the position of opponents of bilingual education, to reveal the falsity of the rationalizations used to deprive minority students of their language rights in the education system.

Political and administrative decisions are often taken on the basis of such false representation of the content, means and outcomes of bilingual education. Such special pleading by and for the dominant group facilitates the operation of pressure groups such as US English, which have the explicit goal of imposing a monolingual version of the United States, hence of depriving minority members of their linguistic rights, not only in education but at the ballot box (with a ban on languages other than English), in public administration, etc. The article may also prod academics who see them themselves as scientifically "neutral" and "apolitical" but who oppose American abuse of its political and military might abroad (Chile, Guatemala, Panama) into becoming more critical of the "debate" on bilingual education.

MART RANNUT's **Beyond linguistic policy: the Soviet Union versus Estonia** describes the successive phases of Soviet language policy, the kind of bilingualism which was evolved, and the ideology underlying such notions as Russian as an "international language". The detailed dissection of Soviet linguistic policy sheds light on the role of language in many conflictual situations in the former Soviet Union and their roots in demographic, political and educational changes from the period of Stalinism to the 1990s.

The paper is written from the perspective of an Estonian scholar who has actively participated in the struggle to achieve cultural and ultimately political autonomy, in a situation where the Language Laws played a decisive role in the late 1980s in bringing about change in the Soviet state. The historical background is described in some detail, which provides a useful backcloth to understanding the current challenges to both the Estonian- and Russian-speaking groups in Estonia. The denial of linguistic rights in an earlier period has been replaced by a complex dialogue between the various groups in contemporary Estonia, and with human rights figuring prominently on the agendas of both the Estonian and Russian governments, but for very different reasons. The currrent challenge is to devise appropriate policies for the Republic of Estonia that has succeeded in regaining its independence and where language policy plays a central role in mediating the relationship between the groups.

TĪMOTI KĀRETU's paper **The Māori language in New Zealand** is written by a representative of a threatened language. Māori has achieved some degree of legal recognition of linguistic rights, but Kāretu's impassioned article shows that success in political and legislative terms must be accompanied by a change in attitudes to marginalized languages. This of course applies especially to Pākehā (non-Māori) New Zealanders, but also to the Māori community. Loss of the linguistic inheritance has in some cases been combined with an internalization of monolingual disinterest in other languages. As with several of the Sámi peoples, Māori first language speakers are in a minority among the Māori, and most Māori youngsters are second language speakers of Māori. The ethnolinguistic vitality needed in a revitalisation process, to undo the linguistic and psychological results of almost 200 years of repression, is still partly shaky, seen from Kāretu's insider's point of view, but to outsiders it is truly amazing. The Kōhanga Reo have inspired similar day care centres elsewhere, both in Hawai'i and among one of the smallest Sámi peoples, the Skolt Sámi in Finland (around 600 people).

OLE HENRIK MAGGA's paper **The Sámi Language Act** describes the position of the Sámi Language in Norway, where recent legislation has substantially increased the language rights of the Sámi. This represents a major reversal of earlier practice (though the church has made extensive use of Sámi). The paper describes the area of application of the law, and is critical of some of its territorial restrictions. There are quite serious problems of implementation, because even if educational provision through the medium of Sámi expands as foreseen, and officials are provided with study leave so that they can learn to function in the language, much corpus planning is still needed, and positive attitudes to Sámi cannot be assumed. A framework has though been agreed on within which extensive language rights can be exercised, and steps have been taken towards achieving equality between the Norwegian and Sámi languages, which is what the law proclaims. For instance, it is not only those whose mother tongue is Sámi who have the right to learn the language, but also Norwegian speakers. Another indicator of democratisation is that children are entitled under the law to decide for themselves whether they wish Sámi to continue as the medium of education after the seventh year of schooling (this reflects Scandinavian pedagogy generally, which in principle involves learners sharing responsibility with teachers for the content of teaching), but again Magga refers to constraints that may counteract this principle.

Both Kāretu, the first Māori Language Commissioner, and Magga, the chair of the Sami parliament in Norway, are convinced of the centrality of language to their culture, and are involved in activities which are leading to a revitalisation of languages that formerly were thought to be rapidly dying. Both the articles are particularly concerned with problems in the *implementation of LHRs* in addition to their *formulation*.

JUREK SMOLICZ' paper **Australia's language policies and minority rights: a core value perspective** describes the shift in recent decades in Australia from a monolingal English policy to the recognition of linguistic rights for both Aboriginals and for more recent migrants from diverse backgrounds. Smolicz draws on his theory of language as a "core value" (originally 1979) to reflect on the variation in the retention of the mother tongue of different migrant communities. His claim is that the dominant group should be able to "tolerate" extensive rights for minority languages (cf Grin), not only on grounds of equity (cf Fishman) but also because it makes political and economic sense. Economic factors have loomed large in official language planning, but the link between rights for *"community" languages* (those of migrant communities) on the one hand and *"international", "geopolitical" and "trade" languages* on the other hand has often been blurred, not least when several of these converge, as they do in the case of, e.g., Vietnamese and Chinese. Not by any means all political signals indicate a favourable attitude to building on the linguistic richness present in Australia's citizens, but there are many indications of policies at federal, State and institutional level that are designed to combat linguicism. These are very much the initial stages of implementing linguistic rights in a state where English is uncontested as the dominant language (as in the USA) but where officially there is an acceptance of a national policy of valuing minority languages (in contrast to the USA).

JOHN GIBBONS, WILLIAM WHITE and PAULINE GIBBONS' paper **Combating educational disadvantage among Lebanese Australian children** is a case study of how the *realization of educational linguistic rights* can be approached. It describes how a school in a poor part of Sydney tackled the question of how to linguistically empower a group that otherwise was likely to be condemned in large measure to educational failure and societal marginalization. The school devised a policy of in-service staff development in order to support teachers in developing both their ESL professionalism and their own awareness of it and of the linguistic potential of the Lebanese Australian children. The organization of a bilingual Arabic-English programme is described, along with its rationale, as is the issue of teaching about linguistic form in a basically experiential learning environment.

While the limitations of the project are also carefully noted, including the tricky issue of its scientific evaluation, it is clear from the description that the St. Mel's school programme has succeeded in evolving a primary school environment in which the minority mother tongue is valued both for itself and as a means of access to more efficient learning of the societally dominant language, English. Among the important goals seems to be *equality of outcome* as much as (or rather than) *equality of opportunity*.

The paper also highlights a number of "extra-linguistic" factors that are likely to be relevant in attempting to achieve effective implementation of educational linguistic rights: high teacher expectations of the pupils' bilingual potential, teacher commitment to a bilingual/bicultural school for *all* children, teamwork among those responsible for the development of each language, and positive parental involvement.

Language policy in the United States
A history of cultural genocide

Eduardo Hernández-Chávez

Except for very brief periods during which private language rights have been tolerated and certain limited public rights have been permitted, the history of language policy in the United States has generally been one of the imposition of English for an ever wider range of purposes and the restriction of the rights of other languages. This paper first describes these developments in their historical context, linking them to changes in sociopolitical conditions that serve as counterpoint to the central linguistic theme. It then focuses on the role of the Civil Rights movement in the liberalization of language policies during the 1960's and 1970's. Finally, it examines the economic and political conditions that fuel the reactions and counterreactions in the current debates over making English the official language of the United States.

English as the official language: the stage is set

It is often noted that, from its original drafting, the U. S. Constitution has been silent on the question of a national language for the United States. Actually, it is silent only in the sense that the framers did not make the official language explicit, an omission cited as a rationale for current official-English activities. However, the Constitution is not silent with respect to the very language in which it was written. This fact was later to weigh heavily in debates about English requirements for naturalization and voting. English was clearly to be the language of the new federation, used not only for citizenship, but also for all legislative, judicial and administrative matters. In addition, over the years there have been a variety of federal statutes and court decisions making English a legal requirement for different purposes, and there are numerous States with similar laws. These all involve government regulation of language, and thus, contrary to the claims of those who wish to establish English constitutionally, there can be little question that the United States has always had an official language and that this language is English.

During the campaign for Anglo-American independence, non-English languages were readily used by the English colonists where it was of political benefit. The various English-speaking areas of the colonies were all contiguous, and it was the English-speakers who were the architects, draftsmen, and builders of the new union. But there were other nationalities in the colonies — Germans, French, and others–who resided in areas where English was not the dominant language. The American-English had needed the collaboration of these nationalities to defeat the British and had used the languages of these groups in declarations and communications with them. The Articles of War, in French, were sent to the Quebecois, as were circulars inviting them to join the insurgency, offers that were later withdrawn because of religious biases. Similarly, the Articles of Confederation were translated to German, and during the War, German-American units fought alongside the English-American troops. Proclamations were issued that appealed to the German population to join the war and that provided information about the war's progress (Kloss 1977: 26–27). Specifying in the Constitution that English was the official language would surely have alienated these allies, and besides, the language of the founding documents would serve the same purpose, though less overtly.

Already prior to the War for Independence (1775–1783), there had been apprehension about the Germans. Benjamin Franklin, writing in 1751, called for a halt to German immigration to Pennsylvania (Piatt 1990: 7). Others tried to suspend voting rights for German members of the Colonial Assembly until they learned English and wanted to make legal documents void if not written in English.

After independence, the English-Americans quickly asserted their political superiority through the Continental Congress which consolidated the status of English as the language of U. S. official documents, ceasing to issue its proclamations in German (Kloss 1977: 28–). Upon the acquisition of Louisiana in 1803, an English-speaking governor was appointed who immediately proposed to draft all laws in English despite the overwhelming number of French speakers in the territory. Indeed, President Jefferson considered sending 30,000 settlers to Louisiana in order to achieve an English-speaking majority. This proposal was quickly withdrawn after a storm of protest (Leibowitz 1969: 15–16; Baron 1990: 2). Nevertheless, the Enabling Act of 1811 and the first Louisiana constitution specified English as the language of State documents. In Michigan, an 1810 petition to translate the laws into French was rejected.

The rise of nativism

Throughout the early decades of the 19th Century, attempts to obtain minority language rights met with stiff resistance, mostly in reaction to new immigrations, especially of Irish and German Catholics. The Native American Association (an organization dedicated to promoting the interests of "native" European-Americans, whence the political label *nativist*) issued a resolution in 1837 calling on Congress to deny citizenship to foreigners (Baron 1990: 90). The same year, the Pennsylvania constitutional convention debated the institution of schools in both German and English. Arguing that allowing such schools for German would cause all other language groups to make similar demands, the legislature turned the measure down (Baron 1990: 74–). In Congress, five separate proposals between 1843 and 1847 to print federal documents in German and French were rejected (Baron 1990: 91–92). Both the 1845 and 1852 Louisiana constitutions continued the earlier requirements that official versions of laws be written in English though unofficial French versions were permitted as well. Major officials and office holders were also required to know English in addition to French (Baron 1990: 84). During this entire period and as late as 1868, Louisiana passed a series of laws requiring English along with French for official notices. The French provisions were later to be removed in the exclusive favor of English (Kloss 1977: 110–).

Toward mid-century, American expansion and the consolidation of German settlements in sparsely populated regions of the Midwest opened up a brief period of liberalization of language policies in those areas. German ethnic organizations had sprung up that acquired considerable political influence and worked vigorously for language rights. This political pressure along with practical necessity and attempts to attract students away from ethnic religious schools soon led Ohio, Pennsylvania, and Wisconsin to permit the teaching of German in their public schools (Baron 1990: 11). Several legislatures, including Ohio, Illinois, Iowa, Indiana, Missouri, and Wisconsin ordered the printing of State laws in German, and numerous executive messages were printed in that language. Even as late as 1863, the U. S. General Land Office was given authority to print its report in German in order to encourage additional European immigration and the settlement of territory newly wrested from indigenous peoples (Kloss 1977: 85–86; Marshall 1986: 11).

However, these immigration and settlement policies continued to bring in large numbers of Catholics, including both Germans and Irish fleeing

European economic depressions, and public attitudes quickly hardened once again (Kloss 1977: 29–). Nativist, mostly Protestant, reaction led to denunciations of the new immigrants and to riots in several East Coast cities (Piatt 1990: 14). In 1843 and and again in 1862, attempts to allow Congressional deliberations and the publication of laws in German were voted down, the arguments against such measures focusing on the question of whether or not the U. S. was to have a single national language (Kloss 1977: 29–). In Louisiana during this period, Anglo-American immigration increased, especially in the northern parishes, and numerous local ordinances were passed requiring English for administrative purposes. This movement culminated in the Constitution of 1868, in which English became the language of instruction in the schools, and in the passage of a new Code of Practice abolishing French as the language of court announcements (Kloss 1977: 118–121).

The indigenous peoples

During the same general period of the 19th Century, the United States had embarked on a series of military campaigns to subdue the indigenous nations west of the Mississippi River, the so-called "opening of the West." (These peoples have historically been named *Indians* by the Europeans, a label that most native people themselves continue to use as a self-designation. Many political activists, however, prefer to use specific tribal names wherever possible and to employ the term *Native American* in a pan-tribal sense.) The eastern tribes had already been decimated and many of their survivors had been relocated, in the infamous Trail of Tears, to areas distant from their homelands. Nevertheless, some of these tribes such as the Choctaw, the Seneca, the Cherokee, and others had established their own extensive school systems, some teaching their own languages as well as English (Fuchs — Havighurst 1972: 6–7; Szasz 1974: 9). These schools would eventually be eliminated by the Curtis Act of 1898.

For well over a century, the federal government pursued the goal of cultural as well as physical extermination of Native Americans. Planned cultural disintegration was carried out through laws establishing tribal governments, police forces, and court systems that emulated white institutions and undermined existing ones (O'Brien 1985: 43).

The most consequential of these practices from the point of view of language was the establishment, beginning in 1879, of a system of boarding schools far from the reservations. By the 1920's, there were seventy-seven such schools whose express purpose was the complete assimilation of Native American children, remolding their conception of life and their attitudes toward the land (Szasz 1974: 8–10). In justifying their removal to these schools, the Commissioner of Indian Affairs noted the difficulty experienced in reservation day schools of "freeing the children ... from the language and habits of their untutored and often savage parents. When they return to their homes at night ... they relapse more or less into their former moral and mental stupor" (U. S. Government Printing Office, 1886: xxiii).

Children from different tribes were transported great distances to these schools, often after being forcibly taken from their parents. Tribal religions were completely suppressed, and the children were forbidden to use their native languages under pain of physical punishment. They were taught to speak, read, and write English as well as to dress and act like white childen. The curriculum had no application to the children's home environment and culture. To finish the process of anglicization, students were placed with white families for three years after the completion of school, the supposed benefits compensated for by the children's labor, and upon their return to the reservation, they were often the objects of ridicule (Fuchs and Havighurst 1972: 224–).

It was not until the 1930's under the leadership of liberal Indian Service administrators that a few innovative bilingual education programs were instituted, but these were to be short lived. The post-World-War II years brought a renewed emphasis on the assimilation of Native peoples, culminating in the "termination" policies of the 1950's by which many dozens of tribes were stripped of official recognition, federal services were terminated, and their members encouraged to migrate to urban areas and to sever their tribal ties.

The Civil Rights Movement of the 1960's and 1970's brought the revival of bilingual education programs (see below). These programs, which continue to the present, tend to permit a certain amount of community involvement in the educational process and the inclusion of culturally relevant curricula. There is still a great emphasis, however, on English instruction and on preparing Native American students to leave the reservation. At present, the native languages of most tribes are rapidly disappearing, and the bilingual programs serve little more than a transitional purpose.

The Mexicans

Following the Mexican War (1846–1848) and the annexations of Texas, California, and New Mexico, policies in the West followed the pattern of anglicization policies in the East and Midwest. Despite the large Mexican population, Texas came to be dominated by Anglos and Germans who had immigrated there in anticipation of secession from Mexico. (*Anglo* is generally used in the Southwest to refer not just to English-Americans but to other, mostly white, Americans of European background. They have generally accepted the English language and Anglo values and customs, and in this sense, they are largely indistinguishable from English-Americans.) Resentment toward Mexicans following the Battle of the Alamo (1836), in which a small contingent of Anglo rebels and Mexican allies were annihilated by the Mexican army, was translated after annexation into completely Anglo-centered policies. In 1841, just five years following its rebellion against Mexico, Texas suspended the printing of its laws in Spanish though in 1846 the Governor of the new State of Texas was authorized to disseminate the laws of the State in either Spanish or German, as he deemed it necessary for their proper administration (Kloss 1977: 175–).

It is clear that such laws concerning the use of Spanish were passed not in the interests of the people, but for the convenience of the State in administering the laws. Thus, the law of 1856 allowed the use of Spanish in the courts only in counties with large Mexican populations. Even so, English was required where one of the parties did not speak Spanish. By 1858, a mere dozen years after Texas became a State, English had become the language of instruction in the schools. In 1870, in response to the immense problems that were encountered in effecting this law, a proviso was added allowing any "foreign language" to be taught, so long as it was in connection with the teaching of English, i. e. the temporary teaching of Spanish in a weak form of transitional bilingual educaton. But by 1905 a new law was passed that specified that, except for foreign language instruction, all instruction had to be in English (Kloss 1977: 177). The linguistic rights of Texas Mexicans became essentially non-existent.

In California, too, Anglos became a majority virtually at the time the territory was ceded by Mexico. The 1849 constitution permitted the publication of laws in Spanish and English and an 1852 statute required their promulgation in Spanish in the counties most heavily populated by Mexicans. In these same counties, summonses in Spanish were required, and court proceedings in Spanish were permitted (Kloss 1977: 181–82). But the constitution of 1855 specified that English was to be the language of instruction, and in 1862–63, legislation was passed that restricted further the laws that could be published in Spanish and the number of counties in which court proceedings in Spanish were to be permitted (Kloss 1977: 182). Finally, the constitution of 1879 dropped all official use of Spanish, stipulating that all government business would be "conducted, preserved, and published in no other than the English language" (California 1879: 801, cited in Baron 1990: 17). California, like Texas, had become officially English.

New Mexico was different: it had no gold like California; it did not have the rangeland of Texas; it was poor. The overwhelming part of its population when it was ceded by Mexico was still made up of *mexicanos/ mexicanas* (hereafter *mexicanas*). (This term continues to be used in modern times by the Spanish-speaking population of New Mexico as a term of self identification. It is essentially an ethnic designation rather than a political one since there remains little loyalty to the Republic of Mexico.) Consequently, unlike other States, New Mexico waited sixty-four years for statehood, until after about fifty petitions to Congress (Kloss 1977: 128). At first, New Mexico was ruled by a series of military governors, but the legislature and the courts were made up largely of *mexicanas*. Their great preponderance in the population made Spanish the *de facto* language of government, though translation to English was required for communications with Washington.

In the petitions for statehood, the fact that Spanish was the normal language in all facets of New Mexican society loomed always as the primary consideration. So, in 1861, the Territory of Colorado was formed, slicing in two the *mexicana* area of the New Mexico Territory (Kloss 1977: 125). It was not until 1912, when the Anglo population surpassed the number of *mexicanas* and many of the community lands had come into its hands, that statehood was finally granted.

Few laws pertaining to language were passed in New Mexico during this period, either by the Territory or by the federal government. Throughout the latter half of the 19th Century, administrative necessity required the continued use of Spanish, but within a few decades, Spanish inevitably gave way to English. Thus, in 1853, a petition to authorize translators was granted by Congress, and in 1884 funds were appropriated for translation and publication of proceedings (Marshall 1986: 41). Also in 1884, a school law permitted either Spanish or English as the language of instruction. But by 1891, another law required English to be taught and the teachers to know English. Spanish-speaking teachers were taught English in the normal school so that they could teach in that language in the schools. At the approach of statehood, Aurelio Espinosa reports that Spanish was completely neglected in the schools of the State (Espinosa 1911: 18).

The New Mexico Enabling Act of 1910 stipulated that schools were to be conducted in English; officials and legislators had to know English; the laws were to be published in both languages for twenty years and thereafter only in English; and teachers would be trained in English. In the courts, however, an accused had the right to an interpreter (Baron 1990: 100). The 1912 Constitution continued most of these provisions and in addition gave the right to vote in Spanish (Kloss 1977: 49). Several State statutes made explicit the constitutional provision of English as the school language with the result that by 1921, Spanish was no longer used in the classroom, and by 1935 it was no longer an official language in the legislature (Kloss 1977: 137). A little later than others, and with more prodding perhaps, but New Mexico has followed the pattern of other States with English as its official language. Only recently has this pattern changed somewhat, as it has in other parts of the country (see below).

Immigration and war fuel xenophobia

During the latter part of the nineteenth century and the early decades of the present century, the country underwent yet another extended period of nativism and xenophobia. The Civil War, the Indian Wars and the land struggles with *mexicanas* had engendered deepseated racist attitudes among many whites. Then in the 1880's, Southern and Eastern Europeans began to immigrate in large numbers, and Chinese workers were brought to work on the construction of the railroads. These immigrations exacerbated the nativist attitudes that already existed and resulted in many suggestions for requiring English as a condition for immigration (Baron 1990: 57). The racially motivated Chinese Exclusion Act was passed in 1882 (Piatt 1990: 15), and in Wisconsin and Illinois, laws were passed requiring English as a medium of instruction in both public and private schools. However, the latter laws were soon repealed under pressure from a German alliance of Catholics and Lutherans (Baron 1990: 96, 119). In the 1890's, courts in New Jersey ruled in favor of English-only notices and in Illinois on the exclusive publication of laws in English. Michigan also passed a statute to require publication of its laws only in English

(Baron 1990: 115). Pennsylvania eliminated its German schools and instituted an English examination for miners (Baron 1990: 83). By 1903, fourteen States required English as a medium of instruction (Baron 1990: 150), and in 1906 an English requirement was imposed for naturalization (Piatt 1990: 6).

Nativism turned into a virtual panic in the years surrounding World War I. Lynchings of Italians and Mexicans were reported (Kloss 1977: 45); National Councils of Defense were formed that lobbied against German; New York passed English literacy laws for voting. In Illinois, German was forbidden in the names of corporations (Baron 1990: 117) and in Ohio, fines were instituted for using German in public. Nebraska passed laws that banned German in open meetings, made English the official language, and forbade foreign language instruction. Fifteen other States quickly followed Nebraska's example (Kloss 1977: 52–). The Governor of Iowa even proscribed the use of a foreign language on the telephone and in religious services (Baron 1990: 110–11). The bans on foreign language instruction in private schools were later overturned by the Supreme Court in **Meyer vs. Nebraska** (262 US390, 1923) and **Farrington vs. Tokushige** (273 US 284,298, 1927). But by the time of these decisions, the deed had been done, and few private schools returned to teaching ethnic "foreign" languages.

The national Immigrant Act of 1917 imposed quotas to exclude immigrants who could not read English, and in the same year, the Trading with the Enemy Act controlled foreign language publications (Baron 1990: 108). In education, the teaching of German was banned in States across the country, and the US Senate introduced a bill, which did not pass, making English the language of instruction in all the country's schools (Marshall 1986: 15).

Anti-foreigner and patriotic sentiment continued after the war. There were requirements instituted to display the flag, especially in schools. "Americanization" programs were started, encouraging foreigners to learn English. By 1923, thirty-four States required English as the medium of instruction (Baron 1990: 150–). Tennessee required teachers to be citizens and, if they taught white students, to be white themselves (Baron 1990: 162). In 1924, Congress passed the National Origins Act, imposing quotas on immigration and prohibiting immigration from Japan (Piatt 1990: 8).

In the following four decades, there was little legislation regarding language, as though the country's energies in this area had been spent. The approach of World War II (1939–1945) led again to certain restrictive measures aimed at the Germans, but by this time the German language in the U. S. could hardly be considered much of a threat. After the war, anti-communist sentiment led to amendments to the Naturalization Act requiring reading and writing in English, and the McCarran-Walter Act of 1950 instituted quotas on immigration (Marshall 1986: 18). By 1959 in California, English became the required language of instruction and of public laws and court proceedings.

Language rights as civil rights

Though it was based on race and ethnicity rather than language, the Civil Rights movement of the 1950's and 1960's was to initiate a number of changes in language policies. The Black Civil Rights movement in the South was paralleled by increased Native American militancy and by the United Farmworker (UFW) struggles of Chicanos/Chicanas and Filipinos/Filipinas in the West. The latter, begun as efforts to organize the union and to improve working conditions in the fields, inspired Chicanas both inside and outside the farmworker movement to seek an end to discrimination and to work toward a renewal of their language and culture. Students joined the movement in great numbers, not only supporting the struggle of farmworkers but also making strong demands on governmental and educational institutions. (For contemporary accounts of the Chicano movement, see for example Galarza – Gallegos – Samora 1969; Valdez – Steiner 1972; and Rosaldo – Seligmann – Calvert 1974.)

One constellation of demands was bilingualism. The leading States in reacting to these demands were California and New Mexico. In 1965, a California law provided for the printing of informational pamphlets in Spanish (Kloss 1977: 182) quickly followed by the Bilingual Education Acts of 1967 and 1972. Between 1971 and 1974, approximately ninety bills were introduced in the California legislature on topics ranging from bilingual informational tracts and commercial contracts to official government services (Blaine 1974: 659).

Although these bills had a poor record of passage, those that did pass had an important impact on language-minority rights. For example, the Bilingual Services Act of 1973 required State and local agencies that render significant public services to linguistic minorities to hire bilingual employees or interpreters (Blaine 1974: 662; Marshall 1986: 53). Other legislation required the publication of bilingual handbooks on police and small-claims-court procedures; home solicitation contracts in the same language as the oral sales presentation; recruitment of bilingual deputy registrars to assist voters; and the provision of information on the Unemployment Insurance Code (Blaine 1974: 657–; Marshall 1986: 53; Kloss 1977: 182). It is noteworthy that most of these laws are designed to protect ordinary persons who would otherwise be at serious disadvantages in society mainly by reason of language.

Other States around the country quickly followed suit, especially with transitional bilingual education programs and protections for voters. In New Mexico, for example, a number of language rights laws were passed including the provision of Spanish voting instructions and assistance to voters; proclamation of elections; bilingual signs in mines; the labeling of pesticides; and, very importantly, the Bilingual Multicultural Act (Marshall 1986: 42–).

At the federal level, three pieces of legislation stand out as being the most important: the Voting Rights Act of 1965, Title VII of the Elementary and Secondary Education Act of 1968, and the Court Interpreters Act of 1978. The Voting Rights Act was intended to eliminate the plethora of discriminatory laws at the State level. One provision outlaws State English-only voting statutes, and in doing so has potentially important societal ramifications. Title VII, known as the Bilingual Education Act, has been renewed and amended on a number of occasions. It basically provides federal funds to local school districts that wish to institute a bilingual education program. The Court Interpreters Act requires judges to employ qualified interpreters in any federal case initiated by the government.

In addition, a number of crucial court decisions were handed down during this period that have had important effects on the direction of language rights. Two key rulings were **Serna vs. Portales Municipal Schools** (351 F. Supp. 1279, D. N. M. 1972) and **Lau vs. Nichols** (414 US 563, 1974). Both of these decisions were similar and had their basis in the Civil Rights Act of 1965. They found that education of non-English speaking children in all-English classrooms violated equal opportunity provisions of the Act. The remedy reached by the court was that some special program of instruction needed to be instituted for these children such as English as a second language or bilingual education. In a different type of case, the Ninth Circuit court ruled that an English-only rule by a union violated the equal participation provisions of the Landman Griffith Act of 1959. The union was ordered to provide interpreter services (Piatt 1990: 75).

This is but a sampling of some of the most important court rulings and legislation involving language rights that came out of the Civil Rights period of U. S. history. A common feature of these various laws is that their fundamental purpose is to provide language-minority persons access to legal rights already accorded English speakers. In this way, bilingual education (or ESL) programs are intended to insure equal educational opportunity, albeit through English; courtroom interpretation provides defendants a measure of due process that is otherwise denied; and voting becomes much easier for speakers of minority languages as does contact with a number of essential governmental and private services. These are generally positive results insofar as they serve to ameliorate discrimination. It is clear that, on balance, they have permitted a much broader and qualitatively more integrative participation in U. S. society by members of linguistic minority groups.

Limitations of linguistic civil rights

Even so, several judicial rulings of the period revealed a countervailing trend to the expansion of language rights. For example, **San Antonio Independent School District vs. Rodriguez** (411 US 1, 1973) held that since education is itself not a fundamental right under the constitution, neither is bilingual education. In **Guerrero vs. Carlton** (9 Cal.3d 808, 512 P.2d 833, 109 Cal Rptr.201, 1973) the California Supreme Court found that adequate and timely notice in an Aid for Dependent Children case did not have to be given in a non-English language. And in **Carmona vs. Sheffield** (475 F.2d 738, 9th Cir., 1973) an appeals court found that Spanish speakers had no right to an interpreter in unemployment hearings.

It is also clear that many of the liberal civil rights laws described above, fail to address other critical issues of linguistic human rights: the right to learn, to use, and to transmit one's native language and to be protected in those rights by the state. For example, Title VII, the State laws, and the judicial decisions regarding bilingual education focus almost exclusively on programs that are transitional in nature. Their original purpose was and continues to be the rapid anglicization of language minority children; the right to an education in one's native language simply does not exist. Without such a right, minority languages will continue to be lost, and so-called "developmental" programs will only hold out the illusion of language maintenance. (See Hernández-Chávez

1978, 1979, and 1988 for discussion and critiques of issues in bilingual education rights.)

The Court Interpreters Act does not cover State cases, does not apply unless the case is initiated by the government, and it suffers from the problems inherent in any provision for interpretation; criminal trials in one's own language are not even considered. Similarly, bilingual voting rights have little practical effect for many Spanish-speaking voters, Chicanas in particular, since the vast majority of them also know English. Such laws are thus principally symbolic. Laws providing for bilingual services are severely limited by population tests, typically requiring a "substantial number" of persons being served, which number is to be determined by the agency in question (Blaine 1974: 662); there exists no basic right to use the native language for official government business since this must generally be exercised through interpreters and is often at the discretion of the agency.

From these perspectives, the laws in question can be seen to have negative rather than positive effects. By providing partial access to the government and using the powerful symbolism of bilingualism, they give the appearance not only of substantial gains in civil rights but also of governmental support of indigenous languages and cultures. However, non-English languages are used officially only with monolinguals (or near monolinguals) and only as a compensatory mechanism, not as a language right. They function both to ease administrative burdens and, ironically, to acculturate members of ethnic minority groups into the bureaucratic system. In this way, minority languages and cultures are undermined at the same time that they are used to gain support among minorities for the programs and to mute their opposition to governmental language policies.

The Official-English movement

In retrospect, a predictable consequence of linguistic civil rights laws, limited as they are, has been the strong negative reaction among those segments of society that feel threatened by gains made by minority groups. Since the early 1980's, one realization of this reaction has been the advocacy of laws explicitly making English the official language of a State or of the country. We have seen above that, in fact, English already functions in many ways as the official language of the U. S. and of the

States, sanctioned by law and by practice. Thus, such official-English statutes might remain principally symbolic, a not unimportant result.

However, State official-English laws typically include clauses that explicitly prohibit any governmental agency from requiring a language other than English and establish mandates to "preserve, protect, and strengthen the English language" (e.g., the English Language Amendent to the Constitution of the State of California, enacted 1986). These types of clauses threaten to invalidate many of the State language rights laws discussed above which require, for example, information, assistance, or interpreting to be given in a non-English language.

No official-English law is now in effect at the federal level, though several such attempts have been made in 1982, 1983, 1985, 1988 and again in 1992 (Marshall 1986: 22–43; Piatt 1990: 20). These attempts are certain to continue. At the State level, Illinois, Nebraska, and Hawaii already had official-English laws prior to 1980. Since then, California has taken the lead by passing an official-English constitutional amendment in 1986. A substantial number of other States have followed California's example, so that by 1992, a total of twenty States have such laws: seventeen with overtly English-only statutes, three with so-called English-plus laws that essentially reaffirm the status quo (English Plus Information Clearinghouse 1990, personal communication). Were an official-English provision to become part of the U. S. Constitution, as advocates propose, it would clearly interfere with the dissemination of laws and proceedings in other languages, the provision of bilingual services, and bilingual voting rights. Indeed, one of the targets of the proposed amendment is the bilingual provision of the Voting Rights Act.

Bilingual education is also explicitly targeted, in particular maintenance-oriented programs. Although advocates of official-English laws generally oppose all forms of bilingual education, they seem willing to allow the continuation of some form of transitional bilingual education so long as the native language is permitted only until students are deemed ready to be "mainstreamed", a euphemism for being placed in English-only classes. However, under a constitutional amendment, programs that have language maintenance as a primary goal would most certainly be seen by the courts as violating prohibitions against native-language requirements as well as detracting from the mandate to strengthen English.

The English-only movement has already affected certain areas of private as well as public life. A common practice, not only in States with an official-English law but also in other States, is the prohibition on the use of minority languages in the workplace. Similarly, government bureaucrats unilaterally reduce or deny essential information or services on the basis of language, using official-English statutes as a justification. The language of business and street signs is controlled by a number of local ordinances. Job applications are denied because the applicant does not speak English or speaks it with an accent, even if the particular job requires little or no communication in English. Border Patrol officers arrest and deport Mexicans solely on the basis of appearance and the fact that they do not speak English. And in public places, strangers accost speakers of minority languages with such reprimands as "This is America. Speak English."

Action and reaction — the new nativism

This linguistic backlash is not tied exclusively, nor even mainly, to language rights themselves. Rather, it is linked to a much wider and more varied set of domestic and international conditions that have created resentment and fear, especially of minorities. Domestically, these conditions include the very gains that minority people have made in education and employment as a direct result of civil rights laws. Demands for equal treatment in employment and education have required meticulous affirmative action guidelines that are seen by the majority as granting undeserved preferential treatment to minorities. Moreover, the recruitment and hiring of minorities, their increased admission to colleges, and their advancement to positions of responsibility and authority create more competition and the perception of fewer positions for the majority. This is especially true in the early years of the present decade as the U. S. economy falls deeper into a recession resulting from the military and market excesses of the 1980's.

On the other end of the scale, the social and monetary costs of under-education, under-employment, and the over-representation of minorities within the criminal justice system are borne by all, including the majority who do not feel they should bear those costs. These minorities are perceived as lazy, lacking in intelligence, immoral, and most importantly, insolently living off the public dole that must be paid for by the white majority.

At an international level, a situation that is at the very core of the backlash and has strong and direct domestic overtones is immigration, especially from Latin America. The greatest perceived threat is migration from Mexico because it represents such large numbers of people. (Many

Chicanas do not consider this migration to involve a legitimate international border since *mexicanas* moving to the U. S. Southwest are entering a historical homeland, occupied by the U. S. since the war with Mexico, 1846–1848.) Most of these people take jobs that are generally not wanted by non-migrants. However, some of them do not, and many of their offspring already compete with U. S. born persons for jobs and resources. Politicians and the major media accuse these new arrivals of taking away jobs and of placing additional heavy burdens on social welfare programs and on taxes. This ignores the fact that these migrants not only accept the most back-breaking and menial labor, but because of their "illegal" status, they are very reluctant to seek any kind of public assistance and tend to pay a disproportionate amount of their own earnings in taxes.

Further resentment of foreigners is generated from a number of international relationships beginning with the still vivid American defeat in Vietnam; the Arab oil embargo of the 1970's; the Iranian hostage crisis; Cuban Marielito, Haitian, and Central American refugees; the technological and economic successes of the Japanese vis-a-vis American companies; the drug "war" in Latin America; and, most recently, the Persian Gulf War. These seemingly unrelated events have in common with the Mexican in-migration that they involve peoples of color and that the Americans are unable to control them.

As in the reactionary periods of the 18th and 19th centuries, these kinds of external events give rise to a new nativism, to an aggressively defensive posture that is identified with the English language and Anglo values. Ruling elites, both inside and outside the government, play upon this underlying xenophobia, molding a fear and resentment of foreigners that is easily transferred to minorities in the US — "foreigners" in the eyes of many. This, it seems, is at the root of the move to institute English-only laws, thinly veiled as calls for national unity or economic benefit.

Summary and conclusion

Throughout U. S. history, the drive for Anglo-American hegemony has demanded the suppression and elimination of non-English cultures. These are acts that today are recognized by the international community as violating human rights (e.g., United Nations General Assembly 1948b, 1966) and even as constituting genocide (United Nations General Assembly 1948a). As early as the colonial period, English slaveholders deliberately and actively separated Africans from their tribes and children from their parents in order to destroy their languages and thus reduce the potential for insurrection (Thompson 1982: 162). Later, English-American settlers continued a similar practice with Native American schoolchildren.

European ethnic groups that retained their languages and cultures were also seen as possible threats to Anglo dominance. As whites and as free people, Europeans could not easily be dealt with in the same manner as Africans or Native Americans. Yet, wherever it was politically possible, laws were passed requiring the use of English or restricting the use of other languages. Toward these ends, the notion of the melting pot was promulgated whose task it was to "... assimilate and amalgamate these people as a part of our American race, and to implant in their children, so far as can be done, the Anglo-Saxon conception of righteousness, law and order, and our popular government ..." (Cubberly 1909: 15–16).

Often with the enthusiastic concurrence of the groups themselves, the result has been the virtually complete cultural and socio-political assimilation of white non-English settlers and immigrants.

With the conquest and annexation of large parts of northern Mexico into the U. S. Southwest the problem became one of anglicizing large numbers of Mexicans. As with the Native and African Americans, the problem was exacerbated by racial differences which worked against full assimilation. Linguistic acculturation is still seen as the *sine qua non* of efforts to forestall the "quebeckization" of *Aztlán*, or U. S. Southwest, by irredentist Mexicans. (See Butler 1985 for "national security" arguments in this vein favoring the elimination of Spanish-English bilingualism among U. S. Mexicans.) The strategies used to accomplish this have included political pressure, gerrymandering, submersion educational programs, and physical and psychological violence. (See Skutnabb-Kangas 1984: 305–327 for a discussion of the role of violence in language education).

Now, the massive and continuous influx of Mexicans into the Southwest has produced additional reactions. Groups such as the Federation of Americans for Immigration Reform (F. A. I. R.) were successful in obtaining passage of the Immigration Reform and Control Act of 1986. Americans for Border Control (A. B. C.) together with members of the Ku Klux Klan and other white supremacist groups intimidate, beat, and kill Mexicans caught crossing the border. Both F. A. I. R. and A. B. C., along with the Council for Inter-American Security, a private group with close links to the intelligence community, have been active in promoting organizations such as U. S. English and English First, whose primary agenda is the passage of official-English laws. In this way, private activity joins with official government action to repress both the civil and the human linguistic rights of language minority groups. (See Jaimes and Churchill 1988 for an analysis of the intricate inter-relationships among all these various groups).

The purpose of these activities is, without a doubt, the disintegration of language minority cultures in the US society in order to eliminate even the possibility of separatist tendencies. Full assimilation into Anglo-American society, however, does not appear to be a real goal as evidenced by the strong reaction to programs that adhere to the doctrine of equal protection of the laws. "Integration" into the dominant society is seen as a proper objective only insofar as this means the cultural adaptation of the minority to the norms of the majority rather than the full and equal participation by all groups (see Skutnabb-Kangas 1991d for discussion). A more cynical analysis might conclude that the true goal is to maintain a racially based system of power and control and of unequal access to resources.

Where strong political pressure has been applied by language minority groups themselves, State and federal language policies in the United States have been at least permissive of the official use of minority languages. This is evident historically from official reactions to political activity of the Germans in the Midwest and the French in Louisiana during the early 1800's and of the *mexicanas* of New Mexico and Texas in the latter half of the century. Similarly, modern language rights legislation and judicial pronouncements are a direct response to demands made during the Civil Rights Movement. Except for such brief periods of forced liberalization, the Anglo-American majority in the United States has followed a determined course of linguistic and cultural genocide whose fundamental purpose is the repression and anglicization of ethnic minority groups.

The discourse of disinformation: the debate on bilingual education and language rights in the United States[1]

Jim Cummins

The term "disinformation" refers to the systematic spreading of false information in order to confuse and disorient the opposition. Although the term is usually associated with media manipulation in the international political arena, the phenomenon of disinformation is no less evident in debates on domestic political issues, such as the merits or otherwise of bilingual education for language minority students.

As cultural and linguistic diversity increases across the globe, an increasing number of countries are engaging in policy debates about the appropriate language(s) of instruction for both language minority *and* majority students. For example, in Canada, many English speaking (majority group) parents have demanded *the right* to have their children educated partially through French in French immersion programs (see Genesee, 1987). However, when minorities demand the right to an education through their own language, the policy debate frequently becomes extremely volatile. Debates about minority language instruction encompass issues of legal and moral rights, issues of cognitive and academic outcomes from different types of programs, and ultimately, issues of the envisaged relations of culture and power in the society as a whole.

As examples of these issues, in Canada, minority francophones outside of Quebec have the legal right to an education through French *where numbers warrant*, and not surprisingly, legal interpretations of what constitutes "sufficient numbers" vary. Several investigators have argued from a moral perspective that the rapid loss of the home language in quick-exit transitional or majority language submersion programs has a devastating impact on family communication and cohesion, and thus, strong promotion of the home language in school should be a linguistic human right (e.g. Skutnabb-Kangas 1984). With respect to the outcomes of bilingual versus majority language immersion or submersion programs, this debate continues in the United States, as I outline below. Under the

U. S. constitution, all students have the right to equality of educational opportunity, and thus, the debate aboüt outcomes focuses on whether bilingual or English-only programs satisfy the equity provision of federal law. Finally, it is clear that any discussion of minority group *rights*, whether linguistic or educational, necessarily involves issues relating to the division of status and resources in the society; in other words, it constitutes a debate about the nature of the power structure in the society.

The present paper analyzes the discourse on bilingual education in the United States context from this perspective. Specifically, I attempt to place the debate about outcomes of different types of programs in the context of the power relations between dominant and subordinated groups.

The bilingual education debate has preoccupied educators, politicians, the media and occasionally the general public in the United States for more than twenty years. Many commentators have warned that bilingual education is not only educationally ill-advised, it also threatens the social and political stability of what (in the United States) is often referred to as "the most powerful nation on earth." Newspaper editorials across the country have detailed a catastrophic scenario of Latina "activists" demanding ever more intensive bilingual education as a ploy both to prevent minority children from learning English and to fuel Latina separatism, resulting ultimately in the disintegration of the United States.

In analyzing the tactics used by opponents of bilingual education to discredit its educational and social rationale, I argue that similar processes are in operation in the attempt to suppress the linguistic and educational rights of minority students as are evident in global relations between rich and poor nations. In both cases, potential social changes that are perceived as a threat to the power of the dominant group (or country) are suppressed and the suppression is rationalized as being in the best interests of the subordinated group. In other words, the fear that has engendered such a negative reaction to bilingual education is the fear of minority group empowerment; if minority groups develop the confidence in their own identity and the knowledge and critical awareness to articulate their rights, then they become more resistant to exploitation at the hands of the dominant group.

The fear and insecurity evident in the rhetoric directed at the "internal threat" of bilingual education (i. e. minority empowerment) is strikingly similar to the paranoia engendered in powerful nations by liberation movements that, if successful, might challenge their hegemony in particular regions. Among the more obvious examples is the support by successive U. S. administrations for brutally fascist regimes in central America (e.g. Nicaragua, El Salvador, Guatemala). The similarities between the suppression of empowerment among domestic minorities and the suppression of liberation movements in the international arena are more than superficial; in fact, the overriding goals of the dominant group are virtually identical in both situations, namely, to reverse a sociopolitical change that they perceive as threatening their ability to control and exploit a traditionally dominated group. The processes through which information is manipulated to promote domestic acceptance of this goal are also very similar. In both cases, empirical realities that contradict the rhetoric are denied or dismissed. This process is supported by the media, and blatant logical inconsistencies in the policies are ignored.[2]

The purpose of pursuing this analysis is to place the bilingual education debate into a broader context of power relations between rich and poor groups (or nations) so that the nature of the debate can be better understood by proponents of empowerment pedagogy for minority students. Many advocates for minority students still view the opposition as essentially well-intentioned but misinformed. They view their major task as informing the opponents about the empirical evidence for bilingual education so that rational decisions can then be made on the basis of this research evidence. While some of those opposed to bilingual education are genuinely well-intentioned and will be swayed by empirical evidence supporting bilingual programs, a considerably larger proportion (as evidenced by media comment) are more concerned with the threat that bilingual education represents to the societal power structure which they would express in terms of the "American way of life". The evidence to date suggests that this component of the dominant group will continue to vehemently reject educational empowerment of minority students. In fact, the more empirical evidence is produced that certain types of programs result in personal and academic growth among minority students, the more vehement will be the denial of this evidence and the rejection of these programs by the dominant group. Thus, the reality is the opposite to that assumed by many proponents of bilingual education who believe that positive results of bilingual programs will increase the likelihood of these programs being accepted and implemented more extensively.

It is important to state here that, *at one level*, the United States has committed itself since the mid-sixties to educational equity more vigorously than many nations. Considerable funds have been expended on research to elucidate the nature of minority underachievement and on intervention aimed at reversing underachievement. This major public commitment has been matched by the dedication of many educators who are genuinely committed to promoting academic and personal empowerment among minority students and their parents.

However, at another level, a very different process is operating. This opposing process is dedicated to maintaining the power structure within the society; in other words, preserving the current ways in which power is divided according to class, ethnicity, "race" and gender (as illustrated, for example, in job status). Maintenance of the societal power structure requires that the impact of attempts to empower minority students and communities be neutralized. As outlined below, this process must be inferred to explain why there is minimal public funding for those programs that have demonstrated their effectiveness in educating minority students, namely, programs that promote additive bilingualism through empowerment pedagogy.

The anti-bilingual rhetoric

Three quotations will convey the concerns of many Americans about the increasing penetration of Spanish into mainstream institutions such as the educational system; the first two come from journalistic attacks on bilingual education while the third is from a monograph by Lloyd Dunn (1987), the author of the widely used *Peabody Picture Vocabulary Test*:

> Bilingual education is an idea that appeals to teachers of Spanish and other tongues, but also to those who never did think that another idea, the United States of America, was a particularly good one to begin with, and that the sooner it is restored to its component "ethnic" parts the better off we shall all be. Such people have been welcomed with open arms into the upper reaches of the federal government in recent years, giving rise to the suspicion of a death wish. (Bethell 1979: 30).

A recent very positive review of Rosalie Pedalino Porter's book *Forked Tongue*, which vehemently attacks bilingual education, communicates well the "fear and loathing" that bilingual education evokes in many Americans:

> What *can* be helped, as Porter demonstrates with case studies from some U. S. cities that have abondoned useless approaches and adopted immersion or semi-immersion, is the continued stubborness, deliberate obstructionism, even, of those who through their

"educational" practices would guarantee in essence that foreign-born kids spend their lives pushing brooms or slapping meat patties on a grill.

Whether or not the goals of "U. S. English" to mandate English as the "official" language of this nation come to fruition ... the gradual dissolution of the United States is manifest, in culture, clothing, music, customs, marital rites, indices of criminality, inner city vs. suburban values, the cinema, television, special-interest politics, and not least in approaches to communicating with the spoken and written word. (Brudnoy 1990: 11).

The final example comes from Lloyd Dunn who in his monograph, attributes the educational failure of Latina students to a combination of genetic inferiority, parental apathy, and the damaging effects of bilingual education.

Under the "maintenance theory" (or excuse), in extreme cases, some Mexican-American pupils are taught almost exclusively in Spanish by Mexican-American activist teachers, who repeatedly point out to the pupils that they are an oppressed group, and therefore obligated to assist in social change. With this focus, it is not surprising that these childern are not prepared to switch over to English at the end of elementary school, and have not adequately mastered the regular elementary school subject matter (Dunn 1987: 67).

The general line of argument against bilingual education is clear: such programs are a threat to national unity and furthermore they are ineffective in teaching English to minority students since the primary language, rather than English, is used for a considerable amount of instruction in the early grades. To opponents, the bilingual approach implies a counter-intuitive "less equals more" rationale in which *less* English instruction is assumed to lead to *more* English achievement. Opponents argue that unless language minority students are immersed in English at school, they will not learn English and consequently will be prevented from participating in the mainstream of American society.

This line of reasoning has been effective in undermining bilingual education throughout the seventies and eighties such that only "quick-exit" transitional bilingual programs have been tolerated in most jurisdictions. Only a small proportion of eligible students are in any form of bilingual education in the United States and most of these programs employ first language (L1) instruction for a minimal amount of time during the school day (often less than ten per cent) (Crawford 1989; Wong Fillmore – Valdez 1986).

By contrast, advocates of bilingual education have argued that quick-exit programs are considerably less effective than programs that strongly reinforce children's L1 conceptual development in the early grades and continue L1 instruction for at least part of the school day throughout elementary schooling and, if possible, beyond.[3] As outlined later in this paper, there is considerable evidence for this position.

The failure in the late 1980's to fund "developmental" and "two-way bilingual" programs, almost universally advocated by researchers as the most promising bilingual program options, suggests that any program that would simultaneously promote academic achievement and students' abilities in their primary language would be regarded as a threat to the societal power structure. Crawford (1989) documents one instance of this process in California in the mid-eighties. Subsequent to articulating a theoretical framework for educating language minority students that places strong emphasis on L1 literacy development (California State Department of Education 1981, 1983), the State Department's Office of Bilingual Education implemented a Case Studies project in five schools throughout the state. Although the schools were both geographically and demographically diverse, all the students had in common poverty, limited English skills and chronic underachievement. Crawford points out that

> By 1986–1987, after five years of the Case Studies treatment, median scores for the 3,500 children in these schools were well above district norms in English reading, writing, and mathematics. News of this dramatic progress ... has prompted a number of other districts to adopt the Case Studies model. ... Therefore, it came as a surprise to many admirers of the Case Studies approach when the U. S. Department of Education decided in 1986 to terminate the project's Title VII grant two years ahead of schedule. (1989: 128)

In the next section, the purpose of limiting language minority students' access to programs that are potentially empowering is considered.

Empowerment as a goal of education

I use the term "empowerment" to refer to the interactional process whereby students develop the critical abilities and the personal confidence in their own identities to acquire the knowledge and skills they need to take control of their own lives and to envisage and plan their futures. The term "empowerment" clearly conveys the fact that "power" is negotiated in schools: between educators and students, and ultimately between dominant and subordinated groups. Thus, the interactions between teachers and students can be analyzed according to the degree to which these interactions reflect or challenge historical and current patterns of dominant-subordinated group relations. This analysis implies that minority students' school failure is rooted in the ways that schools have reinforced patterns of dominant-subordinated group relations in the wider society by eradicating students' language and culture, suppressing their experience and excluding minority communities from any form of meaningful participation in the life of the school. It follows that if notions like *equality of educational opportunity* are to be anything more than a rhetorical facade, they must entail a direct challenge to the societal power structure.

In this sense, the concerns of opponents of bilingual education are justified since the existing societal power structure *is* threatened by programs that provide an interactional context within which empowerment of minority students can occur. Despite the veneer of liberal reforms within the education system, empowerment pedagogy will continue to be resisted because empowered peoples are more difficult to exploit. They are more likely to strike for better wages and working conditions, more likely to resist being sprayed with pesticides and fertilizers while picking fruit or vegetables and more likely to demand a decent schooling for their children. Consider, for example, this account of the Pajaro Valley family literacy project, described by Alma Flor Ada:

> Another parent said she noticed her children are now starting to request that she bring more books home to read, and they are now requesting them in Spanish instead of English. The result, she said, is they are learning about their culture and language, and also realizing that there are as many good ideas in Spanish as there are in English.
> Another parent said the reading and writing program has helped her to be more resolute in dealing with teachers and demanding that they teach her child Spanish, her native language.
> The biggest benefit, however, may be that the children and their parents are being drawn closer by the constant expression and discussion of ideas and books they are working on together.

'Tell your children every day how much you love them, how much you value them and how much you appreciate them,' Ada said in closing. (Estrada, Santa Cruz Sentinel, Friday Oct. 31, 1986)

It is clear that these parents are becoming empowered in the sense of gaining the internal resources, confidence and motivation to begin to exert some control over the forces that affect their lives. The notion of empowerment is similar to what Johan Galtung (1980) has called *autonomy*, which is defined as follows:

> Autonomy is here seen as power-over-oneself so as to be able to withstand what others might have of power-over-others. I use the distinction between ideological, remunerative and punitive power, depending on whether the influence is based on internal, positive external, or negative external sanctions. Autonomy then is the degree of 'inoculation' against these forms of power. These forms of power, exerted by means of ideas, carrots and sticks, can work only if the power receiver really receives the pressure, which pre-supposes a certain degree of submissiveness, dependency and fear, respectively. Their antidotes are self-respect, self-sufficiency, and fearlessness. ... 'self-respect' can be defined as 'confidence in one's own ideas and ability to set one's own goals,' 'self-sufficiency' as the 'possibility of pursuing them with one's own means,' and 'fear-lessness,' as 'the possibility of persisting despite threats of destruc-tion'. ...

> The opposite [of autonomy] is penetration, meaning that the outside has penetrated into one's self to the extent of creating submissiveness to ideas, dependency on 'goods' from the outside, and fear of the outside in terms of 'bads.'" (1980: 58–59).

The resistance of many American women to the Equal Rights Amend-ment during the 1980's is a good example of how the process of inter-nalizing submissiveness and dependency works. Why else would so many women collaborate in maintaining a power structure that denies them equal rights? Similarly, societal institutions such as schools have rein-forced the unequal division of power and resources by convincing mi-nority students of their own inferiority, a process that results in submis-siveness, dependency and fear, i. e. a lack of power-over-oneself or what Galtung describes as "autonomy."

In Galtung's terms, empowerment pedagogy will be resisted by the dominant group because it results in self-respect, self-sufficiency and fearlessness; expressed in more conventional terms, it promotes minority students' self-esteem, ability for independent learning rather than learned helplessness, and confidence in their own academic and personal talents. By doing this, it reduces or eliminates the power of the dominant group to penetrate or control the formerly dominated minority group.

The process of disempowerment

The focus of the analysis in this section is on the rhetoric used to justify continued control and exploitation as being in the best interests of those groups against whom this control and exploitation is directed. In the case of the bilingual education debate, the covert goal of the dominant group is to effect a return to all-English submersion programs (see Skutnabb-Kangas, 1988a, note 5) to lessen the possibility that an even larger number of Latinas will achieve an education that might result in upward mobility; in other words, the goal is to continue the historical pattern of economic exploitation or in Ogbu's (1978) terms, to maintain the "job ceiling" for dominated minorities.

Naturally, the operation of this disempowerment process must be denied if it is to achieve its goals. Much of the debate about the education of minority children in the United States (and in other western countries (see Skutnabb-Kangas 1984) is directed to obscuring contradictions between the rhetoric of equality and the reality of domination. Thus, programs aimed at preserving the learned helplessness of minority children (e.g. all-English submersion programs) must be rationalized as being in the best interests of minority children; in addition, programs that provide an interactional context for minority student empowerment must either be eliminated through denial of funding or their impact controlled through media manipulation. In other words, the "threat of a good example" (Chomsky 1987) must be neutralized (see Table 1). The means through which this control is exercised are almost identical to the disinformation and mystification techniques used by powerful nations to justify their overthrow of legitimate democratic regimes in less powerful nations.

This process involves at least three components:

— limiting the framework of discourse;
— denying/distorting empirically documented counter-examples;
— ignoring logical inconsistencies in the positions being advocated.

Table 1. Neutralizing the threat of a good example in preserving global and domestic power
        structures

A. GOAL

Ensure that the economic and political interests of the dominant group are not
threatened by deviant initiatives that might empower emergent nations or minority
groups.

↓

B. METHOD

Exert economic and political pressure to ensure that implementation of the deviant
initiative is destabilized and outcomes are negative. If positive outcomes emerge
despite this pressure, then either ignore, deny or distort them.

↓

C. OUTCOMES

The failure of the deviant initiative under these conditions will demonstrate that
attempts at dominated group empowerment are ill-conceived and ill-advised. Dominant group control can be re-established under the guise of equality and justice.

The operation of these processes in the international arena will be
considered briefly and then the parallels with the discourse on bilingual
education will be examined.

The process of preserving power structures in the international arena

American foreign policy (and that of many other nations) has consistently
legitimated its intervention in the affairs of other countries in terms of a
choice between "good" and "evil" polar opposites: the options being
"freedom and democracy" ("our way of life") versus "terrorism and
Communist agression" (the threat to "our way of life"). As pointed out
by Chomsky (1987), as a result of the manipulation of discourse by
government and business interests, and the collusion of the American
media, there is virtually no consciousness among the American public
that their government, through the CIA, has systematically inspired
military coups against democratically elected governments in Latin Amer-

ica and elsewhere that have attempted to initiate even mild social changes (e.g. land reform) or were not felt to be sympathetic to the profit needs of multinational companies. Some examples of discourse and action from the international arena will help to document the parallels with the domestic debate on bilingual education.

The democratically elected government of Jacobo Arbenz in Guatemala was ousted by a CIA inspired coup in 1954. Since that time the military dictatorship has been responsible for at least 100,000 people murdered, 38,000 disappearances and 200,000 refugees (Wright 1987). Despite the current veneer of democracy in Guatemala, mass murder of the indigenous population and the disappearance of anyone who speaks for civil rights continues unabated. Smith (1991, A21), for example, points out that 1990 "was the worst for human rights violations in recent memory. In June, the national police reported one killing per hour".

The CIA similarly inspired a coup in Iran in 1953 to impose a regime that according to Amnesty International in 1976 had the "highest rate of death penalties in the world, no valid system of civilian courts and a history of torture which is beyond belief" (cited in Chomsky and Herman, 1979: 13). The Shah's notorious secret police (SAVAK) was trained and equipped by the CIA.

Democratically elected governments in Brazil (1964) and Chile (1973) were also overthrown as a result of CIA supported coups and thousands of men, women and children were tortured and/or disappeared as a result of this "democratization" process. The destabilization of the Sandinista government in Nicaragua by the Reagan Administration in the 1980s was, according to Chomsky (citing Oxfam reports), largely a response to the "threat of a good example" posed by the constructive social programs and absence of widespead torture in Nicaragua; this example contrasted dramatically with many of the military regimes supported by the United States in the region (e.g. Chile, El Salvador, Guatemala).

The unwillingness or inability of mainstream media to acknowledge the "unthinkable", namely that the forces of freedom and democracy could be engaged in overthrowing freely elected democratic governments around the globe, is clearly expressed in a letter to the *New York Times* by Samuel Chavkin (March 12, 1991) and I quote at some length from his letter:

> Some of your comments in "Atrocities and Repentance in Chile" (editorial, Feb. 23) on the Chilean Government report about human rights violations during the Pinochet dictatorship, are commenda-

ble. But your statement that some Chileans, President Patricio Aylwin among them, felt that the chaos prevailing during the elected Socialist presidency of Salvador Allende justified the September 1973 coup, is dismaying. ... what of the majority of Chileans who opposed the coup, the thousands who perished at the hands of Gen. Augusto Pinochet's henchmen and the hundreds of thousands who were tortured in prisons? And you fail to mention that the chaos during the Allende regime had much to do with the conspiracy between the Nixon Administration and powerful Chilean and foreign economic interests to strangle the Allende economy by embargoes and cutting off credits and deliveries of spare parts for Chile's vast motor transport system. In 1975, the Senate Select Committee on Intelligence under Senator Frank Church, reported that before Mr. Allende took office, 'The Central Intelligence Agency was instructed by President Nixon to play a direct role in organizing a military coup d'etat in Chile to prevent Mr. Allende's accession to the presidency.' Also, you say that 'most Chileans agree the Pinochet regime brought useful economic reforms, "but nearly half the population is struggling to survive at a poverty level. ... for those fortunate enough to find jobs, the minimum wage is "31.8 percent lower than it was in 1974.' (Chavkin, *New York Times*, March 12, 1991, p. A22).

In short, when the framework of discourse is restricted to "good vs. evil", "us vs. them", "the American way of life" vs. "threats to the American way of life" it becomes necessary (and easy) to overlook or ignore awkward truths, whether the issue is the threat posed by deviant leftist democratic regimes in Latin America or elsewhere or the threat posed by bilingual education (see Brudnoy quote above). Similarly, logical inconsistencies are blithely ignored in foreign policy; one example among many is the fact that most western governments, including Canada and the leftist government of Gough Whitlam in Australia, looked the other way when the "friendly" government of Indonesia invaded East Timor in December 1975 and proceeded to perpertrate atrocities to the point of genocide on the East Timorese. Yet all expressed outrage when Iraq invaded the non-democratic but "friendly" Kuwait despite the fact that the military build-up in Iraq had been supported by western and Soviet governments who viewed Iraq as a lesser evil than Iran.

The same discoursal processes are very evident in the bilingual education debate in the United States.

Limiting the framework of discourse

Opponents of bilingual education consistently refuse to acknowledge the major variations that exist within bilingual education programs, labelling all forms of bilingual education as "transitional bilingual education" (TBE) and contrasting them with "structured immersion" by which they mean all-English programs that include some programmatic acknowledgement of the fact that children come from non-English backgrounds (e.g. a formal English-as-a-second-language component). They ignore the fact that many North American researchers of bilingual programs (including French immersion programs in Canada that provide French-English bilingual instruction for English-background students) have been extremely critical of "quick-exit" transitional bilingual programs, regarding them as very much inferior to "late-exit developmental" or "two-way" bilingual programs in which schools either attempt to maintain students' L1 abilities or promote an additive bilingualism among both majority and minority students (see, for example, Genesee 1987; Swain 1979).[4] This limitation of the framework of discourse to TBE vs. immersion has had the effect of virtually excluding enrichment programs such as "maintenance" or "developmental" programs (in Europe termed "language shelter programs" (see Skutnabb-Kangas — Bucak, this volume) and two-way bilingual programs from the policy debate. Thus the "threat of a good example," i. e. of enrichment bilingual programs empowering minority students, is contained, partly as a result of such programs having little possibility of being funded and partly because any successful enrichment program will be classified as either transitional bilingual education or structured immersion. In some cases a program may be classified as both TBE and structured immersion; for example, Baker and de Kanter (1981) classify as "an alternate immersion program" the half day English, half day Spanish kindergarten program that Legaretta (1979) reported was significantly more effective in teaching English than programs that had considerably more English instruction. The net effect of these tactics is that the positive results of the few enrichment programs that are evaluated can be aggregated out of existence in the midst of mediocre results from quick-exit transitional programs.

Denying/distorting empirically documented counter-examples

There are several ways in which this has been done in the bilingual education debate. The Baker — de Kanter report set up highly questionable criteria of what they would accept with respect to methodological controls and managed to dismiss many apparently positive results from bilingual programs as a result. More significant, however, is the refusal to examine the research data with respect to their consistency with the theoretical assumptions underlying policy. This refusal permits opponents of bilingual education to ignore the fact that *virtually all* the data they analyze is inconsistent with the assumptions underlying structured immersion (i. e. a direct relation between amount of English instruction and achievement in English) but consistent with those underlying enrichment (empowerment) bilingual programs (see Cummins 1989; Skutnabb-Kangas 1984).

Opponents of bilingual education (e.g. Imhoff 1990; Porter 1990) consistently invoke the principle of "time-on-task" or "practice makes perfect" to argue for immersion in English as the most effective route to academic achievement. For example, one of the lessons Porter derives from the Canadian experience with early total French immersion programs is that early intensive exposure to the target language is essential:

> The evidence of direct correlation between early, intensive second-language learning and high level of competence in the second language is inescapable, as is the time-on-task principle — that is, the more time spent learning a language, the better you do in it, all other factors being equal. (p. 119).

The data just don't support this principle, either for majority or minority students in any type of bilingual or immersion program. For example, the French immersion data show that students who have far less exposure to English (the majority language and their L1) suffer no adverse consequences in English academic achievement (see, e.g. Genesee 1987).

Similarly, the data from late immersion programs (usually starting around grade 7) are inconsistent with the time-on-task principle. Porter devotes only one sentence (p. 113) to late immersion, possibly because the results of late immersion refute the time-on-task principle in that after several years of late immersion there are minimal differences between early and late immersion students in French proficiency despite the fact that the former have had far more exposure to French than the latter (see Harley et al. 1990). The late immersion data also refute Porter's unqualified claim that "starting second-language learning early, at age five or six, with a total classroom immersion in that language, promises the best results in learning that language" (p. 119).[5]

Exactly the same pattern is evident in programs for minority students. This is illustrated quite dramatically by the results of the the Ramirez report (Ramirez — Yuen — Ramey 1991) (so called after its principal investigator, J. David Ramirez of Aguirre International), a longitudinal evaluation of alternative programs for Latina students. The study compared the academic progress of Latina elementary school children in three program types: (a) English "immersion", involving almost exclusive use of English throughout elementary school, (b) early-exit bilingual in which Spanish was used for about one-third of the time in kindergarten and first grade with a rapid phase-out thereafter, and (c) late-exit bilingual that used primarily Spanish instruction in kindergarten, with English used for about one-third of the time in grades 1 and 2, half the time in grade 3, and about sixty per cent of the time thereafter.

One of the three late-exit programs in the study (site G) was an exception to this pattern, in that students were abruptly transitioned into primarily English instruction at the end of grade 2. In other words, this "late-exit" program was similar in its implementation to early-exit. Students in the "immersion" and early-exit programs were followed from kindergarten through grade 3 while those in the late-exit program were followed in two cohorts (K–3 and 3–6).

It was possible to directly compare the progress of children in the English immersion and early-exit bilingual programs but only indirect comparisons were possible between these programs and the late-exit program because these latter programs were offered in different districts and schools from the former. The comparison of immersion and early-exit programs showed that by grade 3 students were performing at comparable levels in English language and reading skills as well as in mathematics. Students in each of these program types progress academically at about the same rate as students in the general population but the gap between their performance and that of the general population remains large. In other words, they tend not to fall further behind academically between first and third grade but neither do they bridge the gap in any significant way.

While these results do not demonstrate the superiority of early-exit bilingual over English immersion, they clearly do refute the argument that there is a direct relation between the amount of time spent through English instruction and academic development in English. If the "time-on-task" notion were valid, the early-exit bilingual students should have performed at a considerably lower level than the English immersion students, which they did not.

The "time-on-task" notion suffers even further indignity from the late-exit bilingual program results. In contrast to students in the immersion and early-exit programs, the late-exit students in the two sites that continued primary language instruction for at least 40 per cent of the time were catching up academically to students in the general population. This is despite the fact that these students received considerably less instruction in English than students in early-exit and immersion programs and proportionately more of their families came from the lowest income levels than was the case for students in the other two programs.

Differences were observed among the three late-exit sites with respect to mathematics, English language (i. e. skills such as punctuation, capitalization etc.) and English reading; specifically, according to the report:

> As in mathematics and English language, it seems that those students in site E, who received the strongest opportunity to develop their primary language skills, realized a growth in their English reading skills that was greater than that of the norming population used in this study. If sustained, in time these students would be expected to catch up and approximate the average achievement level of this norming population. (Ramirez et al. 1991: 35).

By contrast, students in site G who were abruptly transitioned into almost all-English instruction in the early grades (in a similar fashion to early-exit students) seemed to lose ground in relation to the general population between grades 3 and 6 in mathematics, English language and reading.

The report concludes that

> ... students who were provided with a substantial and consistent primary language development program learned mathematics, English language, and English reading skills as fast or faster than the norming population used in this study. As their growth in these academic skills is atypical of disadvantaged youth, it provides support for the efficacy of primary language development in facilitating the acquisition of English language skills. (1991: 36)

These findings are entirely consistent with the results of other enrichment and two-way bilingual programs and show clearly that there is no direct relationship between the instructional time spent through the medium of a majority language and academic achievement in that language. If anything, the bulk of the evidence suggests an inverse relation between exposure to English instruction and English achievement for Latina students in the United States.

Ignoring logical inconsistencies

Three such inconsistencies can be noted. First, during the past decade a variety of influential groups and agencies within the United States have documented the "crisis" facing the United States as a result of its appalling incompetence in foreign languages.

Both international trade and national security are jeopardized by the fact that, in the words of former Secretary of Education, Terrell Bell, American schools are producing "a bunch of monolinguistic bumpkins." Even avowed opponents of bilingual education such as Secretary of Education Bennett and members of the U. S. English organization proclaim themselves to be strongly in favor of improved foreign language programs.

The logic here is that we first ensure that schools eradicate students' native "foreign" language skills and then spend significant amounts of money trying to teach these same "foreign" language skills using traditional non-bilingual methods that have been demonstrated to be ineffective except for a small elite of students. This squandering of the nation's human resources hardly constitutes "excellence" in education. A nation that bases its education system on this type of logic is truly "at risk."

A second logical contradiction concerns the use made of the French immersion results to argue for "structured immersion". The logic here is to argue for a monolingual English-only program, taught largely by monolingual teachers, and aimed at producing monolingualism, on the basis of the success of a program involving full bilingual instruction, taught by bilingual teachers, whose explicit goal is to produce additive bilingualism and biliteracy.

A third logical contradiction involves the push to exit children from transitional programs as quickly as possible. The logic here is that children have been put into bilingual programs on the grounds that they will make better English academic progress in a bilingual rather than a monolingual program. In other words, less English instruction will lead to more English achievement. As noted earlier, the empirical data are consistent with this assumption. Yet the rationale behind exiting students as quickly as possible is that they will fall behind in English unless they are in a program with maximum exposure to English. In other words, the two rationales are logically inconsistent with each other.

The extent of the logical contradiction here can be seen in the fact that minority students in the early grades of transitional programs are expected to make so much progress in the cognitive/academic skills underlying English literacy that after a short period they should be able to compete on an equal footing with their monolingual English'speaking peers who have had all their instruction through English. In other words, the quicker the exit from transitional programs, the more effective one must logically assume that the bilingual program has been in developing English proficiency. If these programs are so effective in promoting English, then what is the educational logic in exiting the child at all?

These logical contradictions and the denial/distortion of evidence promoting empowerment programs illustrate the process whereby the veneer of equity is maintained on the structure that disables minority children. In Galtung's terms, this structure provides the dominant group with "power-over-others" while denying dominated groups (whether children in classrooms or migrant workers in fields) the opportunity to develop "power-over-self."

Conclusion

The major point that I have tried to make is that the structure of institutionalized racism that assaults minority students' cultural identity in schools, denies their linguistic human rights, and prevents empowerment is essentially the same structure in goals and functions as the structure that has attempted to maintain a "favourable climate" in underdeveloped countries for continued profitability for multinational companies. Documents such as the Baker — de Kanter (1981) report and Porter's (1990) *Forked Tongue* serve important functions in legitimating the preservation of dominant-dominated power relations. The process over the past decade has involved paying lip-service to the rhetoric of educational equity by funding various forms of compensatory programs while ensuring that potentially empowering pedagogical programs (i. e. those that challenge institutional racism in schools, e.g. two-way bilingual programs) do not qualify for funding. Thus, the intervention goals are defined narrowly in terms of learning English and, as far as possible, only programs that pose little threat to the power structure get implemented (namely, quick-exit transitional programs). However, since it has transpired that even these programs have affected the power structure by providing jobs for Latinas and other minorities (even though for the most part they have not reversed minority students' school failure), it is regarded as desirable to eliminate them; this becomes an urgent priority in view of the changing demographics which potentially pose a real threat within a democratic country. Thus, the next step must be to demonstrate that these programs (not surprisingly) do not work very well and should therefore be eliminated "in order to help minority children succeed academically". Thus, the status quo (submersion under the label of "structured immersion") can be reinstated while preserving the myth that minority students' needs are being met.

Notes

1. I would like to thank Robert Phillipson, Tove Skutnabb-Kangas, and Alistair Penny-cook for useful comments on an earlier draft of this paper.
2. The analysis in the paper is limited to the more overt aspects of disinformation processes operating in the domestic and international arenas. A more complete analysis would also pursue parallels in the ways in which the infrastructures of inequality are created both domestically and internationally, e.g. through planned economic dependency, development projects that increase dependency, etc. I am indebted to Alistair Pennycook for discussions on this topic.
3. These types of bilingual programs have been termed "developmental" programs when the primary target group has been language minority students and "two-way bilingual" programs when both English-background and language minority students have received bilingual instruction designed to promote bilingualism and biliteracy (see Genesee 1987, for a discussion of such programs).
4. Following Fishman (1976), I will use the term "enrichment" program as a general label for all bilingual programs designed to promote full bilingualism and biliteracy among minority or majority students. Such programs, at the very least, will involve a "late-exit", i. e. L1 instruction continued late into elementary school.
5. For a review of Porter's book *Forked Tongue* see Cummins 1991.

Beyond linguistic policy: the Soviet Union versus Estonia

Mart Rannut

Introduction

The article analyses the linguistic situation in the former Soviet Union, a totalitarian multilingual empire whose linguistic policy was based on the ideological postulates of Communism. The tragedy of speakers of non-Russian languages on the territory of the former USSR is described. Under the pressure of the imperial ideology they were forced to sacrifice linguistic rights for an ideal that was clearly an attempt at linguistic genocide. Two main trends, russification and maintenance of one's language, are analysed in the second part of the article through a detailed study of Russian-Estonian relations. Due to the collapse of the totalitarian regime and the destruction of the USSR, new linguistic policies, involving the protection of local languages, have been introduced. As these are incompatible with previous ideology, and due to the redistribution of power among linguistic groups, these changes have caused considerable tensions, in most cases between immigrant and indigenous populations.

In presenting an historical overview of the linguistic policy in the former Soviet Union, attention is paid to the ideological goals influencing the linguistic policy, to their realisation, and to the results obtained. Although the linguistic policy of the Soviet Union was an indistinct phenomenon, three main periods can be observed, each differing in the methods that were used to achieve ideological goals. Prior to these periods there was no clear overall policy or means, due to the struggle for power in the Soviet leadership.

The first period, during Stalin's regime, was characterized by the vigorous and violent measures employed in order to bring Communist ideals to life. These measures involved the elimination of whole ethnic groups using a class-based approach. During the second period, post-Stalinism, less violence was used, while emphasis was placed upon re-building human nature and eliminating ethnic markers. A special type of education called "international education" was created, and in extreme cases, citizens were sent to psychiatric hospitals and prisons. This period, now referred to as "stagnation", was mainly associated with the name of Leonid Brezhnev. The third period began when M. Gorbachev came to power, and "perestroika" was introduced. Nevertheless, the ideal of the Soviet Union as a Communist empire was maintained, although glasnost was allowed. In other words, there was a delay in taking measures: in a departure from Stalinist linguistic policy, pure and righteous Leninist policy was propagated, but without success. As the right to self-determination was denied, ethnic and linguistic conflicts increased, among them a new tension between imperial-minded, homines sovetici, (who aimed to preserve the Communist Party-led USSR), and the local nations fighting for their cultures, languages and the right to self-determination. The attempted coup of August 1991, and the liberation of the Baltic States (occupied since World War II) terminated this period with the collapse of the USSR (Minsk declaration of 8 December 1991).

In this phase three main processes may be observed simultaneously, each influencing one another: 1) increasing economic malfunctioning accompanied by general chaos; 2) the attempt of indigenous nations to establish political sovereignty or to gain additional political rights for their home territories; and 3) the attempt of indigenous nations to protect their languages and cultures. These processes, together with vain attempts to preserve the status quo have been the basis for monitoring relations after the collapse of the Soviet Union and formation of the Commonwealth of Independent States.

The theory

PHASE I: *No person, no problem*

One of the most widespread postulates of Soviet ideology was the claim that the problem of ethnicity ("the national question") had long been solved, and that there were, and would never be, ethnic or linguistic conflicts between nations or between the central government and these nations. This was claimed because of the structure of the Soviet Union, a multinational empire, created by force on the ruins of the tzarist Russia and maintained by violence. Unatural political boundaries united some nations and ethnic groups by compulsion, while separating others (for example Central Asia, Karabakh).

There are at least two reasons why Soviet linguistic policy was only an implicit one. In the first place, an explicit Soviet linguistic policy never existed per se, as it was merely one dimension of Soviet Communist ideology. Secondly, this implicit policy was never stable, as it had to reflect the current views of the then General Secretary of the CPSU (Communist Party of the Soviet Union). These opinions were spread through CP documents, always backed up by appropriate quotations from Marx, Engels and Lenin. Nevertheless, some general principles influencing linguistic policy can be adduced.

The primacy of class over ethnicity, according to which the logical outcome of the class struggle (which serves as the motor of historical development) is that the most progressive class, the proletariat, must rule society. At the time of the October Revolution, the attempt to introduce such a class-based approach led to the primacy of one million proletarians (the ideologically conscious in Petrograd and Moscow) over 140 million non-proletarians, and further, that the Communist Party apparatus, "the leading and directing force of the society and the vanguard of the proletariat", would reign over all others. To keep this structure in balance, the dictatorship of the proletariat was converted from theory to practice as a euphemism for terror and a totalitarian regime. Such a hierarchical violent structure kept citizens under control and surveillance. As the primacy of class over ethnicity was the necessary, as well as the sufficient condition for a happy society, manifold hierarchies, e.g. those based on ethnic, linguistic or cultural markers, as well as "foreign bodies" such as churches, remnants of other classes and survivals of the pluralistic society were eliminated (cf. ethnicity in the West). Ethnicity in its turn was described as a temporary phenomenon and an inherent feature of capitalism, generated by the capitalist form of production and doomed to perish with capitalism.

Communism as an objective inevitability and historically progressive process, communism as the most perfect order of society has several features, including general happiness and freedom, the absence of state, police and prisons, as well as nations and ethnic groups, and the introduction of monolingualism. Expediency is a universal human vice, even when aiming for positive goals. So it is understandable that during the reign of Stalin (1924–1953), the goal of reaching Communism within the period of one generation meant using severe measures to carry out the policy, including executions, and Gulag facilities (as described by Solzhenitsyn). Thus, according to the first principle of the class-based approach, the state, led by ideological principles, turned against the enemy of the working class. In reality it meant the persecution of intellectuals, including Russian intellectuals. According to the second principle, the state handicapped and eliminated all sorts of nationalists who tried to maintain their native language even in the dawn of Communism (see Nutt 1989). Very little attention was paid to human rights. In fact, an individual had no place in history or in society except as defined in a set of societal relations, behaving according to the principles of class struggle. These relations were first and foremost economic. In the process of liquidating harmful or unnecessary relations, whole nations and ethnic groups were deported and persecuted, including the Kalmyk, the Ingrians, the Cherkess, the Chechens, the Ingush, the Balkars, the Meshi, the Crimean Tartars, the Volga Germans, etc. The fewer the number of languages that remain, the nearer one is to Communism. The solution could not be the substitution of one language by another, but the elimination of the whole ethnic structure, achieved with the help of migrational flows, deportations, the mechanical mixing of people at their work places, and even through mixed marriages.

PHASE II: Persons without ethnicity

In the second, post-Stalin period, less violence was used in ethnic and linguistic policies (prisons and psychiatric hospitals only in extreme cases), and new theoretical concepts were introduced. As the ethnic element restricts free development, one can exterminate the factors which maintain a person's nation and language, rather than eliminating the person him- or herself. Two phases of languages during socialism were posited, *sbliženie* [convergence] and *slijanie* [assimilation]. This represents the replacement of physical violence by psychological or symbolic violence, a progression from the use of sticks to carrots and ideas (Skutnabb-Kangas 1988b).

What emerged was, according to Medvedyev (1986: 95), the following:

1) the convergence of languages and the mutual enrichment of cultures,
2) languages became stylistically diverse (particularly when compared to the period of illiteracy),
3) several writers published their works in Russian instead of in their native languages,
4) phoneme inventories were enriched by new phonemes (e.g. the Kirgiz language added /f/ when the capital of Kirgizia was named "Frunze" in honour of a famous Russian revolutionary).

There are, of course, some constraints in applying the advantages of socialism to language, as pointed out by Desheriyev (1982: 95): "Though language in Soviet society carries an important ideological function, in the Soviet philosophical and linguistic literature it has been proven that language by its nature is a non-class-based phenomenon". This was a great leap forward from Academician N. Marr's Stalinist theory of stages, which linked languages to appropriate socio-economic formations.

To strengthen the positive tendencies in society, the CP-based Leninist ethnolinguistic policy was proposed, which assumed the following (Desheriyev 1982: 12):

1) the absolute equality of languages;
2) the creation of necessary conditions for the evolution and mutual enrichment of languages;
3) an unlimited usage of national languages in all spheres;
4) a guarantee of bilingualism − one's native language and the use of Russian as an instrument of brotherly cooperation between the nations of the SU;
5) the consistent implementation of national-international cross-fertilization, enrichment and convergence, as well as the development of a common Soviet culture;
6) the replenishment of the lexical fund of the languages of the SU nations (cf. academician Y. Trubatchov's theory in Hint 1990).

All the aforementioned assumptions require the internationalization of all spheres of society. Internationalization (*internacionalizatsija*) was a directed and controlled process, influenced by political, economic and ideological, as well as by purely propagandist means. The goal, according to the program of the CPSU of 1961, was to unify the nations − a common economy, common communist features, and a common international culture. This was implemented by means of "international" education (*internacional'noe vospitanie*), including the following subjects: the theory of the national question and propaganda for the cooperation of Soviet Union nations, the inculcation of new international traditions, explanations of the nature of proletarian internationalism, propaganda concerning the importance of the Russian language, sharing the (positive) experience of multinational working parties, the creation of the feeling of belonging to the family of the Soviet peoples, and the struggle against the phenomena of (linguistic) chauvinism and nationalism (Metelitsa 1982). Other researchers added the following topics: the strictly scientific and consistently class-based interpretation of the history of nations, the advantages of socialism in solving national problems, the exposition of the bourgeois falsifications of the national policy of the CPSU, and history of the USSR (see Kandimaa 1989).

The main objective of this education was to produce brainwashed and trustworthy people who had no roots and no ethnic preferences. At the 24th CPSU Congress, these people were given a beautiful name: the Soviet people, having three characteristic features: 1) embodying Marxist-Leninist ideology, 2) having the goal of building Communism, hence 3) supporting non-ethnicity (see Nutt 1989). This new man, born of the Soviet totalitarian regime, was called *homo soveticus*. Other significant symptoms: an address in the Soviet Union, being free of nation and culture, and in lieu of democracy, a struggle for a socialist democracy, always thinking as a *tovarišč* ["comrade"] does, and speaking the language of the future Communist society, Russian, the "international language" (*jazyk mežnacionalnogo obščenija*).

In the 1920s, the chief propagandists spread the theory of the export of Communism, according to which all countries by chain reaction would soon become socialist. The dominant view was that in this scenario, the language would certainly be based on the Latin alphabet, but opinions differed on the choice of language. For example L. Trotzky, Chief-of-Arms of Soviet Russia, promoted the learning of Esperanto and even demanded knowledge of it from his officers until the year 1923.

During the 1920s, the Latin alphabet was introduced for languages which were either not alphabetised or used a non-cyrillic alphabet (the entire literacy campaign aimed at spreading Communist ideology and converting people to Communism). But as this export theory failed in practice, in the 1930s, it was the Russian language that was chosen to fulfil this historic task. This period marked the beginning of the rise of the status of Russian as primus inter pares in order to guarantee effective communication and cooperation in the political, cultural, and economic spheres. The reasons advanced for this were the following: Russian is spoken by Russians, who form approximately one half of the population of the USSR; fraternal cooperation takes place via this language; the Russian people have liberated other peoples and have provided them with fraternal help, common historical traditions, as well as a major part of the Russian culture and science with which to develop the culture of these other nations; Russian is one of the most developed world languages, as it is the language of current scientific, cultural and technological cooperation, and international communication (Desheriyev 1982: 44). In addition, Russian has several unique functions, being the native language of Russians, and it is the freely chosen international language for the peoples of the USSR, as well of the countries of the socialist friendship union. This language contains the richest literature on Marxism-Leninism, as well as socialist economic, cultural, and linguistic construction experiences of the USSR, which are of direct concern to the countries of the Third World (Desheriyev 1982: 47). To reach the inevitable Communism, Russians must keep their language alive and thriving. For non-Russians, the only remaining option was the exchange of their native languages for Russian through voluntary self-assimilation (Khanazarov 1982).

The temporary solution proposed during L. Brezhnev's reign, now referred to as *zastoj* ["stagnation"] was named Russian-national bilingualism (*nacional'noruskoje dvujazyčie*). According to this doctrine, Russian operated as "the second native language" for those Soviet citizens for whom it was not their first language. The "national" native language, unsuitable for scientific and technological purposes, as well as being an obstacle to the scientific progress of the USSR (Kulichenko 1981: 425), was ascribed the functions that Russian could not fulfill (e.g. national folklore). As a result, a two-level linguistic empire was formed, where all the languages were equal, and knowledge of Russian as a lingua franca was obligatory. In reality, this meant diglossia, as the Soviet top administration and diplomacy, as well as the compulsory military service and optional detention in prison required the exclusive use of Russian. Such well-organized russification resulted in the death of approximately seventy languages during the existence of the USSR. These languages perished. Their speakers "surpassed national isolation", and switched to Russian. While the census of 1926 recorded 194 distinct ethnic units, the 1989 census revealed that the current number was only 128. In 1989 in the Soviet Union, education (at least instruction in one's native language) was provided in 40 languages, and higher education was offered in 5 languages.

The entire education system was oriented toward the empire-minded Moscow-centered view (e.g. in history, literature). Native language instruction was replaced with education in Russian. "National" schools were forced to close down. To raise the status of Russian in everyday life, national territories were colonized internally by nominating Russians to top positions in non-Russian areas (for example, in 1988 in Moldova 85% of directors and senior managers were non-Moldavians). In the process of "denationalization of the ethnic environment", the concept of Russian as "the older brother" was also introduced . A new, international non-ethnic culture was created, national in form, but socialist in content.

This socialist realism-based Soviet culture was directly controlled by the CP. Being a subculture, predominantly based on Russian culture, it was a suitable channel for unifying various national traditions by enriching them with socialist advances.

The reality

The all-union linguistic situation

Due to ideological pressure, accompanied by measures restricting the functional use of "national" languages and lowering their status, languages in the Soviet Union operated within the society with differing levels of success. Politically, these languages enjoyed different privileges according to the political status of the ethnic territories of their speakers. Up to the year 1991, ethnic territories in the Soviet Union were divided into 5 categories: the Federal Republic (Russia), Republics (14), Autonomous Republics (20), Autonomous (or National) Areas and Districts (18), and ethnic territories with no political status. The functioning of the language within these territories may be described with the help of the scheme proposed by Denison (1977: 21).

$$A \rightarrow AI/BII \rightarrow BI/AII \rightarrow B$$

where "B" is the ousting Russian language, and "A" the ousted "national" languages, and where "I" indicates the dominant, and "II" the lesser degree of functioning in the society.

The first "A" is where the language does not suffer under the functional pressure of another language, and where other languages operate marginally in the area concerned. "A" was thus represented in the Soviet Union by only one language – the international language of Russian on the territory of Russia (autonomous and national territories excluded). Due to its ideological role, Russian became the main evictor of other languages from the ethnic territories of their speakers. All the other languages, being minority languages as compared to Russian, belonged to the next stages of language decay. The second stage, AI/BII, may be characterized by migrational processes, an abrupt increase in language contacts, ideological pressure, and by a lexical offensive that carries phonetic changes with it. The local language must give up the most prestigious functional areas. In the USSR, the Baltic and Caucasian Republics, the Ukraine and perhaps Moldavia reached this stage.

The Baltic republics of Estonia, Latvia, and Lithuania were annexed by the USSR in 1940. After that, "the national cadres" were mostly deported to Siberia, or to the Far North, or just killed, and in their place, Russians were brought in, according to the program for boosting the economy of periphery areas. Thus the Russian-speaking population in the Baltics comprised from one-fifth to one-half of the population. Nevertheless, the local languages functioned almost equally with Russian in the "national" communities.

In the Caucasian republics, local languages did not enjoy as high a status as in the Baltic States, but due to the demographic situation (the Russian-speaking population was represented marginally), the marginalised languages have continued undeterred in areas where there have been no resources for the alien language offensive. The Ukrainian language experienced this, using the national potential of the Western Ukraine. A more difficult situation obtained in Moldavia. The Moldavians who speak Romanian (the Moldavian language was a socialist invention to justify the partial occupation of Romanian territory in 1940), lived mostly in the rural areas, whereas the towns were mainly russified. Nevertheless, through democratic developments (Moldavians form three-fifth of the population), the linguistic situation was manageable.

The third stage — BI/AII — represents the situation where the language being attacked has its functional positions weakened fatally, as the linguistic potential transferred via the education system is inadequate. Even if support for the alien language ends, extra vigilance is needed to counteract the dangerous tendencies. The local language is ousted by a step-by-step process from all functional areas, and finally from its home. With the loss of every function, the status of the language correspondingly decreases, though it may be hindered by a high birth-rate (e.g. Central Asian republics). Due to the degeneration of the language, passivity as regards national problems appears, and cultural memory, traditional group relations based on language, culture and ethnicity are all lost. If this trend is maintained, it leads to a language's death. At risk were the languages of the Soviet Union in territories that had a national political status of some kind, with at least some legal or administrative protection. As were groups who were a demographic minority in the homeland, though exceptions may be found (e.g. the Komy-Permyak language was the native language of three-fifths of the population of the autonomous district concerned, with no public usage at all).

The fourth stage, "B", is a result of diglossia, where the victim language has lost all functions, and is spoken marginally by bilinguals, or by none at all. In the Soviet Union, this stage was represented by 70 languages operating peripherally, among them the Finno-Ugric languages Liv, Vot and Ingrian (less than 20 speakers). For example the last speaker of Kamassi died in 1985. Language revival is impossible at this stage, even if great resources were available.

In addition to indigenous languages, the Soviet Union was rich in migrant languages, spoken by 60 million people, due to the strong encouragement of massive migration. Being mostly the homines sovetici of the future, migrants enjoyed special privileges (e.g. were awarded state-owned flats without queueing). But as the cultural autonomy system was liquidated during Soviet power, and native language education was not available, the non-Russian migrants were assimilated to the Russian community in the second generation (see Viikberg 1990). Several migrant languages were spoken in the territory where their speakers were deported by Y. Stalin's orders, which has led to some of the current ethnolinguistic conflicts. Russians, making up two-thirds of the migrant population, came to non-Russian areas in order to enforce socialist order, and to fight against possible nationalists. As Russian intellectuals were not interested in these missionary activities, the Russian-speaking migrant communities consist mostly of proletarians who are uninterested in the local culture and language. In the absence of stimuli for contact with the local culture, strong procommunist views suppose that the local people will forget their linguistic and cultural habits, and soon assimilate, and not vice versa.

PHASE III: Gorbachev's perestroika

Improvement in the linguistic situation began during the years of *perestroika* and *glasnost'*, initiated by the then Soviet leader M. Gorbachev. The reason for the new political course was the catastrophic economic situation, induced by the CPSU. Out of dire necessity, perestroika also reached humanitarian spheres (glasnost), though the original intention was to improve the economy only, and to keep the status quo in other spheres (like in China). Due to the liberalization tendencies, political repressions ended, enabling local nations to take measures to save their languages and cultures, and even to dream about their possible independence. Facing an entirely new situation, the official imperial ideology stopped chanting the most unpopular slogans, thus also influencing linguistic policy. However, the main postulates remained the same, receiving only cosmetic revision:

1) language unity (i. e. monolingualism) would be established in the more distant future (rather than the near future),
2) Stalin spoiled Lenin's correct national policy, which therefore had to be restored,
3) Russian as the international language had to have the highest status in the Soviet Union, though local languages might be legally protected (balanced bilingualism instead of unbalanced diglossia),
4) the Soviet Union represented a happy, multinational society with minor ethnic and linguistic conflicts that were solved easily by the SU leadership (a revision of the proclamation of of the USSR as a multinational country without ethnic and linguistic conflicts).

As the main postulate of keeping the Soviet empire together with legislative and executive power in the hands CP officials was highly unpopular, several legal and political conflicts arose. Using the central government's loss of influence in the economy (ruled by Council of Ministers of the USSR) as well as in the ideology (ruled by CPSU), most of the Republics took steps to gain more freedom in economic as well as in humanitarian policy. The following three factors were involved in influencing the linguistic policy:

1) the economic crash, masked by the "perestroika" slogan. As a reaction to this, the creation of an "every man for himself" economic policy in the regions of the SU led to a more autonomous policy in various regions in the SU;
2) idelogical "revisionism" in the form of glasnost, verbal clashes between representatives of the "Old Bolshevik" line and those of the Russian democrats. Here was an opportunity to use ideological chaos as a means of distancing oneself from the Soviet Union's ideology and, in this way, gaining additional political rights (in the case of indigenous peoples, e.g. Yakutiya) or full sovereignty;
3) with increased economic and ideological freedom that promoted a democratic movement, steps were taken by local authorities to terminate the discrimination of languages and to protect the respective cultures. Such policies unavoidably led to conflict with the Russian-speaking population, who interpreted the legal acts restricting the privileges of Russian language usage as a discriminatory step.

Thus language laws were adopted in almost every Republic, the chronological order of adoption reflecting the prestige of the local language on one hand, and the power of pro-Union communities on the other: Estonia (18 January 1989), Lithuania (language decree, 25 January 1989), Latvia (5 May 1989), Tadjikistan (2 August 1989), Moldova (1 September 1989), Uzbekistan (21 September 1989), Kazakhstan (22 September 1989), Kirgizstan (23 September 1989), Ukraine (3 October 1989), Byelorussia (26 January 1990), Turkmenistan (24 May 1990). In Armenia, Georgia, and Azerbaidjan, the constitutional amendment declaring their respective languages to be official languages has existed since 1978, and the need for a special law was not deemed urgent. In Russia the drafting of the relevant law was completed only in 1991 due to the severe linguistic (as well as political) struggle that is currently under way (e.g. in Tatarstan).

Language laws were drafted on a lower political level too, for example in the autonomous republics (e.g. in Mordwa). Several legislative acts produced side-effects as well. Thus in Moldova the language law established that the Moldavian and Romanian languages were identical, because what mainly differentiated them − use of a different alphabet − was eliminated while the enforced use of Cyrillic was annulled, and the Latin alphabet was re-introduced. Similarly, the identity of the Farsi and Tadjik languages was established by the Language Law of Tadjikistan.

All the language laws have several common features. First of all, an increase in the language rights of minorities may be noted. Whereas minority languages had earlier been totally illegitimate, using a minority language is guaranteed in the cultural domain (i. e. cultural autonomy) and in education (the right to establish educational institutions in one's native language). Among the languages obtaining these rights are Modern Hebrew, Yiddish and Romani (cf. the language law of Moldova), each of which had long been marginalised, as their speakers did not sufficiently suit Soviet ideals.

The main point in the legal acts was the redivision of the status of local and Russian languages. In most language laws, Russian was proclaimed to be the international language, officially giving it the same legal rights of the local language (except in the Baltic states). This meant that a private individual had to be educated, administered and served in his/her local language or in Russian, according to his/her choice. However, administrative and business institutions had to switch to the local language in their contacts with others inside the Republic.

It was a major step forward, causing the local Russian-speaking immigrant population working in service industries of in governmental positions to learn at least the basics of the local language. Several functional spheres were not under the jurisdiction of the language laws, e.g. the Soviet Army, in some laws the KGB, and even the railways and Aeroflot, which were ruled directly from Moscow.

As a reaction to the adoption of these language laws, the central government responded by confirming the status of Russian as the official language with the highest status in the Soviet Union in the "Law of the languages of the USSR", adopted on 24 April 1990. This law re-established the old two-level hierarchy of languages, constraining the functional usage of other languages than Russian in the framework of Russian-national bilingualism. However, due to the primacy of the laws of the Republics before All-Union ones, as well as ideological and economic chaos, this law had no significant effect at all. It is evident that these changes were a tremendous step toward the protection of dominated languages, but due to a total lack of enforcement of the laws (except in Estonia and Lithuania), this change has mostly influenced society by serving to focus attention to an increasing extent on the status of local languages. Societal change was also induced by other, more directly political factors.

Post-USSR linguistic policies

The collapse of the Soviet Union and the disintegration of the power structure changed the linguistic situation completely. Instead of one there are 15 different policies, reflecting the number of sovereign states. The similarities between old and new may be observed only in the case of the Russian Federation, where the former autonomous republics were raised to the status of full republics. Though Communist ideology is not used by officials, the clichés of the past are far from extinct. On the other hand the new law on languages in the Russian Federation introduces new democratic principles and promotes awareness of linguistic human rights, also protecting other languages besides Russian.

However, the political reality does not reflect any influence from this law. Implementation of the law is hindered, or totally absent. Activists in this field are persecuted or killed (e.g. the case of the Khanty cultural leader, Sopatchina, beaten to death by local Russian militia, with no investigation afterwards, in May 1993). Conflicts in this domain are frequent. They are regarded by the centre as "nationalist" phenomena threatening territorial integrity, by others as representing ideas of cultural self-determination for the new republics.

The new states of Central Asia have solved the linguistic problems as a by-product of political transformations: due to low living standards, a rising crime rate, and xenophobic attitudes in some areas where little human rights protection is available, groups which are not indigenous nations (e.g. Russians, Germans in Kazakhstan) are moving out and taking refuge in the European part of Russia. Though up till now the language of the elite is still Russian, its status is diminishing continuously. The Cyrillic alphabet will be replaced by the Latin (Turkish) one, or by Arabic in Tadjikistan. Increasing contacts with Turkey, Iran and other Islamic countries have intensified anti-Russian feelings and also increased the need to know local languages. It has led to massive emigration by Russians from Central Asia. Out of 9 million Russians, probably only a small number will stay, mostly in Kazakhstan, where in some areas Russians constitute a majority.

Although to a smaller extent, the same phenomena may be observed in the Caucasian region, with full-scale armed conflicts speeding up the process. There is war in Moldova Dniestr-region, where the right not to know the Romanian language is effectively protected by the 14th Russian Army, which makes a mockery of the principle of non-interference in the internal affairs of other states. Due to the conflicts between Russia and Ukraine (over nuclear weapons and the START agreement, autonomy for Crimea, and the Black Sea Fleet), the status of the Ukrainian language has risen considerably.

The transformation process for these new states (excluding the Baltics, as under international law they are old states that were temporarily occupied) has been painful. Nevertheless, similarities may be observed. Firstly, an increase of ethnic values, a restructing of societies on the basis of ethnic (or linguistic) identity instead of class-based identity. Maintaining one's cultural roots can be seen as positive, but in extreme cases of nationalism (e.g. in Georgia) and linguistic imperialism it (e.g. in Russia), it prevents others from enjoying their cultural and linguistic freedoms. Thus it is often accompanied by an intolerance of minority cultures and languages (e.g. anti-semitism in Russia, anti-German attitudes in Kazakhstan). Curiously, even in the face of aggressive linguicism, mass cultural trends are becoming increasingly popular, even to the detriment to one's own culture.

Secondly there is intensive migration, including repatriation, temporary displacements, refugee flows, and labour migration to areas with higher living standards. It is propelled by two main forces, insecurity which compels people to leave, and the search for one's roots and national identity, which determines the choice of place of settlement. According to some experts, 10 − 15% of the population in the former Soviet Union will be involved in this process.

The third factor is ethnic and linguistic tensions due to the instability of the political systems, the malfunctioning of economies, and difficulties in accommodating one's linguistic habits to the changed linguistic environment.

Political influence on the linguistic situation in the the former Soviet Union

The disintegration of the Soviet Union in December 1991 was just one major step in the restructuring process that began with recognition of the restitution of the independence of the Baltic States. It is incomplete, with several former autonomous republics and regions demanding more political rights and even attempting secession (Chechenia, Tatarstan). The political tensions are not going to reduce, on the contrary, they may erupt into full-scale war.

As a rule the states on the territory of the former Soviet Union regard linguistic issues as a domestic policy concern. The one major exception is Russia, whose linguistic prescriptions are also directed to the "near abroad". The division of foreign countries into "near" and "far" abroad was worked out immediately after the foundation of the Commonwealth of Independent States. The concepts are not geographical (Norway does not belong to near abroad, although bordering on Russia), but rather political, based mostly on the availability of two constituents, Russian military presence and a Russian-speaking, non-integrated diaspora.

The aim of the policy towards near abroad is to maintain Russian influence on the territory of the former Soviet Union, to block unwelcome decisions and to keep the near-abroad countries in the Russian sphere of influence. For this purpose it was necessary to hinder effectively or even freeze the withdrawal of troops, as well as to keep the Russian diaspora non-integrated into local society and thus loyal to Russia. A more detailed scheme was worked out, based on the Karaganov doctrine (1992). This recommends that Russia use Russians in the former USSR to influence policies serving Russian interests. The Russian-speaking population residing in the former USSR was regarded not simply as a debit, but as a powerful asset for Russia. So the first task was to leave the Russian speakers in the regions where they were. This was necessary not only to prevent a flood of refugees, but also because Russia needed to preserve her leverage and maintain influence. The second task was to keep Russian speakers loyal to Russia, simultaneously promising them all political rights in the state concerned. It meant the granting of citizenship by principle of ius soli or at least by option (with a free choice between Russia and the state of residence concerned) or even better, double citizenship. Linguistically it meant a demand for two official languages with Russian being one, or in the event of a hostile reception, to form Russian autonomous "national" areas on the territory of another state populated by immigrants and maintained by Russian military force (like the Dniestr-region in Moldova, or the Crimea, Sevastopol, in the Ukraine). In some cases it turned out to be more effective to take direct military action and install puppet governments (like in Tadjikistan) or provide direct military support to one side in a conflict (e.g. the Georgian-Abkhazian conflict).

If military actions were considered out of place, propaganda about human rights violations was used. In fact the human rights most clearly violated in the near abroad were the right of Russians not to know the local language, the right of Russian military personnel to reside in a place of their choice and, in some cases, to obtain citizenship without meeting the necessary requirements. This occurred in states that were formerly occupied. If any of these special Russian human rights were not respected, it provided an excuse for having Russian military forces on the spot, to protect human rights in the area.

This linkage between human rights violations and the Russian military presence has proven to be politically very valuable. Karaganov asserted that it would not be practical for Russia to overtly state that it is defending the rights of Russians. Instead he recommends that "... we (the Russian Federation) have to make the basis of Russian foreign policy regarding Russian-speaking populations the position that we are defending human rights throughout the entire territory of the former USSR." In favour of Russian domination in the economy, he further states:

> Economically, it is useful for Russia to begin a far-reaching expansion of investments. We need to make use of the huge debt burdens that the former Soviet republics have in order to buy up their enterprises and to become the owners. In this way, we will form a powerful economic political enclave, which will be the basis for our political influence in those countries ...

He does not advocate using force to achieve Russia's goals, but recommends that

"... we [the Russian Federation] need to prepare public opinion and international organizations so that they would acknowledge the need for the limited use of force within a legal framework for Russia ..." Due to the political changes, economic disaster, and the consequent redivision of the status of languages, there will continue to be tensions and conflicts in the territories of the former USSR. Russian imperialistic ambitions are definitely not the right treatment to solve them.

Linguistic policy in Estonia

The annexation of Estonia

The ideology of the Soviet Empire was reflected in its treatment of Estonia. Following the Soviet-German Non-Aggression Pact and its Secret Protocol (known as the Molotov-Ribbentrop Pact), the Soviet Union occupied the independent states of Lithuania, Latvia and Estonia in June 1940. The USSR had a strategic interest in the ice-free harbours of the Baltic Sea. At that time Estonia was an independent, mainly mononational country, whose minorities (Russians, Germans, Swedes, Jews) enjoyed ample cultural autonomy. According to the 1934 census, the ethnic composition of the population of Estonia was as follows: 992,000 (88%) Estonians, 92,000 Russians (8%), 16,300 (1.5%) Germans, 7,600 (0.7%) Swedes, and 4,400 (0.4%) Jews. A majority of the largest minority group (Russians) lived in rural areas, the most "Russian" areas being Narva (29.7%), the territories east of Narva, and the Petseri region. In Tallinn the percentage of Russians was 5.7%.

In response to an appeal from Hitler, most Germans left Estonia in October 1939. In June 1940, 90,000 Soviet soldiers were stationed in Estonia, in addition to the 25,000 already there, in accordance with the treaty on military bases that had been imposed on Estonia in October 1939. This made the forces occupying the territory 115,000 strong, as against an Estonian army of 14,000. Most Estonian military officers, senior police officers and top civil servants were imprisoned and executed. The President of Estonia was arrested, together with his family, and deported to Russia, where he eventually died in an asylum, while part of his family died of hunger.

Estonia was proclaimed a part of the Soviet Union (6 August 1940) and named the Estonian Soviet Socialist Republic, and fell under the rule of the Soviet governmental apparatus and Communist Party. The first phase, Stalinist linguistic policy, was introduced in Estonia, having a serious impact.

Firms were proclaimed to be Soviet property, the Soviet rouble became the only valid currency, and Soviet law and Stalinist terror ruled the country. On 14 June 1941, during a single campaign, more than 10,000 people were deported to Russia. Non-Communist parties and organizations were banned, all schools, societies and clubs of the ethnic minorities were closed, and cultural autonomy was eliminated.

Most journals and newspapers were closed down. Those few that survived were made heralds of Communist ideas. Access to information was channelled through the Soviet official information agency, TASS, and through Moscow Radio. The foreign press was prohibited, and foreign contacts were terminated. Individual arrests, the most common element in the sovietization policy, began from the first day of occupation, 17 June 1940. In the course of the first year of Soviet occupation (1940–41), the population of Estonia decreased by 104,000 (see Kala 1991).

World War II overrode Estonia twice. Germany conquered Estonia in 1941, and in 1944 the country was again occupied by the Soviet Union. At the end of 1941 Estonia was claimed to be Judenfrei by Nazis. In 1943 the Swedes left their homes in the Estonian coastal region and islands for Sweden, in conformity with a German-Swedish treaty. In 1944, before the arrival of the Soviet army, 70,000 Estonians left as refugees (mainly for Sweden and Germany), in fear of a return of the Soviet terror. Many factors contributed to a further decrease in the Estonian population, particularly war damage and deportations, but also the illegitimate transfer of Estonian territory to Russia in 1945. The result was that by 1946 the Estonian population had decreased by one-fifth (200,000) to 854,000. A mere 23,000 (2,7%) of non-Estonians remained as minorities in Estonia.

The first post-war decade in Estonia

During the first post-war decade in Estonia the Stalinist policy continued. According to the ruling ideology of the time, the "people's enemies" were crushed, brute force being used against persons of the "wrong" social background or class. The social basis of the "hostile" class was constrained by means of industrialisation (prefential development of heavy industry, the closing down of small private firms), collectivization (creation of socialist agriculture, the ruining of private farms through the creation of collective farms), and the Literacy Campaign — despite the fact that Lutheran Estonia had been over 90% literate since the 19th century.

Russian workers and collective farmers were invited to Estonia to fulfil their international duty, and to help to set the Estonian working-class free from "the bondage of German and English imperialists and the oppression of local capitalists". In the years 1945–1950, the number of immigrants was 0.5 million, and that of emigrants was half that amount, while natural increase was only 8,700. 170,000 non-Estonians settled permanently in Estonia, over 90 per cent of them in towns. They saw Estonia as part of the USSR, where a new way of life and the Russian language had still to be learned (Kala 1991). Among the reasons for moving to Estonia were a better standard of living (there was hunger in Russia), organized recruitment (construction work, oil shale industry), privileged positions in certain trades where Estonians were not trusted, e.g. navigation and aviation (an opportunity for Estonian nationalists to flee abroad), the railways (the risk of sabotage by nationalists), communications (state secrets), etc. Simultaneously, the oppression of Estonians continued, a reaction to which was the escape of Estonians to the woods (hence the guerilla movement known as the "forest brothers").

The best way to manage the vast task of restructuring Estonian society was to destroy societal integrity and continuity as well as collective ethnic memory. The latter was accomplished by mass deportations of Estonians to other regions in the Soviet Union. In March 1949 over 20,000 Estonians were deported to the Far East and Siberia, the majority women and children. Many died en route.

To alter the collective memory, the material bearers of it were destroyed together with human ones. Approximately 30 million books (including childrens' books!) were burned. Thick volumes were fragmented with the help of an axe (see Meri 1991). At Tartu University library a special position of censor was created, a responsibility held by a monolingual Russian. Access to other materials published in independent Estonia and not used for heating purposes was severely restricted. To eliminate the blank spots in Estonian history a new version was written, describing Russians as Estonia's very peace-loving neighbours, who help Estonians re-establish their own native culture, and who liberated Estonia from German and Swedish occupation.

To make the new version of Estonian history more easily memorable, public places such as streets, squares and parks, as well as institutions and factories and even one town (Kuressaare) were renamed in honour of various revolutionaries and prominent Russian figures presiding over this new history. Simultaneously monuments and statues glorifying the past (among them the statue of the folk hero of the Estonian national epic Kalevipoeg) were demolished and replaced by statues that were to be important in this new past. An attempt was made to deprive Estonians of their literary roots, and to replace the Estonian (Latin) writing system by Cyrillic, but this failed because of lack of enthusiasm.

In several functional domains, Estonian was replaced by Russian, due to Estonia's direct subordination to Moscow, for example in banking, statistics, the militia (Soviet police), railway, naval and air transport, mining, energy production, etc. Some functional activities were completely new in Estonia, having no corresponding Estonian terminology and were therefore carried out in Russian, e.g. Gosplan (state planning) and the KGB. Some were eliminated entirely in Estonian, and for this reason, recreated in Russian, e.g. everything connected with military purposes. Nevertheless terminological work was carried out continuously at the Institute of Language and Literature of the Academy of Sciences in Estonia, thus preserving the functional potential of the language.

In an attempt to mechanically mix peoples, and to destroy their (non-Soviet!) ethnic and cultural environment, the Ingrians (already deported from their mother country in the 1930s) were driven from Estonia in 1947 (Decree of the USSR Council of Ministers of May 7, 1947), from where they had just settled in 1944–1947, finding the new milieu relatively acceptable in terms of language and culture. In 1951, the final deportation took place, the victims being mostly active church-goers, who were no good at adopting the new ideology. During the same year most of the civil servants who had collaborated with the occupiers in 1940 were arrested, and their jobs taken by "trustworthy" workers with a Russian background. During the first decade of occupation, oppressive methods were used to create favourable social and demographic conditions for the destruction of Estonians and their language as well as the remnants of indigenous minorities, replacing them with Russian-speaking, imported, "trustworthy" personnel.

Areas of immigration

Immigration was favoured as a means of producing loyal personnel with "clean papers". The immigrants settled mainly in: 1) the town of Narva (North-East Estonia), which was bombed by the SU air force, and lay in ruins, and where, during the post-war years, resettlement by Estonians was restricted; 2) Sillamäe, an area closed to Estonians as members of a "suspect" ethnic group, due to the uranium mining, and, later, uranium processing; 3) the Kohtla-Järve oil-shale mines; 4) the country's capital, Tallinn (large factories and Soviet bases), and 5) the submarine base Paldiski, where Estonians were turned away, and where all monuments reminiscent of Estonia, including cemetery squares, were demolished.

In connection with the building of large military airfields, the linguistic balance was violated and inter ethnic-relations ruined in Tartu, Tapa, Haapsalu and Pärnu. The army took vast territories and Estonians were simply expelled from these lands without compensation. Estonians who survived the GULAG were deprived of the right to live in their area of origin.

An ancient Estonian profession, off-shore fishing, was forbidden, the boats broken up and burned. Any protest was severely punished: protesters were often either shot or sent to Siberian prison camps for 25 years, while family members were deported to Siberia, and their relatives denied access to higher education and to certain jobs.

As a result, despair and cynicism (the so-called social fatigue syndrome) became prevalent among Estonians, accompanied by a rapid fall in the birth rate, and an increase in the number of suicides. To this day the Estonians have not yet regained their pre-war population numbers. In 1959 the proportion of Estonians in Estonia's general population fell to 74.6%.

The assimilation period

The relatively short mild period of the 1960s, usually associated with N. Khrushchev, brought about a revitalization of Estonian culture. The new generation was socially immune, having acquired the skill of double-thinking and fighting for the Estonian cause under the guise of being devoted to building socialism. But this period did not last long. Even then, some Estonian factory managers, having in mind their material well-being, allowed their factories to grow extensively, and thus supported immigration (the so-called migration-pump effect). After the 1960s, migration diminished, but until the end of the 1980s, the number of newcomers exceeded those leaving by 8,000 – 9,000 per year, in a population of 1.5 million. The total immigration during the Soviet occupation was 1.4 million, emigration 0.8 million, consequently a net inward migration of 0.6 million. As the number of Estonians did not rise to its pre-World

War II level, remaining at less than a million, the proportion of Estonians in the overall population fell from 97.3% in 1945 to 61.5% in 1989.

The newcomers attained a privileged position by getting flats (according to Drobizheva, 1984, 86% of the aliens and only 57% of the Estonians live in flats with all modern conveniences), as well as enjoying other privileges in towns, mainly because 90% of the immigrants were townspeople. The result was a decrease in the percentage of Estonians, falling to 4% of the population in Narva, 3.2% in Sillamäe, 21% in Kohtla-Järve, 2% in Paldiski and 47% in Tallinn, the capital.

According to the 1989 census, the ethnic composition in Estonia was as follows: 963,000 Estonians, 475,000 Russians, 48,000 Ukrainians, 28,000 Belorussians, 16,600 Finns, 4,600 Jews, 4,000 Tartars, 3,500 Latvians and 3,000 Poles. Only two of these ethnic groups — Estonians and Russians — have generally retained their mother tongue. 1/3 of Estonians spoke Russian, which was a compulsory school subject, while 15% of Russians were bilingual in Russian and Estonian. These were mainly local Russians, the resident minority from before 1939.

The third group comprised real homines sovetici, mostly Ukrainians, Belorussians, Jews, Germans and Poles, in whose case the official de-ethnization policy has produced the best results: only a minority of 40% spoke their native languages, 52% were russified, approximately 8% spoke Estonian. The lack of education in their native language created an underdeveloped sense of national identity, which made the national aspirations of the Estonians difficult for them to accept. Although Jews, Germans and Swedes, owing to their cultural autonomy, successfully maintained themselves as ethnic groups in the years between the two World Wars, most left Estonia during World War II. As a result, only one fifth of Estonian Germans and Jews represent a minority of local origin. The rest came to Estonia seeking better opportunities for emigration to the West, as well as being in fear of pogroms in Russia. The 300 coastal Swedes have been assimilated to the Estonians, as were some ethnic Finns, who shifted language from Finnish to Estonian.

Attitudes of non-Estonians

The Estonian-based schools were required to teach Russian as a "second native language", whereas the curricula of the Russian-based schools contained little practical Estonian and no Estonian history or geography whatsoever. Due to the unbalanced education system, two separate communities developed, whose mutual understanding was deficient both linguistically and culturally. Both communities can be classified into several subgroups which differ from each other on two basic parameters: their attitudes, firstly, to Estonian independence, and secondly, to the primary position of the Estonian language on Estonian territory. According to a gallup survey conducted by D. Mihhailov in 1989, the Russian-speaking population can be divided into three main groups:

1. "Internationalists", representing ideological views of the past based on Communism, and numbering between 160,000 and 170,000. They were predominately female, with little formal education, and their cultural needs were met adequately by socialist culture. The main characteristics of this group were an imperial turn of mind (pro-totalitarian Soviet Union), a totally negative attitude to other languages, ethnicities and cultures and to the national independence of Estonia. They were determined to ensure that Estonia remained part of the Soviet Union under the leadership of the Communist Party.

2. Another faction, equal in size to the "internationalists", was a group who cherished their own as well as Estonian culture, ethnicity, language, and the idea of Estonian independence. This group could be subdivided into the indigenous Russians of Estonia on the one hand, who avoided participation in inter-ethnic conflicts and led a settled life, and the democratically-minded ethnic groups (including Russians) on the other who, in their effort to maintain their own cultures, appreciate the Estonians' aspirations and problems.

3. The third group, according to D. Mihhailov, comprised approximately one-half of the non-Estonians. These people were characterized first and foremost by their rootlessness, their lack of interest even in their own culture, language and ethnicity, and complete indifference to the indigenous population.Their main motives seemed to be economic. This group would accept Estonian national independence if it did not interfere with their economic opportunities. This group's attitude towards Estonian was largely negative because they were unable to speak it. To them, a requirement to know the local language suggested discrimination against their economic interests.

This tallies with the opinion data obtained by K. Haav in 1986, according to which four-fifths of non-Estonians in Estonia identified themselves with Soviet people, and not with any particular ethnic group. As the 1989 census showed, the main problem was the abnormal pattern of immigration. Most non-Estonians are first-generation immigrants with socialization outside Estonia. Among people aged 45, the percentage is 95, among those aged 20 it is 80%. Secondly, the second-generation immigrants do not follow the model of the local population. Due to the major pressure of russification, the second-generation immigrants shift to the Russian language. Thirdly, contacts between immigrants and the Estonian population are minimal (different workplaces, cultural habits, and few mixed marriages). Though immigration was brought under control by the Law on Immigration of 1990, the legacy of earlier immigration will be durable and will cause tensions and hinder integration.

Linguistic policy in education

During the post-war period, Estonian as a "language with no future" was discriminated against in the curriculum, not only in Russian schools, but also in Estonian educational institutions. Even so, F. Eisen managed as Minister of Education to retain the obligatory status of the Estonian language and literature in Estonian schools. This was achieved by prolonging the duration of the secondary education given in the Estonian-based "national" schools by one year as compared to Russian-based schools. For other linguistic groups, using one's native language in education was not allowed, and their education was entirely in Russian.

Estonia suffered from a new surge of russification in connection with Decree No 835, issued by the USSR Council of Ministers on 13 October 1978. The document prescribed a considerable enhancement of the quantity as well as quality of Russian taught in the "national schools" at the expense of other subjects. This decree was followed by an upsurge in russifying activities in Estonia. The leaders of the Estonian Communist Party who had been dictating the rules to Estonia in every sphere of life, and the Minister of Education, were replaced by those more fluent in Russian. The new wave of russification was based on a secret decree of the Bureau of the Central Committee of the Estonian CP, of 19 December 1978 (Protocol 105, Article 1). That document legalized the priority of Russian over Estonian, declaring Russian the only means of active participation in social life, while teachers were obliged to "teach their pupils to love the Russian language".

This was followed by Decree No 3, issued by the ESSR Council of Ministers on 8 January 1979, and Orders 367-k (on the teaching of Russian at kindergartens) and 713-k (on the further improvement of Russian teaching). According to these documents, the teaching of Russian received a considerable amount of additional material support that enabled the authorities to raise the salaries of Russian language teachers, and to reduce the number of students in the Russian language classes by dividing them into parallel groups. Publications promoting Russian such as the new Russian methods journal *"Russkij jazyk v èstonskoje škole"* ("The Russian Language in Estonian Schools") as well as propagandist writings eulogizing the Russian language (as Lenin's mother tongue and a language studied with great interest by Marx and Engels) emerged. A new study programme was adopted that contained additional restrictions on the use and teaching of the Estonian language (adopted by the Council of the ESSR Ministry of Education on April 28, 1983). This document presented the 5-year programme for the preferential teaching of Russian in Estonian schools.

If one recalls that besides these influences there was also an almost impenetrable information barrier — propaganda for Soviet life and the iron curtain policy — one can perhaps visualize the situation in Estonia in the mid-1980s.

Perestroika in Estonia

With the exhaustion of the potential of central planning, the arms race and the resulting economic crisis, the leader of the Soviet Union began to realize that a radical political change was necessary. This in its turn required an enhancement of the role of individual judgement. The resultant policy, associated with Gorbachev and the watch-words perestroika and glasnost', created a democratic means for ending the discrimination of Estonians in their homeland. This process of democratization evolved from the acceleration of the all-Union economic crisis and took two main directions, namely the restitution of the national sovereignty of Estonia, and the restoration of the right of existence for the languages and cultures of Estonians and other discriminated ethnic groups.

The two corresponding laws were the Declaration of Sovereignty and the Language Law. The Supreme Council of the Estonian SSR passed the Declaration of Sovereignty on 16 November 1988, declaring the supremacy of Estonian laws over Soviet ones. The proclamation of Estonian as the official state language in Estonia, and its legalisation as such by a corresponding Constitutional amendment, was passed by the Supreme Council on 6 December 1988.

The Language Law was passed on 18 January 1989. The Language Law was a provisional one in its content, matching the needs of the transformational process under way in Estonia. Though it described Estonian as the sole official language, due to political expediency as well as the reality of most of the Soviet-period immigrants not bothering to acquaint themselves with Estonian culture and language, the main principle was based on a requirement of Estonian-Russian bilinguality, which required that holders of certain jobs had proficiency in both Estonian and Russian (in most cases 800 words were sufficient). To reach the required level a 4-year delay was introduced in the law, so that it became effective from 1st February 1993.

In order to coordinate the teaching of Estonian to Russian children, a special office, the Estonian Language Centre, was established on 13 March 1989. A Language Protection Committee was also formed at the collective state organ, the Presidium of the Supreme Council. The task of this Committee was to supervise the execution of the law, but because it functioned as an advisory body only, the Committee's suggestions were largely ignored.

These two acts marked the turning point not only in Estonia, but in the whole of the Soviet Union, igniting the dissemination process so that similar laws were introduced in other republics too, thus decentralizing power and crushing ideological postulates. The only powers left in the hands of the central government of Moscow were the military forces, the KGB, and rouble printshops, all of which were put to use.

The 1990 elections marked the first time in 50 years that Estonians were able to participate in a democratic election, and the result was a change in governmental policy. Even though many Communists and ex-Communists were elected, the majority of the new Supreme Council were pro-Estonian. The Communist Party lost nearly all the legal and executive channels through which it had formerly exercised power over high-level decision-making. The new government followed a more Estonian orientation in its policy. Membership of the discredited party collapsed, and the party split into two, a Russian-speaking imperial-minded CP, and the Estonian-speaking CP with a vaguely "leftist" ideological platform.

Along with the advance of democratic tendencies in Estonian society, the Russian-speaking CP in Estonia ceased to exist among Estonians, but retained its position in the Soviet Army, the KGB, and in the Special Divisions of the Ministry of the Interior. These collaborated with the CP local branch in committing "licence to kill" acts of violence in Estonia, as in the other Baltic states, with the aim of creating an atmosphere of insecurity. These military operations were accompanied by accusations of linguistic and ethnic discrimination against the Russian-speaking population, the sole aim of which was to legitimate their actions against the public.

Several additional pro-Estonian steps were taken, the legalization of the national colours, the restoration of the name of the Republic of Estonia, the declaration of Estonia as being in a period of transition to independence (restitutio ad integrum), and the establishment of immigration quotas. A number of measures were taken in order to restore the Estonian language to its rightful status. In August 1990 the Estonian Government decided to repeal all acts which discriminated against the use of Estonian, and to create a body empowered to supervise the implementation of the Language Law. On 23 November 1990 the National Language Board was established. It is the main body responsible for the implementation of language planning in Estonia, and monitoring the use of Estonian, the official language, as a native language and second language, and also supporting and regulating minority language use among the adult population. Its work is based on the relevant articles of the Constitution, the Language Law, the Law on Education and the Draft Law on Cultural Autonomy as well as on the European Charter on Minority and Regional Languages. The primary functions of the Board are the elaboration of language policy and language planning strategies, including the organization, supervision, and analysis of the implementation of the Language Law, the improvement of language teaching methods, the supervision of normative terminological and onomastic work, and the pursuit of sociolinguistic studies. Due to the favourable political climate, a change has taken place in the consciousness of Estonians, the socio-psychological status of Estonian has risen, and its use has extended in various functional domains.

The linguistic situation in liberated Estonia

After the failure of the August 1991 coup in Moscow and the restitution of Estonian independence after more than 50 years of occupation, the Estonian Government has introduced its normalization programme to overcome deep deformations in the social structure in which two virtually separate communities have entirely different interests. The situation was particularly difficult for Russian-speaking immigrants because the status of their language among Estonians dropped dramatically, state borders between their families and relatives arose, and there was insecurity about the future. Reactions vary, as does governmental policy. It is based on three main principles. Firstly, financial and know-how assistance to those wanting to repatriate, which, according to opinion polls, applies to up to

15% of non-Estonians. Secondly, governmental funding for activities promoting integration, such as Estonian language learning, which 2/3 of the non-Estonian population has shown interest in. Thirdly, financial help for minorities in order to preserve their language and culture.

Repatriation is becoming increasingly popular. The factors hindering it are Russia's indifference, in view of the flow of refugees from Central Asia, and the devastating economic situation in the CIS countries.

Figures for population movement indicate substantiallly more emigrating than immigrating, in 1990: 4000, in 1991: 8000, in 1992: 35,000, in 1993: 35,000 – 40,000. The number of those leaving for their homeland, like Russians going to Russia and Ukrainians to Ukraine, has increased, especially those searching for their roots and national identity. The number has particularly increased among Ukrainians and Byelorussians, due to the disputes between the Ukrainians and Russians mentioned earlier. As Ukrainian law stipulates residence in Ukraine as a requirement for citizenship, many Ukrainians are leaving Estonia for Ukraine. Others are organizing Ukrainian language courses, radio programmes, cultural societies and schools. The Russians are effectively opposing this on the grounds that these are nationalistic activities which are breaking up Slavic unity (assumedly based on the Russian language). This modified notion of the Slavic unity of the Soviet people is retrograde and reactionary, communist-based, anti-Jeltsin, and atheist. The idea of Slavic unity is popular among middle-class Russian-speaking non-Estonians (Russians, Ukrainians, Byelorussians, Jews, Tartars and others) with weak or nonexistent ethnic roots, or who may be ashamed of persecution in the past of their ethnic group. It is also popular among the working class, although here the ideals of the former Soviet Union are more strongly adhered to.

Estonian-Russian areas of conflict

As Estonian legal power was restored after the occupation, de jure as well as de facto, Estonia could not be regarded as a new state. Several legal consequences followed from this, such as reaffirmation of the Law on Citizenship, the validity of the Tartu Peace Treaty between Estonia and Russia of 1920, and the establishment of the inter-state boundary. The 1938 Law on Citizenship was the most liberal in Europe at the time of its adoption. It established the jus sanguinis principle by which citizenship is passed automatically to descendants. Others could obtain it through a naturalisation process, with a residence requirement of $2+1$

years and basic proficiency in Estonian. Under the Law on the Estonian Language Requirements for Applicants for Citizenship, one must

1) have a listening comprehension of everyday texts, such as news broadcasts, announcements and statements;
2) be able to hold a conversation on given topic, such as the family, work, leisure activities and shopping. Some topics require a basic knowledge of Estonian geography, important historical events, culture, national holidays and national symbols;
3) read and provide a short summary of announcements, news reports, newspaper articles, regulations, etc.;
4) be able to complete simple written exercises, such as filling out personal applications, composing a curriculum vitae, writing an address on an envelope, writing an application for study or employment, writing a letter of authorization and filling out standard forms.

It also provides for special examination guidelines for persons born before January 1, 1930, and persons who are considered to be permanently disabled or who are unable to complete an examination in the usual way due to their disability. Persons born prior to 1930 are exempt from the written requirements, they are however required to converse on topics such as the family, work, leisure activities, shopping, places in Estonia and Estonian history, culture and national symbols. Specific guidelines for the disabled vary, taking into consideration the different forms of disability (i. e. hearing, visual, speech impairment). Graduates of public secondary schools, who have completed a final Estonian language examination in accordance with standards established by the Ministry of Culture and Education may apply for citizenship by naturalization without completing a further examination. The current Estonian language curriculum in Russian-language schools, as approved by the Ministry of Culture and Education, fully covers the Estonian language requirements established for citizenship applicants.

These measures were not appreciated by Russia, as they conflicted with the Karaganov doctrine. The Estonian policy meant that immigrants, in order to obtain citizenship, had to go through a naturalisation process instead of having it by virtue of residing in Estonia, though such a principle would violate the IVth Geneva Convention, which states in Article 49:

"Individual or mass forcible transfers, as well as deportations of protected persons from occupied territory to the territory of the

Occupying Power or to that of any other Country, occupied or not, are prohibited, regardless of their motive. [...] The Occupying Power shall not deport or transfer parts of its own civilian population into the territory it occupies".

The problem arose because the half-million immigrant community lost its citizenship with the disintegration of the Soviet Union. The successor of the USSR, the CIS, decided to change the naturalization laws from jus sanguinis to jus soli, thus depriving citizens of the former Soviet Union of their previous citizenship and leaving them stranded. Most countries have a marginal number of these people permanently residing on their territories and consider them Russian citizens unless otherwise proved. Any attempt to declare them "stateless" and thus prolong their residence must face the prospect of imminent extradiction. This solution is politically unsuitable for countries which are neighbours of Russia and have significant Russian immigrant communities, like the Baltic States. Furthermore these people are used as political pawns by Russia, which redefines their status as immigrant rather than minority, thus ignoring the niceties of international law. To protect the "discriminated minority", the presence of Russian troops is seen as being essential.

There have been numerous human rights missions to Estonia, 15 since the restitution of independence, none of which have found any gross or systematic violations of human rights. These missions have made many valuable suggestions concerning linguistic normalization, and their efforts are much appreciated by the Estonian authorities.

Māori language rights in New Zealand

Tīmoti S. Kāretu

As part of its promotion and publicity campaign in 1988 Te Taura Whiri I Te Reo Māori, the Māori Language Commission, issued a poster which featured a photograph of an ancestor Pūkakī and his twin sons with the following caption beneath

"Tōku reo, tōku ohooho
Tōku reo, tōku māpihi maurea
Tōku reo, tōku whakakai marihi.[1]

Language is the key to understanding".

The expression "Tōku reo ..." had been coined two years previously as a catchphrase for Māori Language Week and because of its message, its concision and its lyrical beauty I considered it worthy of retention. Hence its inclusion in the poster.

New Zealand must be one of the few countries in the world where the phrase "Language is the key to understanding" is meaningless and uncomprehended and where linguistic ignorance and arrogance are rife, thriving and rampant. As Dr. Pawley of the University of Auckland said in his paper entitled On The Place of Māori in New Zealand Life: Present and Future, " ... New Zealanders probably have less respect for culture and tradition than almost any other nation − the pioneering peasant mentality still dominates here. If something is no use we have no time for it. And most of the electorate have no use for Māori".

Since 1 August, 1987 when Māori became an official language of Aotearoa, there has been opposition to its active promotion, to its use in the media and its use in the public place. The opposition is not new, it is just less covert and subtle.

When the Commission first took up residence in its present premises there was a negative reaction to Te Taura Whiri I Te Reo Māori being used on the directory on the ground floor. As more notices in Māori and English were put in place the negative reaction grew but as time passes the verbal reactions have dissipated but not the attitude.

The Commission in its endeavours to employ a bilingual, bicultural secretary wished to insert an appropriate advertisement for such a person in the local media, that is "The Dominion" and "The Evening Post", the morning and evening papers of Wellington, in Māori only. In his letter declining our request Mr B. E. Geale, Joint Classified Advertising Manager (Sales) said,

> ".. it is our company policy that all classified advertisements published in languages other than english [sic] should be accompanied by the english [sic] translation so as to give all our readers an opportunity to understand what is being printed".

We were willing to supply a translation for the edification and enlightenment of the staff concerned but did not wish to include it in the advertisement. My point was that I wished to see how many applicants could understand the advertisement, thus giving me some initial indication of the linguistic competence of the applicant. Those having to read it in English would obviously be unsuitable and ineligible and I doubt that such a position would be of interest to the wider reading public of the newspapers concerned. Furthermore, it did not preclude non-Māori with the requisite aptitudes sought from applying. It is interesting to note that the "N. Z. Herald", the morning newspaper of Auckland, accepted the advertisement without hindrance or restriction and while the "Evening Post" remains entrenched in its attitude, it in fact published an advertisement in Māori only in its edition of 14 March 1989.

The Chief Executive of the Commission and I were in a shop in Wellington completing the formalities on a purchase and were conducting a private conversation in Māori as we always do. An objection to our conversation was raised by an assistant who considered it "rude" because she could not understand. Our reaction was swift and as a consequence we received an apology from the Manager who informed us that the said assistant had been duly spoken to. However, that reaction is not an isolated one for as Dr. Pawley states (1988),

> The monoculturalism of New Zealanders can reach extraordinary heights. Kiwis are simply not used to hearing other languages spoken around them. A friend born overseas tells stories of Kiwi office mates who get rattled when visitors come in and converse with her in their mother tongue — who are rattled even when she speaks over the phone in another language. Passengers in buses become uneasy when they hear the sounds of foreign languages

buzzing around them. Some friends, otherwise kindly and liberal folk, are even disturbed by the sound of the Māori news on radio. They can't understand it and it is somehow threatening. Monolingual New Zealanders expect everyone to accommodate by talking English in front of them.

A group calling itself "One New Zealand" wants the word Pākehā, the Māori word for a white person, legally expunged from the vocabulary of New Zealand and accepts that while there are people of Māori descent there are no Māori, only New Zealanders. Furthermore, this group wishes all programmes in the Māori language on television to be captioned. I oppose captions, an unnecessary expense but also because an essential language service is, again, forced to compromise. If people wish to know what is being said then learn the language.

"Te Karere," a news service in Māori, is broadcast on television for 10 minutes every evening at 5.15pm from Monday to Friday. If, however, there are issues more important to the general public of Aotearoa such as a test cricket series between New Zealand and Sri Lanka then the Māori news service is cancelled on those particular days. In the eyes of those who hold the economic and political power it is a very dispensable service.

I doubt, very strongly, that speakers of Māori will desist from including the word Pākehā in their conversation when referring to the fair skinned majority of Aotearoa nor do I see Māori not referring to themselves as Māori. Certainly, this Māori will continue to use both words in contexts where he deems them appropriate, in spite of the rantings of both "One New Zealand" and the more recently formed Kiwi United society.

Te Taura Whiri i te Reo Māori has also been the recipient of anonymous letters. The following is from "Dismayed Citizen" dated 2-3-1989:

Dear Sir,
Your article (enclosed) as per *N. Z. Womans Weekly* causes concern as regards language in New Zealand.
We are predominantly an Anglo Saxon culture with a Westminster style of government and have English as the one and only official language of Aotearoa.
According to your policies we should be trying to accommodate a language that:
1) Is dead, (not used officially since 1840)
2) Has no alphabet or written Records
3) Only useful to 300,000 odd New Zealanders

4) Of no use whatsoever internationally
As an alternative language educational systems should be looking at French, German, Japanese, all of which (and including English) are more intelligent languages.
Ethnic minorities including Māori are supposed to fit in to the English system and "westernise" themselves.
Yours faithfully[2]

To exemplify the racism endemic in Aotearoa many more examples could be cited and while some might consider these circumstances to be isolated, they are symptomatic of the thinking of the majority of New Zealand.

A recent cause célèbre regarding the language was the Ngāi Tamarā-waho affair, the case in which documents filed in Māori were refused by the Registrar of the Tauranga District Court (16 October 1988).

While there was no onus on his part to accept the document, one had hoped that there might be some modicum of humanity and political astuteness on the court's part. However, such was not to be and a translation had to be supplied by the petitioners despite the court's access to interpreters.

Te Taura Whiri as a consequence has recommended, as an extension to the present legislation, that:

(a) any person presenting evidence in Māori be responded to in Māori;
(b) that all evidence given in Māori be recorded in Māori;
(c) that documents filed in Māori be accepted by the court.

Māori language rights are only activated in the official domain when some breach of the law has been perpetrated. Such is the irony of the Māori language situation as it pertains in New Zealand in 1991.

The arrogant assumption is that all should speak English on all occasions and yet as Dr. Tāmati Reedy says in his report, *Developing an Official Māori Language Policy for Government* (1985: 5)," The fact that English is now the only working language for the vast bulk of Māoridom has not brought about the societal unity promised by the anti-Māori language policies of the past 150 years."

I am convinced that language imposition, the criticism levelled by those non-Māori against the language and things Māori in the school curriculum, will not bring unity but greater division. It is not our intention to impose our language on others for we know what it is like to have a language imposed on us and as a consequence of that measure to see our own language in decline. Our philosophy is to make our language available to those who so desire.

One need not be a seer nor a genius to deduce that despite almost 200 years of repression and suppression, both covert and overt, the Māori language has survived, albeit with only 50–75,000 who could truly be said to be native speakers, and a further 120,000 or so who are termed passive speakers. That says much for the resilience of both the language and its speakers, to have withstood the continued onslaught of the ignorant, the arrogant and the racist.

Mere survival, however, is not sufficient to ensure the language's continued survival into the millenia to come. Policies in place at present need to be streamlined, strengthened and improved to guarantee that the students involved emerge with a good command of quality language. I do not deny that language in its natural state changes but unnatural change into a meaningless and slovenly language should be abhorred and averted.

If we consider that there is at present a *native* speaking population of approximately 50–75,000 then it can be said there are, at least, 300,000 or so who are not. Most native speakers are now 45 plus. Second language learners are the young ones learning the language in universities, in schools. Children in Kōhanga Reo[3] number over 13,000 but we still do not know how good their command is. An evaluation is proposed and is being organised at the moment.

Native speakers are dying off at an alarming rate and are being replaced by *second language learners in most instances.*

As second language learners begin to outnumber the native speaking population then the language will begin to change. A battle is already ensuring our correct usage in certain instances but, to date, the battle is being won by native speakers. One can but wonder what the language will be like in 2091!

Rhetoric and resources per se will not guarantee the survival of the language. What is required is a commitment and that I do not see despite Kōhanga Reo, Te Ātārangi, Kura Kaupapa Māori, (Māori language immersion schools of which there are 15 in 1991) bilingual schools, universities, polytechnics and other institutions that are all involved in the teaching of the language. There needs to be a *total commitment on the part of Māori speakers. We have compromised far too long.*

The Māori population more than any other needs to commit itself to the proposition that the language deserves to be retained, maintained and sustained. Once having made that commitment, to ensure that English is no longer employed in predominantly Māori situations but that Māori be spoken on all those occasions. The continued use of English by Māori people, particularly speakers of Māori, among themselves, is to belittle the Māori language itself and to guarantee its extinction.

Language is difficult, hence the concentration on the comparatively less demanding aspects of dance, song, carving and weaving. These skills can be acquired without language but often the knowledge is perfunctory, but these are the skills cited by some as being those which make one Māori.

It is evident from the reaction to Māori language promotion that the bulk of New Zealand cares little whether Māori survives or not. The reactions rather indicate that the preference would be for Māori to disappear altogether but as Dr Reedy states (1985: 5),

> Māoridom today appears to be more bent on remaining Māori despite the poor self-image that post-European history has bestowed on the label "Māori". Clearly, Māori language is being seen by many as a rallying point for a restructuring and piecing together of a much broken and damaged people. It serves to restore an identity for people who see themselves as Māori and want to be recognised as such!

What is ironic is that the same people who would wish Māori were not here use things Māori with which to identify once away from these shores. The Olympic team in Seoul performed its version of the haka[4] as do the All Blacks, New Zealand's premier rugby football team. Schools which pay scant attention to things Māori have a school haka, more often than not a bowdlerised, meaningless form of "Ka Mate", "Utaina" and "Tau Ka Tau", all well-known haka. The sensitivity to Māori people is nil and the message of the haka ignored, a further index of the attitude of most of New Zealand to the culture and language of the Māori.

Legislation will not guarantee the learning of Māori by the majority of New Zealand nor is it sought, contemplated or envisaged. What is sought is a greater tolerance of the right of things Māori to exist, to be nurtured and to grow, the most important of these being the language, for it is the very essence of all things Māori. Without it, all else becomes meaningless and pointless.

The Māori population needs to be convinced of this and then to make it a reality, for despite the intermingling of the two main cultures, Māori and Pākehā, for over 200 years I doubt that there would be 100 Pākehā who are fluent in Māori. To me, no more need be said regarding their attitude to the language.

Economic and social demands have necessitated the Māori's becoming bilingual and bicultural, therein lies the salient difference. There is no economic pressure to become Māori speaking but I would point out the social aspects of doing so are overwhelming. Was it not said on 6 February, 1840, the day the Treaty of Waitangi was signed, "We are one people," meaning that we should appreciate and accept each other for what we are? Most pertinent to that appreciation is the knowledge of each other's language, the key to each other's culture. Since contact it has been a very one-sided affair.

People lament the state of race relations but one can scarcely feign outrage or amazement at the reaction of Māori to the disparaging and vilifying remarks about them and their language.

Like any language, Māori will have to be able to accommodate concepts and ideas that are foreign to the culture. The language did that readily upon initial contact and is continuing to do so, for therein lies its relevance to the present generations whose world it needs to be able to describe. Its more esoteric and classical aspects can be learnt and appreciated at the appropriate stage of development.

I said in a television interview that 50 years from now the language would be struggling to survive if commitment to it were not made. I abide by that remark but what is needed in addition to commitment is a climate that is not blindly hostile and antagonistic but rather one in which those who wish may participate in the learning and use of the Māori language.

No other country in the world can ensure the survival of the Māori language nor guarantee it its place in the sun. It must survive and be meaningful in its own context − not just be seen to be so but be allowed to do so.

1 August, 1987 is an important date in the annals of Aotearoa history for it was on that date that the government declared Māori "an official language" of Aotearoa.

The legislation, the Māori Language Act, 1987, not only declared Māori to be an official language but it also established the Māori Language Commission which is charged to:

(a) Conduct, hold, or attend all such inquiries, hearings, or meetings as the Commission thinks desirable to enable it to determine the views and wishes of the Māori community in relation to the promotion and use of the Māori language; and

(b) Undertake or commission research into the use of the Māori language; and

(c) Consult with and receive reports from Government Departments and other bodies on the use of Māori language in the course of the conduct of the business of those Departments or other bodies, whether by their staff or by people with whom they have official dealings; and

(d) Publish information relating to the use of the Māori language; and

(e) Report to the Minister on any matter relating to the Māori language that the Commission considers should be drawn to the Minister's attention.

I consider the decision by the former Labour Government, defeated in the General Elections of 1990, to have been momentous and far-sighted for it gave political recognition to the indigenous language of Aotearoa. There are many of us who feel the legislation did not go far enough but there are far more who believe the government, just by its acknowledgement of the other language of Aotearoa in its statutes, went too far.

The Māori language will continue to be a political issue. The Māori however is not prepared to see the language languish but will persist until the political pundits are prepared to consider seriously the findings of the Waitangi Tribunal Relating to Te Reo Māori and A Claim Lodged to Hon. K. T. Wētere, Minister of Māori Affairs, 29 April, 1986, page 71 of which states:

RECOMMENDATIONS

We recommend to THE MINISTER OF MĀORI AFFAIRS in each case and:

1. TO THE RIGHT HONOURABLE, THE PRIME MINISTER

that legislation be introduced enabling any person who wishes to do so to use the Māori language in all Courts of law and in any dealings with Government Departments, local authorities and other public bodies (refer para. 8. 2. 8).

2. TO THE HONOURABLE, THE MINISTER OF INTERNAL AFFAIRS

that a supervising body be established by statute to supervise and foster the use of the Māori language (refer para. 8. 2. 8).

3. TO THE HONOURABLE, THE MINISTER OF EDUCATION

that an enquiry be instituted forthwith into the way Māori children are educated including particular reference to the changes in current departmental policies which may be necessary to ensure that all children who wish to learn Māori should be able to do so from an early stage in the educational process in circumstances most beneficial to them and with financial support from the State (refer para. 6. 3. 7)

4. TO THE HONOURABLE, THE MINISTER OF BROADCASTING that in the formulation of broadcasting policy regard be had to this Finding that the Treaty of Waitangi obliges the Crown to recognise and protect the Māori language, and that the Broadcasting Act 1976 (Sec. 20) enables this to be done so far as broadcasting is concerned (refer para 7. 1. 9).

5. TO THE HONOURABLE, THE MINISTER IN CHARGE OF STATE SERVICES
that amendments be made to the State Services Act 1962 and the State Services Conditions of Employment Act 1977 to make provision for bilingualism in Māori and in English to be a prerequisite for appointment to such positions as the State Services Commission deems necessary or desirable (refer para 9. 1. 4).[5]

The former Minister of Māori Affairs trod warily and the present incumbent (Hon.Winston Peters) has yet to state his policy with regard to the language, although he has stated that the Māori Language Commission will continue to exist.

Whakataukī, proverbs, were often used to encapsulate a thought and the following would seem to me to be appropriate,

Mānuka takoto, kawea ake.
(The challenge has been issued, take it up.)

It is apposite for both the Māori population and retainers of political power. Without the concerted efforts of both these ends of the spectrum, the Māori language has little hope of surviving into the next millennium.[6]

Notes

1. "My language, my valued possession
   My language, my object of affection
   My language, my precious adornment"
2. Māori can be comprehended readily by speakers of Hawaiian, Tahitian, Cook Island Māori, Rapanui (Easter Island) and Wallisian. Though speakers of Māori can comprehend what is being said by speakers of Samoan, Tongan, Tokelauan and Niuean, greater concentration is required.
3. Te Kōhanga Reo as a movement commenced in 1982 at the Wānanga Whakatauira where elders asserted that the time had come for Māoridom to take control of the future destiny of the Māori language and to plan for its survival.

In response, the former Department of Māori Affairs promoted Te Kōhanga Reo. The kaupapa, in general terms, is one based on a programme of total immersion in Māori language and values with the aim to educate for life under the directorship of the Kaumātua and the application of the life principles of the Māori. At present there are over 13,000 children enrolled in 710 Kōhanga Reo throughout the country with a present budget from the Government of approximately 9;37,000,000. The movement is going from strength to strength and augurs well for the future of the Māori language.

4. Haka — a vigorous posture dance where males are to the fore.

5. Dated at Wellington in 1986 and signed by E. T. Durie (Chief Judge, Chairman), Sir Graham Latimer (Member) and P. B. Temm (QC, Member)

6. The final section of the Appendix to this volume reproduces the arguments used to counter resistance to the official recognition of te reo Māori, from the report of the Waitangi Tribunal.

The Sámi Language Act

Ole Henrik Magga

Introduction

In October 1990 the Norwegian Parliament took a series of legislative steps to strengthen the official use of the Sámi language in Norway. Together these measures are widely referred to as the Sámi Language Act, a label I shall use for ease of reference. In reality the regulations in question involved changes in three laws, primarily the law on the Sámi Assembly (Parliament), and also laws on education and on courts of law.[1]

During a political crisis in 1980, the Norwegian Government was obliged to establish two investigatory commissions to examine the Sámi people's cultural and legal position in Norway and to make recommendations on future policy. The events that led to this decision were vigorous protests against the Alta River hydro-electric dam project[2] and more general protests against Norwegian policies towards the Sámi population. The Sámi Rights Commission, chaired by Carsten Smith, now presiding judge of the Norwegian Supreme Court, presented its first report and recommendations in 1984. This resulted in the establishment of the Sámi Parliament and the passing of a constitutional amendment with the following wording:

> It is incumbent on the governmental authorities to take necessary steps to enable the Sámi population to safeguard and develop their langue, their culture and their social life.

A draft Sámi Language Act was prepared by the Culture Commission (NOU 1985:14, chapter 8), which submitted three reports. The government has closely cooperated with the Sámi Parliament in drafting the provisions of the Language Act, for enforcement from March 1 1992.

The enactment of these laws has radically changed the principles underlying Norwegian policy towards the Sámi people. In addition, Norway has adopted a broad interpretation of international standards for the protection of minorities. Thus article 27 of the International

Covenant on Civil and Political Rights is understood as imposing an obligation to discriminate positively in favour of the Sámi minority. This means that the authorities shall not merely legislate against the discrimination of Sámi language and culture. The state shall take positive steps to make it possible for the Sámi people to survive as a people. The Ministry of Justice declared this explicitly in 1987.

I shall present the content of the Sámi Language Act and comment on its practical consequences. But before doing so, a few words about the historical background of the Sámi people's situation in Norway may be not quite out of place.

Earlier Norwegian state policy towards the Sámi

When a Canadian lawyer, Professor Douglas Sanders, was asked to provide the Norwegian Supreme Court with an expert opinion on the relationship between the Sámi nation and the Norwegian state, he declared (Sanders 1981): "The relationship between the Norwegian State and the Sámi people is colonial in its origins". Exactly the same is true in the other Nordic states, and in Russia/the Soviet Union. Sámi land was absorbed and divided up by the Nordic states and Russia in a historical process which began with trading, plunder and missionary expeditions. The borders were drawn up in 1751 and 1826, after which the states installed themselves as private owners of all land and water. The Norwegian state launched a systematic war against Sámi culture and language for 100 years, while the other states denied the existence of the Sámi as a people.

Prior to 1700, Norwegian state policy towards the Sámi was unsystematic. Between 1710 and 1720, the "Sámi mission" was organized, and its first leader, Thomas von Westen, strongly advocated the use of the Sámi language in education and the church. After his death, attitudes to the Sámi language were more hostile. This changed again in the 1820s, when a parson, N. V. Stockfleth, started work among the Sámi. Many books were printed and teachers trained. But unfortunately new winds soon swept over the fjords and mountains in Sámi land. From 1850 onwards there was a cold winter for the Sámi language, lasting for a century. This was the time when the young Norwegian state was establishing itself and the true Norwegian nationalist spirit could not bear those "foreigners" (the Sámis and Kvens, i. e. immigrants from Finland). All means were taken into use for the purpose of "Norwegianisation".

Teachers were paid a bonus for good results in this national task. Sámis were not allowed to buy land unless they started to use Norwegian in their homes and learned to write the language. The Sámi resistance was strong initially, but little by little almost all doubt was swept aside: the Norwegian language and culture should prosper in Sámi land and the Sámi language should die.

Then the War came to Norway in 1940, and Norwegians had their own experience of foreign rule, also in the cultural field. After World War II Norway declared that a new course would be followed in the policies towards the Sámi population. The old discriminatory laws were repealed. Little by little a new consciousness had grown among Sámis. Gradually the Sámi organizations in Norway, Finland and Sweden managed to influence government policies so much that the Sámi gained some official recognition. The breakthrough came in Finland, where an elected Sámi Assembly was established in 1973. In Norway things went more slowly. The 1960s and 1970s produced a stream of resolutions, but nothing decisive happened, although the Sámi language was taken into use in primary schools on an experimental basis in 1967. Then came the Alta clash. Within a few years four major reports were submitted to the Government outlining proposals for a principled basis for an official Sámi policy. The Sámi Parliament was opened by the King in 1989. While the Sámi Culture Commission has concluded its work, the Sámi Rights Commission is still at work on the land and water questions.

The Sámi language in Norway

The majority of speakers of the Sámi language live in Norway. Norway has therefore a special responsibility for the future of the Sámi language. Here we find three of the main dialects of Sámi, North, Lule, and South.[3] The northern dialect is the most widespread geographically and has the most numerous speakers. It is also the dialect that has been used most in books and newpapers. There are no precise figures for the Sámi population or for speakers of Sámi, because of the absence of reliable data. Since 1890 the Sámi population has been put at around 20,000. The latest census, in 1970, covered only the 3 northernmost counties of the country (Finnmark, Troms, Nordland). The report summing up the census concluded: "There are probably in Norway some 40,000 persons whose life is in one way or another affected by their Lappish (i. e. Sámi) ancestry" (Aubert 1978: 118). An informed guess at the number of Sámi speakers in Norway is roughly 25,000. Much depends on what is meant by "a Sámi speaker", as the language competence in Sámi of such bilingual speakers ranges from total mastery to only "kitchen Sámi" with an elementary vocabulary.

Since 1967 Sámi has been taught in primary schools. It is also currently both used as a medium and taught as a subject in secondary schools and at 2 universities. Textbooks have been printed, and since the early 1970s 5 – 10 literary books have been published each year. There are 2 newspapers. Regional radio services are in Sámi for a little more than 1 hour daily. Several local authorities have declared that they will use Sámi more in their services. Several laws and information leaflets on health and social welfare have been translated. The Sámi languge has thus been gaining ground for several years.

Hitherto the only references in Norwegian law to the Sámi language have been in the Primary and Lower Secondary Education Act and in the Upper Secondary Education Act. Whenever Sámi has been used for official purposes, this has been entirely at the discretion of the body in question. Individual courts could, under a provision in the Courts Acts, which states that any person who does not understand Norwegian is entitled to an intepreter, decide on the admissibility of Sámi.

The rationale for the legislation

The committee set up to investigate Sámi questions as long ago as in 1956 declared in its 1959 report that the maintenance and development of the Sámi language was decisive for the future of the Sámi people. The same principles lay behind the Sámi Culture Commission's reasons for recommending the enactment of a Sámi Language Law. The parliamentary committee which drafted the bill has stressed several times that language is such a central element in Sámi culture that the existence of the Sámi as a people depends on the maintenance and development of the language. The Parliament has endorsed this principle. The rationale for the legislation is therefore not merely practical needs, such as that individuals must be able to make themselves understood in courts and public offices. Objections from various sides, and in particular from the legal system and the police, were considered insubstantial when compared to the overall goal of cultural preservation and development.

In addition regulations were obviously required to meet practical needs in several areas of social life. The interests of Sámi speakers have been treated in a cavalier way in many domains. The most bizarre arguments have been used in order to justify a refusal to provide services in Sámi. The need to leave this dark period behind was abundantly clear to anyone with the slightest interest in the state granting a degree of equality of treatment to its citizens.

The content of the legislation

Purpose

The purpose of the Sámi Act, as stated in its preamble, is to make it possible for the Sámi people in Norway to safeguard and develop their language, culture and way of life. An additional paragraph in the preamble states that Sámi and Norwegian are equal languages with equal status, pursuant to the provisions of section 3 of the Act. This, together with the paragraphs in the laws on education and justice referred to earlier, guarantees to citizens certain rights to service in Sámi, and imposes corresponding obligations on public bodies to communicate in Sámi both orally and in writing and to provide information to the Sámi population in Sámi.

Area of application

Six local authorities in the counties of Finnmark and Troms, where the Sámi language has a strong position, are defined as the administrative area for the Sámi language.[4] It is within this area that the legal provisions have the most extensive application. The obligations of public bodies (local, county or state bodies) and regional public bodies (county or state bodies) depend on whether they serve an area which wholly or partly includes councils in the administrative area of the Sámi language as defined above.

The Primary and Lower Secondary Education Act refers to "Sámi areas", and these are manifestly not identical to the "administrative area" mentioned above.

The Courts Act mentions the two northernmost counties, Troms and Finnmark, particularly in connection with the language rights of inmates.

When nothing is said about territorial limitations, the law is to be interpreted as applying to all citizens or to those defined in each particular case.

The language rights of individuals and the obligations of public bodies

In the Sámi administrative area

In the Sámi administrative area, *local bodies* are obliged to answer in Sámi if a member of the public initiates contact in the Sámi language, orally or in writing. (This does not apply to oral approaches to public servants carrying out duties away from the premises of the body concerned.) Regional public bodies whose authority extends across the whole or part of the administrative area shall likewise answer in Sámi if they receive written applications from members of the public. The King may extend these duties to other public bodies as well or make exceptions in special cases.

Official announcements which are particularly directed at the population in the administrative area shall appear in both Sámi and Norwegian. Official forms to be used in communications with public bodies in the administrative area shall be available in both Sámi and Norwegian.

In *courts* with jurisdictions which wholly or partly include the administrative area, the following rules apply. Any person has the right to issue writs with annexes, written evidence or other written submissions in Sámi. If the court is to transmit the submission to the other party, it makes provision for translation into Norwegian. Translation may be dispensed with if the other party consents. Any person has the right to contact the court orally in Sámi provided the legislation on legal procedure allows for oral instead of written submission. If the court is under an obligation to take down the submission in writing, the person putting forward the submission may demand that it be taken down in Sámi. Any person has the right to speak Sámi in court. If any person who does not speak Sámi is to participate in the proceedings, use is made of an interpreter appointed or approved by the court. When a party applies for this, the presiding judge may decide that the language of the proceedings shall be Sámi. If the language of the proceedings is Sámi, the presiding judge may decide that the court record shall also be kept in Sámi. The court makes provision for translation into Norwegian. The court makes provisions for court records that are written in Norwegian to be translated into Sámi when a party so demands.

For the *police* and *prosecuting* authorities serving an area which wholly or partly includes the administrative area, the following rules apply. Any person has the right to speak Sámi during interrogation at the office of the body concerned. Any person has the right to use Sámi when submitting an oral report and a notice of appeal.

Any person wishing to use Sámi to safeguard his or her interests vis-a-vis local and regional *health and welfare* institutions in the administrative area has the right to service in Sámi.

Any person has the right to individual ministration by the *Church* in Sámi in the parishes of the Church of Norway in the administrative area.

Employees of a local or regional public body in the administrative area have a right to paid leave in order to acquire knowledge of Sámi when the body has a need for such knowledge. This right may be made conditional upon the employee undertaking to work for the body for a certain time after such educational provision.

In Finnmark and Troms
In Prison Service Institutions in these two counties, inmates have the right to use Sámi with each other and their family. They also have the right to use Sámi for oral notice of appeal to the prison authority.

In "Sámi areas"
Children in "Sámi areas" have the right to receive instruction in or through the medium of Sámi. From the seventh class, it is the pupils themselves who decide on this. Pupils receiving instruction in or through the medium of Sámi are exempted from instruction in one of the two forms of Norwegian (bokmål and nynorsk) at the 8th and 9th class levels.

In general
Laws and regulations of particular interest to the whole or parts of the Sámi population shall be translated into Sámi.

The local council may decide that Sámi shall have equal status with Norwegian in the whole or parts of local administration.

The local council may, after hearing the views of the local education committee, decide that children with Sámi as their mother tongue shall be taught through the medium of Sámi for all nine years and that those who have Norwegian as their mother tongue shall have Sámi as a subject. Instruction in or through the medium of Sámi may also be given to pupils with a Sámi background outside Sámi areas. If there are no fewer than three pupils whose mother tongue is Sámi at one school, they may demand to be taught through the medium of Sámi and have Sámi as a subject.

Any person has the right to be taught Sámi. The King may issue more detailed rules concerning the implementation of this provision.

Appeal

If a public body does not conform to the provisions of section 3 of the Sámi Act, the person who is directly affected may appeal to the body which is immediately above the body the appeal concerns. The county governor is the appellate authority when the appeal concerns local or county bodies. Nationwide Sámi organisations and public bodies with tasks of particular relevance for the whole or parts of the Sámi population also have the right of appeal in such cases. The same applies in cases in which no single person is individually affected.

Sámi Language Council

A Sámi Language Council is to be established. The Sámi Parliament appoints the members of the Council. The Council's field of operation is to preserve and develop the Sámi language, to give advice and assistance to the public and the authorities on language questions, to inform people about their language rights and to produce an annual report on the status of the Sámi language to the Sámi Parliament and the Government.

On the significance of the laws in principle and in practice in various areas

General

The legislation enlarges the area of application of the Sámi language substantially, most strikingly in the courts and the police.

Although Sámi is now in principle equal with Norwegian, these regulations clearly do not ensure full equality. The limitations of territorial application are the strongest restriction. The Sámi do not have the same rights everywhere in the country. There are merely a few general rules which are supposed to apply throughout the country. In most cases, the rights are restricted to a few counties, to the "Sámi district", and finally there is an administrative area where the full range of regulations apply. But even within this area, local authorities have wide discretion in how they should enforce the law. When one notes that in several of the six local authorities, particularly Porsanger and Tana, people have expressed considerable opposition to the Sámi language, one can scarcely expect a whole-hearted effort to follow the letter of the law everywhere.

Local government

The law introduces major changes in local government at the level of the local authority and particularly the county. Some authorities have already done a good deal, using interpreters, translating documents, and taking proficiency in Sámi into account when employing people. Such policies have been decided on voluntarily on the initiative of the authority. At county level virtually nothing of this sort has been attempted. Governmental bodies have used Sámi occasionally at the level of the county and local authority, but in a completely unsystematic way and depending on the will of the body in question.

The clause which gives councils the right to decide that Sámi should have parity with Norwegian as the language of administration will put an end to the strange situation in some councils of everything having to be interpreted into Norwegian even though everyone present at a meeting speaks Sámi. It is improbable that this right will be asserted except in the Sámi administrative area.

The right to a reply in Sámi will prevent such enormities as when a school class wrote to the senior legal administrator ('lensman') in Guovdageaidnu (Kautokeino), who replied "Write in Norwegian!". Most councils will regard the obligation to reply in Sámi as arduous at first, but they will probably not be inundated in communications in Sámi. Spoken Sámi is in fact already used extensively, so little will change here.

The requirement that laws and regulations should be translated does not represent anything fundamentally new in practice. It has already been done to some extent for a long time, but the new regulation will intensify this work. So far as announcements are concerned, this will really make itself felt in some councils, in particular the two counties affected, as they have hitherto used Sámi very little in announcements or publicity.

Courts of law, police, prisons

The new regulations will have a significant impact on the courts and the police, where there is virtually no experience. It was also here that there was most resistance to the new law. The Ministry of Justice was the Ministry which had the strongest objections during hearings on the bill. It has been practice hitherto for the courts to employ an interpreter in individual cases if one of the parties required it. With explicit regulations it will be easier to use Sámi. A request for an interpreter often used to be rejected by the police for the most odd reasons which had little to do with fair legal process. It has been known for an applicant's education to be used as evidence against needing an interpreter.

For inmates to be entitled to talk Sámi to their family is a human right which should have been accepted without question for a long time. What is strange is that this right is restricted by law to the Troms and Finnmark counties. When asked whether the same right should not apply elsewhere, the parliamentary committee dealing with the bill failed to reply.

Health and social welfare

In the health and social security sector Sámi is on its way in, but as yet without formal regulation. An increase in the use of Sámi used to be resisted by the Sámi Mission, which until recently administered nursing homes and old people's homes in many northern Sámi councils. For them it was more important for the staff to have the right faith than for them to be able to communicate with the patients.

Church

In the church widespread use has been made of Sámi, via interpreters. There will be no major changes here. The church has in fact made diligent use of Sámi, particularly in inland Finnmark. The clergy in many parishes have for a century been obliged to learn Sámi. At one time the only training in Sámi available was at the theological college of the University of Oslo. This was so because of the requirement that the clergy should know Sámi. The new law will be easiest to implement in church affairs because the clergy have a long tradition of using Sámi and learning languages. In recent years the Church of Norway has also demonstrated its willingness, in theory and practice, to achieve progress in this area.

The primary and lower secondary school

The regulation on instruction in or through the medium of Sámi will not alter current practice significantly. The letter of the law states that it is enough that Sámi is offered as a subject (instruction *in* Sámi), but there is no right to instruction *through the medium of* Sámi. However, in the past this regulation has been interpreted as meaning that the child has an unconditional right to teaching through the medium of Sámi. This right holds in the "Sámi districts". This territorial restriction, which also applied earlier, is imprecise. It cannot mean the same as the administrative area (the six councils), as in this case the same expression would have been used. It has often been necessary for parents to establish that a council ("kommune") belongs to the "Sámi area" before they have been able to get instruction in Sámi as a subject for their children. It is a weakness in the new law as well that parents will probably still have to struggle to assert their rights through establishing what a "Sámi district" is. The law ought to ensure that those to whom the rights apply should not have to struggle to establish them or to have to engage in legal quibbling about what constitutes a "Sámi district".

On the other hand the law now applies to all children in the Sámi district and not only to Sámi children. Earlier versions of the same law restricted the rights to those who spoke Sámi. This enlargement is definitely an advance. However the obscure term "Sámi district" may prevent the law from achieving its intended effect, at least until the Ministry of Education explicitly lays down what geographical area it covers.

The law states that the children themselves are to decide whether they want Sámi as a subject or as a medium from the seventh grade. Until that point the parents have the right to decide. The right to opt out of something as important in education as one's mother tongue is a dubious one, and shows that the legislators do not quite have faith in Sámi being of equal value in the educational context. We Sámi have for many years been working to establish that the use of Sámi in education is so fundamental for Sámi children and so necessary for all children who live in Sámi areas that it should not be possible to opt out of it. It should in other words be obligatory. There has been a case of a council deciding that Sámi should be obligatory in all their schools. Norwegian-speakers appealed against the decision, and the administrator responsible for overseeing schools in the county reversed the decision on the grounds that she could find no legal authority for insisting on Sámi as an obligatory subject. Under the new law the council authorities are entitled to make Sámi obligatory. I assume that when such a step is taken, pupils will be deprived of their right to opt out, because the council is entitled to make decrees which apply to all nine years of compulsory education.

Language cultivation

A Sámi Language Council will presumably be able to work more systematically with language cultivation than the current Sámi Language Board. It is important that Nordic collaboration, which is of vital importance for the development of the Sámi language as a whole, continues.

Other aspects of the Sámi Language Law

The law mostly benefits North Sámi
The law applies in effect only to North Sámi districts[5], apart from educational provisions. Lule Sámi and South Sámi have been left out of the administrative area. The justification for this was that financial provision was even more difficult, added to which the government and Parliament probably believe that most Sámi here know Norwegian well enough to get along.

Study leave
The right to study leave is absolutely essential, because proficiency in Sámi, particularly written Sámi, is still seriously inadequate throughout local government (Gaup 1991). This right should apply in all bodies in which proficiency in Sámi is needed, and not merely those in the "administrative area". It is by means of study leave that we have managed to build up the competence now present in the education system and local government. It is again particularly unfortunate that Lule and South Sámi have been completely excluded.

The regulations are maximally general
Hitherto one has had to define onself as linguistically "helpless" in order to get interpretation[6], and for this reason it was frequently those who most needed an interpreter who regarded it as a point of honour to do without. The regulations are now maximally general. There is no requirement of having to prove that one is a Sámi or has difficulties in making oneself understood. Except as regards education, the regulations apply to 'everybody'. This therefore makes it impossible, for instance, for the police to refer to level of education and use this as a reason for refusing a request for an interpreter or for translation of a document. This is one very advantageous aspect of the law.

It has not been proposed that there should be rules giving preference to people who know Sámi when filling jobs. It is felt rather that proficiency in Sámi will be a qualification that may be decisive when the body making the appointment needs such proficiency. In this way, proficiency in Sámi is part of overall competence, and there will hopefully not be accusations of discrimination against those who are not Sámi.

Concluding remarks

This new legislation on the Sámi language can be seen as implementing the new clause in the Constitution referred to earlier. It also demonstrates how Norway interprets the clauses on the protection of minorities in international law. The regulations are in line with the International Covenant on Civil and Political Rights, article 27, and ILO convention 169 on indigenous and tribal peoples, which Norway has ratified, both the general clauses (article 4) and those dealing explicitly with language (articles 12 and 28).

In many respects Norway now appears to be a pioneer in indigenous and minority affairs. But even if the legislation represents a major step forward in the Norwegian Sámi context, it is far from unique. The parliamentary committee also noted this and pointed out that many other minorities in Europe have much better legal protection for their languages than what the Sámi in Norway now have. In Finland legislation is being prepared to ensure equivalent rights for the Sámi to those in Norway. In Finland a Language Act is in effect from 1 January 1992. The Finnish legislation accords equal linguistic rights to all Sámi, even those from Norway or Sweden. In Sweden the issues have been discussed in a committee on Sámi affairs, but less progress has been made as compared with Norway and Finland.

The Sámi Language Law is now obviously the primary legal bedrock for the Sámi language in Norway. In addition a distinct law has recently been passed on place names in official documents. Sámi names are explicitly referred to, and there are rules for how officialdom shall deal with them. The main rule is that existing names shall be used and that translations or ignoring names shall not be permitted. These rules will also have great importance for Sámi language and culture.

The problem today is not so much to fight for rights but how to practically implement the Sámi Language Law. The starting point is not auspicious. Broadly speaking, little work on language cultivation and terminology has been done, and few people are good at written Sámi. The education system has had too little time and too few resources to have been able to equip us to meet the many challenges we are confronted with.

On the other hand it is undeniable that the new rules are a big step forward. They will promote the use of Sámi in public administration and can be expected to have a really significant effect on the development of the Sámi language. The best way of tending a language is to make real use of it. This will also decisively improve the status of Sámi. Users of Sámi will no longer have to define themselves as second class citizens. How far the regulations are adequate for achieving the goals of the law, in other words the maintenance and development of Sámi as stipulated in the Constitution, is less certain. But this was the most that it was politically possible to achieve at the time. Both the national Parliament and in particular the Sámi Parliament stressed at the committee stage of the law that we need experience. After some time, and with the benefit of experience, there will be cause to further extend the regulations. What we must hope is that sufficient resources will be allocated for implementing the law so that favourable experience will provide pointers for the future.

It is fair to conclude that despite the weaknesses of the Sámi Language Law the new regulations come very close to what it is now possible to achieve when attempting a balance between legislation and what it is practically possible to carry out.

Translated from the Norwegian by Ole Henrik Magga, Robert Phillipson and Tove Skutnabb-Kangas

Notes

1. The legal amendments of October 1990 mainly involved changes in the law on the Sámi Assembly and other Sámi legal matters (the Sámi Act, Act No. 56 of 12 June 1987). This law is the basis for the Sámi Assembly or Sámi Parliament, which was established in October 1989. A new paragraph was added to the Primary and Lower Secondary Education Act (Act No. 24, 13 June 1969) replacing a part of an earlier paragraph which was repealed. The third law that was affected was the Courts Act (Act No. 5 of 13 August 1915) where a reference to the Sámi Act concerning the use of Sámi in court was added.

2. When the Norwegian Government decided to flood the Alta River valley, there were massive protests. Sámi organised a hunger strike in front of the Parliament in Oslo, Sámi and other demonstrators chained themselves to the rocky mountainside near the dam site to prevent construction of a road, 600 policemen were brought in to remove demonstrators, and another hunger strike began. The construction work was temporarily stopped, but was ultimately concluded after a Supreme Court decision.

3. Sámi has nine main dialects, spoken from the south of Scandinavia to the east of the Kola peninsula in Russia. Differences between them, particularly those that are geographically remote from each other, are substantial, so that many linguists refer to Sámi languages rather than dialects. There are also variations within each main dialect that can be regarded as within the range of ordinary dialect variation.

4. The six communities ("kommuner") are Guovdageaidnu (Kautokeino), Karasjohka (Karasjokk), Deatnu (Tana), Unjarga (Nesseby), Porsangu (Porsanger) and Gaivuotna (Kåfjord). The name forms in parenthesis are "Norwegian" name forms. Most of them are adaptations from Sámi. The form Kautokeino is obviously based on the "Finnish" form Koutokeino, a Finnish adaptation of the Sámi form.

5. Both Finnmark and Troms are within the North Sámi area. The Lule Sámi and South Sámi are traditionally spoken in Nordland, the Trøndelag counties and Hedmark.

6. Within "deficiency theories" problems encountered by minorities are diagnosed as being caused by "deficiencies" in the minorities themselves, for instance their lack of proficiency in the majority language, rather than lack of linguistic rights, where the majority societies do not provide minorities with the same services which they take for granted for themselves, for instance the right to use one's mother tongue in official situations (see Skutnabb-Kangas 1988a: 32−36). In order to obtain this right, the minority person has to agree to be defined as helpless and "deficient". In this way, the costs of interpretation can also be blamed on the minority: it is the "deficient" minority which causes the expense, rather than the monolingual majority or the unequal distribution of linguistic human rights (Skutnabb-Kangas 1991b).

Australia's language policies and minority rights: a core value perspective

J. J. Smolicz

One may wonder why language death (or linguicide), such as has already occurred in the case of so many Aboriginal languages in Australia and threatens still others (of the original 230 no more than nine are spoken by more than one thousand speakers), passes so frequently unlamented, or even unnoticed (Black 1979; Fesl 1988). This appears in contrast to deep feelings of sadness, revulsion and protest at news of the danger of extinction of some rare species of buffalo, or orchid, or a marsupial such as the "Tasmanian tiger". And yet linguicide desecrates the very humanity of whole groups of people whose culture may disintegrate when deprived of the most fundamental core of their heritage, their language. A key to the art of living, laboriously evolved over centuries or millenia, is thereby lost. This does not seem to move the dominant people who appear content to trample upon the human dignity of other, less powerful individuals and groups.

The monolingual urge which fails to recognise the linguistic rights of minorities is rather curious, since language constitutes that particular element of culture which can be shared most readily with people of other backgrounds, without this jeopardizing the ability to use one's own, or first language. In the field of language there is no intrinsic linguistic requirement to choose just one particular language from among competing or co-existing systems, as in the case of religion, family or other group value systems. Instead, one can make use of one or more linguistic systems in various situations and domains of life. Conversi (1990: 50) concurs with this view, when he writes that

> Ethnic languages rather than other values (such as race or religion) offer better prospects for peaceful and successful mobilization of democratic states if these languages are spoken — or at least understood — by a sizeable proportion of the population ... Language has a more inclusive character, inasmuch as it is not used as a barrier to prevent the integration of outsiders.

It is surprising, therefore, that doubts and fears persist in some sections of the Australian community in regard to bilingualism which, in the Australian multicultural context, always involves English and another minority language. No doubt the sensitivity in acknowledging the linguistic rights of others is due to the very great importance that language assumes in our cultural life. Indeed, is it not perhaps the very quintessential nature of language, which permeates our whole existence as humans, that somehow, by the inverse process of self-assertion, makes us so callous towards the rights of others?

As Tsuda (1986: 49) affirms, "Language is far from neutral, but it is actually a system of beliefs, values and interpretations emphasized and handed down in a certain culture. The adoption of a certain language leads to the dominance of that culture's practices and the submission to [its] other cultural values". Hence the fear among subordinate or smaller groups of losing their tongue, since this would cause them to sever their links with fellow speakers in the world and rupture the historical continuity with their own group, as manifested in its oral and literary heritage. As for the majority group, it may come to feel insecure in its dominant position because of the persistence of other languages within one and the same state and society, as happened when fear of the "enemy" language (German) in Australia, at the time of the First World War, led to legislation permitting only English as the language of instruction in schools (Selleck 1980; Harmstorf 1983).

Linguistic core values

The place and use of language in ethnically plural societies and of the varying degrees of "ethno-linguistic vitality" shown by the minorities can be clarified by referring to the theory of core values. This theory argues that some ethnic groups are very strongly language-centred, so that their existence as distinct cultural and social entities depends on the maintenance and development of their ethno-specific tongues. In the case of some groups there may be some debate about which particular aspect of culture is of core significance. Indeed, other cultural factors, such as a specific religion, social structure or "racial" affiliation may prove to be of equal or greater significance than language for some peoples (Smolicz 1981, 1984; Smolicz — Secombe 1989).

While there may be grounds for disputing whether the core of states such as Ireland, Lebanon or the Philippines resides in one particular ethno-specific tongue, there is no doubt that it is the linguistic core which animates not only the French and Québecois of Canada (Laurin 1977), but also the Poles, Greeks, the newly independent Baltic peoples, and many other ethnic groups. The situation of French was most clearly articulated by an economist and Nobel prize winner, Allais (1989), who has expressed his absolute conviction that the French language is the core of his culture, in view of its role in sustaining that nation's identity and vital powers of creativity, as well as its economic well-being.

During a visit to Australia, the secretary of the Ukrainian Writers' Association, D. Pavlychko, was asked why he was such a champion of the Ukrainian language, both in his own country and for Ukrainian-Australians. In a reply that applied with particular force to his own ethnic group, he asserted that

> Language is not only a method of communicating. It's a system of philosophical imagery, its metaphorical, illustrative thinking. Where a language disappears, there you have the disappearance also of the national structure and the national spirit. The death of a language is the death of its people. In trying to save the Ukrainian language we are saying that we are trying to save a nation's memory and a nation's future (quoted in Taylor 1989).

Such comments recognize the special role of language not only as a bridge which furthers *communication* with others, but also as an *identity-maker*, and as a core value which symbolises a person's belonging to a particular community, and no other. Thus when one learns another language within its cultural envelope (and not just its formal grammatical structure or its simplified business version) one enters into *communion* with other speakers of that language and forms a bond which can and should enrich the individual and his or her group. In this way an element of culture which has given rise in the past to in-fighting, and even to cruelty and war, can be turned into a bridge that links and promotes amity and cooperation. Learning a second or third language can then release the culturally and economically productive forces of all citizens, without depriving anyone of his or her right to a particular linguistic heritage. Instead, that heritage is made to work as a linguistic resource for the benefit of the whole society.

Core values and ethnolinguistic vitality of minority languages in Australia

From these considerations it is clear that factors which influence the vitality of a minority language in a plural society (or conversely the shift of its speakers to the majority tongue) are complex and inter-related. Very often the linguistic outcome can be seen as the product of interplay between the core values of the minority group and that of the dominant majority. Some factors are directly connected to the current geopolitical situation of the group. Others are deeply embedded in its culture and history.

The data obtained from the Australian censuses (Jupp 1988) show a regular pattern in the extent to which first generation immigrants have claimed not to use their mother tongue. Indeed the uniformity in the shift to English, as shown by the rank order of major ethnic groups throughout all the states and territories of Australia, is in line with empirically derived insights gained from the study of the Australian scene (Smolicz – Harris 1977; Clyne 1982, 1985; Smolicz – Secombe 1986). The 1976 census data show that Greek-born Australians have the smallest language shift (3%), while the Dutch are the most likely of all the groups to change to English, with a 44% swing in the first generation. Italians, Yugoslavs, Poles, Germans and Maltese occupy intermediate positions on such a scale (Clyne 1982; Smolicz 1986a). In the 1986 census (cf. Clyne 1988) the same order of ethnic linguistic erosion was preserved, both for the first generation immigrants (Greek, 4.4%; "Yugoslav", 9%; Italian, 10%; Polish, 16%; Maltese, 26%; German, 41%; Dutch, 48%) and their children. Those from parents of the same ethno-linguistic background also show loss of the use of the native tongue in the same sequence (Greek, 8.7%; "Yugoslav", 18%; Italian, 29%; Maltese, 59%; German, 73%; Dutch, 85%). Those from "mixed" marriages show a much greater linguistic erosion (Greek, 41%; "Yugoslav", 65%; Italian, 71%; Maltese, 86%; German, 85%; Dutch, 92%).

It is of course necessary to understand the limitations of such census data. For example, just as the "Yugoslav" grouping is linguistically artificial, "Italian" too does not differentiate between standard and dialects, nor between extensive and restricted usage of the language concerned. At best, such data are indicative of the ethnolinguistic vitality of a language, rather than of its significance as a core value of culture. With all these reservations in mind, it is nonetheless remarkable that the ethnic

rank order of the self-reported linguistic erosion of the languages concerned has been maintained over generations and time.

In the case of the Greek language group in Australia, its low shift to
English and high maintenance of the mother tongue can be related to
the many centuries of survival under the Ottoman rule through which
Greeks have acquired "experience" of the ways of defending their identifying cores. Italians, though also subject to centuries of foreign rule,
did not face the prospect of linguicide on the part of a single all powerful
occupier in the same way as the Greeks. Latvians represent a relatively
small group in Australia which has consistently displayed a high degree
of ethnic language maintenance. This reflects not just the role of language
as the chief carrier of the group's culture throughout its history, but also
the most recent bout of russification carried out in Latvia by the post
World War II Soviet regime. In this situation, Latvian-Australians assumed the role of "keepers" of their language to save it from total
extinction.

Another factor which favours ethnic language maintenance is the
presence of other values that reinforce the language. In the Greek and
Italian groups, the closely knit and extended collectivist family structure
plays that role (Smolicz 1985). However, in the Greek case, a further
reinforcement is provided by an ethno-specific Greek Orthodox church,
a situation that is not replicated on the Italian side. The profound
differences between the religiosity of Italian and Anglo-Irish Catholics
(Pitarello 1988) and the work of Italian orders, such as the Scalabrinians
and Cappucines among the Italian community in Australia, would also
suggest that religion may reinforce Italian language maintenance. However, the centralised nature of the Catholic church and an Irish orientation
within its Australian hierarchy have made Italian religious practices more
open than those of the Greeks to the entry of the English language into
their religious devotions (Smolicz 1988).

The situation of the Dutch is rather different. While the importance
of the Dutch language in the Netherlands itself can hardly be questioned,
there are not many countries, whether in Europe or elsewhere, in which
a minister of education could propose that lecturing in his country's
universities should switch to English, as the Dutch Minister, Jozef Ritsen,
did. In commenting on this proposal, Pleij (1991) reports that the protests
were so vehement that the minister had to abandon this initiative. In his
view, what was remarkable, however, was that after making such a
proposal, the minister "simply could proceed governing". Ironically, the
state of affairs is almost the reverse in most African and Latin American

and many Asian countries, in that a Minister of Education is unlikely to suggest a switch to lecturing in an indigenous language.

In Australia, a survey reported by the Department of Immigration, Local Government and Ethnic Affairs (1991) provides results similar to those from the census. Of those born in the Netherlands, and aged five and over, 98% spoke only English at home, as opposed to 15.2% of those born in Poland. The shift from Dutch to English has been explained by reference to the similarity of the two languages and the relative absence of linguistic ethnocentrism among the Dutch in the Australian setting. Such an extensive transition to English could also be related to the overlap of Dutch cultural values with those of the majority, and the ease of mutual social acceptance between the two groups.

English as an overarching value in Australia

In the multilingual society of Australia, the centrality of English as the means of communication shared by all Australians has never been challenged. Yet the development of policies that recognise and give educational support to minority languages has had to overcome the fear among many English speakers that a language policy of this kind would undermine the place of English. An example of such misplaced fears was provided by a former Minister of Immigration, John Hodges, in addressing a National Language Policy Conference organized in 1982 by the Federation of Ethnic Communities Council of Australia. He demanded, in disbelief "Surely you cannot seriously suggest that the numerous other languages being spoken can become interchangeable with English as the common mode of expression" (Hodges 1982).

As noted previously, language is a part of culture which can be regarded as capable of introducing the greatest degree of harmony into society, since it is essentially additive, rather than subtractive. This means that while English plays the key role in Australia, other languages can co-exist within the arch, allowing people to participate in the mainstream of Australian life, while acquiring literacy in a variety of languages, many of which are already spoken in Australian homes (Marjoribanks 1980; Smolicz 1984). By acquiring literacy in their home language, these minority-ethnic Australians are developing bilingualism which can be used for positive and socially constructive ends.

The great advantage which Australia holds over many countries with more rigid overarching frameworks (such as, say, Saudi Arabia or Iran) is that it does not require its citizens to conform to certain fixed beliefs, such as one particular religion, in order to be accepted as full citizens with the same basic rights and responsibilities. There is, however, a general expectation of a knowledge of English which (as noted before) does not preclude the continued development of other community languages, not just for those people from that particular background, but to be shared by all Australians willing to take up the challenge. The flexible, yet stable nature of our overarching values was emphasised by the then Prime Minister, Malcolm Fraser, when he spoke, in 1981, of

> ethnic cultural differences set within a framework of shared fundamental values which enables them to co-exist on a complementary rather than competitive basis.

There is yet another reason why Australia can look upon the maintenance and development of languages other than English without the fear of any threat to our unity, whether cultural or territorial. This is because, unlike other countries, Australia has a unique position in the world, being the only continent governed as a single political entity. In some other countries, minority groups are under a cloud of suspicion that their linguistic and cultural demands shroud political motives of separation and secession. A majority group may be less than happy to see a minority cultivating its own language in some part of the country, only to walk away with the territory either by wishing to join it to one of its neighbours, or to establish an independent state. In Australia none of our ethnic minorities wishes to secede from Australia − our territorial integrity is not in doubt. Hence the desire on the part of non-English-speaking-background Australians to have their linguistic rights recognized represents a demand that the English-speaking-background majority can safely accept. Since it poses no threat to Australia's overarching system of values, the recognition of linguistic pluralism represents an affordable tolerance that is justified not only on the grounds of equity or linguistic human rights but as a matter of economic and political necessity.

The rise of monolingualism in the early twentieth century

The various steps taken by Australia along the path of granting some degree of linguistic rights to minority Australians can be conceptualized, using Skutnabb-Kangas and Phillipson's (1989a) continuum, as a reflection of movement from prohibition of a language to its toleration, non-discrimination, and permission to use it. In Australia, promotion as a goal still appears to be just over the horizon.

The toleration of speakers of other languages has varied in extent and form, with changing perceptions of Australian cultural diversity. The culturally plural Aboriginal era was followed by the superimposition of a great variety of ethnic inputs brought by two hundred years of mainly European settlement. The pluralism, which thrived in the early colonial days and during the years of the gold rushes, was still evident at the beginning of the twentieth century, when there existed in Australia some one hundred bilingual schools (Clyne 1985).

During the course of the First World War, German, and by implication all languages other than English, came to be viewed with suspicion so that their use was regarded as somehow "disloyal", or at least "un-Australian." It was during that epoch that legislation was passed which forbade the use of other languages as the medium of instruction in private schools (Selleck 1980), resulting in the closure of some 80 German Lutheran schools in South Australia alone. This law remained on the statute books of that State until the mid-1970s.

Into the culturally monistic climate that prevailed over the next three decades came the waves of European immigrants from non-English-speaking backgrounds who arrived following World War II. They were met with the expectation that before long they would become almost completely assimilated. Although Australia prided itself on being a democracy, the policy adopted in relation to recognition of linguistic rights can only be described as minimalist. Minority group members were permitted to make use of their tongues merely in a domestic situation and in the restricted area of ethnic clubs and possibly part-time, after-hours ethnic schools. This approach was generally based upon the assumptions that linguistic transmission would be short-lived and that a language restricted in usage to the home would become extinct in subsequent generations, without "disturbing" the monolingual texture of society as a whole.

The assimilationist policy adopted towards the minorities did not mean, of course, that no language other than English was taught in the school portals. But these other languages were seen as either classical and traditional (Latin, Ancient Greek), or modern and foreign (French, German). In this way Australian education strove to develop the image of English society rather than relate itself to the realities of Australian life. This classical linguistic and educational perspective can be seen in language syllabuses for university entrance or matriculation examinations. For example, in South Australia up until 1964, the only four languages available at matriculation, Year 12, level were Ancient Greek, Latin, French and German (Smolicz 1986).

The international language focus

The beginnings of a more international approach were marked by Australia's increasing awareness of itself as an independent nation in world affairs, and a growing recognition of its geographical position in Asia and the Pacific. By the late 1960s moves were evident in Australia to extend the range and image of language, history and culture courses. The "mother country's" perspective was no longer seen as the only valid one, and courses which were more responsive to the Australian context were developed. This included the introduction of the languages, histories and cultures of Australia's, rather than England's, neighbours and trading partners.

Official acceptance of the internationalist approach was acknowledged by the 1970 Report of the Commonwealth Advisory Committee on the Teaching of Asian Languages and Cultures in Australia (Auchmuty Report 1974). It highlighted the growing involvement of Australia in the economy, culture and security of South East Asia. A notable feature of the report was its emphasis on the study of language, as part of a broader cultural concern for the region.

At tertiary level this resulted in the establishment of departments of Asian Studies, involving the teaching of languages such as Chinese, Japanese and Indonesian/Malay. (This was usually done under the slogan, "Australia as part of Asia".) Other "geopolitical" languages introduced were Spanish ("trade with Latin America") and Russian ("trade, defence, sputnik and international power").

In South Australia the languages available at Matriculation level were extended in 1967 by the inclusion of Russian, and this was followed two years later by Chinese, Japanese and Spanish. Malay and Indonesian were added in 1975. The original impetus for the teaching of languages of "international importance" waned in subsequent years, to re-emerge from the mid-1980s, especially in relation to Asian languages.

The multicultural language focus

It was not until the mid 1970s that Australia's gaze turned inwards to "discover" the ethnic, linguistic and other cultural complexities within its own shores — some of them already of second and third generation vintage. This marked the phase of what may be termed "internal multiculturalism", where interest in languages and cultures became innerdirected into Australian society itself and the linguistic rights of minorities began to be acknowledged.

This approach does not negate the previous approaches, since they can co-exist, and usually do, though there may be competition for resources between those who favour the rapid development of languages that foster relationships with other societies (mainly Asian languages) and those who primarily favour the linguistic rights of minorities within Australia and hence advocate the teaching of "community languages". In South Australia, all the languages taught in the two earlier phases continue to be available as Year 12 subjects, although in some cases the emphasis is changing. German is being recognised as a community language, as well as one of general cultural and trading significance. The advent of many Chinese-Vietnamese refugees has helped to make Chinese a community language, as well as an international one.

The first community language introduced in South Australia was Italian, which was included at pre-Matriculation level as early as 1958, and at full Matriculation (University entrance) level in 1967. (Even then it was seen by some more as an "international" rather than an "ethnic" or community language). Italian was followed by Dutch in 1969; Hebrew in 1973; Ukrainian and Lithuanian, 1975; Modern Greek, 1976; Latvian and Polish in 1977; Hungarian in 1978 and later still, Vietnamese. By 1991, Serbo-Croatian, Khmer, Croatian and Farsi had been added, in response to requests from these language communities, some of whose members were recent arrivals in Australia. Three states, Victoria, South Australia and New South Wales, have also successfully introduced language schools run by the State Departments which offer a wide range of community languages outside school hours.

Moreover there have been moves to rationalize Year 12 syllabus development and examinations in 20 community languages so that one state examining authority becomes responsible for assessing students in that language throughout Australia. Under these arrangements, for example, Arabic, Czech, Macedonian, Maltese, Slovenian and Swedish will become available to South Australian students for examination purposes. South Australia is itself responsible for national syllabus development and examining in Polish, Latvian, Lithuanian and Khmer. In 1992 a program to develop a national syllabus framework for Aboriginal languages was announced.

The "Multicultural Focus" policies have resulted in making Australian society more aware of the linguistic rights of children of non-English-speaking backgrounds. Furthermore, there is a growing realisation that it makes sense to build upon the languages concerned and to utilize the great potential locked in two million Australian bilinguals, rather than see those linguistic treasures squandered, only to try to painfully reconstruct them later from scratch through foreign language instruction.

The adoption of national language policies

After the official government adoption of a "multicultural" orientation in the mid-1970s and the acceptance of the Galbally Report (1978), further advances toward recognising linguisitic rights were made through the articulation of language policies during the 1980s. Australia's National Policy on Language (Commonwealth Department of Education, Lo Bianco Report 1987), and the newly declared language policies of states such as South Australia, Victoria, New South Wales and Queensland, promised to make up for at least some of the glaring omissions of the past (*Australian Advisory Council on Languages and Multicultural Education* 1990).

While there still appears to be insufficient acceptance of the need to make the study of a language other than English (LOTE) a compulsory subject, some states have formulated a specific plan to increase language teaching, such as an undertaking to provide at least one LOTE for all primary school students by 1995 (South Australian Ministerial Task Force on Multiculturalism and Education, 1984, Education Department of South Australia 1985). According to the former South Australian Director General of Education (Boston 1989), South Australia "seeks to affirm and promote cultural and linguistic diversity for all students through the application of Culturally Inclusive Education". This includes the expansion of existing LOTE programs in schools that already teach eighteen languages to one third of the State's primary and secondary school students. Boston also affirmed as his Department's "main priority", the "mother tongue development of students", as well as the teaching of "the total range of languages" — including "geopolitical", "traditional" and "community" languages.

The protagonists of Australia's policy on languages have stressed the need for two-way bridge-building which they perceived as a *dual focus* approach in relation to LOTE (Commonwealth Department of Education, Lo Bianco Report 1987). One focus is on the creation of conditions which recognise minority linguistic rights by permitting those Australians who already speak a language other than English as their first language to consolidate and develop it further through literacy, with the chance to learn a third language, in addition to English, if they so desire. The other is for people from English-speaking backgrounds to have every opportunity and incentive to build a linguistic bridge towards their fellow citizens in Australia, and/or to Australia's neighbours in the region, or to people of interest elsewhere — with the possibility that one and the same language may fulfil all these functions, internal, trade, political, etc. (Lo Bianco 1990).

The National Policy on Languages offered a balanced and coordinated approach which combined the elements of social justice in terms of support for linguistic rights, economic and international needs of the nation, and access to a variety of cultural and linguistic perspectives for all Australians. These linguistic goals form an ideal which has not yet been attained, as is demonstrated by contrasting the rich linguistic diversity of the population with the dismally low level of LOTE study in the final year of school, namely roughly 14%.

In the past decade Australia has taken into consideration both the original inhabitants who form its "indigenous minority" (or the Aboriginal people) and its post-war multitude of migrants from non-English-speaking backgrounds. The violation of the rights of the Aboriginal people who, from the beginning of the European influx in 1788, were denied participation in the life of their country, has been progressively rectified in the *political* domain since 1967 (Stretton and Finnimore 1988) and a change of policy on land rights. In *linguistic* terms, however, Australia is far from making full amends for past omissions since "the languages of Australia [a term adopted for the indigenous languages by the Aboriginal people themselves] still continue along the path to extinction" (Fesl 1988). According to the head of the Aboriginal and Torres Strait Islander Commission (ASTIC) "the time has come for a treaty which would be an act of reconciliation between Aborigines and other Australians who are descendants of migrants or migrants themselves". Only then could the tide be reversed so that Aboriginal people were no longer the "victims of immigration" (O'Donoghue 1990).

Legal enactments of linguistic rights

The Human Rights Commission Act of 1981 provided specifically Australian legal machinery to advance and protect the linguistic rights of minorities. Article 1 of the 1959 Declaration of the Rights of the Child (which forms Schedule 2 of the Act) affirms the entitlement of the child to all rights set out in the Declaration without distinction or discrimination on account of race, colour, language, national, or social origins.

However, these rights, guaranteed in law, have still to be translated into actual practices, programs and services in education in order to prevent or eliminate social, economic, and political cleavages and inequities based upon the individual's racial, cultural, and linguistic backgrounds.

The Committee of Review of the Australian Institute of Multicultural Affairs in its 1983 *Report* to the Minister of Immigration and Ethnic Affairs gave top priority to the objective of promoting "equity of access for those whom society disadvantages because of their ethnic or cultural differences" (vol. 2, para. 3.1), and to "promoting the rights of those whom society disadvantages because of their ethnic or cultural identification" (para. 3.3). The significant point which emerges from the Review and from subsequent community consultations is that the pursuit of minority cultural development must be linked to the elimination of ethnically based structural inequalities in those areas of life where they occur. An improvement in the life circumstances and life chances of migrant and ethnic minorities can be effected only if members of ethnic groups are able to maintain and develop their languages and cultures, without this being turned against them and used as a marker of, or even an excuse for, social inequality.

Advances in educational policy have not, as yet, found their reflection in legal terms that would guarantee the linguistic rights of minorities. The Australian Senate's committee report, *A National Language Policy* (1984), questions the need to legislate on language rights, in spite of the demands for such legislation on the part of minority ethnic groups. Such demands were exemplified by the submission of the Federation of Ethnic Communities' Councils of Australia to the Senate Committee which suggested that a "National Language Act would guarantee individual rights to communicate and to have access to information". The Federation requested that the Senate Committee "recommend that draft legislation be prepared for comment by the community" (para. 1.26). The

Committee's response was that it was "not persuaded" that legislation on language rights would have helped in the past or be appropriate at this juncture, although it did not exclude the possibility that "a need for some form of legislation may arise" in the future (para. 1.27).

The principle of equality of opportunity in education has often been interpreted as ensuring that non-English-speaking students have equal access to the curricula and programs provided for the English-speaking background majority in the mainstream schools. While such mainstream services are essential, the minority communities have argued that it is also important to realize that through the right to choose, or in recognition of cultural differences, specific or additional linguistic provisions for the members of minority ethnic groups are also required.

For this reason the South Australian Education Department Policy Statement on *Antiracism* (July 1990) has adopted a wide-ranging view of race which extends beyond phenotype, such as facial features and skin pigmentation, to matters pertaining to culture. With its credo put in positive terms, "The Education Department values cultural diversity and promotes the optimum participation of all students both in schooling and in the wider society". While the policy document is less explicit in defining what actually constitutes racism, it is at its most forceful when condemning the effects of racism:

> Racism impoverishes and undermines our society by demeaning and excluding individuals and groups and by limiting their participation. Racism feeds on prejudices and fears about *cultural* and physiological differences, prejudices and fears which are just as powerful whether these differences are real or assumed (author's underlining).

The wider interpretation given to the concept of race in the Policy Statement is significant, in that it incorporates the phenomena of ethnicism and, by implication, linguicism (Skutnabb-Kangas 1988a). These cause individuals to suffer discrimination not necessarily because of their looks, but because of their ethno-cultural origin, the religion they profess, their family structure, the clothes they choose to wear, the food they eat (in the case of ethnicism), and the language in which they converse with each other, as well as the particular accent with which they speak English (in the case of linguicism). Since neither ethicism nor linguicism are spelled out in legislation, discrimination on these grounds could not be investigated unless it was included under the "racism" label.

Economic relevance and minority rights

The latest danger to minority linguistic rights has appeared from a rather unexpected quarter. The more usual opposition has been based upon warnings of "other" languages within the community as being "divisive", and "expensive". These reasons could be interpreted as expressing the majority group's fear of losing its dominance and being unwilling to acknowledge that minority groups also make their financial contribution to the running of the educational system of the country. The new reason for denying the minority language rights is based upon calls for "economic relevance" of the languages that were being taught in school, with the assumption that virtually all "community languages", with sizeable groups of Australians using them in their homes, were "irrelevant" for "trade" and "economic development". The irony is that this fascination with "economic relevance" — conceived in such narrow and ethnocentric terms — could undermine not only language rights but also its own officially stated goals.

Languages currently gaining popularity are generally perceived as neither European nor community, but Asian and foreign (Asian Studies Council 1988). The danger is that this short-sighted interpretation of "economic relevance" may place a wedge between languages that are actually spoken in the Australian community and those languages which are labelled as "foreign", "trade", and "Asian". The existence of languages that are both Asian *and* community is often ignored by the catch-cry of "trade", and the simplistic belief in a relationship between the acquisition of an elementary knowledge of a foreign language and an automatic trade surplus with the country concerned. Supposed "insufficient trade" is used as a device to ignore Vietnamese, which is spoken at home by many Australian citizens and is on the threshold of becoming a trade language of the future.

The situation is more complex in the case of Chinese. It could hardly be by-passed — since it is undoubtedly "Asian and trade", while the assumption that it is foreign ignores the presence in the country of some 140,000 Australian citizens and residents who make use of a Chinese language in their home, and for whom it has a "community" rather than a "foreign" (or simply "trade") connotation. From the Australian perspective, the significance of Chinese for trade is in fact partly *because* it is also a "community" language — a name that indicates that the Australian business people concerned are not only fluent in the language *per se*, but are also knowledgeable about its cultural context (Smolicz — Lee — Murugaian — Secombe 1990). They are most likely to have the capacity to communicate with their former homeland, whose "cultural envelope" of customs and ways of life they generally understand and cultivate through continuing social contacts. Such people are in a position to collaborate with Australian business people from other backgrounds and provide a bridge of cultural, social and economic links with the countries concerned.

The dilemmas which still face Australia relate to the fact that unless rights of minorities are respected and "internal" linguistic resources fully utilized as part of Australia's attempts to come closer to Asia, "external" cultural and educational efforts may prove inadequate to meet the hopes that are currently placed in them.

It is unfortunate that some of the present policy intentions, far from furthering trade, may actually hinder it. The disregard of the linguistic rights of Asian-Australian citizens and their cultures is being carefully watched by Australia's trading partners in Asia and it is not likely to increase that country's popularity. At the very least, ignoring the existing linguistic potential locked in the Australian bilingual population is a waste of economic assets. In view of such developments, it would be a fallacy to interpret a model of linguistic rights as assuming an invariable progression in a "positive" direction — towards empowering minorities to use and become literate in their mother tongues. However, policies may move backwards, as seems to have happened in Federal government documents of the early 1990s.

The latest challenge

One of the most disquieting features of recent developments was the appearance of official ministerial papers, under such titles as *The Language of Australia* (in the singular — sic) which did not even acknowledge the connection between language learning and literacy (Department of Employment, Education and Training, December 1990).

The report seemed to represent a return to a kind of monolingual myopia, which has proved to be one of the main obstacles to the recognition of minority language rights. The acquisition of literacy was considered in terms of literacy in English as if the study of French, Chinese or Modern Greek did not involve the goal of literacy in these languages. The perception of English as the only "normal" language is disconcerting, since it implicitly devalues minority rights and the significance of other languages in the world, as well as in Australia.

Another uncertainty created by the ministerial paper related to its failure to recognize the way in which the learning of languages other than English could play a vital role in the acquisition of a full range of literacy for those whose first language was English. But the most obvious casualties from the lack of the conceptual linkage between literacy and language learning are the home speakers of minority languages who need to be given the opportunity to acquire literacy in their home or first languages, before being introduced to literacy in English (Cummins 1987b).

In a more positive vein, the Australian federal authorities have recognized the need for greater knowledge of languages in society by offering financial inducements in the form of *per capita* grants to the states for each student completing a Year 12 course in languages other than English (LOTE). Even that offer, however, was limited to 25% of the school student population, as if it had been assumed in advance that no more than a quarter of those completing secondary school needed to have acquired some degree of proficiency in LOTE.

Furthermore, the Federal Ministry considered it necessary to abrogate to itself the right to decide which languages were in the national interest for students to acquire. The financial carrot was dangled only for those students and their schools which chose one of the specified "priority" languages. These were mainly selected on the basis of their "trade", "foreign" and "Asian" label. Initially, the priority language list included "Aboriginal" (as if there was only one such language!)

It is fortunate that States, such as South Australia, have formally adopted a stance that "it is important to ensure that, regardless of the base on which the additional Federal funds are obtained, their distribution [in this state] is to be undertaken on the basis of equality of all languages". Based on this principle, at least some States are expected to provide financial assistance from the Federal government to increase the range of "languages for wider teaching" chosen according to a variety of factors, including "daily use by a considerable number of Australians".

This approach gives hope of the recognition that Australia's great advantages rest within the continent and its gifted people with their manifold linguistic heritage. Its resources lie partly in the native speakers of several community languages whose linguistic human rights need to be affirmed, so that they can develop their proficiency in their mother tongues further for the benefit of themselves and society. To some extent such recognition of minority rights depends on the majority group escaping the confines of monolingualism. Those who start life as speakers of English should be given every encouragement to study other languages and cultures through an educational system that favours the learning of another language for all. The University of Melbourne has given a lead in this direction by its decision in May 1992 to give a bonus mark representing ten per cent of the maximum possible score in one subject to all those final-year secondary school students who have passed one language other than English at Grade D level or above.

In developing the dual focus policy of the acquisition of a second language for the majority and language maintenance for minorities, Australians are becoming conscious of the benefits of multilingualism. In this way the cultural and economic resilience of Australian society is being seen as inextricably linked to safeguarding the language rights of its minorities — whether of Aboriginal or migrant origin.

Combating educational disadvantage among Lebanese Australian children

John Gibbons — *William White* — *Pauline Gibbons*

This paper discusses the curriculum response made by St Mel's Catholic Primary School, Sydney, to the educational needs of Lebanese Australian children, including an Arabic-English bilingual programme in the first three years.

The social context

At the national level, since the Second World War there has been a very large migration into Australia of people speaking languages other than English. Around one quarter of all Australians are from backgrounds where a language other than English (hereafter LOTE) is used. Approximately one percent of Australians are Aboriginal. At the last census for which we have figures (1981) Sydney was home to the majority of Australia's Lebanese. They are now the largest LOTE group in Sydney Catholic schools, comprising eleven percent of the school population (Abdoolcader 1989).

Looking now at the local community, Campsie where the school is located is in essence a poor working class suburb with a substantial number of Lebanese speakers. According to Horvath and Tait (1984) Campsie has more of the following than the Sydney mean: households with an income of less than ;6000 per year; people employed in trades, process work and labouring; unemployed persons. Horvath and Tait also note (1984: viii) that the Lebanese community is among the most residentially segregated and (1984: 19) that "Neighbourhoods in which they (Lebanese) are more numerous have more working class people (R = .38), fewer high income earners (R = -.38), fewer professionals and managers (R = -.32) and fewer people with educational qualifications (R = .34)." On the grounds of the available income, educational background and employment of parents, and of the ethnicity of the area, St Mel's is classified as a disadvantaged school, and receives extra government funding on this basis. The civil war in the Lebanon has also had unfortunate effects on the Lebanese community in Australia.

The educational context

At the national level, there is evidence of majority approval of migration into Australia from countries where LOTEs are spoken, and for necessary support services to be provided for migrants. However, as in other countries, those involved in the education of language minority students feel that more financial support is needed if such children are to have the same educational outcomes as their English native speaker peers. Lebanese Australian children are particularly at risk — for example Horvath (1986: 27—28) examined the likelihood of children from different ethnic backgrounds being placed in lower streams in secondary schools. Among the sixteen migrant groups she examined, Maltese and Lebanese children were the most likely to be in lower streams. Underperformance by Lebanese Australians at secondary school is also documented in Young — Petty — Faulkner (1980) and Meade (1983).

In New South Wales fully developed bilingual programmes to meet the needs of minority groups have yet to be seen as a viable educational option in the way they have in some other states in Australia. In New South Wales approximately one quarter of all primary children attend Catholic schools, so the system is very large, and includes children from all socio-economic backrounds. In Sydney more than half of the children in the Catholic system are from LOTE backgrounds (Abdoolcader 1989) and around one third enter kindergarten with little or no English, although in many cases the children are Australian born. Given the restricted funding available to the Catholic system, specific programmes for children such as these have an inbuilt fragility compared with other perceived educational priorities. Resources are subject to the continuing vagaries of external and internal funding policies.

Within the Lebanese community, parents, while often intensely interested in their children's education, traditionally hold a culturally-based view of teacher and parent roles in which teachers are regarded as totally responsible for the education of children. This tendency is reinforced by the fact that many of the parents are first generation migrants from village communities, and have only basic education. They often have difficulty in understanding and coping with the Western urban society in which they find themselves, and may not therefore feel fully competent or confident in taking part in the life of the school. Children from such working class Lebanese background may enter school having had little exposure to academic Arabic (we refer here to Cummins' (1984) "cognitive academic language"). Their English speaking peers will be exposed to academic varieties of their mother tongue at school, but in most schools this will not happen for Arabic speakers.

St Mel's school is a primary school which takes children from approximately five to twelve years of age. In 1989 the school had 520 pupils, of whom 468 or 90% were from backgrounds where a language other than English was used. 405 or 78% needed, according to teacher evaluation, specialist English as a Second Language support, and 270 or 52% were from Lebanese backgrounds. In a class, aside from the demands imposed by 90% not being native English speakers, there are on average three or more recent arrivals in Australia, three children with significant remedial problems, one or two emotionally maladjusted children, and one child with a significant health problem. Despite the above, this paper is not a piece of "misery research", but a description of how a school, with some support from the system, has responded to this challenge.

The challenge

From the preceding information we hope it is obvious that the Lebanese Australian children entering St Mel's School are in very great danger of being socially and educationally disadvantaged. The challenge is to design a set of educational experiences within a very limited resource base that will give them the same life choices and opportunities as other Australian children. This is of course extraordinarily difficult. As one teacher wrote "this is a place where educational challenge has no limit". If equality of outcome (rather than equality of opportunity only) is a goal of the school, and if all children, despite their linguistic background, have the right to achieve this equality, then the challenge is achieving linguistic and educational rights for all children.

The response

Staff development

Teachers' previous training in effective education for LOTE children is a major variable in the provision of such education. Currently in New South Wales there is little available in the pre-service area which will adequately prepare a classroom teacher for a culturally diverse school. This places upon schools the demand to make some provision for staff development, usually from their own resources. St Mel's response involved a large group of teachers attending an "ESL for Classroom Teachers" course; developing a release time project to enable teachers to discuss cognitive development language issues; organising extensive discussion and in-service input from the Catholic system's multicultural adviser; arranging for cross grade exchanges on such language issues; and actively promoting the need for higher expectations of the students (see "attitude creation" below). As Samuda (1979: 49) writes about the education of language minority children, "The central feature for change must be the teacher's attitude, the teacher's understanding and acceptance which can only come by implementing preservice and inservice education programs ...". In retrospect it was of great importance to accept teachers' current understanding of language learning and the teaching of LOTE children, and to challenge teachers to be able to articulate why they were doing what they were doing. As teachers' awareness and skills in the language areas developed and as their ability to articulate such ideas strengthened, it became possible to redesign the language programmes to more appropriately meet the needs of all LOTE children, and to make more effective use of the two ESL specialists. Other outcomes of such development and professional interaction were the understanding of the need to exploit and develop language across all curriculum areas and a desire to include bilingual approaches as an option (see "the bilingual programme" below). This can be seen as a successful attainment of the major aim of professional development, which was to develop reflective professionals who could scan a variety of language and educational theories and select from them those elements best able to meet the needs of this particular group of pupils.

Attitude creation

Skutnabb-Kangas (1984, chapters 2 and 10) has argued eloquently and convincingly that there is a link between attitudes and the educational underachievement of language minorities. Hernández-Chávez (1988: 48–

54) documents this clearly for the USA case. Howard Giles in many publications (see for example Giles, 1977) has also made a strong case for the role of attitudes in a whole range of language related phenomena such as language loss and death. Hence the attitudes of teachers, children and parents were directly addressed.

Among *teachers* it was necessary to ensure that their expectations of these children were that the children could achieve at the same levels as other children (including middle class native English speakers). Without such expectations, depressed educational achievement can become the norm, since it is well established that low expectations lead to low achievement — see for the principle Rosenthal — Jacobson (1968), and for an example from bilingual education Carrasco (1981). There is a danger that the children's language background may be seen as a disadvantage rather than a potential asset, as an excuse rather than a starting point. Another aspect of teachers' attitude base was their attitudes to themselves, their self image and self esteem in relation to their work. In a profession which is often poorly regarded and shabbily treated in Western societies this is not always easy. In practice this meant developing an appropriate organisational and educational climate in the school, by involving teachers as partners in a continuing educational debate and decision making process of the type discussed in "Staff Development" above. By and large the attitudinal objectives have been attained: the teachers believe (rightly in our view) that their children are capable of a high level of educational achievement, and that they themselves are professionals, who are doing their job well — this has become part of the culture of the school. Evidence for this is provided later, in the teachers' comments.

Among *children* there was a possibility that those from minority language backgrounds might develop low self esteem if their home language and culture were not seen to be valued (see Taylor — Meynard — Rheault 1977). To counteract this (as well as the transitional bilingual programme discussed below) an aggressive staff employment policy was adopted of using teachers of Lebanese background. In addition, Lebanese language and culture were recognised in school practices, procedures, signs and other aspects of the curriculum. Examples include: newsletters in Arabic, the learning of Arabic songs by all children, the recognition and celebration of days important to the Lebanese community and Arabic language programmes for Arab-Australians in years 5 and 6. The success of the policy was demonstrated in the comments given by children and teachers during the evaluation of the bilingual programme performed by the Catholic Education office in September 1989: for example Rodney, a Lebanese background kindergarten child "Do we have Arabic today ... I love Arabic", and from a Lebanese background teacher "For the first time in Australia I feel comfortable to be Lebanese". However, the most important single means of supporting the children's self esteem was enabling them to succeed through the curriculum development discussed below. Attitudes and achievement are of course in a dynamic, mutually influencing relationship, rather than one directly causing the other. Lambert (1977: 25–26) discusses the consequences of similar work with French Canadian children "they apparently have been lifted from the typical low standing on scholastic achievement measures that characterizes many ethnolinguistic groups in North America. An important element in this transformation appears to be a change in the self-views of the French-trained youngsters who, our research has shown, begin to reflect a powerful pride in being French ...".

With regard to Lebanese *parents* an attempt has been made to overcome any culturally based views of schooling which were limiting the level of their participation in the life of the school. This includes involvement in the instructional programme, in the home and/or in the school (compare Ada 1988). Part of this process involved developing the necessary knowledge and skills through a ten session Parent Education Programme, which was designed to assist parents in responding to their children's reading and writing and also included an introduction to current Maths in Arabic. There were language specific meetings to enable parents to raise concerns and issues. Volunteer parents from the Parent Education Programme also work on the bilingual programme, the personal development programme, and take group reading/writing activity. Since more learning takes place on an individual basis in the home than is possible within the school, to regard education as the unique preserve of teachers is an attempt to walk on one leg. The school's target is meaningful (not token) involvement of parents in instruction, either in the classroom or in the home. The acceptance and involvement of parents in the programme is evidenced by this teacher's comment "Parents are feeling very positive about it (the bilingual programme) — they see it as the school reflecting what they want".

The bilingual programme

The bilingual programme at Campsie placed particular emphasis upon the following five principles.

1) The first language is a valuable basis for learning the second (Cummins 1984: 142–144).
2) Allowing the child to learn through the mother tongue
   (a) establishes a socio-emotional environment which provides the basic conditions for learning, (for example Appel (1988: 76) notes that children from a bilingual programme "seemed more "in balance" and less disturbed than the [comparable] children from the regular schools"); and
   (b) permits normal cognitive development — for evidence of the role of the mother tongue in cognitive development see Slade — Gibbons (1987: 104).
3) Maintaining the separation of languages is important, and is achieved by using each language for an extended block of time rather than relying on continual translation and code switching. There are two surveys which give the main reasons for doing so: these are Mc-Laughlin (1985: 121–124) and Swain (1986: 105–109). To summarise briefly, the reasons are: (a) where languages of instruction are mixed, learners ignore the language they understand less well and wait for a translation. This can result in an undesirable slowing in the acquisition of the second language — in the case of our learners, English (Legaretta 1979); (b) separation of languages forces learner engagement with both languages and encourages teachers to use creative and non-verbal means of communication when using the children's weaker language; both of these promote learning of language (Wong Fillmore 1982); (c) continuous interpreting is exhausting for teachers (Swain 1986: 107); (d) perhaps most importantly, unless specific time is set aside for the minority language, even in bilingual programmes the majority language tends to take up to 90% of the instruction time as a consequence of its socio-cultural dominance (Wong Fillmore — Ammon 1984).
4) Bilingualism should be a bonus — it is important to avoid subtractive bilingualism (Lambert 1977: 19) in which the child's mother tongue is replaced by an (often) incomplete knowledge of the second. A good bilingual programme recognises that the child is a potentially competent and balanced bilingual with all the cognitive and social advantages that this brings. A well researched illustration of the potential advantages of being bilingual is Bain — Yu (1978).
5) Provision of a bilingual programme demonstrates to the community that minority languages and cultures are valued.

The bilingual programme at St Mel's is transitional, based on principles one and two above, so it runs in the first three years of schooling, which is the most critical time, since this is when the children's Arabic is most fragile (principle 1) and their English least developed (principle 2). We recognise that a continuing bilingual programme would be desirable, but this would demand resources that would be removed from other even higher priorities. Following principle 3, the timetable for each school day is divided into blocks of time. At certain times all children are taught the following through the medium of English: English, Social Science, Religion, Health, Art and Craft, Music and Physical Education. For one and a half hours four days a week the year group is divided into Arabic medium and English medium streams, and Mathematics and Science are taught, with reinforcement later in the English medium time blocks. After the Arabic medium block the Bilingual Aides provide within class support to the Arabic dominant children across other curriculum areas. To make this possible, class teachers, bilingual aides and the ESL teachers meet every day after school to plan the curriculum for the next day, in order to ensure that the same content is covered in both language streams, and also to discuss any problems that have arisen or may arise. This does involve extra time and commitment from the teachers. It also means that teachers to some extent "own" the bilingual programme, rather than perceiving it as an inappropriate formula imposed from outside. The print materials and resources are the English medium ones, since written Arabic is not used, only the spoken Lebanese dialect. Standard spoken and written Arabic are taught as a subject (rather than used as medium) in years 5 and 6.

The Catholic Education Office's evaluation elicited many comments in support of the use of Arabic. Among the more interesting were (from year one teachers)

> "it's made a huge difference to Joseph and Charbel ... they switch on quickly ... there's never a problem with maths and science concepts" and "About concept development — we've been doing surface area — those children (from the bilingual programme) — they hadn't heard the English before but they were able to transfer straight over. By the end of the lesson they were using the structures back to us that we were modelling in English. They were saying: 'I estimate that ...' ".

Focussed work on literacy and numeracy

In recent years, we have seen in primary education, and particularly among some primary teacher trainers in Australia and other parts of the world, somewhat idealistic beliefs concerning language development.

These include a belief in the ability of children to assume total responsibility for their own language development and a belief that such development will occur osmotically through immersion. This may derive from a misinterpretation of current educational theories concerning the nature of "whole language" and experiential approaches to language learning.

There is a range of definitions as to what constitutes a whole-language classroom and the philosophy that underpins it. It has often been seen, incorrectly we believe, as at the far process end of a process-product continuum, and as involving little or no direction or intervention by the teacher, including a rejection of work which focuses on language systems or language skills. For some children such an approach may be sufficient. For others however, including many children from culturally different or linguistic minority backgrounds, we would argue that it is not sufficient, and a more readable and explicit classroom is necessary. We feel that there are very great gains to be made in the learning of language, literacy and numeracy if there is (in addition to an unfocussed osmotic approach) a deliberate focus on certain elements of them within the context of a holistic language programme.

While the programme at St Mel's does not reject current theories concerning the value of a holistic and experiential approaches to language, the curriculum does allow for focussed work in specific language skills. In practice there is a focus on the language (i. e. Cognitive Academic language – Cummins 1984) demanded by all curriculum areas. Teaching programmes include focussed work on particular language areas, whether notions/functions (such as classifying or contrasting), grammar (such as tenses) or genres (such as exposition or reports). Similarly, in reading development activity phonics and other word attack skills are included as part of the development of a set of reading strategies, and writing is quite carefully modelled and guided. It is an eclectic approach founded in an understanding of both language theory and learner needs.

Evaluation of the programme

Formative evaluation has been carried out twice each year, and the programme has been substantially revised and improved through this process. The comments quoted through this paper were mostly gathered during the formative evaluations. The best measure of success comes from the former year 3 teachers who have commented that formerly in that year 40 – 50% of children were non-functional readers/writers. Today this has been reduced to approximately 10—15%. and it is hoped to reduce this further. This provides convincing evidence of the school's success, and we believe that the curriculum at St Mel's is a good model worthy of wider propagation.

However its success needs demonstrating to a sceptical world. There are severe problems in performing an objective summative evaluation of the programme. First there is the problem of finding appropriate instruments which would fairly reflect the curriculum. Secondly it is difficult to find meaningful measurable intermediate objectives for our long term aim of enabling these children to have the same life chances as native speaking middle class peers. Third we feel it would be invidious and unprofessional to deliberately set out to prove the success of the programme if this would entail destructive comparisons with the attainments of other children and other schools. We are now attempting to find a form of evaluation that would overcome these problems and whose findings would be reasonably acceptable to everyone.

Coda

To continue to resource schools on the assumption that they are primarily monolingual and monocultural runs the risk of developing a second class citizenry which has never had the opportunity to develop to its fullest potential through the provision of appropriate educational programmes that acknowledge the linguistic rights of the children. Until decisions by government funding agencies and at upper levels in any educational hierarchy involve professionals who have had experience at primary level with large numbers of LOTE children, decisions will lack deep and genuine understanding both of the problems faced by children entering an educational system which uses a language other than their own, and of the necessity for the profound re-adjustment of the entire education system which is required to cope with this reality. Without such informed decision making, the nature and funding of programmes for such children will continue to be determined from an inadequate base.

III POST-COLONIAL DILEMMAS AND STRUGGLES

Section introduction

RAINER ENRIQUE HAMEL's first paper **Indigenous education in Latin America: policies and legal frameworks** describes the main types of indigenous education that have been practised, and the fundamental ambivalence of Latin American states towards indigenous education in the state-building enterprise. If bilingualism is regarded as desirable, but not biculturalism, as in Mexico, this shows a similar half-heartedness towards the distinctiveness of minority cultures as in immigrant education in Western countries, where bi- or multiculturalism is nominally accepted but seldom bilingualism. Both disconnections are violations of rights. Indian (Hamel explains why he uses this term in footnote 2) educational and linguistic rights have become central in the struggle for Indian cultural survival. The issue of the importance of education through the medium of the mother tongue is considered in the light of experience, particularly from Mexico and Brazil. Hamel's paper draws on a wealth of evidence from throughout Latin America.

RAINER ENRIQUE HAMEL's second paper **Linguistic rights for Amerindian peoples in Latin America** summarizes the position of indigenous minorities throughout Latin America, and concentrates on a comparison between Mexico and Brazil. The study shows how inconsistent and ambivalent official policy is vis-a-vis Indian groups, and that when constitutional documents accord few substantial rights, of whatever kind, to these Aboriginal peoples, *individual* rights are inadequate (a position which is strongly supported by the representatives of Indigenous Peoples, commenting on the First Revised Text of the Draft Declaration on Rights of Indigenous Peoples, see IWGIA 1990: 159). If the destruction of Indian cultures is to stop, rights need to be *collective*, the property of the group. There is a complex relationship between individual and *territorial* rights, and a different position in each country, which HAMEL's country studies bring out clearly. *LHRs and cultural rights are interwoven with rights to land and water, and to autonomous control of resources and education.* HAMEL also shows that there is a fundamental *incompatibility between a Western-inspired legal system and Indian customary law* (which is older than that of the invader). The vital questions are what legal framework would facilitate the survival of Amerindian groups, and what role LHRs would play.

LACHMAN KHUBCHANDANI's paper **"Minority" cultures and their communication rights**, *questions* several implicit *assumptions and concepts in "western" homogenizing language planning* efforts, while his article also criticizes some of the policy decisions in South Asia, using the position of Sindhi speakers in India as an example. He mentions the increasingly active role of State machineries in promoting linguistic homogeneity and in misinterpreting or even misusing ethnic upsurges. He claims that to organize plural societies politically along linguistic lines (as when Indian Provinces were reorganised in 1956) completely transforms the concept of language pluralism. When the right to territory (i. e. Province borders) was made exclusively dependent on language, language identity changed from being one among the many fluid, non-static, low-key, combinable identities with no clear-cut borders, either sociolinguistically (borders between different languages, dialects, sociolects and stylistic varieties being fluid) or socioculturally (religious, regional, educational, professional and majority/minority identities merging into each other but not being coterminous) to becoming The Defining Characteristic in a new stratification order. For a country where native speakers of a language do not necessarily form a coherent speech community geographically (they may live in several countries and in many provinces, and be minorities everywhere) or in terms of accepting (or needing) the same linguistic norms and standards (or formalised linguistic standards in the first place), language planning models or concepts about what are or should be linguistic rights, developed in more homogeneous or homogenizing societies, are not necessarily positive.

Khubchandani rejects monistic, puritanical norms, razor-edged boundaries between languages, attempts by dominant languages (and their political representatives) at homogenizing and eradicating plurality. He makes a plea for accepting situational norms, heterogeneity, inherent fluidity in the speech spectrum, and claims that it not only may meet the demands of social justice and the needs of "minority" cultures and languages better — but that it also makes more sense.

MAKHAN TICKOO's paper **Kashmiri, a majority-minority language: an exploratory essay**, presents an unusual Indian linguistic situation, describing Kashmiri, one of the 15 languages (out of the 1652 mother tongues reported in the 1963 census) which have been given official political recognition in the Constitution as literary languages. Despite being official and the absolute majority language (the mother tongue of 97% of the population) in the valley of Kashmir, Kashmiri is not used in the official administration or as a medium in primary school. In addition to being the language of home, neighbourhood and market place, Kashmiri has a literary heritage going back several centuries. It is being studied in upper secondary school as a subject, and at university level.

Myths about Kashmiri being inadequate, only a dialect, having an incomplete grammar, etc, are still abundant. Tickoo sees many of the myths (about the negative consequences of bilingualism; several languages being a burden rather than enrichment; the "necessity" of choosing between a "world language" with all its riches and a small, backward mother tongue, only good for ethnic identity; time spent on the mother tongue being time taken off English) as consequences of the linguicist misinformation which the unilingual west has successfully propagated in "Third World"/Asian countries. The myths have been spread by "men who, like their ancestors among the Platonic cavemen, refuse to look beyond their comfortably walled worlds."

Tickoo describes the consequences of the displacement of the Kashmiri language for the individual child, for families, literacy efforts, the economy and the general social structure (a new "caste" system is rapidly developing, with an English-knowing elite, alienated from the Kashmiri-speaking ordinary people). The consequences of linguicism which he describes echo the similar experience of minorities and powerless majorities all over the world. The more oppressed the people feel, the more intense will become their desire for a separate political status, which would restore the mother tongue and people's pride in themselves.

Tickoo's alternative resembles that of many African thinkers/researchers: the mother tongues have to be restored, and have their rightful place in all official spheres, most importantly education. English (like other dominant languages) also has to have its rightful place, a status as "a strong additional language" and not that of "a language of social survival". What is needed for the alternative to succeed is a proper action-oriented strategy (plans for the script problem, for curricula, materials and teacher training etc) as well as a subsidiary attitudes-oriented strategy which starts dismantling the myths and educating all those who lack faith in the capacity of Kashmiri to serve as a language for learning.

Tickoo makes a strong case for applied linguistics and ELT being radically re-thought. His strictures on the *irrelevance and inappropriacy of language pedagogy devised in the West and dispensed in the East* echo that of other Indian specialists (e.g. Kachru 1986; Pattanayak 1981, see also Phillipson 1992). Tickoo's description of Kashmiri studies flourishing at university level but being deprived of their rightful place in the school system also has an exact parallel in Africa: "the paradox of mother tongue education in many African countries is that while it is negligible at primary level, it seems to flourish at university level" (Bamgbose 1991: 101).

ROBERT PHILLIPSON and TOVE SKUTNABB-KANGAS' paper **Language rights in postcolonial Africa** notes that although lip-service is paid in government circles to the desirability of promoting indigenous African languages, it is still the former colonial languages which are accorded pride of place. A major cause of this is that the linguistic hierarchy that was established in the colonial period, in each colonial empire, is still largely in place. The hierarchy is maintained partly through structures, essentially the allocation of resources and functional roles to some languages rather than others, and through attitudes towards the relevant languages, some being perceived as more equal/useful/modern/etc than others. There is substantial evidence of inequality between languages, and the way government and donor policies perpetuate this. As a result most Africans are deprived of the right to learn their mother tongues in the education system or use them in law courts or in dealings with the authorities.

Many African scholars have devised policies for multilingual language planning which would involve greater enjoyment of linguistic rights. At the Pan-African level, the OAU (Organization for African Unity) has elaborated a charter of linguistic rights and related policy documents.

TOVE SKUTNABB-KANGAS and SERTAÇ BUCAK's paper **Killing a mother tongue — how the Kurds are deprived of linguistic human rights** deals with the most extreme form of linguistic oppression, describing how the elimination of the Kurdish language is enacted in the Turkish Constitution and legislation. The rich history and contemporary variety of the Kurdish language are summarized, as are some of the complications of the language evolving differently in adjacent but distinct states: Kurdish is written in different scripts, takes in loans from different languages, Kurdish is politically fragmented. The position of Kurdish is thus in some respects comparable to that of Sámi and several major African languages which are spread over several states because of the way state borders were drawn by the colonial powers in 1884–1885.

Turkish language legislation and policy is in conflict with countless human rights covenants, and runs counter to many current international initiatives aimed at the protection of minorities. Turkey, as a country aspiring to membership of the European Community, and in the aftermath of worldwide concern for the fate of the Kurds after the Gulf war of 1991, wishes to convince the outside world that human rights are respected in Turkey. It has therefore deliberately sought to create the impression in the Western media that the Kurdish language is no longer restricted. The reality is unchanged, as even a cursory glance at the Anti-Terror Law of 1991 shows. Speakers of Kurdish are still systematically deprived of fundamental linguistic rights.

The second part of the article relates the current position in Turkey to definitions of "mother tongue" (by origin, identification, competence and function) and the way these constituents of the term mother tongue relate to human rights awareness, to language legislation (drawing on the grid presented in Phillipson — Skutnabb-Kangas, this volume) and oppression of a language. This part also exemplifies conceptual clarifications needed for declarations of linguistic human rights.

Indigenous education in Latin America: policies and legal frameworks[1]

Rainer Enrique Hamel

In Latin America most Indian[2] peoples are still far from enjoying the fundamental indigenous rights[3] which are considered essential to create a context for autonomous development and thus the survival of indigenous ethnias.[4]

In the first place, the right to use their own languages for official and educational purposes has been denied to the vast majority of Amerindian peoples since colonization, because the dominant societies considered the languages an obstacle to assimilation and national homogenization. Second, to grant the right of self-determination and control to a minority would contradict fundamental legal, ideological, and socio-economic convictions about the nation and the state, including the military doctrine of national security imposed by the USA during the era of military dictatorships since the sixties.

The central controversy underlying this conflict refers to the question whether it is possible to build plurilingual and pluricultural states that are able and willing to reconcile the forging of a national identity and unity with the preservation of linguistic and cultural diversity.

It is doubtless the project of building homogeneous, monolingual and monocultural nation states shaped on the European model that emerges as the main obstacle to an independent, ethnicity-based development of Indian education. After independence most Latin American constitutions based on a liberal and positivist philosophy extended the general principles of freedom and equality to all citizens including the Indians. Since no one should be discriminated against because of their race, language, gender, or religion, education had to be equal for everyone and was supposed to contribute to the overall objective of creating a homogeneous population. As we shall see later, the inherent contradiction between the postulated formal equality and the factual inequality turned the abstract legal principle into its opposite and helped to maintain discrimination in most cases.

In this paper I shall first give some basic data about the indigenous population in Latin America. Next, the main strategies and models of indigenous education in Latin America will be outlined, including some data on the legal framework of education. Third, Indian education will be exemplified with the cases of Mexico and Brazil, Latin American's most important countries, that contrast in almost all aspects of indigenous population and education. Finally, I shall draw some conclusions about differences and similarities in indigenous education in Latin America.

Amerindian population

Today more than 30 million Indians representing aproximately 400 ethnolinguistic peoples[5] live in Latin America.[6] An extreme diversity of numbers[7], demographic density, linguistic (and sociolinguistic) differentiation, and degrees of assimilation are characteristic of their actual conditions of life. Taking into account this heterogeneity, three main groupings could be distinguished among Amerindian peoples (cf. *América Indígena*, L, 1, 1990: 20).

The first and most important comprises at least 80% of the indigenous population and is concentrated in two *macro-ethnias* located in the areas where highly differentiated societies existed before the European conquest; one occupies the *Mesoamerican plateau* containing central Mexico (6 to 8 million), Guatemala (3.4 million), and Belize (24.000)(cf. Suárez 1983). Some 80 languages are spoken by this ethnic family, among them Náhuatl (the main language of the ancient Aztec empire) and Mayan as the most important ones. The other one is located in the *Andean area* from the south of Columbia to the north of Chile, including Ecuador, Peru, and Bolivia as the most important countries with Amerindian population (cf. Rodríguez et al. 1983). Here 2 languages, Quechua (12 millions) and Aymara (3 million), are dominant.

The second grouping is subdivided into more than 300 languages and comprises some 7 million members scattered over the whole of the Latin American territory. Their main areas of residence are located in Central America (except Guatemala and Belize), the Caribbean coast of South America, the Amazonian basin, and the extreme south of the continent (Argentina and Chile). Different from the first, this ensemble of Amerindian micro-ethnias is characterized by low demographic density, high linguistic diversity, and a wide variety of stages on the continuum of socioeconomic and cultural assimilation that range from still fairly isolated hunter and gatherer societies to almost fully assimilated groups.

The third and relatively new grouping is growing fast at the expense of the other two (cf. *América Indígena*, L, 1, 1990): it comprises the *urban indigenous population* of several millions that share the living conditions of the urban sub-proletariat dwelling in the huge shanty-towns that surround Latin American big cities. Capitals like Lima, Mexico and Guatemala City, La Paz, or Quito bear the mark of an increasing Amerindian population that interfere decisively with recent urban processes and the forging of new multicultural societies.[8]

From the perspective of the national states and their indigenous population, Latin America could be subdivided into 5 groups of countries: 1. *Uruguay* and *Caribbean* countries like *Cuba*, where the Indian population has been exterminated; 2. countries like *Brazil* (0.17%) *Costa Rica* (0.8%), *Argentina* (1%), *Venezuela* (1.5%), *Columbia* (2.2%), *El Salvador* (2.3%), *Paraguay* (2.3%)[9], and *Honduras* (3.2%) with a minute or relatively small percentage of Amerindian population; 3. countries like *Chile* (5.7) with a somewhat larger indigenous population but with relatively little weight in socioeconomic and political terms; 4. *Mexico* (9%)[10], *Peru* (27%), and *Ecuador* (33.9%) where the aboriginal population plays a significant historical, ideological and political role since they descend from ancient highly complex cultures, apart from their demographic weight; 5. and finally countries like *Bolivia* (59.2%) and *Guatemala* (59.7%), where the Indian peoples not only belong to ancient cultures but also amount to more than half of the population.

Indigenous education in Latin America: basic strategies

In Latin American history two radically divergent types of indigenous policies were translated into action to deal with the "Indian problem". One considered trying to integrate the Indian population impossible or of little value; consequently, this policy combined segregation with genocide causing the total extermination of the aboriginal population in Uruguay and most Caribbean countries; a reduction to extremely small numbers in Argentina[11], Brazil, and some other countries where genocide has still been practised in recent years; or it brought about a partial extermination as in Chile until the end of the 19th century.

The other position considered the so-called "integration"[12] of Indian populations a necessary and possible policy that would lead to a dissolution of aboriginal tribes through their mixture with the colonial society and the "white race", as happened in Mexico, Guatemala, and, partially, in the Andean states.

In the latter countries two basic strategies to reach the proposed aims developed over time in the fields of language policy (cf. Heath 1972; Orlandi 1988; Escobar 1988; Albó 1988a, b; Plaza — Albó 1989, etc.) and education for Indians (cf. Rodríguez et al. 1983; Zúñiga et al. 1987; López 1989; López — Moya 1990).

The first and generally dominant strategy considered the assimilation (i. e. dissolution) of Indian peoples and the suppression of their languages as a prerequisite for building up a unified nation state. A second position favoured the preservation of Indian languages and cultures in this process, without giving up the ultimate aim of uniting nation and state. Up to a certain point, this controversy was reflected in education and Spanish teaching — the main pillars of cultural policies for the Indians — through two basic approaches which differed considerably in their cultural and educational philosophy and methods, their view on socio-cultural integration, and, above all, in their procedure of using and teaching Spanish as the national language.

The first strategy imposed direct Hispanization: the national language was considered to be the only target and medium of instruction; teaching materials, content, and methods were the exclusive preserve of the dominant society, in accordance with the objective of assimilation. Speaking in modern terms, we would call this procedure a *submersion programme.*

Transitional programmes reflected the second strategy; they applied diverse bilingual methods where the Indian language played a subordinate, instrumental role as language of instruction and for initial alphabetization. This alternative emerged in the 1930s and 1940s as experimental programmes[13] because of the absolute sociopolitical and educational failure of the submersion programmes. The Indian languages were no longer considered to be an obstacle, but a useful tool for cultural transition. The principle that anyone learns better in her or his mother tongue was becoming generally accepted at that time.[14]

No clear *maintenance programmes* materialized in that period. Nevertheless, some of the most progressive pilot projects led by pro-Indian anthropologists did contain elements of maintenance programmes, mainly through L1 literacy and a series of contextual ethnic activities. Given their limited pedagogical resources, and — in the long run — political support, however, they eventually turned into transitional programmes.

Important changes have begun to surface since the 1970s. The emergence of Indian movements throughout the continent (cf. Grupo de Barbados 1979; Bonfil 1981; Rodríguez et al. 1983), progressive nationalist governments in some countries, and a growing awareness of the multilingual and multiethnic nature of their states among the more critical sections of society — all these elements are contributing to the rise of alternative, genuinely bilingual, intercultural and pluralistic models of Indian education. Such projects appeared as official policy or pilot projects in Peru in the 70s, and in Ecuador, Mexico, Guatemala, and Nicaragua in the 80s.

Clearly opposed to previous models, the new programmes are based on a pluricultural conception of the state and full respect for Indian peoples and their ethnic rights. They claim as their target the maintenance or revitalization of Indian cultures and languages (cf. América Indígena, XLVII, 3, 4, 1987). According to the new philosophy, indigenous culture in the curriculum should not be restricted to content (Indian folktales and songs), but cover the full range of material, social, cognitive, and linguistic aspects of culture.[15] The consequent pursuit of such a perspective has even raised doubts about the appropriateness of formal education — an occidental, dominant institution par excellence — for Indian peoples as such.

Until today, however, pluriethnic programmes of Indian education represent a goal, sometimes an officially declared policy, rather than a real practice (cf. Varese 1983). Important backlashes, as in Peru, or ambiguities, as in Mexico, often occur due to changing political constellations. And, of course, many theoretical, methodological, and practical problems remain unsolved. (cf. Amadio 1987a; Modiano 1988).

Pluriethnic education and the Indian movement

Whereas in the submersion and transitional models, Indian groups and individuals played a more passive than active role, and legal aspects remained rather marginal, in the struggle for a pluralist maintenance model of education, both *Indian movements* and the question of *Indian educational and linguistic rights*[16] become a central issue.

It appears that the most conscious Indian organizations have already gone beyond traditional demands such as access to education that could be satisfied within the established system. The new element in their struggle consists in the fact that some movements now question the *legitimacy* of the state to design and impose models of assimilation, transition, or even maintenance in indigenous education. A genuine bilingual intercultural model of native education would seem to require at this stage that there exists an Indian movement strong enough and capable of taking over control and developing a basic programme for native education, possibly with the support and advice of experts outside the ethnia; and that the dominant classes of the state cede sufficient economic, political, and cultural autonomy and resources for the minority peoples to organize themselves according to their own principles. Only then a new relationship of *integration*, i. e. a process of mutual negotiation and change (cf. Skutnabb-Kangas 1991d), could be initiated that might eventually lead to minority programmes of maintenance and enrichment without segregation.

The legal basis and the multicultural awareness of both minorities and dominant groups for such a framework of autonomy is, however, far from the reality in Latin America. Although all countries in the area grant the right to public education and equality of access in their constitutions, more than half of them do not establish any specific legislation concerning the education of linguistic minorities. Among those that do, *Bolivia*[17], *Peru* and *Mexico* stipulate that literacy should be achieved through L1 to facilitate transition to L2 as soon as possible. Others like *Brazil, Columbia*[18], *Ecuador, Panama* and *Guatemala* decree bilingual intercultural education without any specific definition of purpose (transitional or otherwise) or limit education in the indigenous languages to the audio-oral skills like Paraguay.

Peru represents a fairly unique case in the recent Latin American history of Indian education (cf. Paulston 1988a; López — Moya 1990). Between 1968 and 1975, a progressive military regime under Velasco Alvarado initiated a series of radical reforms including the expropriation of strategic resources and large land estates ("latifundios"). In this context, the military government also tried to break the power of the urban and rural oligarchy in the domains of culture and language in order to establish a genuinely multiethnic space for the indigenous cultures. For the first time, education was not considered only an instrument to hispanize and assimilate the Indian population, but a tool for permanent bilingual and bicultural development beyond the narrow barriers of the school (cf. Escobar 1975, 1983; Pozzi-Escot 1988; Cerrón-Palomino 1989). However, the violent reaction of the white and mestizo bourgeoisie against being forced to learn Quechua impeded any real bilingual programme for the majority to be put to practice.

Generally speaking, the overall objective of almost all constitutions and educational laws is to assimilate the Indians as individuals into the nation. Legal prescriptions range from covert prohibition of use of the Indian languages at school to rare cases of overt maintenance-oriented permission.[19]

Indian education in Mexico and Brazil

As an example of the wide range of cases I shall examine the programmatic debates and practical implementations of Indian education in Mexico and Brazil, the two most important countries in terms of economic, political and demographic weight (80 and 140 million inhabitants) in Latin America. At the same time they represent polar cases that contrast in most aspects concerning Indian minorities: their quantitative role, the countries' history of colonization ("mestizage" and assimilation vs. genocide and segregation), legislation (non-recognition but acceptance as citizens vs. paternalistic legal tutelage), and educational programmes (governmental policies and monopoly institutions vs. negligence and private initiatives).[20]

Mexico

Mexico corresponds to the general picture of language policy and Indian education sketched above.[21] There was no question about the necessity and possibility of integrating the native peoples, who formed the majority of the population until the second half of the 19th century; systematic genocide has never been a real option as in some other Latin American countries. The question was rather *how* integration should be achieved. Throughout history the two basic approaches — direct Hispanization vs. transitional bilingual education — developed and were used at different times (cf. Sánchez Cámara — Ayala 1979; Scanlon — Lezama Morfin 1982).

In 1988, 7,671 pre-primary and 18,446 primary school teachers, all of them Indians, offered services to some 690,000 children of school age. Until 1988, 84 primers and teacher's manuals in more than 36 of the 56 Indian languages were printed, together with other teaching materials (cf. González Gaudiano 1988).

During the past administration (1982 to 1988) the Office of Indian Education (Dirección General de Educación Indígena — DGEI) in the

Federal Ministry of Public Education, developed a programme of bilingual and bicultural education that was to provide instruction to all Indians from pre-primary (kindergarten) through grade 6.

The programme proposed a radical change of perspective as compared to previous curricula in that it recognized the necessity of teaching literacy in the vernacular language. The education of monolingual Indian children should start at the age of 5 with 2 years of alphabetization in the vernacular language (pre-school year and 1st grade). Spanish audio-oral skills for communicative and academic purposes should be introduced in the 2nd year; and only in the 3rd grade were reading and writing skills to be taught in Spanish, in the hope that transfer strategies would help to acquire these skills relatively fast. During the 7 years of elementary education (pre-school + 6 grades), the Indian languages should function as the main languages of instruction in all subjects. Furthermore indigenous cultural topics were to be introduced in the curriculum.

Generally speaking, this curriculum takes into account important findings from international research (cf. Cummins 1984; Cummins — Swain 1986; Harley et al. 1990). It contains the necessary characteristics of a maintenance programme which could in principle, depending on modalities of application, produce additive bilingualism and foster cultural and ethnic identity. At the same time, it could contribute to reaching satisfactory levels of academic achievement and communicative skills in both languages.

During the 1984—85 and 1985—86 school years, the programme and existing teaching materials were tested in some 40 pilot schools in the Nahuatl, Zapotec, Mixtec, and Mixe language areas. Unfortunately, no results of this evaluation are known. The pilot projects were interrupted and the massive adoption of the programme that had been planned for 1987 has been suspended because of political opposition that was never made public.

Since 1990 we face a new setback in relation to prior decisions in educational policy. Thus L1 literacy is again being severely questioned in the context of an overall programme of educational modernization (cf. SEP 1990) that claims to prepare Mexican students for the new challenges in connection with the new Free Trade Agreement with the USA and Canada.

At the present a great variety of pedagogicial practices are in use in the Indian Educational System. They include direct Spanish teaching as the basic method, using the monolingual Spanish primer as the only textbook, intuitive (i. e. non systematic) use of the vernacular as language of instruction, and many other improvised procedures. These reflect the inadequacies of teaching materials, and the immense range of ethnic, sociolinguistic, and administrative diversity which is characteristic of Mexican Indian education (cf. Hamel 1984, 1988b).[22]

The central debate in Mexico, a controversy that is hardly ever carried out in public, focusses on the following issues:

1. To what extent is the government prepared to grant relative autonomy to the system of Indian Education? By the end of the last administration in 1988, it seemed that autonomy was granted to teach literacy and other content matters in L1 where appropriate; but teaching content had to be kept homogeneous and must follow the national compulsory curriculum for Spanish-speaking children. In other words, bilingualism was accepted to a certain extent, yet biculturalism was not.
2. To what extent are Indian-language literacy skills and content matters desirable for the pedagogical development of the child? Are there research findings that not only prove or demonstrate the convenience of developing literacy and other cognitively demanding skills in L1, but also convince the Mexican politicians and experts who are the policy-makers? Up to now, almost no research findings from studies in Mexico on these topics are available.
3. To what extent is a programme based on L1 literacy acceptable to Indian communities who have always considered the public school as a means of Hispanization and assumed upward social mobility? Most inquiries among Indians only reproduce the well-known stereotype that Indian communities really want to use only the official language at school.[23]
4. To what extent do the emerging Indian movements develop educational objectives and models of their own that may enter and, eventually, substitute the official curricula?[24]

Brazil

Brazil is a typical representative of those countries that combined genocide with segregation and paternalistic tutelage in the past (cf. Ribeiro 1970), reducing the indigenous population from some 5 million at the time of colonization to 200.000 today.[25]

For a long time, Indian peoples lived under military control. The government made little effort to provide Indians with public education.

By 1980, only 5 language groups out of 170 received specific education by state agencies. Catholic missions and over 25 foreign protestant sects set up local educational projects that ranged from submersion programmes to fully bilingual programmes with L1 instruction (cf. Melià 1979; Montserrat 1989). Altogether less than 10% of the Indian population of school age were offered formal education by 1980 (cf. Varese — Rodríguez 1983). According to my own experience in 1989, this situation has improved significantly, due to the work of a number of non governmental organizations (NGOs), some of which have developed very promising experimental programmes and produced some teaching materials.[26] Unfortunately, very few of these programmes are sufficiently documented[27], and virtually no solid research on bilingual education exists.

On the other hand, important gains for Indian rights were achieved with the new Constitution in 1988 (cf. Hamel, this volume). Article 210 concerning public education establishes that Portuguese is the language of instruction in primary education. Nevertheless, Indian communities are granted the right to use their mother tongues and their own learning procedures during primary education. Throughout 1989 and 1990 intensive debates took place to elaborate proposals for specific laws, decrees, and the regulation of Indian education. For instance, a new bill on education (Diretrizes e Bases da Educaçao Nacional, article 52) submitted to Parliament in 1989 (cf. *Boletim Jurídico*, 1, 5, 1989:3) contains important specifications for Indian community education. They demand bilingual and intercultural education for Indian peoples that helps to foster Indian social organization, cultures, customs, languages, beliefs, and traditions. Programmes should strengthen the sociocultural use of mother tongues and elaborate specific methods for L1 and L2 teaching. Teacher training for Indian staff, flexible curricula, evaluation programmes and procedures, as well as differentiated teaching materials and time-tables according to agricultural cycles, etc. are also on the agenda.

All these legal improvements could no doubt inspire optimism if it were not for the well-kown fact that legal protection did not prevent the dominant society from committing acts of genocide over many years. At the time of writing, it is still too early to evaluate or even know in detail the outcome of the legislation process. Even less do we know what real changes in Indian education may emanate from legislation.

Compared to Mexico the situation of many Indian peoples in Brazil is that of relative isolation and preservation of important traits of their traditional tribal culture; they have been subjected though to rapid change during recent years. The clearcut ethnic boundaries (cf. Barth 1969) between the Brazilian dominant, non-Indian society and the Indian peoples has a considerable influence on the debate about Indian education. Different from Mexico again, there is hardly any question that Indians need some kind of specific education of their own.

Two chains of argument concerning *literacy in L1 or L2* could be identified.

1. The first advocates of *literacy in L1* based on a justification that is common elsewhere (cf. Montserrat 1987): *Technical and professional* arguments support the view that alphabetization in L2 is difficult due to learners' limited competence in that language; literacy in L1 is faster, afterwards strategies of transfer to L2 can operate. *Political and cultural* arguments include the higher valorization of Indian culture through L1 education; every individual's right to acquire literacy in her or his own language; and that literacy in L1 contributes to a modernization and standardization of Indian languages which is necessary for their survival.

2. The other position advocates *L2 literacy*. Whereas in Mexico L2 literacy is justified on the basis of folk theories like "maximum exposure", and with the necessity to assimilate, to grant upward mobility, etc., in Brazil the sharp ethnolinguistic dualism serves to justify L2 literacy (cf. Ladeira 1981) on the *technical* grounds that literacy in L1 would only produce "semi-literates" anyway; or the support of L2 literacy is based on *political and cultural* arguments such as Fishman's well-known postulate that cultural and linguistic maintenance could only be guaranteed if a clear division of functions and forms between the cultures and languages (diglossia and di-ethnia) is preserved.[28] Since the school is considered to be an instrument of the dominant occidental society and belongs to the "they-code" universe, Indian languages and cultures should be kept out of school in order to avoid their hegemonization, assimilation, and refunctionalization.[29] Furthermore, literacy in L1 is supposed to provoke violent changes in a non-literate society and reflects an ethnocentrist view which takes the written language as the best form to transmit knowledge, even cultural knowledge from a society based on orality. Furthermore, literacy in L2 (and oral acquisition of Portuguese) are needed for contact and wider communication; their learning avoids most of the problems mentioned before.

The two positions represent specific variants of the international controversy between proponents and opponents of L1 literacy (cf. Skutnabb-
Kangas 1986). In my view it would be inadequate in the Brazilian case
to identify opponents of L1 literacy altogether with an assimilation-
oriented, generally conservative position, and, vice versa, proponents
with progressive supporters of maintenance, as happens in the USA and
elsewhere.[30] The two sets of arguments reflect different views of ethnicity,
cultural contact, the role of the school as an institution, and political
control in a socio-economic and cultural context which contrasts significantly with other situations (e. g. migrants in industrialized countries).
On the whole, basic psycholinguistic issues related to language choice
and acquisition are dealt with much less than the central political question
of political and ethnic control, which occupies a salient position in the
Brazilian debate. Thus, alphabetization as an occidental mode of world
view, cognition, and communication are seen as a menace to orality-
based Indian cultures as such, irrespective, up to a certain point, of the
language chosen. Inspired by Freire's tradition of grounding alphabetization in the creation of political and cultural awareness, researchers and
activists are involved in developing methods, techniques, and materials
that are meant to reduce the effect of alienation and help Indian ethnias
to achieve control over their education.[31]

In sum, Brazilian education for Indian minorities shows both weaknesses and encouraging perspectives in its legal and educational aspects.
Given small numbers, extreme linguistic diversity, and a comparatively
low − but growing − level of Indian participation and control, the
position of Indian organizations is still rather defensive. On the other
hand, important steps forward have been made in recent years in terms
of political organization, the legal framework, national and international
awareness[32], and educational experience. According to most observers,
the Indian movement made considerable gains in Indian ethnic rights
with the new constitution (Sierra 1993 b). As claims Montserrat (1989),
the immediate task is now to formulate and promulgate specific laws and
regulations, and to design a national policy of Indian education.

At the level of local projects, significant experience has been gained
through pilot projects which show the viability and also the limits of a
wide range of approaches. The most innovative, successful, and partici-
pative projects and experiences of Indian bilingual and bicultural education are carried out by NGOs. One central problem in most initiatives
is little endurance and continuity, lack of materials and professional

support, as well as absence of documentation and research about ongoing projects.

In my view, the most important strategy to follow at present would be to support, encourage and initiate local projects, starting wherever possible from an Indian initiative. New experiments and pilot projects would have to be accompanied by integrative, multidisciplinary research capable of evaluating and testing specific aspects of the process, and of furnishing constant feedback to the educational process itself.

Mexico, Brazil, Latin America: convergence and divergence

This brief comparison highlights Mexico and Brazil as two contrastive poles on a continuum of Latin American legal frameworks, educational programmes, and debates on indigenous education. Many of the differences are due to fundamental contrasts in the Indians' historical, socioeconomic, and cultural modes of existence in each country.

Whereas in Mexico the historical role of Indian peoples for the foundation of the nation and their reciprocal, inclusive identity – as Indians *and* Mexican citizens – is hardly denied by anyone, Brazilian Indians remain separated from the nation in the consciousness of probably a majority in both societies. In addition to small numbers, this explains, at least in part, why it seems much easier in Brazil than in Mexico (or Peru, Bolivia, and Ecuador) to grant a certain autonomy in education as regards cultural content, methods, and language. In Mexico, by contrast, the "raison d'état" does not allow an important, supposedly integrated portion of the national population to break away from "mainstream" society in such a crucial, highly ideological field as public education.

In general terms, the dominant groups in Latin American societies persist with varying strategies in their resistance against sharing power with the indigenous minorities and against transforming their nations into pluricultural states. Education is one of the crucial fields in this controversy. The hegemonic strategy still pursues assimilation through a variety of submersion or transitional programmes. Exceptionally programmes can be found that come at least near to real bilingual maintenance courses, mainly through various different processes: either through initiatives launched and strongly supported from outside the indigenous group[33]; in situations where indigenous groups succeed in subverting existing programmes, or where their movements gained enough strength to establish a certain degree of autonomy in education (e. g. the Shuar in Ecuador, cf. Laje 1983; Kummer 1985). In the long run, true bilingual maintenance programmes will probably have a chance to consolidate where they are based on indigenous movements strong enough to have achieved autonomy and control over their own education.

Notes

1. Investigation for this paper is related to the Research Project "Language acquisition and academic development of Indian primary students", sponsored by the Mexican National Council for Research and Technology (Consejo Nacional de Ciencia y Tecnología — CONACYT) under the title D113−903962. A travel grant provided by CONACYT under title A128CC0E900410 to present this paper at the IX World Congress of Applied Linguistics in Thessaloniki, Greece, is gratefully acknowledged. I am also grateful to Tove Skutnabb-Kangas and Robert Phillipson for their very valuable comments on an earlier version of this and my other chapter in this volume.
2. Ever since the definition of the new territories as part of the Indies ("El Consejo de las Indias", etc.) at the beginning of Spanish and Portuguese colonization, the term "Indian" has become a widespread symbol of identification in Latin America in many concepts like "Indoamérica, indianidad"; today it bears no relationship with India for Latin American speakers. No doubt the word "indio" had and still has a discriminating connotation in a number of contexts and has therefore been replaced by the less specific "indígena" (= indigenous) in public and academic discourse. Over the past decades, however, the Indian population themselves have increasingly vindicated the term "indio" and its derivatives (cf. Bonfil 1981), perhaps in a similar process that made black people in the USA want to be called just blacks. For all these reasons, I shall adhere to the common habit in Latin America of using "Indian", most of the times in its combination "Amerindian", alongside with indigenous.
3. See e.g. the Draft Universal Declaration of Indigenous Rights (1989) which not only demands the recognition of an abstract right to use indigenous languages and to have access to education through the native idiom, but connects these demands with the fundamental claim of autonomy to organize and control the contexts of local language use and education according to the ethnia's own cultural patterns and traditions, and to dispose of the necessary resources for this purpose.
4. Schermerhorn's (1970) criteria (real or putative ancestry, memories of shared historical past, cultural focus on one or more symbolic elements for an ethnic group) may serve as a starting point to define ethnic groups on the macro-level topics dealt with in this article. My own sociolinguistic studies about Mexican Indians on the micro-level of social and verbal interaction (1988a), however show the limits of such global definitions. Very often, if not normally, ethnicity, like identity (cf. Wald — Poutignat 1982), exists in a fragmentary and contradictory way in the ethnic members' consciousness and action. It is constantly negotiated and has to be seen rather as a relation (like power, hegemony, etc.) than a substance (cf. Skutnabb-Kangas' (1990) concept of ambo-definitions (relational identifications) of ethnicity).
5. It is not my purpose to engage here in the complex debate about language classification. Typologies range from 300 to 600 languages for the American continent, according to

intrinsic principles of linguistic classification (cf. Arana de Swadesh et al. 1975; Suárez 1983; Muntzel – Pérez González 1987; Maurais 1991). Important classifications are Ruhlen (1987) for Amerindia, Suárez (1983) for Mesoamerica, and Rodrígues (1986) for Brazil.

6. Statistics about Indian demography are very poor in most countries; moreover, criteria to define membership of an ethnic minority are extremely difficult to establish since they imply complicated aspects of identification, identity, and ethnolinguistic consciousness (cf. Stavenhagen 1984; Rodríguez et al. 1983), among other criteria. Thus, the Mexican census of 1910 counts 51 language groups, the one of 1950 only 30, and the 1980 census 41 (cf. Valdés 1988). As almost everywhere, official census data tend to underestimate the indigenous population, whereas figures forwarded by indigenous groups and activists sometimes grossly overrate the aboriginal population.

7. According to Ruhlen (1987: 204), only 17 languages count more than 100,000 speakers (figures in millions): Quechua (7.00), Guaraní (3.00), Aymara (1.50), Náhuatl (=Aztec)(1.00), Quiché (Mayan) (.87), Yucatec (Mayan) (.53), Zapotec (.50), Mapudungu (=Mapuche, Araucarian) (.44), Cakchiquel (Mayan) (.41), Mazahua (.35), Totonac (.27), Kekchi (Mayan) (.27), Mam (Mayan) (.26), Mixtec (.25), Hñan'hñú (=Otomí)(.22), Mazatec (.12), Tzotzil (Mayan) (.11). The rest of the language groups only have a median of 1,400 speakers. (Note that Ruhlen 1987 gives much lower figures than other sources do).

8. State authorities do not normally recognize this urban population as belonging to an ethno-linguistic minority. Since there has been very little research on these new groups until recently (but see Pellicer 1988), they will not be dealt with in this text.

9. Paraguay is a special case; some 40.000 Amerindians organized in 17 language groups exist today (cf. Bartolomé 1989). Apart from these ethnic groups, the majority of the population speak Guaraní, which is divided into two distinct varieties: indigenous Guaraní, an ethnic langue used mainly in the domain of religion; and Paraguayan Guaraní, the supra-regional "lingua franca" strongly influenced by its contact with Spanish (cf. Meliá 1974, 1988). Paraguay is the only country in Latin America with a predominantly bilingual population: in 1982, 48.3% Paraguayans were bilingual (Guaraní and Spanish), 41.1% monolingual in Guaraní, and only a tiny minority of 4.2% spoke only Spanish (cf. Corvalán 1989; von Gleich 1989).

10. Figures about indigenous population in Mexico diverge significantly. The smallest is given by the national census of 1980 with 9.0% (5.18 million, counting the indigenous population above 5 years compared to the total population above 5 years, cf. Valdés 1988: 38); the largest by Mayer – Masferrer (1979): "La población indígena en América Latina", in: *América Indígena,* XXXIX, 2, with 12.4% for about the same period (quoted in Masferrer 1983).

11. During the last century, when Independence was already achieved and Indians were granted citzens' right, the government organized various military expeditions into Indians' land to exterminate the native population in a very similar procedure to the USA (cf. Stavenhagen 1988 a).

12. The use of the term "integration" (vs. assimilation) follows a long tradition in Latin American debates about indigenous minorities (cf. Amadio 1987a for a classification, also Hamel 1988b). Its use is no doubt extremely ambiguous. Following the dominant philosophy of the homogenous nation state, it means in most of the cases "assimilation", i. e. the covert incorporation (= "salvation") of the *individual* into the dominant society at the price of giving up her/his ethnic group identity. Nevertheless, important efforts

have been made throughout this century to achieve the difficult aim of integrating Indian ethnias *without* destroying their cultural base, as we shall se later on. For a more detailed typology from Europe that includes definitions of submersion, transitional programmes, etc., see Skutnabb-Kangas (1988a).

13. The school of Warisata in Bolivia in 1931, cf. Montoya (1983), or the well-known Tarasco project in Mexico since 1939, cf. Aguirre Beltrán (1983).

14. It was perhaps not coincidental that the Mexican delegation, representing the Tarasco project, excercised a substantial influence on the UNESCO Conference at Paris in 1952 where the famous resolution on vernacular language education was adopted (cf. UNESCO 1953).

15. See the advances of Native Inuit education in Canada in relation to cultural curriculum (Stairs 1988; Stairs − Leavitt 1988).

16. On the topic of linguistic and educational human rights, and their relation to indigenous movements in Latin America, see my other chapter in this volume.

17. A recent overview of indigenous education programmes in Bolivia is Amadio − Zúñiga 1989).

18. Columbia is the only Latin American country that delegates the whole responsibility of Indian education to the Catholic church through a concordat with the Vatican (cf. Stavenhagen 1988 a).

19. Cf. the analytical framework in Skutnabb-Kangas − Phillipson (1989a), Skutnabb-Kangas (1990a), and Skutnabb-Kangas − Phillipson, this volume.

20. My discussion benefits from information and experience from two on-going, collective research projects I am currently involved in. Their fundamental aim is to analyze, evaluate, and partially intervene in specific local processes of Indian bilingual education. The one in Mexico (cf. Hamel − Muñoz et al. 1989) is carried out by a team of researchers from various Mexican universities; it studies the process of L1 and L2 development during 2 successive school years in 5 Indian schools in 3 different language areas (Nahuatl, Mixe, Totonaca) that clearly contrast in their characteristics and levels of ethno-linguistic and cultural vitality (maintenance vs. shift). The Brazilian project is carried out by a team from Campinas university (UNICAMP) in a Guaraní area near Sao Paulo (cf. Cavalcanti et al. 1989). It is helping to set up and start an experimental programme of bilingual bicultural primary education based on the guidelines established by the community. It also trains young Guaranís from the village to become teachers and ethnic researchers.

21. The standard book on the history of language policy in Mexico which is particularly useful for the colonial and independent period is Heath (1972).

22. Contrary to what many authors (Varese 1983; Varese 1987; Hernández Moreno − Guzmán G. 1982; Amadio 1987b; Modiano 1988, etc.) affirm about contemporary Mexico, in 1991 systematic alphabetization in vernacular languages is not the real policy in public Indian education, and in probably more than 90% of the schools in the bilingual system it does not take place.

23. The complexity and − in part − ideological fallacy of Indians' expectations regarding school objectives and programmes in Latin America are analysed elsewhere (cf. López 1988a; Hornberger 1988, 1989; Hamel 1988b).

24. In one village from the Mixe region (see the Mexican research project mentioned in footnote 20), the community decided in 1989 that they wanted to develop their own curriculum for literacy in L1 which is now being implemented in the 1st and 2nd grade (cf. Hamel 1990b).

25. For the first time in history, the Brazilian Indian population has begun to increase again in absolute numbers since 1930 (cf. Rodrígues 1986).

26. On the other hand, the process of gaining autonomy in this domain is constantly menaced by contracts on Indian education between the government (via its principal state agency, the Fundaçao Nacional do Indio, FUNAI) and foreign religious missions like the well-known Summer Institute of Linguistics, or even much more radical and culturally disruptive sects like MEVA, MNTB, etc. The first freely elected government for almost 30 years that took office in 1990 initiated a restructuration of FUNAI which operated as a militarized apparatus of control in the past (cf. Sierra 1993 b).

27. Among the few exceptions cf. Comissao Pró-Indio 1981; Projeto Interaçao 1987; Montserrat 1989; Cavalcanti et al. 1989).

28. The postulate that establishes diglossia and di-ethnia (i. e. a clear-cut separation of forms and functions) as a *conditio sine qua non* for linguistic minority maintenance (Fishman 1964, 1967, 1980; see also 1989) seems to survive over time as one of the strongest axioms in the sociology of language, in spite of numerous refutations by native (Pedraza Jr. et al. 1980; Dejean 1983) and other (Eckert 1981; Hamel 1988a, 1990a, 1990c) researchers.

29. See Spolsky — Irvine (1982), Hornberger (1989), and many others who support the hypothesis that, under certain circumstances, ethnic group refusal to use their language at school may not reflect language shift but maintenance.

30. The debate demonstrates once more that the opposition between L1 and L2 literacy does not constitute a sufficient theoretical framework in itself to explain both psycho-linguistic and socio-political processes involved in minority education. Cummins (1984, 1988, 1989, etc.) and others (cf. the discussion in Rivera 1984) have sustained this caveat against both a number of well-established popular theories (maximum exposure, mismatch), and a reductionist interpretation of Cummins' own theoretical framework.

31. "Alphabetization, which is not necessarily related to the school, is a necessity generated by the situation of contact. To alphabetize is not a neutral activity. When operationalized in a way that minimizes interference in traditional Indian education, it could be a weapon that helps the Indian in her/his relationship with the dominant society; inasmuch as it substitutes traditional education it becomes a weapon against the Indian, a factor of social division in a society that used to be egualitarian ..." (my translation; from a debate on Indian education, cf. Sampaio Grizzi — Dalva — Lopes da Silva 1981: 17).

32. The transition from a military to a civilian regime, and intensive debates about Indian rights in the Constituent Assembly that formulated the new Constitution during 1987 and 1988 drew national and international attention to the deplorable situation of Brazilian Indians. Many Brazilian citizens no doubt realized for the first time that Indians existed in their country.

33. E. g. the Puno project in Peru which developed and implemented primers in Quechua and Aymara for all 6 grades of primary education that was sponsored by the German GTZ, a governmental development agency, between 1976 and 1989 (cf. López 1988a, forthcoming; Hornberger 1988, 1989); or a recent programme on bilingual intercultural education in Ecuador sponsored by the same institution, (cf. *Pueblos indígenas y educación*, 15, 16, 1990).

Linguistic rights for Amerindian peoples in Latin America[1]

Rainer Enrique Hamel

Linguistic rights for minorities[2] are increasingly associated with fundamental human rights in the international debate. Both theoretical discussion and empirical experience are creating a growing consciousness that linguistic rights can only be fully granted if their collective (in addition to their individual) dimension is acknowledged.[3] This presupposes that the state recognizes formal equality between language communities, and provides preferential treatment for minority groups for real equality of not only opportunity but also outcome.[4]

It could indeed be argued that linguistic human rights admirably demonstrate the fundamentally collective character of most human rights for minorities.[5] The acceptance of collective rights, however, can only be based on a pluriethnic, pluralistic concept of society, since it implies the recognition of ethnolinguistic minorities as — at least partially — autonomous groups or peoples inside the state. Yet such a recognition runs counter to the ideology of the monolingual and monocultural nation state that prevails in many areas of the globe, not least in former Spanish and Portuguese colonies.

Legislation for indigenous peoples in Latin America

Ever since independence at the beginning of the 19th century, the young republics have interpreted linguistic and ethnic difference as backwardness, marginalization, and an obstacle to communication within the national society. Programmes to develop Indian communities were therefore based on strategies of socio-economic integration, cultural assimilation, and linguicide; their aim was to "de-Indianize" the Indian peoples.[6] This strategy explains the fact that the constitutions in many Latin American nations do not even recognize the existence of aboriginal peoples on their territories, or include extremely vague references. Liberal and positivist philosophy that inspired most Latin American constitutions extended the general principles of freedom and equality of all citizens to the Indians as individuals. No-one should be discriminated against because of race, language or religion.[7]

In principle, reference to indigenous minorities (via language or education) can be found on three distinct levels within a state's legal framework: constitutional articles on the status of languages and about fundamental educational rights; general educational laws which refer to ethnolinguistic minorities; and decrees and other lower level regulations about specific forms of education for minorities (cf. Stavenhagen 1988a; von Gleich 1989).

Among the constitutions that do mention the existence of Amerindian groups, some like Argentina have a general reference to aboriginal groups; some have a specific article on Indian protection as part of collective social and cultural rights, such as Guatemala and Panama. Others including Chile, Columbia, and Ecuador refer to human rights and include special legal regulations about Indian communities. Still others have established special statutes on a constitutional level like Brazil, Nicaragua, and Paraguay.

Some countries like Mexico and Peru concede specific economic and agrarian rights to the peasants, a social class based to a large extent on Indian traditions, without however mentioning the indigenous population explicitly.[8]

In most countries with an Indian population, even in those with no constitutional reference to Indian rights, there are isolated laws or groups of laws and decrees concerning indigenous minorities in the areas of agrarian, civil, criminal, educational, and linguistic legislation.[9]

Legislation in some countries limits the incorporation of Indian subjects into the dominant society by assigning the status of minors or other legally disadvantaged groups to them, as in Brazil. In general terms, the integration of two opposed legal principles into the legal framework — formal equality before the law versus legal diversity in the face of unequal situations — has led to a contradictory treatment of Indian legislation (Stavenhagen 1988a: 96) where the existence of indigenous peoples is normally seen as a problem. Almost nowhere do we find a recognition of cultural, ethnic, and linguistic differences as values in their own right[10], i. e. as a potential contribution or resource in the building of a multicultural nation state (cf. Ruíz 1984).

In most cases linguistic rights are not expressed as such, but implicit in educational rights. The general principle that prevails in educational legislation coincides with the overall objective of indigenous laws. According to the official terminology, education has to accomplish the function of "integration", "civilization", and transition to the national language (castellanización).[11]

Spanish is the only official language of the state in *Chile* and *Costa Rica*. Other countries like *Ecuador, Nicaragua*, and *Peru* establish Spanish as the only official language, but grant a specific status to indigenous languages. In Ecuador, with 33.9% of indigenous population, Quechua, Aymara and other aboriginal languages are only recognized in vague terms as belonging to the national culture. Paraguay, the only country in Latin America with more monolinguals (40%) in an Indian language (Guaraní) than in Spanish (4%), has no clear constitutional recognition of Guaraní.

Perhaps the only historical attempt to avoid reducing linguistic minority rights to transitional education and to extend the political and legal role of an Indian language (Quechua) to a whole nation took place in *Peru* during the progressive military regime between 1968 and 1975, as mentioned earlier (Hamel, this volume). Nowadays, Quechua and Aymara are stipulated national languages; they have co-official status (Spanish being the official language), with territorial and sectorial delimitations.[12] The other Amerindian languages of the country (mainly those spoken in the Amazonian basin) are defined as belonging to the patrimony of the nation.

Mexico and Brazil: two polar cases

In order to exemplify the wide range of different situations in Latin America, I shall briefly analyse language policy and legislation in Brazil and Mexico, the two most important countries in terms of population, that contrast in almost all aspects in relation to Indian peoples.

Mexico: National identity and liberal legislation

With its 9% of Amerindian population, Mexico represents a very particular case regarding Indian policies that can only be explained in the context of the historical search for national identity. On the one hand, we encounter a peculiarly strong version of the nationalist ideology of a centralized, monolithic nation state that Mexico shares with most Latin American countries; on the other, the historical reference to the Indian classic cultures of the past, the Aztecs and Mayas, plays a central role in the construction of a national identity.

Ever since the 19th century and even more so after the Mexican revolution (1910–1920), national identity and its ideology have been grounded in the symbiosis of two races and cultures, the occidental Spanish and the New World Indian. This mixture created the new Mexican state and its citizen, the Mestizo, in a conceptual framework where neither the white nor the Indian played an important role any more (Heath 1972; Stavenhagen 1984, 1985).

On the level of language policy and legislation, the still unaccomplished cultural integration of the nation challenges Mexican society to succeed in both finding an internal cohesion and in drawing boundaries on three cultural and linguistic fronts (cf. Villoro 1950; Lara 1987):

— Vis-à-vis Hispanic culture and Spanish, the unquestioned national language and mother tongue of about 90% of the population, specific Mexican norms had to be established which differ from the Castilian standard.
— Vis-à-vis the present day aboriginal ethnias, the necessity of integration and "Mexicanization" places Indian languages in a paradoxical position where they are at the same time a necessary point of reference and a supposed obstacle to national unity.
— Vis-à-vis the US American neighbour, the Spanish heritage creates bonds of solidarity that help to resist the penetration of English and cultural aggression from the north.[13]

This complex constellation provides a framework within which to explain a number of puzzling contradictions, such as the contrast beween the limited economic and demographic weight of the Indian population, and its prominence in public discourse and governmental institutions; or the contradiction between the pioneering role Mexico played in Latin American Indigenist policies, programmes, and institutions as opposed to the lack of constitutional recognition and Indian legislation until very recently.

Nowhere in the colonial, republican, or post-revolutionary constitutions is Spanish defined as the official language of the country. It only became the means of communication for a majority of the population during the 19th century.[14] Neither did the Mexican constitution recognize the existence of Indian peoples as distinct ethnias until 1991. It thus denied the multiethnic reality of the nation. In all areas of legislation the principles of generality and formal equality prevail. Consequently, no specific chapters in agrarian, civil, criminal or educational law refer explicitly to Indian individuals or communities until now, although certain forms of organization created to preserve Indian and other peasant traditions such as the "ejido", a kind of collective land tenancy with specific individual rights and obligations, are protected by the constitution and specific laws.

In contrast to legislation, indigenist and language policies have been much more explicit in Mexican history. Ever since colonization there have been two basic positions concerning indigenous ethnias that have taken shape after independence at the beginning of the 19th century (cf. Hamel, this volume): the dominant line considered the assimilation of Indian peoples and the supression of their languages to be a precondition for the construction of a unified national state. The other one, generally subordinated to the first, defended the preservation of Indian cultures and languages in the process of building a pluricultural national state.

Given the strong ideological tradition of legal liberalism which objects to any recognition of structural differences such as race or religion as a matter of principle, it is extremely surprising that in 1989, the Mexican federal government launched a proposal to amend the constitution in order to recognize Indian cultural rights.[15] The proposal (Iniciativa ... 1990), submitted to Congress in December 1990 and approved by the House of Representatives in July 1991, suggests that the following text be added to article 4 of the Constitution, an article which protects the social rights of specific groups (women, minors):

"The Mexican nation has a pluri-cultural composition which is based originally on its Indian peoples. The law will protect and promote the development of their languages, cultures, usages, customs, resources, and specific forms of social organization. It will grant their members effective access to the jurisdiction of the state. In the agrarian judgements and processes in which they are a party, their practices and legal customs will be taken into account in terms that will be established by law." (my translation).

Most independent observers and experts agree that the governmental initiative as such is a positive step in the right direction that will establish the constitutional basis for more specific laws that protect Indian rights. It is also hoped that the debates stimulated by the proposal will help to raise the level of consciousness in both majority and minority society about the multicultural, multiethnic, and multilingual nature of the country.

At the same time, the proposal is severely criticized as too limited in content and scope since it seems to be extremely difficult to grant and protect indigenous *cultural* rights in isolation, without granting at the same time their economic, social, political, and educational rights. A full recognition of the Indian peoples would therefore imply amendments to a number of articles in the constitution, a proposal that is not acceptable to the government and the political party in power.[16]

The central controversy is whether the state is prepared to recognize the pluricultural nature of the nation in all its dimensions, which includes the recognition of *autonomy of the Indians as peoples, even as nations*. In this respect the text is considered to be ambiguous at least. Given the past and current policy of the Mexican government it seems to be highly unlikely that such autonomy would be conceded.

In relation to *linguistic* rights, it is considered to be insufficient to grant linguistic rights only as individual rights, as the abstract human right to express oneself in one's own language (cf. Cifuentes — Hamel — Lara 1990; Hamel 1990d). Beyond the right of *expression*, the constitution would have to warrant the collective right of *communication* to the Indian peoples. According to international experience in the protection of minority rights, this presupposes that two aspects be granted: 1. The principle of formal equality must be accorded not only to the members of minority and majority groups, but also to the linguistic communities as such. 2. Specific measures will have to be adopted so as to permit maintenance of the differing ethnic characteristics of the Indian peoples (cf. Braën 1987; Wildhaber 1989; Turi 1989).

In sum, the Mexican case shows with particular neatness some of the general characteristics which are typical of a certain type of Latin American indigenist language policy and legislation: a liberal constitution that places formal equality of all citizens over and above all other principles, and above the reality of economic, social, ethnic and cultural inequality; the effort to build a homogeneous, centralized, monolingual and monocultural nation state; and the consequent orientation to assimilate ethnic minorities into the dominant society via education and other programmes. All this means that minority rights in general and linguistic rights in particular only benefit from comparatively weak protection. Given a political tradition where the law used to play a minor role in the political and economic struggle, it is no surprise that most activities of ethnolinguistic resistance movements developed in a space where reference to legality, even to legitimacy, did not have a major effect.

This fact reflects a remarkable independence between linguistic as well as educational policies, on the one hand, and their legal, namely constitutional framework in the past, on the other hand, an independence which allows a series of contradictions to persist over a long period of time.

The situation, however, is rapidly changing. A movement that demands respect for the law and for human rights in all domains constitutes at present one of the most explosive political challenges to a seventy year-old political system that is undergoing a difficult process of transformation, from a corporate, extremely centralized one-party-regime to the declared aim of a pluralistic democracy. In such a context, the respect for Indian peoples and other minorities becomes a touchstone of democratic transformation.

Brazil: juridical paternalism and political-military genocide

In many aspects of Indigenist policies and legislation, Brazil's tradition stands in sharp contrast with that of Mexico. Ever since colonization Brazil has applied a policy that combined elements of segregation with those of − at least potential − assimilation, if the Indian peoples or individuals were willing to give up their ethnic identity. As a matter of fact, the overall result was genocide and extreme fragmentation of indigenous peoples. The 200,000 Amerindians that have survived are subdivided into 170 language groups.[17]

In Brazil the constitutional principles of freedom and equality of all citizens were not extended to the Indians. Until the present, the principles of paternalism and tutelage rooted in the 19th century characterize Brazilian Indigenist policy and legislation. A special statute both segregated and protected the Indian peoples from the mainstream society.[18] The Brazilian constitution in force until 1988 contained various articles and a special statute (Estatuto do Indio, promulgated in 1974) concerning Indian rights (cf. Carneiro da Cunha 1987; Menezes 1989). Indian individuals[19] were classified as either "isolated", "on the way to integration", or "integrated" (meaning assimilated). In criminal law, for instance, a restricted liability is considered to apply in cases where non-"integrated" Indians are involved.

The civil code (article 6) defines non-"integrated" Indians as having an intellectual and social capacity comparable to minors between 16 and 21 years who need a legal tutor. This function was formerly exercised by juvenile court judges; since 1967 it has been administered by the National

Indian Fundation (Fundaçao Nacional do Indio, FUNAI), a govermental agency which came under the Ministry of Defence or the National Security Council during the military regime.

The Federal Constitution (articles 4, 198) grants *territorial rights* to the recognized Indian peoples of immemorial settlement in a specific area. These include the right to exploit the surface natural resources, and grant a share in the exploitation of mineral resources, which belong to the Union.[20]

Furthermore, the "Estatuto do Indio" granted restricted citizenship, the recognition of Indian habits and customs (*customary law*), the right to make use of national instruction and to receive *alphabetization* in the Indian languages. Education should be geared towards gradual "integration", respecting the cultural heritage, artistic values, religions, beliefs, and rites (cf. Stavenhagen 1988a: 249).[21]

After a long period of debates in the constitutive assembly, a new constitution was finally promulgated in 1988 as a legal fundation for a democracy after more than 15 years of military rule. To the surprise of many observers and participants, one of the topics that stimulated most controversy, public debates, demonstrations, and international attention, was Indian rights (cf. Gaiger 1989a).

Most specialists agree that important gains for Indian rights were made (cf. Rodrígues, 1988; Gaiger 1989b; Carneiro da Cunha 1990), although the principle of state tutelage was not altogether abandoned. Improvements include the abolition of the explicit assimilationist view including the classification of Indians; a better protection of territorial rights; and the guarantee of bilingual Indian education.[22]

In sum, linguistic indigenous rights are on the whole weakly protected in Brazil. Nowhere is the status of the languages clearly defined (Rodrígues 1988), but Brazilian legislation and practice implicitly assumes that Portuguese is the national language. As with Mexico, education represents the only area with some explicit prescriptions about Indian languages. Nevertheless, the new 1988 constitution and several subsequent laws reflect important progress, since they define cultural and educational language rights in a much more specific way than has been the case until now in Mexico. On the whole, different parts of legal texts range on a continuum (cf. Skutnabb-Kangas – Phillipson, this volume) between covert assimilation-oriented toleration (Estatuto do Indio) and a weak maintenance-oriented permission which is in part overt in relation to educational rights.

Indian movements, the struggle for autonomy, and collective linguistic rights

The analysis of Amerindian linguistic rights in Latin America shows a number of common features despite the diversity of cases. No doubt linguistic rights for a minority as such have so far played a minor role in the debates and confrontations, although the aboriginal languages are in most cases a key element for establishing ethnic boundaries from the inside and outside.

The history of Indian movements in Latin America, however, reveals the potential centrality of linguistic rights among other minority rights due to their intrinsically collective nature and their close interdependence with other rights of a collective character.

At the beginning of colonization, the Indians defended their land through violent battles against the conquerors. The confrontation shifted then to the field of legality and negotiation. Indian subjects and groups claimed full recognition as citizens of the colonies or young republics, the jurisdiction of their land and some privileges such as tax exemption. During the past 10 or 15 years, however, the most advanced Indian organizations gone beyond traditional demands that could be satisfied within the established legislation.

The new quality of the struggle consists in the fact that Indian movements — who still represent a minority among the indigenous population — are now increasingly claiming autonomous territories and authority to organize the lives of their communities according to their own traditions and customs. They thus question the legitimacy of the state to organize their lives, and invade the arena of politics and the law, demanding autonomy and self-determination as peoples, even as nations.[23], a challenge that tends to disrupt the juridical basis of the national states, and confronts one legal system with another (Iturralde 1989; Díaz-Polanco 1989, 1990; Varese 1987).

As postulated earlier, the key obstacle to a recognition of such claims is the deeply rooted doctrine of the homogenous nation state that establishes formal equality among its citizens as individuals and denies a specific legal status to any collectivity, at least on an ethnic or linguistic basis.[24]

Indian demands include the claim to respect their territories, to grant official status to their languages, and to recognize their religions, their medical and legal practices. Increasingly a central argument is reference to customs and habits in use since time immemorial and the fact that *their* legal system is even older and thus more legitimate than the one imposed by the invaders (cf. Stavenhagen 1988b).

This explains why the opposition between positive state law and Indian customary law is central to this conflict, as recent studies reveal (cf. Stavenhagen 1989b; Stavenhagen — Iturralde 1990). Most claims for autonomy in various fields of social, political, economic, and cultural organization are related to legal practices, habits and customs that collide with the legal framework of civil and criminal state law.

Sociolinguistic studies in Mexico point out that there is a close relationship between customary law and Indian languages. Customary Indian and positive state law can be interpreted as two conflicting language-based symbolic systems related to the two languages in contact (cf. Hamel 1990a). Specific cultural styles and discourse structures of Indian languages are basic to the development of activities in the domains of local government, dispute resolution, conflict solving, ethnic organization, etc. (Sierra 1990, 1991, 1993 a). And in the clash between customary law and the imposition of positive state law on Indian individuals and groups, language conflict and inter-ethnic miscommunication play a major role. This is a field outside education where claims for linguistic human rights are vital and more research is called for.

The question is then what would be the minimal legal framework necessary to render the ethnic survival of Indian peoples possible? And what role could Indian languages and linguistic rights play in this context?

Whether favourable conditions for language maintenance and ethno-linguistic revitalization obtain will depend on the role indigenous movements assign to their languages as central or peripheral elements of ethnic identity, and as tools for organization and action.

The debate about linguistic rights reveals the complex relationship between individual and collective rights, and their correlates in language policy, the principles of personality and territoriality. The new constitutional amendment in Mexico is predominantly based on the principle of personality and individual rights granted to members of an ethnic group. Access to the juridical institutions of the state (and "fair treatment" taking into account Indian customs, using interpreters, etc.) may at best solve an *individual* problem of justice, but only within the legal framework of a different, the dominant culture. It can never replace the *collective* needs of a people to organize their own legal system based on their beliefs, customs, and languages.[25] Collective rights and the principle of territoriality thus appear to be a necessary basis for granting linguistic (and other) rights to the Amerindian peoples.

Since most observers agree that the future of Latin American Indian minorities is closely related to territorial autonomy in most cases, and the right to organize economic, social, political, and cultural life according to their own ethnic principles, it seems evident that a series of fundamental changes affecting the legal basis of Latin American states will have to be put into practice, including a recognition of distinct legal systems based on indigenous cultures.

Given the diversity of situations, traditions, numbers and density of population, degrees of acculturation or ethnolinguistic vitality, there is certainly no one single answer for all cases.

In the Amazonian Indian regions for example, the state of ethnic development, relative isolation and geographic distribution of Indian communities may allow for solutions based on the principle of territoriality for language use, education, and socio-economic organization. The clearcut dualism of ethnic boundaries between the Indian and non-Indian society in Brazil may help to mobilize the principle of personality as a resource as well.

Mexico, on the other hand, is characterized by a long tradition of contact between in part highly complex Indian cultures and the "mainstream" society. Sociolinguistic research[26] reveals that the cultural and linguistic hegemony of the dominant Mestizo society has significantly affected most Indian domains and regions. Cultural syncretism, language conflict, and social bilingualism are therefore typical for most Indian ecosystems.

In several areas with a high density of Indian population in the south and south-east of the country (Oaxaca, Chiapas, Yucatán), indigenous movements are beginning to demand partial autonomy based on the principle of territorial control and government (cf. Díaz-Polanco 1990).[27] Like in other Latin American regions with a high concentration of Amerindian population (Guatemala and the Andean areas of Bolivia, Perú, and Ecuador), a certain combination of the two principles of language policy could be envisaged. In specific pluriethnic, predominantly indigenous regions (territoriality) with partial autonomy, members of Indian ethnic groups (personality) would have the right to use and to demand use of their languages in specific public and social domains like local administration, and public service institutions in the areas of health, justice, and education. No doubt the conquest of new functional domains for Amerindian languages from a position of local control would contribute significantly to the maintenance and revitalization of indigenous idioms and initiate a process of language planning and extension.

Certainly ethnic survival will not depend on legislation as its main support. As I have argued throughout this chapter, the recognition of Indian minority rights, including linguistic human rights, will only be successful in the long run as part of the developing Indian movements, their gains in ethnic and political awareness, and their capacity to struggle for ethnic survival. At the "First Continental Meeting of Indian Peoples" held in Quito in July 1990, indigenous representatives decided to improve international Amerindian cooperation, and they approved a line of action which includes the struggle for self-government, territorial autonomy, and control of their resources.[28]

Given the increasing relationship between the traditional demands of the Amerindian movements and new international issues like human rights and the preservation of the world-wide ecological balance[29], some aboriginal movements and their struggle have acquired considerable international support that brought pressure to bear on national governments in a very effective way.[30] Thus world-wide globalization also helps indigenous movements in Latin America to improve their international coordination and to channel external support for their struggle within which the claims for linguistic and educational rights are central.

Notes

1. Financial support from the Mexican National Council for Science and Technology ("Consejo Nacional de Ciencia y Tecnología", CONACYT) under title A128CC0E900410 (CS-7) is gratefully acknowledged.
2. Although in this chapter I shall only deal with autochthonous minorities, the terminology I use (linguistic minority rights, linguistic rights of minorities) refers in principle to all kinds of minorities, including those not recognized by international law, such as migrants.
3. For a debate, see de Witte (1989) and several other contributions in Pupier — Woehrling (1989).
4. In Latin America there is an extensive debate on this topic; cf. Arizpe (1988), Díaz-Polanco (1988, 1989), Iturralde (1989), Stavenhagen (1988c, 1989a).
5. See the debate on the relationship between the right of expression vs. right of communication in Braën (1987), for Latin America see Hamel (1990a).
6. It is the merging of the concepts of "state" and "nation" that renders governmental recognition of the Indian ethnies as "peoples" or "nations", and not only as minorities, so extremely difficult.
7. The first republican constitution in Argentina from 1819, for example, grants in art.

28 the same rights to Indians and abolishes all kinds of feudal services as well as slavery (art. 29) (cf. Stavenhagen 1988a: 48).

8. In Peru to address Quechuas and Aymaras as "Indios" is considered an insult, even more so than in many other countries. The term was practically abolished and replaced by the term "Campesinos" after the military revolution in the sixties. Only the Amazonian Indian groups on Peruvian territory are still called "Indians".

9. Since territoriality is considered to be a prime source of conflict and at the same time the single most important feature of Indian peoples' identity, it is not surprising that legislation on land ownership, particularly the collective possession of community land, occupies a salient place in Indian legislation (cf. Aylwin Oyarzún 1990 for the Chilean case).

10. One of the most interesting exceptions in recent times is Nicaragua's new constitution (approved in 1986 during the Sandinist Front government) which recognizes the multiethnic nature of the nation and grants extensive autonomy including education and language use to the ethnic groups on the Atlantic coast (cf. Comisión de Autonomía 1987; Lau 1983). Whether these rights that were conquered with so much sacrifice will be respected by the new Nicaraguan government remains to be seen.

11. On educational legislation, see my chapter on indigenous education in this volume (cf. also Hamel 1990d).

12. The only domain where this legislation is still relevant is education. It mus be noted that these definitions contained in the 1978 constitution are a step backwards in relation to previous decrees from 1972 (decree-law 19326 on education and 21156 on the status of Quechua) which established Quechua as official language in the whole country with equal status to Spanish.

13. Indian language policies in Mexico can indeed only be explained consistently if the complex and contradictory policies concerning the national language are taken into account. This fact raises doubts about the commonplace practice in sociolinguistics of investigating language policies for minority languages without considering the correlating − usually implicit − policies concerning the majority language(s) (cf. Hamel 1988c).

14. In 1981 an attempt was made to establish Spanish as the official language in the constitution, a proposal that never even reached parliament. This initiative was part of a governmental campaign to "defend" the Spanish language against the spread of English in a period of political tension with the USA (cf. Lara 1987).

15. Some critics regard this initiative as an attempt to anticipate and thus weaken the claims for autonomy and recognition as independent peoples put forward by the growing Indian movements (cf. Díaz-Polanco 1990). Intensive public debates took place throughout 1989 and 1990 with the participation of indigenous organizations, political parties, and academic specialists (cf. Marcó del Pont 1990).

16. Note that the text that was finally submitted to Congress contains some important reductions as compared to the original proposal launched by the government, which established the consideration of Indian legal customs in *all* kinds of legal affairs: "In the processes of federal and local order to which an Indian is a party, ...".

17. The largest groups are the Makuxi (14,500) and the Yanomami (8,400) in the areas of Roraima and Amazônia. Only 5 languages have more than 5,000 speakers, 13% up to 1,000, and more than 25% have less than 100 members (cf. Rodrígues 1986; Spires 1987).

18. This policy created a non-inclusive ethnic identity and reproduced ethnic boundaries,

maintaining a clearcut opposition between Brazilians (= whites, blacks, all immigrant races) and non-Brazilian Indians in the consciousness of both sides.

19. The "Estatuto do Indio" defines Indians as persons of pre-colonial descent who belong to ethnic groups with cultural characteristics that differ from those of the national society. They are supposed to live in communities that are either completely isolated or in contact with but not integrated into the national community (cf. Stavenhagen 1988a).

20. Here again a marked difference with legislation in Mexico has to be acknowledged. In Mexico no territorial rights for Indians exist. All mineral and water resources belong to the state. This position was reinforced with the expropriation of the big British and US-American oil companies in 1938.

21. Although it includes a set of measures, the "Estatuto" does not explicitly establish the right to *benefit* from education, i. e. to receive the type of instruction that enables the indigenous student the learn and succeed, given his cultural, sociolinguistic, and pedagogic circumstances.

22. Article 210 concerning public education establishes that primary school education is in Portuguese. Indian communities are granted the use of their mother tongues and their own learning procedures during primary education (see my chapter on Indian education in this volume).

23. Recognition as nations would change their legal status significantly, since international law grants the universal right of self-determination only to nations, and not to minorities as such, international support of which encounters severe legal restrictions (cf. Wildhaber 1989; Díaz Müller 1991).

24. The identification of the nation with the state, i. e. the ideological belief that each state is a nation (cf. Seton-Watson 1977), prevails in spite of a counterfactual reality, because the dominant ethnies identify themselves with the state as nations (cf. Stavenhagen 1988b) and tend to establish their cultural and ideological hegemony over all other ethnies with the ultimate aim of assimilating or exterminating them.

25. In the same way, alphabetization in L2, the dominant language, can perhaps satisfy *individual* literacy needs, but only education in L1, the ethnic group's own language, will be able to solve the *collective* problems of literacy and lead to an appropriation of a writing system for their own culture, provided the ethnic language still serves as their principle means of socialization and communication within the community.

26. Only a few publications can be referred to here; cf. Aubague et al. (1983), Hill – Hill (1986), Roth Senneff et al. (1986), Hamel (1988 b, c,) Hamel – Muñoz Cruz (1982, 1988), Hamel – Lastra de Suárez – Muñoz Cruz (1988). An extensive bibliography is to be found in Hamel (1988a).

27. E.g. the "Independent Front of Indigenous Peoples (FIPI)" demands that the state should grant autonomy at the district and regional level, and recognize their own indigenous authorities and representatives (cf. Castellanos Guerrero 1990).

28. See the Declaration of Quito 1990.

29. E.g. the indigenous reserves in the Amazonas basin, where 40% of the earth's reserves of fresh water are threatened with destruction.

30. Some critics note that the sudden interest in, e.g., Amazonian Indians which comes along with bushels of money (see the Sting foundation "Mata Virgen") causes perhaps more disruption than help. They also point out the opportunist basis of the unforeseen "support" of Indian movements, say, by the Dutch government (Holland would be immediately affected by a melting process at the poles as a consequence of ecological

destruction in the Amazonas basin) which is not rooted in a genuine interest in the indigenous peoples themselves; and that the connection between indigenous and ecological demands is therefore tactical, and perhaps of short duration. Nevertheless the factual relationship between the two types of claims supplies the Amerindian movements with a magnificent strength at present on which they have managed to capitalize for their own struggle.

"Minority" cultures and their communication rights[1]

Lachman M. Khubchandani

Introduction: the State as sole guardian or manipulator

Very few populations in the world can be considered totally homogenous in terms of ethnic affiliation. In an ethnographic account of 862 distinct ethnic groups covering 132 states all around the world,[4] Said and Simmons (1976) consider only 9% of the groups to be totally homogeneous and 19% to be 90% homogeneous. In 30% of the cases no single group comprises a majority, and in over 40% there are 5 or more significant groups.

However, many forces promote cultural and linguistic homogenisation in communication, often coercively, in favour of the adoption of dominant group language identities. Such pressures often generate insular tendencies in plural societies and lead to less aperture in cross-cultural communication.

The contemporary "welfare state" doctrine has often led to an increase in the role of the State machinery in intervening in social welfare and cultural promotion domains which primarily concern the cultural and moral fabric of its people. The dependency of the individual on the State is on the increase. Many sections of society look to the State as the "sole guardian" (the *maaii baap* − literally "mother and father"), or as a manipulator.

The State's obsession with such concerns (e.g. policies based on religious fundamentalism; language chauvinism; "sons-of-the-soil" doctrine; finding justification for differential treatment of different sections of its population) erupts into direct confrontation between the State and ethnicity-based movements. The State may consider these as representatives of narrow loyalties, woven around ethnicity and impeding the processes of nation-building.

In recent decades the South-Asian region as a whole has become an active theatre of such traumatic developments subsequent to the holocaust of the 1947 India-Pakistan Partition arising out of the frenzy of the "two-nation" theory. Many regional movements in South-Asia have been questioning State policies concerning the nature of the relations between "mainstream" and "minority" cultures, and between "developed" and "developing" languages.

Demands for linguistic homogeneity are fraught with many complexities, regardless of whether it is a question of old "nation-states" or newly-independent states. The dominance of technology in a society does not necessarily lead to cultural homogenisation (Fishman 1989). This is also confirmed by the agitations concerning the identity assertions of minority groups in many Western countries (such as the United States, Canada, Belgium, Spain) and the recent ethnic upsurges in many republics in the former Soviet Union and Yugoslavia. No doubt, as "external" evidence of primordial identities gets blurred due to "modernisation", these often provide the "reasons" for anxiety among minorities looking for *corporate safeguards* for group rights.[3]

To cope with the apparent contradictions in relation to linguistic and ethnic minorities in the education and communication spheres in contemporary plural societies, it is imperative to take into account the role of the democratisation and legal processes, economic mobility and mass media.[4]

Fluid cultural and linguistic identities

It is a sad reality that in the contemporary world the relationship between small and big cultural entities is not organised on *reciprocity*. The "big" cultures all round the world, supported by enormous political and economic advantages, tend to carry internal tendencies which go radically against the basic intentions of a *fair* communication. In this process weaker groups and their languages get subjugated and their cultural identity gets imperilled (Skutnabb-Kangas 1988a, 1991c).

The tendency to obtain supremacy over other cultures, to be hegemonic, is subtly present even when the majority cares for but patronises "small" cultures. Such a climate carries the seeds of small cultural entities being driven on the defensive to protect their identities through demands for reciprocity and parity in a heterogenous situation. Discussing the struggles of the Nagas and other Tibeto-Burman minorities in North-east India, Rustomji (1983: 2−3) succinctly observes: "Nothing gives rise to so much anger, hostility, even hatred, as the apprehension of cultural aggression ... Much of the discord on the borders is a reaction to this attitude of patronising condescension ... The failure has been for the most part, not so much in intention as in the empathy and sensitivity".

At the same time, a "small" culture carries within itself the potential of contributing to the larger ethos. Every culture, irrespective of being big or small, serves as a *bridge* between others and as an instrument of interaction which is humanly universal (Pogačnik 1986). In this regard, Gandhiji rightly explains the interdependence of individual units in a society through an analogy of "concentric circles in an ocean"; these circles keep on widening to the outer periphery, but never ascending like a "pyramid with the apex sustained by the bottom". In such a pluralistic pattern, the "inner circle" forms an integral unit of the "outer oceanic circle", and will not be crushed by the overwhelming power of the outer periphery. On the contrary, each should give strength to the other (Kripalani 1958).

In the post-colonial era, many newly-independent countries have been going through the trauma of language transition. One of the most radical turnabouts in recent history has been the explicit recognition of language claims over *exclusive* territory. This happened with the linguistic reorganisation of Indian Provinces (enforced in 1956), based primarily on the language identity of the dominant pressure groups. This transformed the concept of language pluralism on the South-Asian subcontinent. In recent decades, the question of numerical "majority" and "minority" (based on language) in a particular territory has arisen in connection with many acts of legislation on administration, education and socio-cultural development. This has led to a shift in language identity, an upsurge away from a low-key *instrumental* role in a framework of stratificational pluralism, to a top-gear *defining* characteristic in the new emerging order of pluralism.

In the context of language identity, it is relevant to make a distinction between a *"body of language speakers"* and a *"speech community"*. In many communities in which the language has been standardised, native speakers of a language are members of its speech community. A German native speaker belongs to the German speech community as far as her/his affiliation with education, literature, cultural heritage are concerned, though politically the body of German language speakers is divided among at least four different nations: unified Germany, Austria, Switzerland and Luxembourg.

On the other hand, a plural society such as India abounds in cases where native speakers of a language do *not* necessarily form one *coherent* speech community. Identities of Panjabi, Hindi and Urdu speakers in both Indian and Pakistani Punjab provide a vivid example of this phenomenon. Inter-language boundaries in many of these regions have remained fuzzy and fluid (for details see Khubchandani 1979).

This non-static, fluid plurality without distinct boundaries applies likewise at other levels in conceptualising language. In formal communication, literate societies generally treat language as an *autonomous* system with its distinct history and tradition. Language is evaluated through the conventions as standardised in its spelling rules and other prescriptive devices of correction in grammatical and lexical usage along with the "etiquette" rules for choosing styles and idioms from its heritage. In short, language is regarded as an independent "institution". This notion is reflected in the unending debates on language policy in many "new" nations of Asia and Africa. These debates assume that each language is a monolith, a "crystallised whole" (Khubchandani 1991: 39).

One cannot however lose track of the fact that speech activity is an ongoing process responding to a variety of communication settings. Labels such as Chinese, English, Hindi, Spanish, Swahili, Urdu are as much products of *environment* as of normative *tradition*. To gain a clear perspective of the role of language in the lives of individuals and in society, it is necessary to examine how "traditions" are socially constructed and the "echo" systems available to a speech community.

Consideration of all this variety, criss-cross relationships of dialects, literature, socio-cultural practices, religious and regional affinities provide strong evidence for treating India as a plural society, where boundaries of neither socio-cultural nor socio-linguistic traits are clearly marked.

Plural societies

Individuals in a plural society belong to several different socio-cultural and socio-linguistic identity groups (such as nationality, ethnicity, religion, language, dialect) and share only a *core* of experiences, criss-crossing in more than one manner, hardly coterminating with the same boundary. Each of these differences may be important under some circumstances in a plural society but no single division is so important that it would operate to distinguish one group (identified through speech, religion, economic or social strata etc) from another in all traits. "Individuals joined by a single trait are generally marked by their *variety*, their *lack* of unity, and their tendency to act as fairly discrete groups relative to the pulls and pressures of time and space" (Khubchandani 1983: 6).

This phenomenon is characteristic of the South Asian region as a whole. An example is the many small groups belonging to different religions, and affiliated to different socio-cultural identities (such as Kachhi, Khoja, Memon, Jaisalmeri, Waghdi, all classified as varieties of the Sindhi language) who have for years shared a common cultural heritage. These legacies transmit from one generation to another some prominent values of interaction: ways of interpreting and sharing experiences, known collectively as the communication ethos.

Profiles of small cultures can provide many insights into the probing of such questions as how to channel the concerns of ethnic identity in a positive and sublime manner to enrich the nation's heritage, instead of provoking linguistic and religious conflicts between "majority" and "minority" cultures/languages, or accepting the assimilation of small cultures into the dominant culture.

Whorf (1956), a neo-Herderian champion, makes out a strong case for "multilingual/multicultural awareness", supporting Oriental, Hebrew and Greek social philosophers. He pleads for "a world in which "little peoples" and "little languages" are not only to be respected but valued (Fishman 1982). In Steiner's view (1975) also, a mathematical "universalist" model of language is bound to fail to account for the nature of relations between languages (or speech varieties) as they actually exist and differ: "A genuine philosophy of language must grapple with the phenomenon and rationale of the human "invention" and retention of anywhere between five and ten thousand distinct tongues"; thus he rejects a theory of *language* in favour of a theory of *languages*. Varying degrees of boundaries between languages, dialects, or speech varieties in the Indian subcontinent can only be explained through a pluralistic view of language.

Sindhi: an example

Socio-cultural characteristics: scattered, urban, literate, bilingual

Sindhi, a language of the North-western Indo-Aryan group (a member of the Indo-European family), is spoken by over 15 million people (1981 estimate) in the Indo-Pakistan subcontinent. Out of these about 2 million are in India, a microscopic minority, 0.25%, of the country's total population.

With the exception of the Sindhi-speaking population in the Kutch-Saurashtra region (known as Kachhis) and the Barmer-Jaisalmer belt on the Indo-Pakistan border, most of Indian Sindhi-speakers, associated with the post-Partition migration from Sindh, are spread throughout the urban and semi-urban centres in the country, with concentrations in Maharashtra, Gujarat, Rajasthan, Madhya Pradesh and Delhi. Only three districts in the Indian Union have Sindhi-speaking populations of above one hundred thousand[5] (Kutch in Gujarat (409.000), Greater Bombay (195.000) and Thane in Maharashtra (140.000)). In addition, Sindhi migrants are scattered in over fifty other districts, mostly in the Western and North-central regions where their number exceeds five thousand in each district (Khubchandani 1991, Table 10, 88 – 89).

The "transplanted" Sindhi language in pluralistic India is acquiring new roles in an environment vastly different from its original habitat in Sindh (now in Pakistan). One can identify three distinct socio-cultural characteristics among the scattered Sindhi migrants in India: *1. urbanisation, 2. near-universal literacy and 3. bilingualism/multilingualism.*

76.7% of the Sindhi-speakers are declared "urban", as compared with an all-India ratio of less than 25%. The majority of the non-urban Sindhi-speakers are reckoned to be Kachhi and Jaisalmeri-speakers. Thus, migrant Sindhis in India have become highly *urbanised*, with very little pull from the rural hinterland.

In India, a rapid growth of literacy is more pronounced in urban areas, and among the classes above the poverty-line. Most of the Sindhi migrants belong to relatively better-earning strata. Hence, the community has achieved *near-universal literacy*, particularly among the younger generation. According to the 1991 provisional figures of the Census of India (Nanda 1991), the overall literacy rate in the country is 52.1%. The gap between male and female literacy continues to be quite wide: while male literacy has increased to 63.9%, female literacy is only 39.4%

Four decades after the initial wave of Sindhi migration to India, it is rather difficult to find Sindhi speakers, regardless of age, who are unable to understand and to make themselves understood in Hindi or in another language of the region, though in some cases with only a smattering of that language. To say that all Sindhis are *bilingual* would be going too far, but an overwhelming majority under 30 years are so.

Language rights and language-identity maintenance

When the Constitution of India was adopted in 1951, the Sindhi language did not find its place among major Indian languages on the pretext that the entire Province of Sindh was carved out to Pakistan. Consequently Sindhi language was given the treatment of a non-literary language in governmental circles. Its contribution to the literary heritage of undivided India was not taken into account. The Sindhi community did not accept this anomaly during the early phase of settlement. A sustained nation-wide campaign was launched for including Sindhi as a major literary language among the polity of Indian languages. It resulted in the recognition of Sindhi by the Sahitya Akademi (the Academy of Letters) in 1956, and its inclusion in the VIII Schedule of the Indian Constitution in 1967 (as the fifteenth language).

Decennial records of Indian census provide a strong evidence in favour of maintaining Sindhi as a distinct language identity. Approximately 800.000 Sindhis were reported to have migrated to India during the 1947–48 turmoil. Subsequent census claims of Sindhi as a "mother tongue" show a steady increase, parallel to the growth in the all-India population: 1951: 1. 250. 000 claimants of Sindhi (this includes the non-migrant Sindhi-speaking population of Kutch and Jaisalmer), 1961: 1. 370. 000, 1971: 1. 680. 000, 1981: nearly 2 million Sindhi speakers. The claims of mother tongue in the census need to be taken as an indication of language *identity*, rather than that of language *proficiency*.

Changes in the functions, status and content of Sindhi

The change of habitat naturally brings changes in the functions, status and content of a language. Sindhi, a language of homogenous surroundings in the pre-Partition Sindh Province (comparable to Kerala and Gujarat in India), is now relegated to limited functions among Sindhi settlers in India. It is mostly restricted to family, neighbourhood and intimate circles and cultural-educational needs. A probe into the communication networks of the Sindhi community reveals that the native language of bilinguals is usually displaced in the formal settings such as occupation, administration, court affairs, trade, etc, and, in some cases, even in informal as well as personal correspondence between Sindhi speakers), in favour of diglossic use of English and/or Hindi. A Sindhi native speaker often uses this bilingual facility as a means of *identity*, manipulating language choice to one's advantage, a common trait of plurilingual societies in the Indian context.[6]

Indian languages, by and large, are also known for their "loan proneness". Sindhi too does not show much resistance to borrowing from other languages, particularly pan-Indian languages such as Hindi, Urdu and English (Khubchandani 1969: 89 – 90).

On the one hand the transplantation processes among a microscopic minority of Sindhis in the midst of enormous diversity have brought about a considerable reduction in the functions of the Sindhi language in formal settings; on the other, the forces of maintaining a distinct cultural identity have led to an upsurge in literary expression, theatre, and the performing arts through religio-cultural festivals at the popular level. The constitutional recognition of the Sindhi language has no doubt given a psychological boost to cultural activities, without however assuring the use of Sindhi in education, the mass media and local administration. Thus far the identity maintenance factors seem to be much stronger than assimilation-promoting traits. To some extent this explains the paradox that the migrant "mainstream" Sindhis have not been so enthusiastic about forging identity-links with Kachhi and Jaisalmeri speakers (who are rooted in their "own" territory on the Indo-Pakistan border) but share assimilatory traits with the surrounding dominant groups, namely Gujaratis and Rajasthanis.

One notices similar trends of *exclusiveness* in the treatment of Sindhi literature as well. To cite one example, in the absence of any worthwhile academic infra-structure for the study of Sindhi language and literature in India, the mantle of giving direction to literature has fallen on journalistic reviews through literary periodicals. In this process, only the self-styled avant-garde writings are considered worthy of serious scrutiny, while the free, uninhibited and creative expression manifested in traditional genres in the forms of *Sufi* and other syncretic writings does not receive adequate attention from literary critics; though the second category of literature (syncretic, spiritual) paradoxically attracts much wider readership than the first one.

Three significant variables affecting the function and content of Sindhi were identified in an earlier study (Khubchandani 1963): *1. language environment, 2. generation gap, 3. educational opportunities.* Homogenous Sindhi enclaves (refugee camps and colonies) have considerably shrunk in number and size, and the proportion of scattered Sindhis has been fast increasing, with a drastic effect on profiles of language use. The second and third generation immigrants reveal a remarkable shift in profiles of language use. The grasp of mother tongue is significantly conditioned by the educational opportunities for learning Sindhi available to the second and third generation migrants. Some have studied in Sindhi-medium schools. Some have only studied Sindhi as a subject. Some have neither been acquainted with Sindhi as a medium nor as a school subject. In order to maintain their distinct identity, many community leaders are keen to introduce the study of Sindhi culture and language outside the formal school curriculum, through distance education, Sunday schools and the like.

Conclusion: linguistic and cultural rights in plural societies

The Constitution of India (Article 345) provides full freedom for the states to choose a language (or languages) in a region as the "official" language(s), allowing linguistic minority groups to receive education in their mother tongues and to set up institutions of their choice for this purpose (Article 30). In multilingual federal India, education was until over a decade ago the responsibility of the states, the constituent units. By a constitutional amendment, education is now brought on the "Concurrent List", allowing both the Union and the state governments to initiate legislation on educational policies. Hopefully this amendment can now pave the way for reflection at the national level on how the educational language rights of linguistic minorities can be promoted. Since the formation of linguistic states in 1956, many state agencies have been preoccupied with the problems of promoting education through the "dominant" languages of their respective states and have seldom championed the cause of "minority" languages (beyond introducing a few tribal languages as "token" media in the initial years of schooling).

When dealing with education in plural societies, we should do well to realise the risks in attempting uniform solutions. Various impediments to the spread of education are attributed to the multiplicity of languages, whereas the real issues are the confrontation between "tradition" and "modernity" concerning the role of language in education and dogmatic rigidity in claiming privileges and parity for different languages in educational curriculum in the thrust for autonomy (Khubchandani 1981: 42–68).

The present-day goals of teaching mother tongue or second language, being primarily conditioned by the criterion of excellence in the pedantic sense, have, in a way, been instrumental in leading to the erosion of some of the humanistic qualities in everyday communication. The *Barbiana Letter* (1970), raising an accusing finger at the teacher who represents the higher-class values of speech, points to the fundamental right of individuals: "All citizens are equal without distinction to language. But you honour grammar more than constitutions".

A brief survey of the Sindhi acculturation processes in a plurilingual milieu highlights

  (i) the *ascribed* nature of primordial identity (i. e. given by tradition),
 (ii) observance of specific traits associated with identity is generally *fluid* (subject to the sensitivity of the group or to individual goals), and
(iii) commitment or loyalty to a particular identity is *relative* to the context (and not absolute), and can at times even be voluntary.

In view of this, linguistic rights are essentially *cultural*, generally transcending the bounds of political and administrative institutions. These are usually fostered through the strengths of "diasporic" solidarity (*birādarī* in Persian), as in the worldwide Jewish case. The question of linguistic rights for minorities is tied up with the role of the state in sociocultural development and of cross-state diaspora asserting linguistic rights in order to secure their cultures. Fresh thinking on these issues should endeavour to create a climate in which cultural identities can be sublimated, rather than submit to the aggressive assertions of narrow loyalties.

Granted the enormous diversity in the speech behaviour of plural societies, it would be erroneous to interpret it on the basis of monistic norms and evaluate the communicative competence by razor-edged boundaries between languages, by the dominating extension of standard usage, and by the notions of language purity and language elaboration (through meticulous coinage of technical terms and translations). One cannot easily brush aside spatial characteristics such as situational norms, and heterogeneity and inherent fluidity in the speech spectrum, as mere interferences in an "ideal" language system, as has been implied in many language planning programmes (Neustupný 1974).

The overall guiding spirit should be service of a language environment which makes sense (Britton 1970) and meets the demands of social justice, bearing in mind the specific needs of "minority" cultures (and languages).

Notes

1. The author is particularly grateful to Tove Skutnabb-Kangas and Robert Phillipson for their valuable suggestions.
2. Said — Simmons' account is based on the Ethnographic Atlas prepared by Murdoch (1967). They quote Gordon's definition (1964: 29) of ethnic group with approval: 'The

unities of race, religion and national origin.' The state is defined in terms of territory, populations and government, essentially a territorial form of organization.
3. For a detailed discussion distinguishing structural and organic pluralism in a global perspective, see Gordon 1981 and Khubchandani 1983. The Schema of four types of pluralism (Khubchandani 1991, Table 2, 13—23) elaborates the salient features of manifestation and organization of speech and external pressures exerted on speech in a society.
4. Theoretical implications of some of the constructs expounding the characteristics of plural societies in the Indian context, such as fuzziness of language boundaries, fluidity of language identity, diglossic complementation across language boundaries, and *tradition* and *echo* systems affecting the verbal repertoire are discussed in Khubchandani 1983, 1986, 1991.
5. Unless otherwise stated, all figures come from the 1981 Census.
6. For a detailed treatment of Hindi and English as contact languages in the Indian milieu through code-switching and other devices, see Khubchandani 1989, and 1991: 55—72, and 95—113.

Kashmiri, a majority-minority language: an exploratory essay

Makhan L. Tickoo

The task

My subject is my mother tongue. Much like the Swiss, we Kashmiris are known to suffer from an excessive degree of sentimental attachment to both our land and our language. A belief in their exceptional beauty, richness and charm may at times make it difficult to take a totally objective view of what has been happening to both. A lot has been happening.

A word first about my principal qualification and main motivation for attempting this essay. I am a teacher of E(F)SL (English as a second [or foreign] language); have been so for a little over forty years. This has taught me to value the innumerable advantages that working in and with the help of this dominant world language bestows on those non-native users who succeed in making it their instrument of growth, professional or social-interactional. Proficient use of English often earns rewards which, in material terms, are almost unique.

However, an uneasy feeling that I have been paying an unaffordable price for this highly valued acquisition has been growing inside me. In the last decade in particular I have been experiencing the deadening weight of the cumulative losses as they manifest themselves in my roles at the workplace and as part of a nuclear family.

This essay relates some of these personal losses to the larger issues that arise in trying to understand the current state of my mother tongue as a majority-minority language. In thus focussing some of these issues it also, in the final section, attempts to outline a possible alternative that should make it unnecessary for future generations to pay this price.

The situation

Kashmiri is one of those fourteen languages that found a place in the 8th Schedule of the Indian Constitution. These languages, now numbering eighteen, were singled out by the makers of that historic document as literary languages which deserve "political recognition at the national level" (Ekka 1984).

One of a small group of languages in the Dardic group (Grierson 1919) which forms a sub-group within the Indo-Aryan family, Kashmiri today is the only language in this group that has established itself as a literary language. It is the mother tongue of most people (about 97% of the total population: Census, 1971) who inhabit the valley of Kashmir and is thus the language of everyday use in the land of its birth and growth. In this sense it is undoubtedly a majority language.

But something sets it apart. Notwithstanding its more than forty-year strong constitutional recognition as a language of literacy and learning and despite the fact that it satisfies every criterion and qualification for being assigned a preeminent place and status at the state level, it has been accorded no roles whatever in either schooling or statecraft. In its land of birth this language has been reduced to the status of a "domestic vernacular" (Smolicz 1986) with no functional domains except those that cannot be taken away from it by decree. As Ekka (1984: 10) rightly points out "Kashmiri presents a unique case in that no facility for mother-tongue teaching exists in the language even though it forms the dominant language in the region".

Apparently based on inaccurate official data, Ekka and others conclude however that Kashmiri is taught as a subject in the first three years of the primary school (1984: 13). This is not true, although it could have been so had the successive state governments not given up their policy decisions on its use made some forty years ago. In 1950 it was the stated objective of the state government to make Kashmiri the sole medium of instruction at the primary level. Within three years of that decision it was felt however that it would not be possible to make it work. Nor do Pattanayak's twin statements on Indian national languages reflect the reality as far as Kashmiri is concerned. His view that the "majority languages" of India are spoken by between ten and eighty million people obviously excludes this majority language; fewer than four million people (perhaps as few as three) speak this language as their mother tongue and the majority of them (fewer than 2.5 million according to the census report of 1971) live in the valley. It is also not true that "barring Sanskrit, Urdu, Sindhi and English, for which special provisions are made, the other languages are dominant in one or more states" of India (Pattanayak, 1981: 68–69).[1] Kashmiri in fact suffers both ways; on the one hand it has been assigned no place and allowed no roles in education or administration; on the other, because it cannot be placed among minority languages, its speakers cannot seek consideration under the special provisions made for such languages in the Indian Constitution. Despite the fact that it has the weight of a whole state behind it, Kashmiri has no status in education or administration. Having become reduced to the status of a minority language, it lives in the shadow of more than one dominant languages which have, individually and collectively, displaced it totally from its rightful domains of public roles and educational responsibilities. Much like a few other similarly placed languages in some other parts of the world Kashmiri appears to have become a victim of "linguicism"(Skutnabb-Kangas 1988) which democratic India's enlightened linguistic policy ought normally to make a virtual anathema.

But although Kashmiri is not taught either as subject or as medium in the primary school, its literary value has for some time been receiving recognition at the highest academic levels. The University of Kashmir has a department of Kashmiri which offers PhD level courses; by mid-1989 eight scholars had received postgraduate (MPhil and/or PhD) degrees in Kashmiri from that university. The department also offers a postgraduate diploma course in literary Kashmiri and an MA in Kashmiri language and literature including poetics, structure of language, political history and a study in depth of one Kashmiri author. In addition, beginning with the academic year 1983–84, Kashmiri has been offered as an elective subject at the undergraduate level in four colleges of the valley; in a small number of schools it also exists as an elective subject at the higher-secondary level and in a few as an additional-optional subject in the two top classes of the ten-year secondary school. More than forty books in Kashmiri on various literary and scientific topics have, in the last few years, been published by the department which also runs an annual research journal on Kashmiri. Works in Kashmiri by Kashmiris are also being sponsored and encouraged by the state government's Academy of Art, Culture and Languages.[2]

The neglect suffered by Kashmiri and its uniquely subordinate status among national languages are thus not at all relatable to any known limitations of the language as an instrument of life or learning. With a long history of literary works (Grierson, 1919; Bamzai 1973) Kashmiri is a living language capable of serving all those purposes that are served by other languages of the 8th Schedule. What then are the main reasons for its deprival?

The reason(s) why

One main reason lies in the valley's history. From the early years of the 14th century to the middle of the 20th (1947), Kashmir and its people remained under foreign domination. This began with the Muslim invasion in the fourteenth century which brought Kashmir under Mohammedan rule for about four and a half centuries. During this period the Sultanates (1339–1586) were followed by Mughal Rulers (1586–1753) and the Afghans who ruled the valley briefly (1753–1819) but harshly. The Sikhs (1819–1846) came next and then the Dogras (1846–1947). As part of this long and sad history of conquest and enslavement the valley was on 16 March 1846 sold by the British to the Raja Gulab Singh for the paltry sum of Rs 7,500,000 (about a quarter million of today's US dollars!) under the Treaty of Amritsar (see Wakefield 1975 for the text of the Sale Deed). Each dynasty treated the conquered people differently — from the harshest to what was, in relative terms, judged as benign. On one thing they differed but little: in all cases a language other than Kashmiri became the language of the court, of state administration and of scholarly discourse. In its land of birth Kashmiri never got promoted to the status of either the official language or the language of formal schooling.

Several consequences have followed. The language did not develop a script of its own, with the result that several different groups (e.g. the creative artists of the two main religious communities or the religious scribes among the Hindus) made use of different scripts which at one time numbered five. This is still largely true, despite the present government-sponsored script and its use by a steadily increasing percentage of Kashmiri speakers. Second, living under foreign yoke for over six hundred years, the decision-makers have developed a "colonized consciousness" (Fanon 1968) which, as we shall soon see, governs their attitudes and behaviours, policies and programmes regarding the place and use of this language. Third, something that is still largely true of even the leading intellectuals among the two religious communities, the firmly entrenched belief in the close association of one or another dominant language with their respective religious faiths and its divine word which, by comparison, makes Kashmiri a mere human language, thus reducing it to a lowly status among the highly influential Hindu pundits and Muslim maulviz. Fourth, and perhaps the most destructive because it came from not just a seemingly superior (and historically more successful) "race" but from those to whom the Nabobs and Maharajas owed allegiance, the highly jaundiced views on Indian languages in general (e.g. Lord Macaulay's "the dialects commonly spoken among the natives of India ... Poor and rude and in need of enrichment from some other quarter", Young 1935: 348) but Kashmiri in particular by British politicians and pundits alike e. g.

> The language of Kashmiris is, like their dress, peculiar, and distinct from that spoken in any part of India, or of the adjacent countries. It may be considered a patois rather than a language proper, and there is harshness and uncouthness about the pronunciation which betrays it as such ... Difficult to pronounce and difficult to acquire, it is generally incomprehensible to strangers" (Wakefield 1975: 107–108);

or it "is of Hindu origin ... may be supposed (to be) rich in agricultural terms ... But the vocabulary is small and inadequate for present-day use, being conspicuously weak in terms both for the implements and materials of modern civilized life and for abstract ideas" (Neve 1912: 84). Such uninformed views unfortunately continue to govern the minds and actions of the present rulers as much as they did those in the days of the Raj.

A second set of reasons is both a product of history and an offspring of current received wisdom in applied linguistics. Together the two have nurtured attitudes, beliefs and practices which militate against not just informed policies on languages and their teaching but ultimately against the very concept of educating the whole person. Historically, modern western education and more particularly education under systems that served widely as models in the third-world, has been premised on the dogma that unilingualism is the preferred state and that bilingualism or worse still, multilingualism, invariably hampers the progress of children at school, causes excessive mental fatigue, represses originality and leads to parrot learning (e.g. West 1926). The reasons for this are clear; latterly they have not only been forcefully restated (e.g. Pool 1972) but equally forcefully contested and in good measure exposed (e.g. "high levels of bilingualism/biculturalism benefit every child", Skutnabb-Kangas 1984). And yet the belief remains fully entrenched. Educational systems in many third-world countries strive hard to reduce the language-learning "load" and reform their curricular programmes with a view to "saving" the majority of "average" pupils against the "debilitating effects" of one or more additional languages.

To this historical baggage of language as a burden rather than as a possible source of enrichment and empowerment, have recently been added several influential ideas based either on a partial understanding of facts or on a select use of data to suit their proponents. Some of these including, for example, the view that languages are divisible into productive and unproductive ones (Mackey 1984: 45), that language choice in bilingual societies is often essentially between that which saves children by allowing them access to the riches of a language of wider use and that which sacrifices them at the altar of mere ethnic identity, are either-ors which make nonsense of the linguist's ideas about the comparable potential of human languages. Some others, which are in part based on the genuine concerns of teachers of English and other world languages (e.g. that time spent on the mother tongue is time taken off English or that different languages on the school curriculum stand in opposition rather than cooperation) seem not only to trivialize the issues (Fishman 1984) but may often have come from men who, like their ancestors among the Platonic cavemen, refuse to look beyond their comfortably walled worlds. But whatever their motivations and however limiting their world view, they happen, in most cases, to carry conviction in educational and administrative systems because their ideas and prejudices come not only with the weight of established and forcefully promoted authority but with the impressive material affluence of their respective countries of origin.

Exploring the Phenomenon

"What are the main problems of learning through an "other" language?" "What losses and gains accrue from having to rely on it for growth, either personal or professional?" These and related questions are basic; most remain unanswered. In this section I shall draw upon various sources[3] to sketch a few relevant facts about (a) an individual Kashmiri learner (b) a Kashmiri family and (c) the speech community as a whole.

The learner

Children acquire the basics of their mother tongue as part of growing up (cf Halliday 1975, "languaging") — at home, in the neighbourhood, with playmates. A Kashmiri child is no exception. Soon however (s)he faces the challenges of using a classical language — Arabic or Sanskrit, to recite the sacred word in the "best" book. Not every child passes through this experience; nor need it come so early. What may be worthy of study in this early childhood experience however is the impact that such esoteric symbols and strange sounds that enshrine eternal wisdom which they neither need nor seek to understand, have on children's cognitive growth and linguistic development.

In a majority of cases the child enters school soon after celebrating his/her fifth birthday. Schooling means the use of an "other" language (Urdu or in some cases English and Hindi) to gain entrance into the world of learning. Not enough is yet known about the pros and cons of such early dependence on second/foreign languages. A few relevant and attested inferences are possible nevertheless. First, such learning becomes difficult because it is built on a total and totally damaging divide between home and school. What makes it worse is a situation wherein learning has to be mediated through instructional materials that belong to an alien culture and a totally dissimilar world view.

For the ordinary Kashmiri child worse soon follows: their first language of learning (in most cases Urdu) gets in competition with a second (or two others) even before they have had a chance of gaining any mastery over it. In most cases therefore it is confined to the tasks of lower-order learning and gets learnt as a limited resource. Very few children need gain active mastery over it and few need realize its potential as a language of "use". The average Kashmiri child thus remains a poor user of Urdu or Hindi.

English soon takes over and in time assumes the role of the dominant language which is assigned "higher order" roles as the medium of science and scholarship and, at the higher reaches of schooling, serves as the sole medium of education. For the secondary level student however the motivation is once again instrumental: s/he works to make English serve as a weapon against the dreaded exams, and may, in the majority of cases, stop at that. A third national/regional language forms part of the school curriculum and, for a percentage of children, there is often an additional optional language.

Languages thus follow each other in quick succession; they come and go. They crowd the curriculum, are regarded as a major learning load — and have been known as a perennial educational concern. For the average student this almost always amounts to semilingualism. Deprived of the opportunity to learn through their own language, placed in a system where the home and neighbourhood and what they experience in them are no part of valued learning, they view languages much the same way as they do other subjects: they are somehow to be put up with to help them cross one barrier after another. Such a child often leaves school with no language that they can call their own and none that they enjoy using creatively or, in a majority of cases, none that serves even the narrowly defined instrumental needs without making them feel inadequate. Having spent many valuable hours for several years on three or more other people's languages, they end up making several acquaintances but no single dependable friend. Average school-leavers thus have no language that they can call their own, none that they can use with confidence even in limited "public" domains. Multilinguals they may be; they definitely have no language that is usable as a critical or creative resource. In most cases they must find their linguistic experience a deadweight that begets little and equips them for much less. And even in those few cases where such children learn how to use one or another language reasonably well, they have to live the rest of their lives in the unenviable situation where even the least lettered native speaker of each language is, by definition, the final authority on what is acceptable and why.

The family

How a family views the different languages must depend on what each offers. For parents who know, languages assume varying degrees of importance as the child passes through different stages of the school. In government schools Urdu occupies an important place in early schooling but before long it gives place to English. In private schools English has pride of place from early on as it serves as the sole medium of instruction. In most cases the official language − Hindi − is also part of the curriculum. In all cases however, since the economic factor is the most potent one in decision-making, parents invest heavily in giving their children the distinctions (real or make-believe) that English alone offers.

Inside the family, reactions tend to vary. For the vast majority of those who live inside the valley, the divide may often be simple. Kashmiri is the language of home, the mosque, the temple and the marketplace. However it ceases to be of any use as a written language except for a "fanatical" few who use it for personal letters among themselves.

Of interest here should however be a peep into a family that deliberately strives to climb the socioeconomic ladder. To understand its typical behaviour I shall use a few extracts from a case-study.

This Kashmiri family lives in one of India's large capital cities. Both husband and wife, with university degrees from the English-speaking world, are well-paid professionals. They use English at work and code-mix English and Hindi/Urdu during their leisure hours. Kashmiri continues to be their language of intimacy, but, conscious of the need to help their two children to feel at ease with the English-dominated upper crust of the Indian middle class and to enjoy its special privileges, they have all along deliberately avoided the use of Kashmiri with them. Both children were educated in English-medium, "Public" schools where the Queen's English was the badge of respectability and where Kashmiri was and is neither heard nor spoken. Altogether therefore they have grown into adulthood with little contact with Kashmiri. To this extent the parents have succeeded.

A heavier price has had to be paid however and it is becoming manifest in the many-sided alienation that the family now suffers. The children are ill at ease with members of the larger family (uncles, aunts, grand-parents, cousins) and they fail to appreciate the joys and excitement of major festivals, religious functions and community get-togethers. In having to keep up with the world-view and values the children have embraced, the parents have been experiencing the tensions of having to live in two different worlds at the same time; they also feel alienated from their kith and kin in the valley. What gives the parents much pain are the feelings of rootlessness and, latterly, the dreaded long-term implications of what they now see as thoughtless masochism in having deprived the children of the most valuable gift that Nature endowed them with. Much less obvious but not far below the surface is the incalculable harm being done by the totally unnatural and clearly unnecessary divide between their own world-views and that of their children and its impact on the fast widening generation gap.

The society

Four related statements — each of them large and all of them admittedly bald, should sum up the losses experienced by the society:

(i) For most *pupils*, dependence on languages all of which are measurably different from Kashmiri in sound, syntax, structure and pragmatics, must make learning both arduous and painful. In the majority of cases this must be a main reason for not just semilingualism but, as Pattanayak suggests (1981: xii), for educational wastage and stagnation. A study of state-level educational budgets shows that in relative terms the investment on a child's primary schooling is much higher in Jammu and Kashmir than it is in many other states of India and yet the state ranks among the lowest as far as its impact is concerned. Despite the fact that the valley's salubrious climate ought to make life inside ordinary schoolrooms much less taxing than in most other parts of India, education in Kashmir shows one of the highest rates of "wastage" in the country. Barring Sikkim where the official language is English, Kashmir also has the lowest literacy rate (21.7%).

(ii) The problems of becoming literate and numerate through a foreign medium get greatly aggravated in the case of *adults*, with the result that notwithstanding Kashmir's very early and innovative involvement in adult literacy programmes, the achievement is once again dismally poor. What makes sense and impacts better in the case of ordinary adults is the as yet limited but increasing use of radio and TV which make use of Kashmiri to inform and educate the farmer/worker about the issues that matter to their lives and work. For the rest the inevitable divide between life and learning that results from total dependence on an "other" language seems to make the task of education a self-deafeating exercise.

(iii) Related to both (i) and (ii) is a socially divisive phenomenon whose horrendous consequences have received little attention from politicians or pundits. With the mother tongue unable to serve most of its rightful roles and other languages operating in a mutually destructive hierarchy, the gap between the educated, more particularly the English educated elite, and the masses has grown into a chasm. As a result, education through English has been paving the way for a society where a new type of debilitating "caste" system is doing incalculable harm.[4]

(iv) The fourth set of issues is potentially the most dangerous. The subordination of the Kashmiris' mother tongue to the status of a domestic vernacular and the continuance of this statusless existence for many generations has, among other things, built a feeling of inferiority and a loss of cultural identity, only parts of which surfaced in looking above at what happens to individuals and families. One sees this in many other spheres including, for example, both Kashmir University's and the State Education Department's continuing lack of faith in a Kashmiri's ability to serve as their chief executive. Much more harmful however may be the long-term political consequences of this many-sided alienation which though barely understood, is bound to serve as a main cause of state-level separatism resulting from Kashmir's ages-old search for a separate identity and for recognition of its uniqueness. The longer their language remains a domestic vernacular with a totally displaced or deprived status — a language of no more than the home and the back-streets marketplace — the more oppressed they will feel and the more intense will become their desire for a separate political status. Already there are more than telltale signs of this happening.

Towards an alternative

Having looked at some aspects of the situation as it exists today, we are now in a position to work towards a possible alternative which, in the light of our present understanding, can be both viable and in time capable of resolving the major problems.

Among the alternatives suggested in recent literature on minority education (e.g. Skutnabb-Kangas and Cummins 1988) the one that appears to offer a good starting point is, in my judgment, what Fishman calls the stopping of the hemorrhaging of the main arteries (Fishman 1984). This he says is best done by focussing upon and shoring up the primary intergenerational arena, which includes the home, the neighbourhood, the primary school, the workplace and the places of worship. For Kashmiri in Kashmir this mainly amounts to giving the language the central place in primary schooling not just as a subject, which the government has already decided to do beginning in 1991, but as the sole medium of education throughout the primary school. To this I would add adult literacy programmes which too must be given entirely in the learner's own language.

What must be done to make Kashmiri an efficient instrument of true literacy? In order to make this a reform which will not only not end up abortively but will become the basis for a more desirable system of education and, in the long run, for restoring to its speakers what they have lost through generations of callous exploitation and oppression, it will be necessary to lay the groundwork for it through two separate but mutually supporting strategies, an *action-oriented strategy* and an *attitudes-oriented strategy*.

The *action-oriented strategy* rests on the understanding that to make Kashmiri serve as the first language of literacy and as a main instrument of life-long learning, the state-level policy planners and language educators will act on a well-thought-out programme of linguistic and educational initiatives. Three main aspects need attention: script, curricula and instruction.

A close study and review of the officially approved *script* is needed to make sure that it does not remain the roadblock it is said to have become. When it was designed and given official recognition in 1947, it was viewed with a degree of suspicion by a number of Kashmiri linguists. Braj Kachru, for example, wrote (1969: 298) "In the final decision for accepting this script mostly non-linguistic matters were considered. The usefulness of the Perso-Arabic script for Kashmiri is still doubtful". Several teachers in Kashmiri schools who responded to my questionnaire also blame this script as being partly responsible for both the non-teaching of Kashmiri in schools and for their failure to use the language as a written medium. But whether they are right or wrong, what is important is to educate the policy-planner about the basic linguistic fact that far from being an inalienable part of a language, a script may be no less and no more than a garment of convenience. What may help in this is a studied understanding of how, for example, Malaysia or Indonesia have been making use of the Roman script to help their predominantly Muslim populations to master the national language as an instrument of Islamic thought and culture alongside secular scientific learning. What is being proposed here is however not the adoption of Roman or any other script but a scientific attitude to the question of how best to make the script serve its functions as a facilitator for teaching the language widely and well.

But good or bad, a script does not teach a language. For effective teaching/learning to take place societies depend on schooling systems — their *curricula and courses*, their instructional *materials* and above all, willing and able teachers. A greater challenge than that of evolving a script that can "easify" learning will therefore be to attract and set to work the ablest linguists and language teachers in the valley to design and develop good syllabuses, effective literacy materials, including both source and course books, learners' dictionaries and pedagogic grammars, audio and visual aids and materials to build learner self-reliance and the ability to learn how to learn. Unless and until quality literacy materials are made widely available at affordable prices, no attempts at giving Kashmiri its place among languages of learning will have any worthwhile impact. And most important of all, there will have to be a carefully designed *teacher-education* programme for all those trainers and teachers who will be entrusted with the responsibilities of using Kashmiri as the sole medium of primary-level and adult-literacy programmes.

The object of the *attitudes-oriented strategy* is to educate everyone who is in any way involved in the use of this language — parents, pedagogues, language policy planners and politicians, through basic facts about displaced languages in general and this language in particular. This has become necessary not only because the folklinguistic platitudes that prevail in the valley are doing incalculable harm but also because the dominant beliefs among sizeable, informed and influential sections of our profession are no less harmful. I shall address a few of each to illustrate

the major beliefs and, where possible, some possible steps towards re-
mediation.

On Kashmiri as a language and its potential for use in its land of birth
there is need to provide a whole host of facts as a basis for positive
thinking and action. Statistics (Koul — Schmidt 1983) on its current use
inside Kashmir reveal a continuum. Spoken Kashmiri is dominant in the
family — with 91% use between married couples whereas it is used just
about 33% at work or study. As a written language however its use is
no more than marginal. Only about 10% write in it to "even the nearest
relatives" and they too, in most cases, are those who are "emotionally
involved in the support of Kashmiri and its development at all levels"
(Koul — Schmidt .1983: 30). Statistics show too that the majority of
Kashmiris support its use as a medium of instruction — some 83%
showing a preference for its use as the medium for primary education,
about 50% at the secondary level and about a quarter (24%) at the
university as well. The above survey, as well as my own small-scale
questionnaire study show that even educated Kashmiris, including those
who are aware of "its long literary tradition" and the fact that for
centuries it has served as a viable medium for creative artists, are often
unsure about its suitability for increased educational responsibilities for
three powerful reasons: in their view it has an "incomplete grammar", is
"only a dialect" and "has yet to sort out its script problems".

The first step towards restoring to the language its rightful status, roles
and domains has therefore got to be the education of all those who today
lack faith in its ability to serve as a language of learning. It needs to be
categorically stated that a language that serves its people as a spoken
medium on all occasions, has for centuries proved itself as an instrument
of literary creativity and, notwithstanding the neglect it suffered through
century after century of callous disregard of Kashmiri culture and aspirations, is being found worthy of scholarly research and study at the
highest level, cannot be found wanting in "grammar". Equally important
is to make it clear that because Kashmiri shares with or borrows parts
of its vocabulary from other languages (viz Sanskrit, Persian, Urdu,
Hindi), it does not become a dialect of any of those languages. What
may help here is, for example, the awareness that the English language
of today, the most international of world languages, is perhaps much
more a result of loans and borrowings than any other world language
and that despite the fact that its borrowings far exceed its original Anglo-
Saxon vocabulary, English can in no way be thought of as a dialect of
any other language, classical or modern. Also, Kashmiri may belong to

the same Indo-Aryan family of languages as some of these other "lending" languages, but it is measurably different from each one of them in its system of sounds (with a number of vowels and consonants which speakers of Urdu/Hindi find extremely difficult to learn), its syntactic structure and in its basic word-order. Finally it may be necessary to point out that changing scripts do not alter the nature or character of a language.

Why, it may be asked, should there be a need to educate the planner and policy-maker on how best to deal with displaced languages if all that we seek is a replacement of one medium by another? The answer is that to smoothe the prospects of the alternative functioning productively many aspects of current received wisdom in bilingual education will require rethinking.

A part of this wisdom is that the time devoted to lesser languages is time taken away from the accredited languages of science and scholarship. This understanding, which has obviously grown in the West where unilingualism was for many generations seen as the norm, need not apply to countries like India where three languages are already provided for in the nationally upheld school-level curriculum. For good returns on learner time and effort, a most important consideration in decision making and programme planning should be that there are many visible and several invisible gains in placing two or more languages of learning facilitatively rather than displacively. Studies done over several decades provide support for this understanding.

Working in India almost seventy years ago, Michael West arrived at the following conclusion on the basis of a series of controlled experiments in primary schools: reading is a general ability which once learnt in one language is almost fully transferable to another (1926). West's findings have received both confirmation and extension in the longitudinal Canadian immersion programmes and other "language shelter" programmes (Cummins and Swain 1986) and research into bilingual education and language shelter programmes (Alderson 1984; Perkins et al. 1989). What they have shown is that one's mother tongue is a good way to lay the foundations of literacy and "literacy-related socio-cognitive skills and dispositions" (Fishman 1984; Harley et al. 1990) and that learning through the mother tongue is by far the surest means towards cognitive development and, something directly supportive of West's main finding, that once the child's overall intellectual and conceptual skills are developed in the mother tongue, they are easily transferable to another language.

A second related point is that the prevailing practices in EF(S)L (English as a foreign [or second] language) teaching — courses, methods and measurement — which have for thirty odd years been serving as a kind of model for the teaching of Indian languages as mother tongues or as second languages, need to be carefully reexamined. The model is not only inappropriate and limiting, its impact on the status and scope of teaching Indian languages has been restrictive and retrograde.

For the vast majority of Indian students, education through the medium of English fails to produce true competence in the more challenging cognitive (not to speak of creative) domains. The two dominant approaches of TEFL (teaching English as a foreign language) of the last forty years, viz the structural and the 'communicative", are, in almost equal measure, applied linguistic responses to specific-purpose needs that have very little in common with those of English in India or in most other third world/Asian countries. Both stop short of what Jerome Bruner calls the "analytical ability" (Bruner, 1976) and Henry Widdowson terms "capacity" as opposed to competence (Widdowson, 1983); both cater for specific and limited aspects of language in use and both exclude more than they include. The alternative must address the fact that languages of learning are meant to serve in context-reduced cognitive domains (Cummins 1984) for which Western Europe and North America make use of their own languages.

In the alternative proposed here, the teaching of the mother tongue must aim at laying the foundations of those cognitive abilities which are required to meet the demands of true learning at the same time as it addresses the demands of successful human interaction. The emphasis must shift from oral communication to language use for cognitive, creative and affective domains. Also, the three (or more) languages of the school curriculum must work in close cooperation with well-defined and shared curricular commitments, prioritizing the "pervasive intellectual, emotional and self-definitional development of the individual learner" (Fishman 1984). In the school curriculum for languages, the aim must be to totally overhaul the system in which currently a majority of the children come out of school to join the ranks of a growing "undereducated underclass" (Skutnabb-Kangas — Cummins 1988). In its place must be put approaches, methodologies and materials which can bring into harmony the goals of all the languages used for learning and which by ensuring maximum transfer of training and learning across languages, can cooperate effectively to produce the type of bilingualism that will meet the outstanding needs of the vast majority of learners in the state.

If in doing so the status of English or other currently dominant languages gets redefined and delimited and its goals altered (e.g. from being taught as a language of social intercourse with a mythical native speaker in mind to being learnt as a strong additional language of learning), that too should be a welcome development. For far too long education through English has been assigned roles that rightfully belong to one or another Indian language, with the result that mother tongue teaching has suffered prolonged and unwarranted neglect. What needs to be prioritized is to enable the mother tongue to play the central role in a child's total education and to teach English for purposes that it alone can serve best. The Education Commission's view (Education Commission 1964–1966) that English be taught mainly as a library language has obviously been both misunderstood and misrepresented. English in India continues to be taught as though it were a language of social survival rather than a strong additional language whose unique contributions lie in relating scientific and technological developments to the country's socioeconomic needs, aspirations and challenges.

But Kashmiri has suffered most in being deprived of its linguistic rights, its roles in schooling and statecraft and in being reduced to the status of an inferior handmaiden to other languages. She has to assume her proper roles as the first and the most powerful language of literacy which must be charged with the responsibility of laying the foundations of true life-long learning. As the one language with which ordinary Kashmiris associate with ease and the only language that gives them a sense of belonging and of common goals and aspirations, the joys of being allowed a separate identity and a relationship with shared values, experiences and achievements of the past, the Kashmiri language must in time be harnessed to take on all the roles and responsibilities of a dominant first language for its speakers.

Notes

1. Pattanayak also writes that "Languages which become minority language either outside or inside their home state range from 4.96% in Kerala to 84.54% in Nagaland, of their respective populations" (1981: 40–41), again forgetting Kashmiri.
2. Kashmir University's involvement in the study and development of Kashmiri began in the early 1970s. Some other agencies that share this interest are referred to in Kachru 1969.
3. Apart from recent publications on Kashmiri which are listed in the bibliography, I have made use of a questionnaire study of the current situation regarding its use. To

the teachers who responded to my questionnaire and in particular to Dr Mohammad Shafi Lone (Shauq) of Kashmir University, I would like to express my sincere thanks for their helpful information and comments.

4. Prime Minister Nehru was perhaps the first Indian to expose the problems being caused by this new caste system. He made fun of it on several occasions in his speeches in the 1960s.

Language rights in postcolonial Africa

Robert Phillipson — Tove Skutnabb-Kangas

Introduction

Language policy is of vital importance for the political stability and legitimacy of the state. Most contemporary African states are experiencing acute economic, social and political problems. In education there are many symptoms of crisis (World Bank 1988). The capacity of African governments to meet the expectations of their citizens is increasingly in question, and the legitimacy of the state is in doubt from Algeria and Morocco to South Africa, from Liberia to Sudan.

The majority of Africans are governed in a language that they do not understand, but few African states have given serious attention to language policy. As Ayo Bamgbose, the Nigerian scholar in his recent book on *Language and the nation: the language question in Sub-Saharan African* puts it:

> There is a general feeling that language problems are not urgent and hence solutions to them can wait. ... Language policies in African countries are characterized by one or more of the following problems: avoidance, vagueness, arbitrariness, fluctuation and declaration without implementation. (1991: 6, 111)

A clear example of declaration without implementation at the continental level is the failure of African governments to act on the *Cultural Charter for Africa*, which OAU (Organization for African Unity) Heads of State and Government adopted in 1976. Article 6(2) of this states that member states should "promote teaching in national languages in order to accelerate their economic, political and cultural development", while Article 18 urges them "to prepare and implement reforms necessary for the introduction of African languages in education" (quoted in Bamgbose 1991: 132). The OAU Language Plan of Action for Africa, adopted in 1986, and which covers the promotion and encouragement of African languages as media of education and mass literacy, has likewise not yet led to any wider use of indigenous languages (Bamgbose 1991: 127–128; see also Mateene 1980 and Kalema 1985).

A principal explanation for this state of affairs is that one of the most durable legacies of colonialism has been language policies. The new leaders have retained the languages of the former colonial powers and even strengthened their position, whereas African languages have seldom been declared official languages of contemporary African states and are often not even acknowledged as "national" languages. The OAU Inter-African Bureau of Languages sombrely concludes that current policies are unlikely to change the marginal position of indigenous languages (OAU-BIL 1985: 7):

> Years after the attainment of political independence, the majority of African independent states have continued to practise linguistic policies inherited at the time of independence, where, on the whole, foreign colonial languages are more favoured than the languages indigenous to the African continent.

(This OAU body was scrapped in 1986, ostensibly for financial reasons, and its director, Kahombo Mateene, transferred to other OAU work. No doubt it was also relevant that the Bureau was championing the cause of African languages, an explicit goal of the OAU, rather more vigorously than most African political leaders.)

The colonial inheritance

Although the imperial powers had slightly different education policies, and considerable autonomy was allowed to the many Christian missions who bore the brunt of teaching, the goals of the imperial powers were very similar.

The Dutch colonial government in Indonesia deliberately restricted the opportunities of Indonesians to learn Dutch (Alisjahbana 1990: 316). A similar view was also widespread in settler colonies in British Africa, but the Colonial Office was convinced that English was a vital medium for Western influence. From the mid 19th century a grammatical knowledge of the English language was regarded as "the most important agent for the coloured population of the colonies" (quoted in Ashby 1966: 150). The colonialist ideology is encapsulated in Earl Grey's remarks in 1899 (quoted in Hodson 1902: 158):

> Probably everyone would agree that an Englishman would be right in considering his way of looking at the world and at life better

than that of the Maori or Hottentot, and no-one will object in the abstract to England doing her best to impose her better and higher view on these savages ... Can there be any doubt that the white man must, and will, impose his superior civilization on the coloured races.

The same refrain could be heard in the French empire, where the "civilizing mission", including the role of the European language, was energetically articulated. The goal was to make the overseas subjects "French in language, thought, and spirit" (Foncin 1910, quoted in Ashby 1966: 365). A statement by Rambaud, the Minister of Public Education, in 1897 displays a keen awareness of the role of language in ensuring ideological control in the phase succeeding physical violence. It is also perceptive in identifying the key sites for linguistic control (quoted in Colonna 1975: 40):

The first conquest of Algeria was accomplished militarily and was completed in 1871 when Kabylia was disarmed. The second conquest has consisted of making the natives accept our administrative and judicial systems. The third conquest will be by the School: this should ensure the predominance of our language over the various idioms, inculcate in the muslims our own idea of what France is and its role in the world, and replace ignorance and fanatical prejudices by the simple but precise notions of European science.

According to French government sources, when the French arrived to "civilize" Algeria, the literacy rate in urban Algeria was 40%, far higher than in France at the time. When the French left in 1962, after 130 years of colonization, the literacy rate among Algerians was, in an optimistic reckoning, 10–15% (Colonna 1975).

Indigenous languages were marginalized and stigmatized, branded as mere "dialects" "idioms", "vernaculars" or "patois", in the same way as the languages of the "periphery" in Britain and France. French and English on the other hand were glorified, French as the language of reason, logic and human rights, English as the language of modernity, parliamentary democracy, technological progress and national unity (Skutnabb-Kangas – Phillipson 1986b; Phillipson 1992, chapter 9). In racially hierarchical South Africa the Boers saw themselves as a "chosen race". As God had selected them, then Afrikaans was logically the language of God. A similar ideology exists in the Arab world, where the language of the Koran is regarded as God's language. This provides a foundation for a belief in the absolute superiority of Arabic to other languages (Calvet 1987: 38–). Independent states in North Africa have institutionalized this "classical" Arabic, which can only be learned through formal instruction, hence prejudicing and restricting the rights of speakers of Berber and demotic Arabic. Despite the crass ignorance betrayed by the assertion of an American headmaster to an immigrant pupil "If English was good enough for Jesus it's good enough for you", there is a tendency for the same type of rationalizations to be used to legitimate all dominant languages, whether by reference to "logic", "technological advance and modernity" or "God".

The structural and ideological entrenchment of the dominant language in colonial empires had predictable results. "English was the official vehicle and the magic formula to colonial elitedom." (Ngũgĩ 1985: 115) "Education to many people came to mean simply the ability to speak and write English (from a history of Ghana, 1963, quoted in Mazrui 1968: 186). The tiny *"evolué, assimilé"* African elite were in theory as good as French. Their successful "education" implied a rejection of African linguistic and cultural values.

Education fulfilled a similar structural role in each colonial empire. It reflected the pattern through which racism is affirmed, namely glorifying the dominant (group/language), stigmatizing the dominated (groups/languages), and rationalizing the relationship between the two, always to the advantage of the dominant (Preiswerk 1980). Colonial education is characterized in the list that follows: the first two points reflect the stigmatization of the language and traditions of the dominated, the next four the glorification of the language, culture and educational traditions of the dominant (for more detail see Phillipson 1992, chapter 5).

— Local languages had low status, whether they were used in education (for initial literacy, as in the British and Belgian empires, and in South Africa and pre-independence Namibia) or not (as in the French empire in Africa), such literacy in no way challenging the dominance of the colonial language in secondary and higher education, administration, etc;
— local traditions and educational practice were ignored, despised and decried (see for instance, Jomo Kenyatta's plea to European educators to familiarize themselves with indigenous traditions (Kenyatta 1979, chapter 5, first published 1938);
— the master language of empire was attributed civilizing properties;
— Western-oriented, bookish education was offered (aimed at producing a class of compliant clerks and a loyal elite);

- from the secondary level upwards, education attempted to copy what was on offer in Europe, and was monolingual;
- though a very small proportion of the population was in formal (Western) education, particularly after the initial phase, education was seen as playing a central role in "civilizing the natives" and giving them access to "scientific knowledge" instead of "superstition".

The active underdevelopment of African languages is directly parallel to the economic underdevelopment (Rodney 1973) of these societies. In both domains, metropolitan values and norms dominated. Thus in education, resources and time were primarily allocated to teacher training, textbook development and teaching in the dominant language and not the dominated ones (Phillipson 1992, chapter 5). Apartheid in the education system involved a grossly unequal hierarchy of resource allocation. While it is true that a great deal of missionary effort went into alphabetizing indigenous languages, and providing initial literacy and translations of the Bible and edifying tracts in them, and that this provides a valuable resource for further development, the colonial education systems treated the learning of such indigenous languages as purely transitional, and a decisive shift was made to the dominant language after a few years in the primary school.

Linguistic human rights in contemporary Africa

A consequence of this linguicist favouring of the dominant languages is that "Africans have been psychologically conditioned to believe that only European languages are structured to aid development" (Kashoki, quoted in UNIN 1981: 41). Little has changed in educational policy in independent Africa: "the colonial legacy seems to determine current educational practices as it has proved virtually impossible in all but a few cases to break away from the inherited practices." (Bamgbose 1991: 8). According to Gilbert Ansre, the Ghanaian sociolinguist, a key factor is linguistic imperialism, which he describes as

> ... the phenomenon in which the minds and lives of the speakers of a language are dominated by another language to the point where they believe that they can and should use only that foreign language when it comes to transactions dealing with the more advanced aspects of life such as education, philosophy, literature, governments, the administration of justice, etc. ... Linguistic imperialism

has a subtle way of warping the minds, attitudes and aspirations of even the most noble in a society and of preventing him from appreciating and realising the full potentialities of the indigenous languages (Ansre 1979: 12).

As a result of linguistic imperialism, the vast majority of languages in former colonies have not gone through the processes of development (wide use of the written form, expansion of discourse functions and vocabulary, etc) which many European languages have in recent centuries. Their growth and expansion have been kept in check by the presence and favouring of the former colonial languages, and the vested interests, national and international, associated with these.

After independence, one of the most important education goals was the achievement of Universal Primary Education (UPE) as soon as possible. This was seen as a way of implementing Article 26 of the Universal Declaration of Human Rights, which essentially affirms everybody's right to free and compulsory education at the elementary level. During the early 1960s the goals for all the regions of the world where UPE was not a reality were formulated at UNESCO conferences. The African conference was held in Addis Abeba in 1961. The question of *which* language Africans should become literate in was not raised, meaning by implication it was assumed that the policies of the colonial period would continue.

The UPE ideal was intimately linked in planners' minds to two basic economic and political ideas (Skutnabb-Kangas 1990a: 24–26). "Education for development" within a modernization paradigm was to lead to economic growth, a panacea for underdeveloped countries. "Nation-building" was to be supported by developing via UPE an awareness of belonging to one nation and an instrument, a common language, for practising this national unity. "Both basic motivating principles behind UPE thus led away from local and regional mother tongues, because both education for development and nation building seemed to "require" common languages with more currency" (Skutnabb-Kangas 1990a: 25). The result was a linguicist concern with the learning of the official colonial language and neglect of the African mother tongues. A vast amount of the "aid" effort has gone into teacher education and curriculum development in and through the former colonial languages, and disproportionately little into other African languages. UNESCO's insistence on education through the medium of the mother tongue (UNESCO 1953) was countered by economic and political arguments (i. e. arguments which can be accommodated under the leaky umbrella of the modernization paradigm and nation building), and branded as naive, romantic and idealistic (e.g. Bull 1955) and quietly forgotten (see Skutnabb-Kangas 1990a, chapter Mother tongue literacy and UPE).

A survey of the place of African languages in former French sub-Saharan colonies concludes (Djite 1990: 97–98):

> The myth of French as a neutral and precious unifying factor has faded and is today essentially an 'elite closure' indicator — a linguistic boundary which limits access to socioeconomic mobility and political power to those societal members who possess the requisite linguistic patterns of the elite and which especially results when the official language is used by the elite in circumstances where a more widely known indigenous language would suffice. ... The use of the language of the former colonizer as a national and official language, a case of language policy by default for reasons of efficiency and efficacy, is no longer tenable. How efficient can a nation be when 90 percent of its population, as we have just indicated, is illiterate in the official language?

The former French colonies in North Africa have a somewhat ambivalent language policy, with French retained as the legitimate language of "modernization", and Arabic promoted as the language of political and religious legitimacy. Thus post-independence Algeria has undergone a major process of decolonization and arabization, but the new modernized Koranic Arabic, used in official domains and the media and learned in school, has taken the place of not only French but also the Arabic and Berber mother tongues (Grandguillaume 1990). The situation is diglossic, with the state attempting to impose its vision of society by monopolizing access to and use of official Arabic. Legislation in 1990, which was aimed at reducing the influence of French, attempted to impose the exclusive use of written Arabic in official functions. The effect was also to confirm the outlawing of the mother tongues of a significant section of the population, languages which most of the population have been prevented from becoming literate in during both the colonial and post-colonial periods. Speakers of demotic Arabic and Berber are effectively deprived of basic linguistic rights in relation to their mother tongues.

Ignoring the linguistic complexities of African countries also characterized the educational planning documents for individual former British colonies as each approached independence — scant attention is paid to language in the reports, and when the issue is raised, attention is mostly confined to the learning of the former colonial language (Cawson 1975, a Ford Foundation survey by a former senior British Council staff member). In the report which served as the basis for expanding higher education in independent Nigeria, prepared by Ashby, a British academic, the local languages are not referred to — there is no mention of Hausa, Igbo or Yoruba (Firth 1961: 15), let alone the other 400 languages native to Nigeria (Bamgbose 1991: 2).

Official policies, abetted by "aid" in the language and education field have impeded the elaboration of local solutions to meet local problems, just as aid in many other fields has been inappropriate (Hancock 1989). In Africa alone there are an estimated 80,000 foreign "experts", a larger number of expatriates than in the colonial period (Hancock 1989), and the degree of success is meagre. When the former colonial languages have been used as media of education in schooling, the gulf between the educated elites (estimated as 10–15% of the total population) and ordinary people has widened. This worry has been expressed in a succession of reports throughout this century (for references see Phillipson 1992), and is still a valid concern. One result is that the interest of the elites tends to be equated with the interest of the nation (Bamgbose 1991: 19).

Awareness of the complexities of the language in education issue is notably absent from recent World Bank reports on the educational crisis in East Africa. These focus mainly on inefficiencies of implementation and budgeting (Psacharopoulos 1990, summarizing the World Bank series on *Comparative African experiences in implementing educational policies*). A World Bank survey of the failure of African governments to achieve declared educational goals concludes (Craig 1990: 59) that

> ... our knowledge of issues bearing on the implementation of educational policies in Sub-Saharan Africa remains seriously deficient. Although many scholars have commented on such issues in passing, the subject has yet to receive the sustained and careful attention that it merits.

An analysis of research issues and perspectives in language in education in Africa draws a bleak conclusion on the contribution of research to this field. Despite "a vast array of urgent research questions, the research community is small, the research outcome disappointing, and even marginal" (Obura 1986: 415). There is however substantial evidence that many aid projects in this field were culturally and educationally flawed: (for a Ford Foundation analysis describing the failings of their projects, see Fox 1975; for an analysis of linguistic imperialism and the role of

English Language Teaching and applied linguistics in the "Third World", see Phillipson 1992).

Tanzania is often held up as an example of a country with a successful African language policy. A large majority of the many mother tongues are structurally related to Swahili, meaning that Swahili, which is the medium of education in the primary school, is much easier for most Tanzanians to learn than English would be. Swahili is increasingly used in social and political life. At the local level, the mother tongues are used in places of worship, business, village administration and courts, and in a supporting role in schools (Rubagumya 1990: 11). However although there is a close fit between the use of Swahili in primary school and outside it, English is still favoured at the secondary school level and above, despite the fact that English is manifestly a foreign language in Tanzania, is used in very few domains and is unable to function effectively as a medium of education (Rubagumya 1990). The "improper" favouring of English in secondary and higher education is self-defeating, as it prevents the achievement of Tanzanian societal goals (Rubagumya 1990). Tanzanian educational language policy is therefore in conflict with social realities. Support for Swahili has been ambivalent and inadequate. The linguistic hierarchy remains, with English dominant vis-a-vis Swahili, and mother tongues below, confined to local and private functions.

In other East African countries, English is even more favoured. Thus in Zambia all children are officially taught through the medium of English from the first class, though in practice this is virtually impossible to implement (Chishimba 1981) and recent reforms have acknowledged that mother tongues are a useful support. Zambian languages are used in adult literacy programmes (Kashoki 1989), but the role of English as a supra-ethnic language of nation-building is secure though not unchallenged. Educationally and culturally, the language policy cannot be regarded as a success (Africa 1980).

Akinnaso's study of Nigeria (1991) distinguishes between exogenous languages (English, French, Arabic), indigenous languages (approximately 400), and the "neutral" pidgin English which has almost taken over the role of lingua franca in informal domains, and is increasingly resorted to in education. A status classification distinguishes between 3 "national" languages, 9 "regional" languages, and the remaining "local" languages. Although only the 12 major languages are known to be actively used as media of instruction in primary schools, it is estimated that nearly 50 different Nigerian languages have been developed and used for initial literacy in primary schools (Akinnaso 1991: 53). In the linguistic hierarchy

English ranks highest because of its status as "official" language. However in Nigeria "language loyalties override all other social and political ones. ... Nigerians are as loyal to their mother tongues as they are contemptuous of other languages" (Akinnaso 1991: 44–45). Language planning involves attempting to reconcile the competing claims of languages for different societal purposes, the conflicting claims of unity versus diversity, state versus local interests. "... the ideologies underpinning language policies in these countries and the orientations of the policies may be in perpetual conflict as are the models of education adopted to promote their implementation." (Akinnaso 1991: 57).

Many African scholars document the complexity of the linguistic scene in individual countries and plead for multilingual language planning (e.g. Africa 1980; Tadadjeu 1980; for a continent-wide survey of the alphabetization and standardization of African languages, and available literacy materials, see Mioni 1989; for a major survey of language planning issues in Sub-Saharan Africa, including the use made of indigenous languages in education, and the gap between academic research, policymaking and implementation, see Bamgbose 1991).

A general survey of language policy in Africa documents the need for change (Heine 1990). A policy paper by the OAU bureau referred to earlier regards the emphasis on learning a foreign language as being distinctly harmful as well as costly (OAU Inter-African Bureau of Languages 1985: 10): it is "delaying the popularisation, among the majority of the population, of basic scientific and technical knowledge, a prerequisite to the general overall development of Africa."

Increasing use of African languages would promote better communication between rulers and ruled, harness the energies of the rural population to the development of their environment, and stimulate more scientific study of African languages (OAU Inter-African Bureau of Languages 1985). The Bureau makes specific proposals for creating linguistic unity at the national level, and recommends a small number of languages (Kiswahili, Hausa, Arabic, Lingala and Zulu) as languages for regional and continental contact and unification. They make a plea to African governments to turn their attention to language policy, promote African languages, and elaborate a "Linguistic Charter for Africa".

Such a Charter is proposed elsewhere in the same publication, which along with proposals similar to those of the OAU Bureau includes the following proposals (Dalby 1985: 29):

2. That the *equal linguistic rights of every individual* be recognised, together with the need to provide *access to literacy in every living African language.*

3. That as many languages as possible in each African state, depending on the number of speakers, be given the status of *national languages*, with an established place in the national education system and in the media.

4. That at least one African language in each state be given the status of *official language*, to replace or be used alongside any existing "foreign" official language.

Sadly, there is little sign of any change in language policy in African countries, while the economic, political and social problems accumulate. The relationship between language policies and such problems has not been explored in any detail, but there is no doubt that present policies serve to educate an elite which is closely tied to Western interests and to marginalize the majority of the population.

Recent moves towards creating structures in which more democratic participation in African societies is permitted are likely to see an increasing demand for linguistic human rights. Current national constitutions and practice seldom guarantee such rights. Nor does the continental African Charter on Human and Peoples' Rights, proposed in 1981, under UN auspices, and in force since 1986, having by then been ratified by a majority of African states. This Charter has a non-discrimination clause in Article 2 covering many criteria, including language. It specifies the right of every individual to education, but does not stipulate in what language this should be (article 17). Several articles aim at strengthening indigenous cultural values (e.g. articles 20 and 29) but the linguistic heritage of Africa is not referred to.

For Fanon, a major theorist of African liberation, the problem of language in the relations between the dominant and the dominated was of "capital importance" (Fanon 1952: 21). For Ngũgĩ, the brilliant Kenyan writer whose novels and political writings aim at "decolonizing" the African mind, language has always been at the heart of the struggle between imperialism and liberation from domination (Ngũgĩ 1985: 109). There is a genuine conflict of interest between a centralized, "modernizing" state with a restrictive official language policy and the huge cultural potential that the de facto ethnic and linguistic diversity of Africa represents. Hopefully greater democratization will lead to greater enjoyment of linguistic human rights and to the solution of some of Africa's grave social, economic and political problems.

Killing a mother tongue — how the Kurds are deprived of linguistic human rights

Tove Skutnabb-Kangas — Sertaç Bucak

Introduction

We will start with a short description of how it is to grow up as a Kurd in the Turkish part of Kurdistan. The extracts come from the testimony of Esref Okumus to the Conference on Minority Rights, Policies and Practice in South-East Europe, Copenhagen, March 30th–April 1st 1990, organised by The Danish Helsinki Committee and The Minority Rights Group, London. Esref Okumus is a Kurdish journalist in his early thirties, now working in Sweden:

> As a Kurd in Turkey you are born in a village or a town the name of which is not valid, because names of nearly all Kurdish villages and towns I know are today changed into Turkish.[1]
>
> If your parents wish to give you a Kurdish name, your name will not be registered by the authorities. It will be changed into Turkish. If your parents still insist to keep your Kurdish name, they will be prosecuted and forced by a court to change your name into a non-Kurdish name.[2]
>
> When you, seven years old, go to school, you won't be able to communicate with your teachers. At least if you, just like me, have parents who do not speak Turkish. It will take 4 or 5 years before you at all can speak with your teachers.[3]
>
> When you have become an adult, you must be aware of all the laws which prevent you from keeping your Kurdish identity.
>
> First of all, you are not allowed to claim that your mother tongue is Kurdish. The third section of law no. 2932 tells you what your mother tongue is: 'The mother tongue of Turkish citizens is Turkish.' You are not allowed to speak Kurdish in public places (citations from law no. 2932) ... If you, in spite of all this, speak Kurdish, you can be sentenced to a maximum of 2 years of imprisonment according to section 4 of the same law.

... (quotations from laws prohibiting all forms of expression in Kurdish) ... All this means that you, as a member of the Kurdish minority in Turkey, are deprived of all fruits of your culture. I want to emphasize this: ALL fruits of your culture. If you don't want to accept this, and clearly show your disapproval by, for instance, writing to a newspaper, then you can be prosecuted for 'weakening of national feelings', according to section 143 of the Penal Code. You can be sentenced to a maximum of 10 years of imprisonment. If you, as a Kurd in Turkey, 'build or attempt to build an association' to maintain your culture and language, you can be sentenced to a maximum of 15 years of imprisonment, according to section 141 of the Penal Code.
Thousands of Kurds have been sentenced according to these laws. If you try to explain this situation abroad, exactly as I am doing at this moment, you can be sentenced to 10 years of imprisonment for 'damaging the reputation of the Turkish state'.[4]

Sertaç Bucak, in a report to the same Conference (1990: 2), said: "Every day there are reports in the newspapers about the confiscation of a journal or a book because it has written or reported about the Kurds" (regardless of the language in which it is written). Using words like "the Kurds" or "Kurdistan" has been enough for confiscation (see also note 11).

Okumus's conclusion is that if Kurds in Turkey assimilate completely and deny their Kurdish identity, they are accepted as a citizen equal to all others. They can even become presidents, like the former Turkish president Turgut Özal (who is reputed to be of Kurdish origin). But if Kurds in Turkey attempt to use only some of the most fundamental minority rights, to speak and maintain their own language, identify as a Kurd, and enjoy and maintain Kurdish culture through books, films, cassettes, etc or through a Kurdish cultural organisation, they can be sentenced to at least 50 years of imprisonment.

This paper[5] brings together some of the extensive documentation of how the Kurds in Turkey are prevented from using their mother tongue, in defiance of international covenants on human rights that Turkey is a signatory to — or, in some cases very significantly, is NOT signatory to (see later). It also discusses some of the consequences of this for Kurdish culture and Kurdish children and adults, both in Turkish parts of Kurdistan, in Turkey proper and elsewhere. At the same time it shows how a clarification of concepts, here demonstrated by the concept of mother tongue, can help us in analysing lack of linguistic rights and in formulating requirements which a universal declaration of linguistic human rights must fulfill (see Skutnabb-Kangas — Phillipson, this volume). Since it is not always easy to get reliable information about the Kurdish language, we start with a short description of the linguistic situation.

Kurds and the Kurdish language

Kurdistan, the land of the Kurds, 500.000 square kilometers, comprises an area larger than the combined areas of Great Britain, the Netherlands, Belgium, Switzerland and Denmark. The Kurdish population totals approximately 25 — 30 million today. The Kurds constitute the majority of the population in their homeland, which is divided between Iran, Iraq, Syria and Turkey.

The Kurds are one of the oldest peoples of the Middle East. Kurdistan has its place among the great ancient civilizations of Mesopotamia. In his work *Anabasis* the Greek historian and military leader Xenophon speaks of Kurdish tribes, mostly self-sufficient farmers without religious rulers, in the regions which the Kurds still claim as their homelands today (Roth 1978: 17). The ancestors of the Kurds lived there for thousands of years, founded villages and cities, lived from farming, constructed irrigation systems and canals, and used cuneiform writing.

Kurdish is, like German and English, an Indo-European language and belongs to the northwestern Iranian family (e.g. Pott 1840: 59). It is closely related to Farsi/Persian (as Danish or Dutch are related to German, Mönch-Bucak 1989). It is *not* related to Turkish (an Altaic non-Indo-European language) or to Iranian and Syrian Arabic (a Semitic non-Indo-European language). Linguistic proof of Old Persian dates back 4000 years. New Persian amd Kurdish developed after Old Persian. Kurdish developed as an independent language in an area where Iranian languages have been spoken for at least 3.000 years, and has been documented since, at the latest, the time of the Arab conquest, i. e. for nearly 1300 years (Mönch-Bucak 1989).

There are two main dialects/varieties of Kurdish, and several smaller dialects/varieties:

- *Kurmanci* (north Kurmandji, North Kurdish), spoken in Turkish and Syrian Kurdistan, in the northern parts of Iranian and Iraqi Kurdistan and in (former Soviet) Armenia.

— *Sorani* (south Kurmandji, South Kurdish, sometimes also called middle Kurdish), spoken in the southern parts of Iranian and Iraqi Kurdistan.

Some linguists also classify southeastern dialects (Sinei, Kirmansahi, Leki) as a distinct variety. In addition, speakers of some central Iranian (grouped together as Zaza and Gurani) and southwest Iranian (e.g. Luri) varieties, also claim Kurdish ethnic and linguistic identity. These varieties are not easily mutually intelligible with Kurmanci and Sorani, but speakers of Zaza and Gurani learn Kurmanci very easily, whereas the opposite is not true (e.g. van Bruinessen 1978: 30). There are no strict dialect boundaries; the dialects merge gradually (for details, see Hassanpour 1989).

Most Kurdish literary critics consider Kurdish art poetry to have started with Baba Tahir Hamadani (935–1010) (Shakely 1989: 51), but the oldest Kurdish literary text, *Pir Salyar's wisdom*, dates from the period before the islamization of Kurdistan. Orature (oral literature) has always played an important part in the development of the Kurdish language, partly because of the oppression of Kurdish literature. Many Kurdish poets and historians have also written in other languages from the 1200s onwards. The Kurdish national epic, *Mem û Zîn*, written in 1694 by Ekhmede Khani (Ahmed-i-Xani), is partly based on an old folk tale, Meme Alan. It combines a beautifully told romantic-tragic love story with Kurdish longing and struggle for liberation, a frequent Kurdish combination.

Much Kurdish literature, both old and new, has as one of its central themes the struggle against oppression (e.g. Fuad 1988: 22). For instance, the great Kurdish poet Cegerxwin (The Bleeding Heart; pseudonym for Hasan Sheikmous) follows this theme, from poems about the Kurdish smith Kewa who slew the child-brain-eating tyrant (Iranian king Ejdehak/ Zuhak) and liberated the Kurdish people, (still celebrated on March 21, Newroz, the Kurdish national day) to poems on international solidarity and the fight against colonialism (e.g. the poem Heval Pol Robson/ Comrade Paul Robeson). (Cegerxwin's publisher again faces a sentence for some of the poems — see note 11). Also Kurdish newspapers (the first, *Kurdistan*, in 1898 in Cairo) and magazines (e.g. *Jin* 1918–19) bear witness to the need to strengthen Kurdish resistance.

The Kurdish language community — divided, dispersed and oppressed

The Kurdish language community differs from many others in several respects which, taken together, have restricted a more "normal" development of the language. The Kurds have been and are still divided, dispersed and oppressed.

Firstly, the Kurdish language community is divided and dispersed. Kurds are subjected to colonial rule in four states, Turkey, Iran, Iraq and Syria. Hundreds of thousands of Kurds have been deported[6] or more or less forced to move from Kurdistan to other parts of the occupying states or to other countries.

Thus it has been and is difficult for the Kurds to develop their language in a way which is normal in closely-knit non-dispersed language communities. This has resulted, among other things, in the fact that written Kurdish today uses three different alphabets and there are at least three centres for the development of a standard variety. The Bedir-Xan variety (Bedir-Xan — Lescot 1970) (or HAWAR-variety), introduced in 1932 in Damascus and Beirut by Celadet Ali Bedir-Xan in the magazine Hawar, based on Kurmanci (mainly as spoken in the south-eastern parts of Turkish Kurdistan), uses the Latin alphabet. The Sulemaniye variety, the standard language of the Kurds in Iraqi Kurdistan, based on the Sorani variety of Kurdish, uses a modified variety of the Arab-Persian script (and the Arabic script was also used in Turkish Kurdistan until 1928–1929). Standard Kurdish in the former USSR, based on Kurmanci as spoken in the southern parts of Armenia, uses the Cyrillic alphabet, but the Latin alphabet was used for Kurdish in the USSR until the late 1930s.

Geographical dispersion and the many changes in script type have, in addition to the oppression of the language itself and the denial of education to Kurds in general and specifically of instruction in Kurdish, made much Kurdish written literature inaccessible to most of the Kurds themselves. Mehmet Emin Bozarslan is the author of both the first Kurdish primer in Turkey, *Alfabe* (which was banned and led to his imprisonment in Turkey) and numerous children's books. He is teaching his compatriots literacy in exile (despite threats from the Turkish Embassy in Denmark — see Skutnabb-Kangas 1989a: 279–280) while rescuing, transcribing, translating and writing comments on some of the old literature (e.g. *Kurdistan, Jin, Mem û Zîn*), all this virtually without financial support. This shows vividly some of the difficulties in Kurdish literary work. Very few Kurds in the world would be able to read what has been published even during this century in Kurdish, even if there were no prohibitions. Few literate language communities in the world face such cumulative difficulties.

Therefore, the Kurdish vocabulary has also evolved in different directions in different parts of Kurdistan. The Kurdish language is not related to the dominant majority language of 3 of the 4 occupying states. As Kurds are obliged to operate for many official purposes in the dominant official languages (which are very different from their mother tongue), despite (often) limited proficiency in them, there is widespread borrowing from them into Kurdish. This complicates the mutual intercomprehensibility of different varieties of Kurdish.

The Kurdish language has been oppressed in most occupying countries, most severely in Turkey, as will be described later. The oppression has made the development of the Kurdish language extremely difficult.

The majority of Kurds in Iran, Syria and Turkey are considered illiterate in their native tongue. In these countries official policy has prevented the autonomous development of a literary variety by denying Kurds education in their own language as well as the right to distribute printed material in Kurdish. Linguistic and literary projects have thus been restricted to clandestine activities of oppositional movements" (Matras 1990: 1).

Most of the recent development of Kurdish as a literary language has taken place during the few periods of relative freedom[7] in Iraq and to some extent Syria, but particularly in the former Soviet Union. To an increasing degree this work is being undertaken by Kurds in exile. Such work is made more difficult by the fact that the ban on Kurdish is also transferred to other countries: there is no teaching in or through Kurdish in most western European countries where Kurds live as migrants or refugees. While most other migrants can get help from the embassies of their countries of origin in upholding their language and culture, Kurds are actively prevented by theirs from maintaining and developing their language (see again note 2 for naming practices).

Together these facts make the situation of the Kurdish language community different from that of others. No other literate language communities in the world are today forced to maintain and develop their language under equally oppressive and difficult circumstances, without linguistic human rights. Because of geographical dispersion and political division between several states (something that Kurdish shares with many other languages in the world) and the severe cultural-political oppression, which includes the most brutal linguistic oppression in the world enacted with the force of law, the Kurdish language has had extremely difficult conditions for its development.

Despite the repression, Kurdish is a fully-fledged language, ready to take its place among official state languages in the world. When enough resources are devoted to the development of the Kurdish language, Kurdish can relatively rapidly be developed into a language which can fulfill all modern needs in education, (see *Muttersprache Kurdisch* 1980; Meyer-Ingwersen 1989) administration, etc (see Hassanpour 1989). "Despite irregularities, inconsistencies and variation there is no doubt about the fact that a literary variety of the Kurdish language exists and is used in publications to express a wide range of subjects", Yaron Matras concludes in his study of Kurdish orthography (Matras 1990: 8).

The legal situation of the Kurdish language in Turkey is in violation of universal and European agreements

A history of oppression

This is how the Bremen Declaration on Human Rights in Kurdistan, adopted at an international conference in April 1989, described the situation of the Kurds in Turkey:

> Kurdish children (in Turkey) have no right to education and training in their mother tongue. Use of the Kurdish language is forbidden by law. Any publication in the Kurdish language, the production, sale and playing of Kurdish music, and the celebration of national and traditional festivals have been declared to be crimes. The Turkish government has replaced Kurdish place names and geographical names with Turkish ones. Kurds are imprisoned and sentenced for crimes of conscience (*Human Rights in Kurdistan* 1989: 231).

Although oppression of the Kurdish language has been Turkish policy since the time of Atatürk, and was enshrined in the Constitution of 1923, this oppression has been intensified in recent years in a number of new laws. The deprivation of linguistic human rights in Turkish Kurdistan has been formalised in the Turkish Constitution of 1982 and in several recent laws.

We shall relate the relevant Turkish constitutional and legal enactments to international covenants some of which Turkey is a signatory to, and to those European covenants and regulations that Turkey, as a member of Council of Europe and an aspiring member of the European Community, should conform to. It is also significant that Turkey has NOT signed some of the most central human rights instruments, for instance the International Convention on the Elimination of All Forms of Racial Discrimination, ratified or acceded to by 128 countries (1991) and The International Covenants on Economic, Social and Cultural Rights (100 countries) or Civil and Political Rights (93 countries; see *UN Human Rights Fact Sheets* 12, 15 and 16).

Prior to that it is important to stress that the Turkish Constitution and the Laws quoted are in clear defiance of the Treaty of Lausanne (July 21, 1923), part of which — Section III Concerning Protection of Minorities — deals specifically with Turkey. In Article 37 of the Treaty of Lausanne,

> "Turkey undertakes that the stipulations contained in Articles 38 to 44 shall be recognised as fundamental laws, and that no law, no regulation, nor official action shall conflict or interfere with these stipulations, nor shall any law, regulation, nor official action prevail over them".

Most of the Treaty deals with what are referred to as "non-Moslem minorities" (and most Kurds are Muslims), but Article 39 states clearly that "No restriction shall be imposed on the free use by any Turkish national of any language in private intercourse, in commerce, religion, in the press or in publications of any kind or at public meetings." Likewise, article 39 states that "Notwithstanding the existence of the official language, adequate facilities shall be given to Turkish nationals of non-Turkish speech for the oral use of their own language before the Courts". As will be seen in the Extracts below, Turkey violates in its Constitution and other laws the linguistic rights which it has itself specifically guaranteed in the Treaty of Lausanne.

We shall refer to three categories of laws in what follows. Firstly we shall refer to laws which are in force and have been so since their promulgation in the early 1980s, most importantly the Turkish Constitution of 1982, and the Turkish Penal Code. Secondly, we shall refer to laws which were in force until April 12 1991, but which were annulled then (Law No. 2932 of October 22 1983 on Publications in Languages Other Than Turkish; Law No. 2820 of 22 April 1983 on Political Parties;

and several paragraphs (140, 141, 142 and 163) in the Penal Code). And thirdly, we shall refer to the Law to Fight Terrorism of 12 April 1991 (Law No. 3713), a law which recapitulates most of the prohibitions on the use of Kurdish in the earlier, annulled laws, but often in a more covert form.[8] It might be important to explain that the somewhat cryptic formulation, defining what "languages prohibited by law" are, namely "languages other than those which are the primary official languages of states recognized by the Turkish State" (Law 2932/2 and other laws) is formulated thus so as to avoid referring explicitly to the Kurdish language, an act which itself was prohibited by law (section 81 of Law No. 2820 — see below). Kurdish is a secondary official language in Iraq, hence the circumlocution.

Under the laws annulled in 1991 thousands of Kurds were imprisoned, killed and tortured (see e.g. *Helsinki Watch Update* 1990; *Human Rights in Kurdistan* 1989, 1990). Most of the prohibitions are still in force through law 3713, but in a more covert form. The only ban on the Kurdish language which has been lifted is that on private use, provided it does not fall under the other paragraphs. Thus Kurds are now allowed to speak Kurdish in their homes and sing Kurdish love songs in their gardens, but if a Kurdish child complains to a parent in a private garden, while picking beans, about not being allowed to speak Kurdish during the breaks in school, this act is still a terrorist crime.[9]

Samples of Turkish law restricting Kurdish

Still in force:

> The state of Turkey is in its state territory and state citizens an indivisible whole. Its language is Turkish. (Constitution, Article 3).
> Everyone bound to the Turkish state through the bond of citizenship is a Turk. (Constitution, Article 66, Paragraph 1).
> No language prohibited by law may be used for disclosure or publication of ideas and opinions. Written or printed materials, records, tapes, videotapes as well as other means of expression that are in violation of this prohibition will be confiscated ... (Constitution, Article 26/3).
> No publications or broadcasts may be made in any language prohibited by law. (Constitution, Article 28/2).
> No language other than Turkish may be taught as a native language to citizens of Turkey in instructional and educational institutions. (Constitution, Article 42/9).

Annulled 12 April 1991:

The mother tongue of Turkish citizens is Turkish. (Law 2932/3).
It is prohibited to disclose, publish or broadcast ideas and opinions
in languages other than those which are the primary official languages of states recognized by the Turkish State." (Law 2932/2).
Section 3/b of the same law specified that this also includes posters,
records, films and tapes.

Article 142/3 of the Turkish Penal Code prohibited the dissemination of
"separatist propaganda", and Article 143 "the weakening of national
feelings".
Section 81 of Law No. 2820 on Political Parties (22 April 1983) stated:

It is forbidden to claim that there exist minorities in Turkey. It is
forbidden to protect or develop non-Turkish cultures and languages.

The new Law to Fight Terrorism (3713), in force since 12 April 1991,
defines in its Article 1 terrorism as follows:

Terrorism is any kind of action conducted by one or several persons
belonging to an organization with the aim of changing the characteristics of the Republic as specified in the Constitution, its political, legal, social, secular and economic system, *damaging the
indivisible unity of the State with its territory and nation*, endangering
the existence of the Turkish State and Republic, *weakening* or
destroying or seizing *the authority of the State*, eliminating fundamental rights and freedoms, or damaging the internal and external
security of the State, public order or general health by any one
method of pressure, force, violence, terrorization, intimidation, oppression or threat.
An organization as described in this Law is constituted by *two* or more
people gathering under a common aim.

We have emphasized some of the formulations which can be used to
prosecute a person who claims linguistic human rights. Most political
parties in democratic countries could also be considered terrorist organizations according to this definition.

Article 2 defines Terrorist Criminals:
A member of an organization, founded to attain the aims defined
in Article 1, who commits a crime in accordance with these aims
individually or with others or a member of such an organization,

though not committing the intended crime, is called a terrorist criminal.

Those who are not members of the terrorist organization, but commit a crime in the name of the organization count as terrorist criminals and are punished like members of the organization."

Articles 3 and 4 define what Terrorist Crimes and Crimes Committed for Terrorist Purposes are.[10] Article 8, Propaganda against the indivisible unity of the State, stipulates

Written and oral propaganda and assemblies, meetings and demonstrations aiming at damaging the indivisible unity of the State of the Turkish Republic with its territory and nation are forbidden, *regardless of the method, intention and ideas behind it.* Those conducting such an activity are to be punished by a sentence of between 2 and 5 years' imprisonment and a fine of between 50 million and 100 million Turkish pounds. (our emphasis)

For reasons of space, we cannot quote the Articles from the Penal Code which define terrorist crimes, but we will only give two recent examples (for more see note 11; for further information see Besikci 1989 — a Turkish sociologist who himself has again been imprisoned on accusations of violating Article 8); (Ali) Bucak 1989; Rumpf 1989 and references there). There are numerous similar measures against books and journals written in Kurdish or about the Kurds.

Mehmet Bayrak was prosecuted in October 1991, and risks up to 8 years of imprisonment, for editing and publishing the book *Kürt Halk Türküleri* [Kurdish folk songs], Öz-Ge Yayinlari [Öz-GR Publishers] Nr 3, Ankara. The book is a collection of Kurdish folk songs along with the music. No verdict has yet been pronounced.

When the book *Kürdistan'da Türk Endüstrisi* [Turkish Industry in Kurdistan] by Ömer Tuku was published in Istanbul in November 1991 by DOZ Publishers and Druck GmbH, the book was confiscated in pursuance of a decision by the State Security Court. The publisher is being prosecuted; the author lives in Germany (Decision No. 991/511, Investigation No. 991/1035).[11]

A note on recent developments

After the Turkish General Election of 20 October 1991 a coalition government was formed by the conservative Right Way Party (DYP), led by Süleyman Demirel, and the Social Democrat People's Party (SHP), led by Erdal Inönü. The partners agreed on 15 November 1991 on a "democratising package", on 19 November a coalition protocol was signed, and on 25 November the government's programme was proclaimed in Parliament. On 30 November the Turkish Parliament passed a vote of confidence in the new coalition government.

According to the "democratising package" there would be a thorough revision of the law on political parties imposed by the military dictatorship, and of the repressive trade union law. International covenants on human rights, in particular those that Turkey has ratified but never in reality implemented, would finally be brought into force. Police custody, during which torture has been standard practice, is to be reduced to 24 hours. A new law should permit a lawyer to be present during police custody. The Anti-Terror law too, passed in the spring of 1991 by the Motherland Party of President Özal, was supposed to be subjected to a major revision. The same applies to the law on the police. The laws which sanction banning and censoring should even be scrapped completely. Higher education, radio and television should regain their autonomy. Likewise there should now be an end to governing by means of "decrees with the force of law", the standard instrument of the Motherland Party, in order to escape parliamentary control. The government would also like to change the constitution.

"The state of Turkey is in its state territory and state citizens an indivisible whole. Its language is Turkish", says the Constitution still (see above). On the other hand Kurdish identity is supposed to be recognized. Kurdish books and newspapers, music cassettes and the like are supposed to be published freely. There should also be no restriction on writing about them.

Even so, there are no plans for allowing Kurdish to be taught in schools in future. Nor are radio or television programmes in Kurdish permitted. Kurdish parties are still forbidden. In other words no fundamental change of direction in the essentials of policy vis-à-vis the Kurds is visible, at least when this article goes to press (June 1994). The Kurdish question is still considered a "security problem" — and the oppression has in fact escalated.

Sample international and European covenants which Turkish language law is in defiance of

Here we merely list a selection of paragraphs from international covenants and European resolutions/recommendations that Turkish language law is in defiance of. Most of the paragraphs mentioned can be found in the Appendix of this volume:

— *The Charter of the United Nations* (1945), paragraphs 6.11, 55.
— *The Universal Declaration of Human Rights* (1948), paragraphs 2, 26
— *The International Covenant on Economic, Social and Cultural Rights* (1966, in force since 1976), paragraph 13.(1) (Turkey has not ratified it, though).
— *The International Covenant on Civil and Political Rights* (1966), Art. 27
— *The Convention on the Rights of the Child* (1989), Art. 30
— The Concluding Document, Vienna Meeting of Representatives of Participating States of the *Conference on Security and Co-operation in Europe* (the CSCE, the Helsinki accords), January 1989, paragraph 45, in the section on "Information"; Document of the Copenhagen meeting of the Conference on the Human Dimension of the CSCE, 1990, paragraphs 32, 33, 34, 35, 38, 40; Charter of Paris for a New Europe, November 1990, CSCE
— The Arfe resolution of the *European Parliament* of 16 October 1981 and the Kuijpers resolution of October 1987, specifically the domain of education; The *European Parliament* resolution on the use of languages in the community (*Official Journal of the European Communities*, no C 127/139, 1984), Preamble, 2.

Turkey is also in defiance of all the draft resolutions about the protection of minorities being prepared at a regional level by the Council of Europe and the European Parliament — see the Appendix and Skutnabb-Kangas — Phillipson, this volume, for some of these.

Implications of the Turkish policy in Turkish parts of Kurdistan, in Turkey proper, and elsewhere

Linguistic genocide — the UN definition

During the preparatory work for formulating the Convention against Genocide (accepted by the United Nations in 1948) the possibility of including cultural genocide was discussed. Cultural genocide may take the form of linguistic genocide (or linguicide). In the final draft of the Convention linguistic genocide was included, and defined as follows in Article III, 1 (quoted from Capotorti 1979: 37):

Prohibiting the use of the language of the group in daily intercourse or in schools, or the printing and circulation of publications in the language of the group.

The article (III,1) about cultural and linguistic genocide was in the end vetoed and not included in the final Convention. (This omission partly explains the intensive work presently going on under Unesco auspices to guarantee linguistic human rights (see Phillipson — Skutnabb-Kangas, in this volume). What we have left, though, is a definition, agreed upon by many states, of what linguistic genocide means. It is easy to see that what Turkey does, falls within the definition of linguistic genocide, as defined by the UN.

What happens to the Kurdish mother tongue

In order to analyse in more detail what Turkey does when it tries to kill the Kurdish language and culture, we have to relate this to those rights which a language should have. Since linguistic genocide can only happen in relation to a group's mother tongue, we have to start with defining what a mother tongue is.

Definitions of a mother tongue
We have earlier defined it on the basis of several criteria. Table 1 summarises the criteria and the corresponding definitions:

Table 1. Definition of mother tongue

Criterion	Definition
ORIGIN	the language(s) one learned first
IDENTIFICATION	
a. internal	the language(s) one identifies with
b. external	the language(s) one is identified as a native speaker of by others
COMPETENCE	the language(s) one knows best
FUNCTION	the language(s) one uses most

We have four theses about the definitions:
A. The same person can have different mother tongues, depending on which definition is used.

B. A person can have two or more mother tongues according to all criteria used.

C. The mother tongue can change during the course of a person's life, even several times, according to all other criteria except origin.

D. The definitions can be organised hierarchically, according to the extent to which they respect linguistic human rights. The definitions by function and competence are more primitive, while definition using a combination of origin and internal identification shows more awareness of linguistic human rights. This presupposes that others accept the internal identification of a person.

For the purposes of linguistic human rights, mother tongue(s) is/are the language(s) one has learned first and identifies with. For most Kurdish people, their mother tongue is Kurdish.

In our view, a universal declaration of linguistic human rights should guarantee at an *individual* level that, in relation to

The mother tongue(s), everybody can
— identify with their mother tongue(s) and have this identification accepted and respected by others,
— learn the mother tongue(s) fully, orally and in writing (which presupposes that minorities are educated through the medium of their mother tongue(s)),
— use the mother tongue in most official situations (including schools); *other languages*, that everybody whose mother tongue is not an official language in the country where s/he is resident, can
— become bilingual (or trilingual, if s/he has 2 mother tongues) in the mother tongue(s) and (one of) the official language(s) (according to her own choice); *the relationship between languages*,
— any change of mother tongue is voluntary, not imposed.

If these rights are not guaranteed, deprivation of the mother tongue may follow. Deprivation of the mother tongue has profound consequences both at an individual level and at a group level. At the group level deprivation of the mother tongue of a group amounts to linguicide, which is what Turkey attempts.

Phases in mother tongue deprivation

We will analyse different phases in mother tongue deprivation with the help of two scales which describe the attitudes towards minority languages. In the first one Juan Cobarrubias, a Basque researcher living in the USA, presents (1983: 71) a "taxonomy of official attitudes toward minority languages, [where] the following can be distinguished:

1. attempting to kill a language;
2. letting a language die;
3. unsupported coexistence;
4. partial support of specific language functions;
5. adoption as an official language".

An absolute minimum of minority rights would require at least partial support of specific language functions (4 above). Even unsupported coexistence (3), leads in most cases to language death within some generations and represents mother tongue deprivation. There are still many cases of letting languages die (2), worldwide. But the attempt to kill the Kurdish language (1) by Turkey represents the most blatant example of linguicide this century. To our knowledge, in no other country in the world today has attempting to kill a language been formally codified in the constitution and related laws.

Killing a language expresses what happens at a group level. But the group consists of individuals, who have the threatened language as their mother tongue, the language they have learned first, a language they know and use and identify with. To kill a language you have to either kill the individuals speaking it or make these individuals change their mother tongue. Turkey tries to change the mother tongue of the Kurds and make Turkish their mother tongue. If you are not allowed to identify with your mother tongue and ethnic group, to learn your mother tongue and to develop it in school, and to use it publicly, the consequence in the long run is that the language is killed. We show how Turkey through the laws quoted above systematically tries to replace the Kurdish mother tongue in all its functions. We also contrast Turkey with other countries.

There are other countries which, directly or mostly indirectly try to change the mother tongues of some or all of their minority populations according to the criteria of function and competence (several articles in this volume describe such situations). Most such countries do so in a covert way, by not explicitly promoting the use of minority languages in education and in official situations. Not being able to use a language in all contexts, especially in schools, leads to a diminishing competence, and this may lead to language death over several generations. But no other countries prohibit in their Constitutions the *internal identification* with a language (i. e. forbid self-identification with one's mother tongue), or try to change the mother tongue by *origin* (i. e. regulate what parents can name their children, which language they can talk to their children in private and/or public places), or change by force the *external identification* of mother tongues (claim that a group's mother tongue or ethnic identity is something else than what it is). A few other countries do some of these things covertly, but no other country has overtly encoded them in the Constitution.

Legislation on language can either thwart or promote equality between languages. In an attempt to capture some of the relevant distinctions, we (Skutnabb-Kangas – Phillipson 1989a) have devised a grid charting some of the important dimensions of language rights (see the description of it and figure 1 on page in our joint article in this volume). The two dimensions used are degree of overtness and degree of promotion. The promotion continuum starts with *prohibition* of a language, continues via *toleration*, to *non-discrimination prescription*, to *permission* to use the minority language. At the other end of the continuum we have *promotion* of the minority language. This is obviously oriented toward maintaining it. For a minority language to be maintained, overt promotion is needed, if the language is to survive over several generations. This is especially true in situations where minority children get formal education in schools: schools are one of the most important means for assimilation of Kurdish children.

In the next section we will place Turkey on the grid in relation to the extent that Kurdish is promoted or suppressed by Turkey, according to each of the mother tongue criteria presented above, in Kurdistan, Turkey proper and elsewhere, and also relate this to Cobarrubias' phases.

Turkish oppression of Kurdish: changing the mother tongue

The easiest aspect to try to change through laws and regulations is the mother tongue by the criterion of FUNCTION. There are extremely few countries in the world where the full official use (Cobarrubias' point 5) of any minority language would get the same overt promotion in official use as the majority language/s. But there are examples (French in Canada, Swedish in Finland, French and Flemish in Belgium, French, German and Italian in Switzerland), even if there are territorial (and other) restrictions involved in many of them. But many countries show some degree of permission or at least non-discrimination prescription. *Turkey* has placed itself in the far left top corner on the grid, with *the highest possible degree of legally encoded overt prohibition.*

Turkey can to a large extent uphold this prohibition in the Turkish part of Kurdistan and in Turkey proper, with the help of killings, imprisonment, torture and intimidation. Turkey also tries to uphold the prohibition in other countries where Kurds from Turkey live as labour migrants or as political refugees, and it has managed, with the help of threats and intimidation of the Kurdish population, coupled with a shameful ignorance and silence on the part of the countries in which expatriate Kurds live, to diminish the completely legal public use of Kurdish in other countries too.

In regulating the mother tongue by COMPETENCE schools play a decisive role. If a minority language is not used as a medium of education, it is very unlikely that it is maintained over several generations as a language which the children learn in all domains, including literacy at a high level. Teaching a minority language as a subject in school is mostly not enough (see e.g. Boyd 1985). Many indigenous languages which were upheld for generations, despite colonization, when there were no schools, disappeared in a generation or two, as soon as the children started to get formal education (e.g. Jordan 1988).

Most countries in the world at least tolerate the development of mother tongue competence, but many permit the teaching of minority mother tongues, at least if it happens outside the school hours and if the state does not need to meet all the costs. Also here *Turkey* is in the far left top corner of the grid, with *the highest possible degree of legally encoded overt prohibition*, which it manages to uphold in Turkish parts of Kurdistan and in Turkey proper. Through false information about the Kurdish language and through prohibiting the publishing of Kurdish materials Turkey has also severely restricted the possibilities of using Kurdish as the medium of education in other countries and even the teaching of Kurdish as a subject. Both happen though, to a minor extent and on an experimental basis, in a few countries, for instance in Sweden.

In regulating the mother tongue by the criterion of **external identification** most countries in the world can be placed on either overt or covert permission or on promotion. The type of regulating that sometimes does occur is when dialects of the same language are grouped together in census statistics under one name. This was, for instance, done in India in the census of 1961, when the 1.652 mother tongues claimed by Indians were reduced by the Central Institute of Indian Languages to some 400 different languages. For instance Hindi was reported under almost 100 different names (e.g. Pattanayak 1981). It should be emphasized that this is mostly done by linguists, on linguistic grounds, because the "languages" can be seen as varieties of one language[12] (see also Skutnabb-Kangas, in press). In sharp contrast to the large majority of countries in the world,

Turkey insists on a false external identification of Kurdish speakers, and is again in the far left top corner of the grid, with *the highest possible degree of legally encoded overt prohibition*, which it manages to uphold completely in Turkish parts of Kurdistan and in Turkey proper. And again it manages by intimidation and the ignorance of other countries to uphold the prohibition to some extent in other countries too, even if it is mostly a question of covert prohibition. There may be a few other countries in the world which try to prohibit external identification with a minority mother tongue covertly, but Turkey is the most harsh example in the world of doing it overtly.

In regulating mother tongue by **internal identification**, again most countries in the world can be placed on either overt or covert permission or on promotion. As far as we know, no other country in the world has *legally encoded overt prohibition* of internal identification. *Turkey* is alone in the far left top corner.

It is difficult to regulate mother tongue by ORIGIN overtly. Covertly it is done in many countries, where the overt or covert message given to minority parents has been and is: speak the majority language to your child. This assimilationist message has, of course, been delivered under the cover of "it is best for the child, if you want your child to get ahead". But the Turkish way of even forbidding Kurdish names, both in the Turkish parts of Kurdistan and in Turkey proper, comes closer to overt prohibition even here than other countries.[13] *Turkey* can thus be placed in the middle of the far left, *prohibition which is between overt and covert*. Many other countries are in the far left lower corner. Turkey also tries to extend this prohibition to Kurds in other countries (see note 2). Turkey does more overtly what in many countries is done more covertly, namely trying to kill the language by persuading the parents voluntarily to assimilate the children.

We claimed above that the mother tongue definition which shows the highest extent of respect for linguistic human rights is a combination of origin and internal identification: the mother tongue is the language one has learned first and identifies with. For majority populations it is self-evident that this language is also the one they know best and use most. These aspects, knowing and using a language, are less immediately central to identity than the two others, origin and self-identification. Therefore attacking these represents attacking the existential roots of a human being and a group. If a language is not passed on by parents to children (if it does not become the children's first learned language) and if the children do not identify with a language, it dies. Parents can of course *choose* not to pass on their language and discourage their children from identifying with it. They as speakers "own" the language, and they have the right to make the choice not to let the language live on in their children, even if we as sociolinguists may regret it. But parents can also be *forced* to act in this way or to accept that their children do not learn their mother tongue and do not identify with it (and, consequently, neither learn it properly nor use it). This is tantamount to killing a language.

Conclusion

This brief review, together with the documentation in the references, can be regarded as showing, that, seen in a global context, Turkey does more, with more brutal means, and more overtly, than any other country in the world to actively kill a language, Kurdish. Turkey, using all the means at its disposal, seeks to deprive all the Kurds, regardless of whether they live in the Turkish parts of Kurdistan, in Turkey proper, or as migrants/refugees in other countries, of their identity, their language and their cultural heritage. In addition, Turkey tries to deprive Kurds in Turkey proper of their fair share of the resources which they participate in creating and their fair share of power in Turkey proper. And Turkey tries — and this is at the root of all the other forms of deprivation — with all the means at its disposal, to deprive Kurds in the Turkish part of Kurdistan of the fruits of their labour, the resources which they create, and the power to determine their own future in their own country, Kurdistan.

In this, Turkey uses all the means that can be used for exerting power: *sticks, carrots and ideas*, i. e. *punitive* force (physical and psychological violence), *remunerative* force (bargaining) and *ideological* force (persuasion) (Galtung 1980). Turkey (and other countries occupying Kurdistan) kill and torture Kurds and threaten those who refuse to give up their language, identity and cultural heritage. Turkey holds up the carrot of a successful career for assimilated Kurds, trying to persuade them not to be Kurds. And Turkey tries through lies and silence to persuade Kurds of the non-existence, unhelpfulness and un-worthiness of their language, culture and ethnic identity and of their lack of right to self-determination as a nation.

When a people is too numerous to kill physically (as the Kurds are), linguicide and cultural genocide are the only "alternatives" for the occupiers. What cannot be accomplished through physical genocide in one generation (to annihilate the Kurds) can maybe be accomplished over several generations through cultural and linguistic genocide. That is one of the main reasons why it is as important to demand cultural and linguistic human rights as it is to demand economic and political rights.

It is urgent and imperative that the international community, and the organizations that represent it, take steps to force the Turkish government to grant to the Kurds and the Kurdish language basic linguistic human rights.

Significant sections of the international community are increasingly voicing protests against Turkish oppression of the Kurds. This was, for instance, a major concern of the conference on "Minority Rights — policy and practice in South-East Europe", organized by the Danish Helsinki Committee and the Minority Rights Group, London, and held in Copenhagen March 30–April 1, 1990. At the Ninth World Congress of Applied Linguistics, held at Thessaloniki, Greece, April 15 – 20, 1990, some 80 distinguished professors and other researchers signed a protest against the violation of the linguistic human rights of the Kurds in Turkey. They agree that basic linguistic human rights are being violated in a brutal manner in Turkey.

The international community is aware that Turkey follows a policy of genocide, physical and cultural, and linguicide. Linguistic freedom is the precondition for the realization of many other fundamental rights. If one is not allowed to use and develop one's own mother tongue, it is difficult to enjoy such other rights as the right to the free expression of opinion (Article 19 of the Universal Declaration of Human Rights), the right to enjoy cultural rights (Art. 22 of the UDHR), the right to education (Art. 26 of the UDHR), the right to freely participate in the cultural life of one's community (Article 27.1 of the UDHR). All of these rights (and several others) are significantly limited in their scope if basic linguistic freedom is not granted. Is the international community to continue to covertly accept this violation of human rights, or is it time that the Kurds were guaranteed basic justice? So far, the international community has done very little.[14]

Notes

1. "The villages in Kurdistan, of centuries old Kurdish origin, have been given new Turkish names." Often villagers first heard these new names at the gendarmerie when they were asked which village they came from and gave the Kurdish name of their own village.

They were physically punished for using the old Kurdish name which "did not exist" (Mönch-Bucak 1989).

2. Kurdish first names and last names are not allowed. "Kurds have been given Turkish names, preferably family names of extreme Turkish nationalism such as Öztürk ("pure Turk") (Mönch-Bucak 1989). Members of the Political Affairs Committee and the Subcommittee on Human Rights of the EC Joint Parliamentary Committee, European Parliament, asked Turkey 26 questions on human rights 7 March 1991 (PE 148.128). One of these was "Will parents be allowed to give Kurdish first names to their children?" The Turkish answer, dated 26 March 1991 (PE 150.056) says that "... parents have always been free to give customary names which are not in contravention of the basic linguistic features of the Turkish language to their children".

Our comment: Since Kurdish is an Indo-European language, it is not at all related to the Altaic non-Indo-European Turkish language. Its structure (phonology, morphology, syntax) is completely different from Turkish. Most "basic linguistic features" of the Kurdish language are thus "in contravention" with those of the Turkish language. The formulation above can thus be interpreted so that every Kurdish first name can be regarded as inadmissible by the Turkish authorities. "Silence is killing them" (1994: 40) reports on the registration of the publishing company, now called "Pele Sor" in Istanbul. The publisher was prevented from registering the company "because of the '^' sign above the last 'e' of the company name 'Pele'. They told me this spelling was not Turkish and therefore registration would not be permitted. Consequently I had to refrain from registering my company."

The practice of not allowing Kurdish first names has also been extended to Kurds in European countries. Turkish Embassies have been known to refuse to record children with Kurdish names (as a recent case in Denmark again showed), in birth certificates, for instance for passports. Turkish Embassies have lists with "names allowed to be given to Turkish citizens".

3. See Clason — Baksi 1979 and Skutnabb-Kangas 1984a for examples.

4. The sentences mentioned by Okumus have been increased in the new Law 3713. Article 5, Increase of sentences, says:
"Penalties of imprisonment and fines imposed according to respective laws in respect to those committing crimes as described in Articles 3 and 4 are to be increased by one half. In doing so the penalties may exceed the maximum penalty for that particular or any kind of crime. However, in case of heavy imprisonment the penalty may not exceed 36 years, in case of imprisonment 25 years, and in case of light imprisonment 10 years' imprisonment."

5. For more detail see Bucak, S. 1989, 1990, 1991; Erdem — Skutnabb-Kangas 1989; Phillipson — Skutnabb-Kangas 1990; Skutnabb-Kangas 1984a, 1991a; Skutnabb-Kangas — Phillipson 1989a, 1990, 1991, 1993).

6. E.g. Baran 1989; Bucak, S. 1989; Chaliand 1980; Kuutman 1984. *Silence is Killing Them* (1994: 55–57) lists the names of the villages which were destroyed only in 1993 — there are altogether 392 of them.

7. TURKEY has had few such relaxed periods. The Turkish Constitutions 1923, 1961 and 1982 have all banned the Kurdish language. In 1924 the schools (many of of which had existed for several centuries), in which lessons took place in the Kurdish mother tongue, were closed. From then until the present time, the only language allowed in the schools in Kurdish areas has been Turkish. Teachers are, almost without exception,

from western Turkey and do not understand Kurdish (Mönch-Bucak 1989; Clason – Baksi 1979).

Despite poison gas warfare, mass deportations and other expressions of extreme political repression, IRAQ continues to recognize Kurdish as the second official language. Especially from 1958 to 1960 and from 1970 to 1974, Kurds in Iraq were linguistically and culturally in a better position than Kurds in other parts of Kurdistan. Kurdish was allowed orally and as medium of education in schools. Kurdish literature was allowed to be published and read. Kurdish folk dances were presented as Kurdish. A Department of Kurdish studies was opened at the University of Baghdad and it had at its peak period some 500 students. The University of Sulemaniye also had a Kurdish Department (for details, see Hassanpour 1989).

During the Republic of Mahabad (1946–1947) in IRAN, Kurdish was used as a medium of education and Kurdish language literature, newspapers etc were published. After the leaders of the republic were hanged in the market place in Mahabad on March 31 1947, Kurdish book bonfires lit up the streets in Mahabad (Kuutman 1984: 41).

There was a relative cultural and linguistic freedom for the Kurds in SYRIA during the period between the world wars, and many Kurdish intellectuals from other parts of Kurdistan settled in Syria. Kurdish magazines and books and Kurdish radio were allowed. From the early 1960s on, this was replaced by severe political and cultural repression, including forced repatriation and forced arabization. Kurdish has largely been forbidden since.

Kurdish has had reasonable conditions for development in the former SOVIET UN-ION. It has been used in schools and on the radio, and used and developed extensively in written publications.

8. At the time of the writing of this article, there is no official translation into English of law 3713. We have, in addition to the original (published in Turkish in the Official Gazette *Resmi Gazete*), used the unofficial translation provided by the Human Rights Foundation of Turkey/Turkiye Insan Haklari Vakfi.

9. Turkey does not even try to deny that this is the case, as was clear from the Turkish Embassy's reply ("Kurderne", by Counsellor Osman Centintas, 20 October) to my article ("Terroristerne: Jeg, Anker og PKK", 30 September 1993) in the Danish daily *Information*.

10. These are crimes defined in Articles 125, 131, 146, 147, 148, 149, 156, 168, 171, 172, and Articles 145, 150, 151, 152, 153, 154, 155, 169, and 499 (second paragraph) of the Turkish Penal Code, respectively, and Article 9 (parts b,c and e) of the Law 2845.

11. *Silence is killing them* (1994) has examples and lists of thousands of Kurds having been murdered, tortured, being beaten up, disappearing, etc in the Turkish part of Kurdistan in 1993, with attacks on cities and villages, most of them allegedly by state authorities or with their cooperation. All this *only* because they are Kurds. It also contains tens of examples of court cases against writers and journalists. Using the word "Kurdistan" or "Kurd" is considered "separatist propaganda" and has led to severe prison sentences in several cases, likewise displaying the national Kurdish colours, (red/yellow/green) in journals, on weddings, in clothes, in theatre performances, etc. Journalists, authors, owners of newspaper kiosks, publishers, editors, correspondents, newspaper vendors on the streets, all are murdered and attacked by security forces, taken into custody, tortured, sentenced to long periods of imprisonment and high fines for violation of the Anti-Terror Law. Books, newspapers and journals are confiscated, their offices and other assets likewise. *Only* because they write about Kurds. Authors and/or publishers

of books like the following face massive fines and long prison sentences or are already imprisoned: *Dersim Tütküleri — Taye Lawike Dersim* [Folk Songs from the Dersim Region], author Mustafa Duzgun; *Dersen Zmani Kurdi — Kürtce Dil Dersleri* [A Grammar of the Kurdish Language], author Baran; *Cumhuriyet Halk Firkasi Programi ve Kürt Sorunu* [The Kurdish Question and the Program of the Republican Popular Party], author dr. Ismail Besikci; *Kime ez — Ronak* [Who am I — Enlightened], a book of poetry by Cigerxwin, the best known contemporary Kurdish poet who died in exile in Sweden 1984; *Cagdas Kürdistan Tarihi* [Contemporary History of Kurdistan], author Lucien Rambout; *Kürt Ulusal Hareketleri ve 15. Yüzyilda Günümüze Ermeni-Kürt iliskileri* [The Kurdish National Movement and the Relations Between the Armenians and the Kurds from the Fifteenth Century Until Today], author Garo Sasuni; *Sonsuzluk ülkesinder Masallar* [Fairly Tales from the Land of the Endless], author Metin Ciyayi. And so on. If anyone reading this article wants to have more information about (and perhaps protest against) these gross violations of human rights, including basic linguistic rights, they can contact The International Association for Human Rights in Kurdistan, Postfach 10 45 51, D-28045 Bremen, Germany, fax 49—421—70 38 85.

We could also take this article as an example. There are two authors, and we have a common aim, to write a scientific article about the linguistic rights of the Kurds. We would be considered a terrorist organization according to Article 8. Claiming that the Kurds exist and that they should have what is here defined as linguistic human rights is a terrorist crime, as defined in Articles 1 and 8 in Law 3713. If we were Turkish citizens, we could be sentenced under the Anti-Terror law, Article 8, with heavy imprisonment and fines. In addition, both the publisher of this book and the series editors could be imprisoned and fined severely, and their assets could be confiscated. So could the assets (e.g. buildings) of our places of work (Universities if Bremen and Roskilde) and the publisher's assets. If you, dear reader, wrote a review of this article in a scientific journal and said that you agreed that Kurdish children should have the right to learn Kurdish, or if you joined a local Committee for the Human Rights of the Kurds (as the former Danish Prime Minister Anker Jørgensen who is on the Board the Danish Committee), you would likewise be considered a terrorist criminal, and could be imprisoned, according to Article 2, even if you never did anything for the Committee or for the education of Kurdish children.

12. An example for non-linguists: Indians who regard themselves as speakers of Bhojpuri or Maithili (i.e. names reflecting internal identification) are classified by linguists as Hindi speakers (external identification). This is comparable to classifying Opal, Clappes Favourite and Victoria (all varieties of plums) as plums. But when Kurdish mother tongue speakers are classified as Turks (external identification), it is as incorrect as calling a Victoria plum an apple.

13. For instance Indonesia encourages ethnic Chinese to shed their Chinese names, and has a variety of measures restricting the use of Chinese — see Jernudd, in this volume.

14. See von Nostitz 1989 on the European Parliament and the Kurdish question, Voigt 1989 on The Human Rights Provisions of the 1975 Helsinki Accords and the Kurds, Saado 1989 on the UN and the Kurds (but see European Parliament, note 2) and *Helsinki Watch* 1990.

Appendix

Extracts from selected UN and regional documents covering linguistic human rights, proposals for such and resolutions on language rights

1. United Nations Charter, 1945
2. Universal Declaration of Human Rights, 1948
3. International Covenant on Economic, Social and Cultural Rights, 1966
4. International Covenant on Civil and Political Rights, 1966
5. United Nations Declaration Regarding Non-self-governing Territories, 1945
6. The United Nations Convention on the Rights of the Child, 1989
7. United Nations Declaration on the Rights of Persons Belonging to National or Ethnic, Religious and Linguistic Minorities, 1992
8. American Convention on Human Rights "Pact of San Jose, Costa Rica", 1969
9. American Declaration of the Rights and Duties of Man, 1948
10. European Charter for Regional or Minority Languages, 1992
11. Convention Concerning Indigenous and Tribal Peoples in Independent Countries, ILO (International Labour Organisation), Convention 169, 1989
12. United Nations Universal Declaration on Rights of Indigenous Peoples, draft 1991
13. Resolutions from the First Continental Conference on 500 Years of Indian Resistance, 1990
14. Document of the Copenhagen Meeting of the Conference on the Human Dimension of the CSCE, 1990
15. Proposal for a European Convention for the Protection of Minorities, Council of Europe, European Commission for Democracy through Law, 1991
16. Submissions of the Waitangi Tribunal, Objections to the Recognition of te reo Maori as an Official Language of New Zealand, 1986
17. Declaration of the Tallinn Symposium on Linguistic Human Rights, 1991
18. TESOL (Teachers of English to Speakers of other Languages), Resolution on Language Rights, 1987
19. Linguistic Society of America Resolution, 1986
20. FIPLV (Fédération Internationale des Professeurs de Langues Vivantes), Draft articles for A Universal Charter of Basic Human Language Rights, 1993
21. Towards Equality and Self-reliance, Resolution of the Xl World Congress of the World Federation of the Deaf, 1991
22. World Federation of the Deaf Commission on Sign Language recommendation: Call for recognition of sign languages, 1991
23. Bonn Declaration, "The Kurdish People — No Future without Human Rights", 1991

1. UNITED NATIONS CHARTER

Chapter I. Purposes and Principles

Article 1

The Purposes of the United Nations are: ...

3. To achieve international cooperation in solving international problems of an economic, social, cultural, or humanitarian character, and in promoting and encouraging respect for human rights and for fundamental freedoms for all without distinction as to race, sex, language, or religion.

Chapter IV. The General Assembly

Article 13

The General Assembly shall initiate studies and make recommendations for the purpose of: ...

b. promoting international cooperation in the economic, social, cultural, educational, and health fields, and assisting in the realization of human rights and fundamental freedoms for all without distinction as to race, sex, language, or religion.

Chapter IX. International Economic and Social Cooperation

Article 55

With a view to the creation of conditions of stability and well-being which are necessary for peaceful and friendly relations among nations based on respect for the principle of equal rights and self-determination of peoples, the United Nations shall promote: ...

c. universal respect for, and observance of, human rights and fundamental freedoms for all without distinction as to race, sex, language, or religion.

Chapter XII. International Trusteeship System

Article 76

The basic objectives of the trusteeship system ... shall be ...

c. to encourage respect for human rights and for fundamental freedoms for all without distinction as to race, sex, language, or religion.

---

2. UNIVERSAL DECLARATION OF HUMAN RIGHTS

Article 2

Everyone is entitled to all the rights and freedoms set forth in this Declaration, without distinction of any kind, such as race, colour, sex, language, religion, political or other opinion, national or social origin, property, birth or other status.

Article 26

1. Everyone has the right to education. Education shall be free, at least in the elementary and fundamental stages. Elementary education shall be compulsory. Technical and professional education shall be made generally available and higher education shall be equally accessible to all on the basis of merit.

2. Education shall be directed to the full development of the human personality and to the strengthening of respect for human rights and fundamental freedoms. It shall promote understanding, tolerance and friendship among all nations, racial or religious groups, and shall further the activities of the United Nations for the maintenance of peace.

3. Parents have a prior rights to choose the kind of education that shall be given to their children.

Article 27

1. Everyone has the right freely to participate in the cultural life of the community, to enjoy the arts and to share in scientific advancement and its benefits.

---

3. INTERNATIONAL COVENANT ON ECONOMIC, SOCIAL AND CULTURAL RIGHTS

Article 2

2. The States Parties to the present Covenant undertake to guarantee that the rights enunciated in the present Covenant will be exercised without discrimination of any kind as to race, colour, sex, language, religion, political or other opinion, national or social origin, property, birth or other status.

Article 13

1. The States Parties to the present Covenant recognize the right of everyone to education. They agree that education shall be directed to the full development of the human personality and the sense of its dignity, and shall strengthen the respect for human rights and fundamental freedoms. They further agree that education shall enable all persons to participate effectively in a free society, promote understanding, tolerance and friendship among all nations and all racial, ethnic or religious groups, and further the activities of the United Nations for the maintenance of peace.

2. The States Parties to the present Covenant recognize that, with a view to achieving the full realization of this right: ...

(b) Secondary education in its different forms, including technical and vocational secondary education, shall be made generally available and accessible to all by every appropriate means, and in particular by the progressive introduction of free education;

(c) Higher education shall be made equally accessible to all, on the basis of capacity, by every appropriate means, and in particular by the progressive introduction of free education;

3. The States Parties to the present Covenant undertake to have respect for the liberty of parents and, when applicable, legal guardians to choose for their children schools, other than those established by the public authorities, which

conform to such minimum educational standards as may be laid down or approved by the State and to ensure the religious and moral education of their children in conformity with their own convictions.

Article 15
1. The States Parties to the present Covenant recognize the right of everyone:
   (a) To take part in cultural life;
   (b) To enjoy the benefits of scientific progress and its applications;

Article 25
Nothing in the present Covenant shall be interpreted as impairing the inherent right of all peoples to enjoy and utilize fully and freely their natural wealth and resources.

---

4. INTERNATIONAL COVENANT ON CIVIL AND POLITICAL RIGHTS

Article 2
1. Each State Party to the present Covenant undertakes to respect and to ensure to all individuals within its territory and subject to its jurisdiction the rights recognized in the present Covenant, without distinction of any kind, such as race, colour, sex, language, religion, political or other opinion, national or social orlgm, property, birth or other status.

Article 14
3. In the determination of any criminal charge against him, everyone shall be entitled to the following minimum guarantees, in full equality:
   (a) To be informed promptly and in detail in a language which he understands of the nature and cause of the charge against him;
   (f) To have the free assistance of an interpreter if he cannot understand or speak the language used in court;

Article 18
4. The States Parties to the present Covenant undertake to have respect for the liberty of parents and, when applicable, legal guardians to ensure the religious and moral education of their children in conformity with their own convictions.

Article 19
2. Everyone shall have the right to freedom of expression; this right shall include freedom to seek, receive and impart information and ideas of all kinds, regardless of frontiers, either orally, in writing or in print, in the form of art, or through any other media of his choice.

Article 24
1. Every child shall have, without any discrimination as to race, colour, sex, language, religion, national or social origin, property or birth, the right to such measures of protection as are required by his status as a minor, on the part of his family, society and the State.

Article 26

All persons are equal before the law and are entitled without any discrimination to the equal protection of the law. In this respect, the law shall prohibit any discrimination and guarantee to all persons equal and effective protection against discrimination on any ground such as race, colour, sex, language, religion, political or other opinion, national or social origin, property, birth or other status.

Article 27

In those States in which ethnic, religious or linguistic minorities exist, persons belonging to such minorities shall not be denied the right, in community with the other members of their group to enjoy their own culture, to profess and practise their own religion, or to use their own language.

5. UNITED NATIONS DECLARATION REGARDING NON-SELF-GOVERNING TERRITORIES

Article 73

Members of the United Nations which have or assume responsibilities for the administration of territories whose peoples have not yet attained a full measure of self-government recognize the principle that the interests of the inhabitants of these territories are paramount, and accept as a sacred trust the obligation to promote to the utmost, within the system of international peace and security established by the present Charter, the well-being of the inhabitants of these territories, and to this end:

a. to ensure, with due respect for the culture of the peoples concerned, their political, economic, social and economic advancement, their just treatment, and their protection against abuses.

6. THE UNITED NATIONS CONVENTION ON THE RIGHTS OF THE CHILD

Article 2

1. States Parties shall respect and ensure the rights set forth in the present Convention to each child within their jurisdiction without discrimination of any kind, irrespective of the child's or his or her parent's or legal guardian's race, colour, sex, language, religion, political or other opinion, national, ethnic or social origin, property, disability, birth or other status.

2. States Parties shall take all appropriate measures to ensure that the child is protected against all forms of discrimination or punishment on the basis of the status, activities, expressed opinions, or beliefs of the child's parents, legal guardians, or family members.

Article 5

States Parties shall respect the responsibilities, rights and duties of parents or, where applicable, the members of the extended family or community as provided for by local customs, legal guardians or other persons legally responsible for the child, to provide, in a manner consistent with the evolving capacities of the child, appropriate direction and guidance in the exercise by the child of the rights recognized in the present Convention.

Article 7

1. The child shall be registered immediately after birth and shall have the right from birth to a name, the right to acquire a nationality and, as far as possible, the right to know and be cared for by his or her parents.

Article 8

1. States Parties undertake to respect the right of the child to preserve his or her identity, including nationality, name and family relations as recognized by law without unlawful interference.

2. Where a child is illegally deprived of some or all of the elements of his or her identity, States Parties shall provide appropriate assistance and protection, with a view to speedily re-establishing his or her identity.

Article 9

1. States Parties shall ensure that a child shall not be separated from his or her parents against their will, except when competent authorities subject to judicial review determine, in accordance with applicable law and procedures, that such separation is necessary for the best interests of the child. Such determination may be necessary in a particular case such as one involving abuse or neglect of the child by the parents, or one where the parents are living separately and a decision must be made as to the child's place of residence.

Article 13

1. The child shall have the right to freedom of expression; this right shall include freedom to seek, recieve and impart information and ideas of all kinds regardless of frontiers, either orally, in writing or in print, in the form of art, or through any other media of the child's choice.

2. The exercise of this right may be subject to certain restrictions, but these shall only be such as are provided by law and are necessary:

   (a) For respect of the rights or reputations of others; or

   (b) For the protection of national security or of public order (*ordre public*), or of public health or morals.

Article 14

1. States Parties shall respect the right of the child to freedom of thought, conscience and religion.

2. States Parties shall respect the rights and duties of the parents and, when applicable, legal guardians, to provide direction to the child in the exercise of his or her right in a manner consistent with the evolving capasities of the child.

Article 16

1. No child shall be subjected to arbitrary or unlawful interference with his or her privacy, family, home or correspendence, nor to unlawful attacks on his or her honour and reputation.

2. The child has the right to the protection of the law against such interference or attacks.

Article 17

(d) Encourage the mass media to have particular regard to the linguistics needs of the child who belongs to a minority group or who is indigenous.

Article 18

2. For the purpose of guaranteeing and promoting the rights set forth in the present Convention, State Parties shall render appropriate assistance to parents and legal guardians in the performance of their child-rearing responsibilities and shall ensure the development of institutions, facilities and services for the care of children.

Article 19

1. States Parties shall take all appropriate legislative, administrative, social and educational measures to protect the child from all forms of physical or mental violence, injury or abuse, neglect or negligent treatment, maltreatment or exploitation, including sexual abuse, while in the care of parent(s), legal guardian(s) or any other person who has the care of the child.

Article 20

1. A child temporarily or permanently deprived of his or her family environment, or in whose own best interests cannot be allowed to remain in that environment, shall be entitled to special protection and assistance provided by the State.

2. States Parties shall in accordance with their national laws ensure alternative care for such a child.

3. Such care could include, *inter alia*, foster placement, *kafalah* of Islamic law, adoption or if necessary placement in suitable institutions for the care of children. When considering solutions, due regard shall be paid to desirability of continuity in a child's upbringing and to the child's ethnic, religous, cultural and lingustic background.

Article 28

1. States Parties recognize the right of the child to education, and with a view to achieving this right progressively and on the basis of equal opportunity, they shall, in particular:

(a) Make primary education compulsory and available free to all:

(b) Encourage the development of different forms of secondary education, including general and vocational education, make them available and accessible to every child, and take appropriate measures such as the introduction of free education and offering financial assistance in case of need;

(c) Make higher education accessible to all on the basis of capacity by every appropriate means.

Article 29

1. States Parties agree that the education of the child shall be directed to

(a) The development of the child's personality, talents and mental and physical abilities to their fullest potential:

(b) The development of respect for human rights and fundamental freedoms, and for the principles enshrined in the Charter of the United Nations;

(c) The development of respect for the child's parents, his or her own cultural identity, language and values, for the national values of the country in which the child is living, the country from which he of she may originate and for civilizations different from his or her own;

Article 30
In those States in which ethnic, religious or linguistic minorities or persons of indigenous origin exist, a child belonging to such a minority or who is indigenous shall not be denied the right, in community with other members of his or her group, to enjoy his or her own culture, to profess and practise his or her own religion, or to use his or her own language.

Article 40
(b) Every child alleged as or accused of having infringed the penal law has at least the following guarantees;

(vi) To have the free assistance of an interpreter if the child cannot understand or speak the language used.

---

7. UNITED NATIONS DECLARATION ON THE RIGHTS OF PERSONS BELONGING TO NATIONAL OR ETHNIC, RELIGIOUS AND LINGUISTIC MINORITIES

The General Assembly,

REAFFIRMING that one of the basic aims of the United Nations, as proclaimed in its Charter, is to promote and encourage respect for human rights and for fundamental freedoms for all, without distinction as to race, sex, language or religion,

REAFFIRMING faith in fundamental human rights, in the dignity and worth of the human person, in the equal rights of men and women and of nations large and small,

DESIRING to promote the realisation of the principles contained in the Charter of the United Nations, the Universal Declaration of Human Rights, the Convention on the Prevention and Punishment of the Crime of Genocide, the International Convention on the Elimination of All Forms of Racial Discrimination, the International Covenant on Civil and Political Rights, the International Covenant on Economic, Social and Cultural Rights, the Declaration on the Elimination of All Forms of Intolerance and of Discrimination Based on Religion or Belief, and the Convention on the Rights ofthe Child, as well as other relevant international instruments that have been adopted at the universal or regional level and those concluded between individual Member States of the United Nations,

INSPIRED by the provisions of article 27 of the International Covenant on Civil and Political Rights concerning the rights of persons belonging to ethnic, religious or linguistic minorities,

CONSIDERING that the promotion and protection of the rights of persons belonging to national or ethnic, religious and linguistic minorities contribute to the political and social stability of States in which they live,

EMPHASISING that the constant promotion and realisation of the rights of persons belonging to national or ethnic, religious and linguistic minorities, as an integral part of the development of society as a whole and within a democratic framework based on the rule of law, would contribute to the strengthening of friendship and cooperation among peoples and States,

CONSIDERING that the United Nations has an important role to play regarding the protection of minorities,

BEARING IN MIND the work done so far within the United Nations system, in particular the Commission on Human Rights, the Subcommission on Prevention of Discrimination and Protection of Minorities and the bodies established pursuant to the International Covenants on Human Rights and other relevant international human rights instruments on promoting and protecting the rights of persons belonging to national or ethnic, religious and linguistic minorities,

TAKING INTO ACCOUNT the important work which is carried out by intergovernmental and nongovernmental organisations in protecting minorities and in promoting and protecting the rights of persons belonging to national or ethnic, religious and linguistic minorities,

RECOGNISING the need to ensure even more effective implementation of international instruments with regard to the rights of persons belonging to national or ethnic, religious and linguistic minorities,

PROCLAIMS this Declaration on the Rights of persons Belonging to National or Ethnic, Religious and Linguistic Minorities:

Article 1

1. States shall protect the existence and the national or ethnic, cultural, religious and linguistic identity of minorities within their respective territories, and shall encourage conditions for the promotion of that identity.

2. States shall adopt appropriate legislative and other measures to achieve those ends.

Article 2

1. Persons belonging to national or ethnic, religious and linguistic minorities (hereinafter referred to as persons belonging to minorities) have the right to enjoy their own culture, to profess and practise their own religion, and to use their own language, in private and in public, freely and without interference or any form of discrimination.

2. Persons belonging to minorities have the right to participate effectively in cultural, religious social, economic and public life.

3. Persons belonging to minorities have the right to participate effectively in decisions on the national and, where appropriate, regional level concerning the minority to which they belong or the regions in which they live, in a manner not incompatible with national legislation.

4. Persons belonging to minorities have the right to establish and maintain their own associations.

5. Persons belonging to minorities have the right to establish and maintain, without any discrimination, free and peaceful contacts with other members of their group and with persons belonging to other minorities, as well as contacts across frontiers with citizens of other States to whom they are related by national or ethnic, religious and linguistic ties.

Article 3

1. Persons belonging to minorities may exercise their rights, including those set forth in this Declaration, individually as well as in community with other members of their group, without any discrimination.

2. No disadvantage shall result for any person belonging to a minority as the consequence of the exercise or non-exercise of the rights set forth in this Declaration.

Article 4

1. States shall take measures where required to ensure that persons belonging to minorities may exercise fully and effectively all their human rights and fundamental freedoms without any discrimination and in full equality before the law.

2. States shall take measures to create favourable conditions to enable persons belonging to minorities to express their characteristics and to develop their culture, language, religion, traditions and customs, except where specific practices are in violation of national and contrary to international standards.

3. States should take appropriate measures so that, wherever possible, persons belonging to minorities have adequate opportunities to learn their mother tongue or to have instruction in their mother tongue.

4. States should, where appropriate, take measures in the field of education, in order to encourage knowledge of the history, traditions, language and culture of the minorities existing within their territory. Persons belonging to minorities should have adequate opportunities to gain knowledge of the society as a whole.

5. States should consider appropriate measures so that persons belonging to minorities may participate fully in the economic progress and development in their country.

Article 5

1. National policies and programmes shall be planned and implemented with due regard for the legitimate interests of persons belonging to minorities.

2. Programmes of cooperation and assistance among States should be planned and implemented with due regard for the legitimate interests of persons belonging to minorities.

Article 6

States should cooperate on questions relating to persons belonging to minorities, including exchange of information and experiences, in order to promote mutual understanding and confidence.

Article 7

States should cooperate in order to promote respect for the rights set forth in this Declaration.

Article 8

1. Nothing in this Declaration shall prevent the fulfillment of international obligations of States in relation to persons belonging to minorities. In particular, States shall fulfill in good faith the obligations and commitments they have assumed under international treaties and agreements to which they are parties.

2. The exercise of the rights set forth in this Declaration shall not prejudice the enjoyment by all persons of universally recognised human rights and fundamental freedoms.

3. Measures taken by States to ensure the effective enjoyment of the rights set forth in this Declaration shall not *prima facie* be considered contrary to the principle of equality contained in the Universal Declaration of Human Rights.

4. Nothing in this declaration may be construed as permitting any activity contrary to the purposes and principles of the United Nations, including sovereign equality, territorial integrity and political independence of States.

Article 9
The specialised agencies and other organisations of the United Nations system shall contribute to the full realisation of the rights and principles set forth in this Declaration, within their respective fields of competence.

---

8. AMERICAN CONVENTION ON HUMAN RIGHTS "PACT OF SAN JOSE, COSTA RICA"

Part 1 — State Obligations and Rights Protected

Chapter 1 — General Obligations

Article 1 — Obligation to Respect Rights
1. The States Parties to this Convention undertake to respect the rights and freedoms recognized herein and to ensure to all persons subject to their jurisdiction the free and full exercise of those rights and freedoms, without any discrimination for reasons of race, color, sex, language, religion, political or other opinion, national or social origin, economic status, birth, or any other social condition.

Article 8 — Right to a Fair Trial
2. Every person accused of a criminal offense has the right to be presumed innocent so long as his guilt has not been proven according to law. During the proceedings, every person is entitled, with full equality, to the following minimum guarantees:

(a) the right of the accused to be assisted without charge by a translator or interpreter, if he does not understand or does not speak the language of the tribunal or court;

Article 12 — Freedom of Conscience and Religion
4. Parents or guardians, as the case may be, have the right to provide for the religious and moral education of their children or wards that is in accord with their own convictions.

Article 13 — Freedom of Thought and Expression
1. Everyone has the right to freedom of thought and expression. This right includes freedom to seek, recieve, and impart information and ideas of all kinds, regardless of frontiers, either orally, in writing, in print, in the form of art, or through any other medium of one's choice.

3. The right of expression may not be restricted by indirect methods or means, such as the abuse of government or private controls over newsprint, radio broadcasting frequencies, or equipment used in the dissemination of information, or by any other means tending to impede the communication and circulation of ideas and opinions.

5. Any propaganda for war and any advocacy of national, racial, or religious hatred that constitute incitements to lawless violence or to any other similar illegal action against any person or group of persons on any ground including those of race, color, religion, language, or national origin shall be considered as offenses punishable by law.

Article 18 — Right to a Name

Every person has the right to a given name and to the surnames of his parents or that of one of them. The law shall regulate the manner in which this right shall be ensured for all, by the use of assumed names if necessary.

---

9. AMERICAN DECLARATION OF THE RIGHTS AND DUTIES OF MAN

Chapter 1. Rights

Article II All persons are equal before the law and have the rights and duties established in this Declaration, without distinction as to race, sex, language, creed or any other factor.

Right to equality before the law

Article IV Every person has the right to freedom of investigation, of opinion, and of the expression and dissemination of ideas, by any medium whatsoever.

Right to freedom of investigation, opinion, expression and dissemination.

Article XII Every person has the right to an education, which should be based on the principles of liberty, morality and human solidarity.

Right to education.

Likewise every person has the right to an education that will prepare him to attain a decent life, to raise his standard of living, and to be a useful member of society.

The right to an education includes the right to equality of opportunity in every case, in accordance with natural talents, merit and the desire to utilize the resources that the state or the community is in a position to provide.

Every person has the right to receive, free, at least a primary education.

Article XIII Every person has the right to take part in the cultural life of the community, to enjoy the arts, and to participate in the benefits that result from intellectual progress, especially scientific discoveries.

Right to the benefits of culture.

Chapter 2. Duties

Article XXXI It is the duty of every person to acquire at least an elementary education.

Duty to receive instruction.

10. EUROPEAN CHARTER FOR REGIONAL OR MINORITY LANGUAGES

Preamble

The member states of the Council of Europe signatory hereto,

Considering that the aim of the Council of Europe is to achieve a greater unity between its members, particularly for the purpose of safeguarding and realising the ideals and principles which are their common heritage;

Considering that the protection of the historic regional or minority languages of Europe, some of which are in danger of eventual extinction, contributes to the maintenance and development of Europe's cultural wealth and traditions;

Considering that the right to use a regional or minority language in private and public life is an inalienable right conforming to the principles embodied in the United Nations International Covenant on Civil and Political Rights, and according to the spirit of the Council of Europe Convention for the Protection of Human Rights and Fundamental Freedoms;

Having regard to the work carried out within the CSCE and in particular to the Helsinki Final Act of 1975 and the Document of the Copenhagen Meeting of 1990;

Stressing the value of interculturalism and multilingualism and considering that the protection and encourament of regional or minority languages should not be to the detriment of the official languages and the need to learn them;

Realising that the protection and promotion of regional or minority languages in the different countries and regions of Europe represent an important contribution to the building of a Europe based on the principles of democracy and cultural diversity within the framework of national sovereignty and territorial integrity;

Taking into consideration the specific conditions and historical traditions in the different regions of the European States,

Have agreed as follows:

PART I GENERAL PROVISIONS

Article 1 Definitions

For the purposes of this Charter:

a. the term "regional or minority languages" means languages that are

   i. traditionally used within a given territory of a State by nationals of that State who form a group numerically smaller than the rest of the State's population, and

ii. different from the official language(s) of that State;

it does not include dialects of the official language(s) of the State or the languages of migrants;

b. "territory in which the regional or minority language is used" means the geographical area in which the said language is the mode of expression of a number of people justifying the adoption of the various protective and promotional measures provided for in this Charter;

c. "non-territorial languages" means languages used by nationals of the State which differ from the language or languages used by the rest of the State's population but which, although traditionally used within the territory of the State, cannot be identified with a particular area thereof.

Article 2 Undertakings

1. Each Party undertakes to apply the provisions of Part II to all the regional or minority languages spoken within its territory and complying with the definition in Article 1.

2. In respect of each language specified at the time of ratification, acceptance or approval, in accordance with Article 3, each Party undertakes to apply a minimum of thirty-five paragraphs or sub-paragraphs chosen from among the provisions of Part III of the Charter, including at least three chosen from each of the articles 8 and 12 and one from each of the articles 9, 10, 11, and 13.

Article 3 Practical Arrangements

1. Each contracting State shall specify in its instrument of ratification, acceptance or approval, each regional or minority language, or official language which is less widely used on the whole or in part of its territory, to which the paragraphs chosen in accordance with Article 2, paragraph 2, shall apply.

2. Any Party may, at any subsequent time, notify the Secretary General that it accepts the obligations arising out of the provisions of any other paragraph of the Charter not already specified in its instrument or ratification, acceptance or approval, or that it will apply paragraph 1 of the present article to other regional or minority languages, or to other official languages which are less widely used on the whole or part of its territory.

3. The undertakings referred to in the forgoing paragraph shall be deemed to form an integral part of the ratification, acceptance or approval and will have the same effect as from their date of notification.

Article 4 Existing regimes of protection

1. Nothing in this Charter shall be construed as limiting or derogating from any of the rights guaranteed by the European Convention on Human Rights.

2. The provisions of this Charter shall not affect any more favourable provisions concerning the status of regional or minority languages or the legal regime of persons belonging to minorities which may exist in a Party or are provided for by relevant bilateral or multilateral agreements.

Article 5 Existing Obligations

Nothing in this Charter may be interpreted as implying any right to engage in any activity or perform any action in contravention of the purposes of the Charter of the United Nations or other obligations under international law, including the principle of the sovereignty and territorial integrity of States.

Article 6 Information

The Parties undertake to see to it that the authorities, organisations and persons concerned are informed of the rights and duties established by this Charter.

PART II OBJECTIVES AND PRINCIPLES PURSUED IN ACCORDANCE WITH ARTICLE 2, PARAGRAPH 1

Article 7 Objectives and principles

1. In respect of regional or minority languages, within the territories in which such languages are used and according to the situation of each language, the Parties shall base their policies, legislation and practice on the following objectives and principles:

a. the recognition of the regional or minority languages as an expression of cultural wealth;

b. the respect of the geographical area of each regional or minority language in order to ensure that existing or new administrative divisions do not constitute an obstacle to the promotion of the regional or minority language in question;

c. the need for resolute action to promote regional or minority languages in order to safeguard them;

d. the facilitation and/or encouragement of the use of regional or minority languages, in speech and writing, in public and private life;

e. the maintenance and development of links, in the fields covered by this Charter, between groups using a regional or minority language and other groups in the State employing a language used in identical or similar form, as well as the establishment of cultural relations with other groups in the State using different languages;

f. the provision of appropriate forms and means for the teaching and study of regional or minority languages at all appropriate stages;

g. the provision of facilities enabling non-speakers of a regional or minority language living in the area where it is used to learn it if they so desire;

h. the promotion of study and research on regional or minority languages at universities or equivalent institutions;

i. the promotion of appropriate types of transnational exchanges, in the fields covered by this Charter, for regional or minority languages used in identical or similar form in two or more states.

2. The Parties undertake to eliminate, if they have not yet done so, any unjustified distinction, exclusion, restriction or preference relating to the use of a regional or minority language and intended to discourage or endanger the maintenance or development of a regional or minority language. The adoption of special measures in favour of regional or minority languages aimed at promoting equality between the users of these languages and the rest of the population or which take due account of their specific conditions is not considered to be an act of discrimination against the users of more widely-used languages.

3. The Parties undertake to promote, by appropriate measures, mutual understanding between all the linguistic groups of the country and in particular the inclusion of respect, understanding and tolerance in relation to regional or minority languages among the objectives of education and training provided

within their countries and encouragement of the mass media to pursue the same objective.

4. In determining their policy with regard to regional or minority languages, the Parties shall take into consideration the needs and wishes expressed by the groups which use such languages. They are encouraged to establish bodies, if necessary, for the purpose of advising the authorities on all matters pertaining to regional or minority languages.

5. The Parties undertake to apply, *mutatis mutandis*, the principles listed in paragraphs 1 to 4 above to non-territorial languages. However, as far as these languages are concerned, the nature and scope of the measures to be taken to give effect to this Charter shall be determined in a flexible manner, bearing in mind the needs and wishes, and respecting the traditions and characteristics, of the groups which use the languages concerned.

PART III MEASURES TO PROMOTE THE USE OF REGIONAL OR MINORITY LANGUAGES IN PUBLIC LIFE IN ACCORDANCE WITH THE UNDERTAKINGS ENTERED INTO UNDER ARTICLE 2, PARAGRAPH 2

Article 8 Education

1. With regard to education, the Parties undertake, within the territory in which such languages are used, according to the situation of each of these languages, and without prejudice to the teaching of the official language(s) of the State, to:

a. i. make available pre-school education in the relevant regional or minority languages; or

ii. make available a substantial part of pre-school education in the relevant regional or minority languages; or

iii. apply one of the measures provided for under (i) and (ii) above at least to those pupils whose families so request and whose number is considered sufficient; or

iv. if the public authorities have no direct competence in the field of pre-school education, favour and/or encourage the application of the measures referred to under (i) to (iii) above;

b. i. make available primary education in the relevant regional or minority languages; or

ii. make available a substantial part of primary education in the relevant regional or minority languages; or

iii. provide, within primary education, for the teaching of the relevant regional or minority languages as an integral part of the curriculum; or

iv. apply one of the measures provided for under (i) to (iii) above at least to those pupils whose families so request and whose number is considered sufficient;

c. i. make available secondary education in the relevant regional or minority languages; or

ii. make available a substantial part of secondary education in the relevant regional or minority languages; or

iii. provide, within secondary education, for the teaching of the relevant regional or minority languages as an integral part of the curriculum; or

iv. apply one of the above measures provided for under (i) to (iii) above at least to those pupils who, or where appropriate whose families, so wish in a number considered sufficient;

d. i. make available technical and vocational education in the relevant regional or minority languages; or

ii. make available a substantial part of technical and vocational education in the relevant regional or minority languages; or

iii. provide, within technical and vocational education, for the teaching of the relevant regional or minority languages as an integral part of the curriculum; or

iv. apply one of the measures provided for under (i) to (iii) above at least to those pupils who, or where appropriate whose families, so wish in a number considered sufficient;

e. i. make available university and other higher education in regional or minority languages; or

ii. provide facilities for the study of these languages as university and higher education subjects; or

iii. if, by reason of the role of the State in relation to higher education institutions, sub-paragraphs (i.) and (ii.) cannot be applied, encourage and/or allow the provision of university and higher education in regional or minority languages or of facilities for the study of these languages as university or higher education subjects;

f. i. arrange for the provision of adult and continuing education courses which are taught mainly or wholly in the regional or minority languages; or

ii. offer such languages as subjects of adult and continuing education; or

iii. if the public authorities have no direct competence in the field of adult education, favour and/or encourage the offering of such languages as subjects of adult and continuing education;

g. i. make arrangements to ensure the teaching of the history and the culture which is reflected by the regional or minority language;

h. provide the basic and further training of the teachers required to implement those of paragraphs (a) to (g) accepted by the Party;

i. set up a supervisory body or bodies responsible for monitoring the measures taken·and progress achieved in establishing or developing the teaching of regional or minority languages and for drawing up periodic reports of their findings, which will be made public.

2. With regard to education and in respect of territories other than those in which the regional or minority languages are traditionally used, the Parties undertake, if the number of users of a regional or minority language justifies it, to allow, encourage or provide teaching in or of the regional or minority language at all the appropriate stages of education.

Article 9 Judicial authorities

1. The Parties undertake, in respect of those judicial districts in which the number of residents using the regional or minority languages justifies the measures specified below, according to the situation of each of these languages and on

condition that the use of the facilities afforded by the present paragraph is not considered by the judge to hamper the proper administration of justice:

a. in criminal proceedings:

i. to provide that the courts, at the request of one of the parties, shall conduct the proceedings in the regional or minority languages; and/or

ii. to guarantee the accused the right to use his/her regional or minority language; and/or

iii. to provide that requests and evidence, whether written or oral, shall not be considered inadmissable solely because they are formulated in a regional or minority language; and/or

iv. to produce, on request, documents connected with legal proceedings in the relevant regional or minority language,

if necessary by the use of interpreters and translations involving no extra expense for the persons concerned;

b. in civil proceedings:

i. to provide that the courts, at the request of one of the parties, shall conduct the proceedings in the regional or minority languages; and/or

ii. to allow, whenever a litigant has to appear in person before a court, that he or she may use his or her regional or minority language without thereby incurring additional expense; and/or

iii. to allow documents and evidence to be produced in the regional or minority languages

if necessary by the use of interpreters and translations;

c. in proceedings before courts concerning administrative matters

i. to provide that the courts, at the request of one of the parties, shall conduct the proceedings in the regional or minority languages; and/or

ii. to allow, whenever a litigant has to appear in person before a court, that he or she may use his or her regional or minority language without thereby incurring additional expense; and/or

iii. to allow documents and evidence to be produced in the regional or minority languages

if necessary by the use of interpreters and translations;

d. to take steps to ensure that the application of sub-paragraphs (i) and (iii) of paragraph (b) and (c) above and any necessary use of interpreters and translations does not involve extra expense for the persons concerned.

2. The Parties undertake:

a. not to deny the validity of legal documents drawn up within the State solely because they are drafted in a regional or minority language; or

b. not to deny the validity, as between the parties, of legal documents drawn up within the country solely because they are drafted in a regional or minority language, and to provide that they can be invoked against interested third parties who are not users of these languages on condition that the contents of the document are made known to them by the person(s) who invoke(s) it; or

c. not to deny the validity, as between the parties, of legal documents drawn up within the country solely because they are drafted in a regional or minority language.

3. The Parties undertake to make available in the regional or minority languages the most important national statutory texts and those relating particularly to users of these languages, unless they are otherwise provided.

Article 10 Administrative authorities and public services

1. Within the administrative districts of the State in which the number of residents who are users of regional or minority languages justifies the measures specified below and according to the situation of each language, the Parties undertake, as far as this is reasonably possible, to:

a. i. ensure that the administrative authorities use the regional or minority languages; or

ii. ensure that such of their officers as are in contact with the public use the regional or minority languages in their relations with persons applying to them in these languages; or

iii. ensure that users of regional or minority languages may submit oral or written applications and receive a reply in these languages; or

iv. ensure that users of regional or minority languages may submit oral or written applications in these languages; or

v. ensure that users of regional or minority languages may validly submit a document in these languages;

b. make available widely used administrative texts and forms for the population in the regional or minority languages or in bilingual versions;

c. allow the administrative authorities to draft documents in a regional or minority language.

2. In respect of the local and regional authorities on whose territory the number of residents who are users of regional or minority languages is such as to justify the measures specified below, the Parties undertake to allow and/or encourage:

a. the use of regional or minority languages within the framework of the regional or local authority;

b. the possibility for users of regional or minority languages to submit oral or written applications in these languages;

c. the publication by regional authorities of their official documents also in the relevant regional or minority languages;

d. the publication by local authorities of their official documents also in the relevant regional or minority languages;

e. the use by regional authorities of regional or minority languages in debates in their assemblies, without excluding, however, the use of the official language(s) of the State;

f. the use by local authorities of regional or minority languages in debates in their assemblies without excluding, however, the use of the official language(s) of the State;

g. the use or adoption, if necessary in conjunction with the name in the official language(s), of traditional and correct forms of place-names in regional or minority languages.

3. With regard to public services provided by the administrative authorities or other persons acting on their behalf, the Parties undertake, within the territory in which regional or minority languages are used, in accordance with the situation of each language and as far as this is reasonably possible, to:

a. ensure that the regional or minority languages are used in the provision of the service; or

b. allow users of regional or minority languages to submit a request and receive a reply in these languages; or

c. allow users of regional or minority languages to submit a request in these languages.

4. With a view to putting into effect those provisions of paragraphs 1, 2 and 3 accepted by them, the Parties undertake to take one or more of the following measures:

a. translation or interpretation as may be required;

b. recruitment and, where necessary, training of the officials and other public service employees required;

c. compliance as far as possible with requests from public service employees having a knowledge of a regional or minority language to be appointed in the territory in which that language is used.

5. The Parties undertake to allow the use or adoption of family names in regional or minority languages, at the request of those concerned.

Article 11 Media

1. The Parties undertake, for the users of the regional or minority languages within the territories in which those languages are spoken, according to the situation of each language, to the extent that the public authorities, directly or indirectly, are competent, have power or play a role in this field, and respecting the principle of the independence and autonomy of the media:

a. to the extent that radio and television carry out a public service mission:

i. to ensure the creation of at least one radio station and one television channel in the regional or minority languages, or

ii. to encourage and/or facilitate the creation of at least one radio station and one television channel in the regional or minority languages, or

iii. to make adequate provision so that broadcasters offer programmes in regional or minority languages;

b. i. to encourage and/or facilitate the creation of at least one radio station in the regional or minority languages, or

ii. to encourage and/or facilitate the broadcasting of radio programmes in the regional or minority languages on a regular basis;

c. i. to encourage and/or facilitate the creation of at least one television channel in the regional or minority languages, or

ii. to encourage and/or facilitate the broadcasting of television programmes in the regional or minority languages on a regular basis;

d. to encourage and/or facilitate the production and distribution of audio and audio-visual works in regional or minority languages;

e. i. to encourage and/or facilitate the creation and/or maintenance of at least one newspaper in the regional or minority languages; or

ii. to encourage and/or facilitate the publication of newspaper articles in the regional or minority languages on a regular basis;

f. i. to cover the additional costs of those media which use regional or minority languages, wherever the law provides for financial assistance in general for the media; or

ii. to apply existing measures for financial assistance also to audio-visual productions in regional or minority languages;

g. to support the training of journalists and other staff for media using regional or minority languages.

2. The Parties undertake to guarantee freedom of direct reception of radio and television broadcasts from neighbouring countries in a language used in identical or similar form to a regional or minority language and not to oppose the retransmission of radio and television broadcasts from neighbouring countries in such a language. They further undertake to ensure that no restrictions will be placed on the freedom of expression and free circulation of information in the written press in a language used in identical or similar form to a regional or minority language. The exercise of the above mentioned freedoms, since it carries with it duties and responsibilities, may be subject to such formalities, conditions, restrictions or penalties as are prescribed by law and are necessary in a democratic society, in the interests of national security, territorial integrity or public safety, for the prevention of disorder or crime, for the protection of health or morals, for the protection of the reputation or rights of others, for preventing disclosure of information received in confidence, or for maintaining the authority and impartiality of the judiciary.

3. The Parties undertake to ensure that the interests of the users of regional or minority languages are represented or taken into account within such bodies as may be established in accordance with the law with responsibility for guaranteeing the freedom and pluralism of the media.

Article 12 Cultural activities and facilities

1. With regard to cultural facilities and activities — especially libraries, video libraries, cultural centres, museums, archives, academies, theatres and cinemas, as well as literary work and film production, vernacular forms of cultural expression, festivals and the culture industries, including *inter alia* the use of new technologies — the Parties undertake, within the territory in which such languages are used and to the extent that the public authorities are competent, have power or play a role in this field, to:

a. encourage types of expression and initiative specific to regional or minority languages and foster the different means of access to works produced in these languages;

b. foster the different means of access in other languages to works produced in regional or minority languages by aiding and developing translation, dubbing, post-synchronisation and subtitling activities;

c. foster access in regional or minority languages to works produced in other languages by aiding and developing translation, dubbing, post-synchronisation and subtitling activities;

d. ensure that the bodies responsible for organising or supporting cultural activities of various kinds make appropriate allowance for incorporating the knowledge and use of regional or minority languages and cultures in the undertakings which they initiate or for which they provide backing;

e. promote measures to ensure that the bodies responsible for organising or supporting cultural activities have at their disposal staff who have a full command of the regional or minority language concerned, as well as of the language(s) of the rest of the population;

f. encourage direct participation by representatives of the users of a given regional or minority language in providing facilities and planning cultural activities;

g. encourage and/or facilitate the creation of a body or bodies responsible for collecting, keeping a copy of and presenting or publishing works produced in the regional or minority languages;

h. if necessary create and/or promote and finance translation and terminological research services, particularly with a view to maintaining and developing appropriate administrative, commercial, economic, social, technical or legal terminology in each regional or minority language.

2. In respect of territories other than those on which the regional or minority languages are traditionally used, the Parties undertake, if the number of users of a regional or minority language justifies it, to allow, encourage and/or provide appropriate cultural activities and facilities in accordance with the preceding paragraph.

3. The Parties undertake to make appropriate provision, in pursuing their cultural policy abroad, for regional or minority languages and the cultures they reflect.

Article 13 Economic and social life

1. With regard to economic and social activities, the Parties undertake within the whole country, to:

a. eliminate from their legislation any provision prohibiting or limiting without justifiable reasons the use of regional or minority languages in documents relating to economic or social life, particularly contracts of employment, and in technical documents such as instructions for the use of products or installations;

b. prohibit the insertion in internal regulations of companies and private documents of any clauses excluding or restricting the use of regional or minority languages, at least between users of the same language;

c. oppose practices designed to discourage the use of regional or minority languages in connection with economic or social activities;

d. facilitate and/or encourage the use of regional or minority languages by means other than those specified in the above sub-paragraphs.

2. With regard to economic and social activities, the Parties undertake, in so far as the public authorities are competent, within the territory in which the regional or minority languages are used, and as far as this is reasonably possible, to:

a. include in their financial and banking regulations provisions which allow, by means of procedures compatible with commercial practice, the use of regional or minority languages in drawing up payment orders (cheques, drafts, etc.) or other financial documents, or, where appropriate, ensure the implementation of such provisions;

b. in the economic and social sectors directly under their control (public sector), organise activities to promote the use of regional or minority languages;

c. ensure that social care facilities such as hospitals, retirement homes and hostels offer the possibility of receiving and treating in their own language persons using a regional or minority language who are in need of care on grounds of ill-health, old age or for other reasons;

d. ensure by appropriate means that safety instructions are also accessible in regional or minority languages;

e. arrange for information provided by the competent public authorities concerning the rights of consumers to be made available in regional or minority languages.

Article 14 Transfrontier exchanges
The Parties undertake:

a. to apply existing bilateral and multilateral agreements which bind them with the States in which the same language is used in identical or similar form, or if necessary to seek to conclude such agreements, in such a way as to foster contacts between the users of the same language in the States concerned in the fields of culture, education, information, vocational training and permanent education;

b. for the benefit of regional or minority languages, to facilitate and promote co-operation across borders, in particular between regional or local authorities in whose territory the same language is used in identical or similar form.

PART IV APPLICATION OF THE CHARTER

Article 15 Periodical Reports
1. The Parties shall present periodically to the Secretary General of the Council of Europe, in a form to be prescribed by the Committee of Ministers, a report on their policy pursued in accordance with Part II of this Charter and on the measures taken in application of those provisions of Part III which they have accepted. The first report shall be presented within the year following the entry into force of the Charter with respect to the Party concerned, the other reports at three-yearly intervals after the first report.

2. The Parties shall make their reports public.

Article 16 Examination of the reports
1. The reports presented to the Secretary General of the Council of Europe under Article 15 shall be examined by a committee of experts constituted in accordance with Article 17.

2. Bodies or associations legally established in a Party may draw the attention of the committee of experts to matters relating to the undertakings entered into by that Party under Part III of this Charter. After consulting the Party concerned, the committee of experts may take account of this information in the preparation of the report specified in paragraph 3 below. These bodies or associations can furthermore submit statements concerning the policy pursued by a Party in accordance with Part II.

3. On the basis of the reports specified in paragraph 1 and the information mentioned in paragraph 2, the committee of experts shall prepare a report for the Committee of Ministers. This report shall be accompanied by the comments which the Parties have been requested to make and may be made public by the Committee of Ministers.

4. The report specified in paragraph 3 shall contain in particular the proposals of the committee of experts to the Committee of Ministers for the preparation

of such recommendations of the latter body to one or more of the Parties as may be required.

5. The Secretary General of the Council of Europe shall make a two-yearly detailed report to the Parliamentary Assembly on the application of the Charter.

Article 17 Committee of Experts

1. The committee of experts shall be composed of one member per Party, appointed by the Committee of Ministers from a list of individuals of the highest integrity and recognised competence in the matters dealt with in the Charter who shall be nominated by the Party concerned.

2. Members of the committee shall be appointed for a period of six years and shall be eligible for reappointment. A member who is unable to complete a term of office shall be replaced in accordance with the procedure laid down in paragraph 1, and the replacing member shall complete his predecessor's term of office.

3. The committee of experts shall adopt rules of procedure. Its secretarial services shall be provided by the Secretary General of the Council of Europe.

PART V FINAL PROVISIONS

Article 18

This Charter shall be open for signature by the member States of the Council of Europe. It is subject to ratification, acceptance or approval. Instruments of ratification or approval shall be deposited with the Secretary General of the Council of Europe.

Article 19

1. This Charter shall enter into force on the first day of the month following the expiration of a period of three months after the date on which five member States of the Council of Europe have expressed their consent to be bound by the Charter in accordance with the provisions of Article 18.

2. In respect of any member State which subsequently expresses its consent to be bound by it, the Charter shall enter into force on the first day of the month following the expiration of a period of three months after the date of the deposit of the instrument of ratification, acceptance or approval.

Article 20

1. After the entry into force of this Charter, the Committee of Ministers of the Council of Europe may invite any State not a member of the Council of Europe to accede to this Charter.

2. In respect of any acceding State, the Charter shall enter into force on the first day of the month following the expiration of a period of three months after the date of the deposit of the instrument of accession with the Secretary General of the Council of Europe.

Article 21

1. Any State may, at the time of signature or when depositing its instrument of ratification, acceptance, approval or accession, make one or more reservations to paragraphs 2 to 5 Article 7 of this Charter. No other reservation may be made.

2. Any Contracting State which has made a reservation under the preceding paragraph may wholly or partly withdraw it by means of a notification addressed to the Secretary General of the Council of Europe. The withdrawal shall take effect on the date of receipt of such notification by the Secretary General.

Article 22

1. Any Party may at any time denounce this Charter by means of a notification addressed to the Secretary General of the Council of Europe.

2. Such denunciation shall become effective on the first day of the month following the expiration of a period of six months after the date of receipt of the notification by the Secretary General.

Article 23

The Secretary General of the Council of Europe shall notify the member States of the Council and any State which has acceded to this Charter of:

a. any signature;

b. the deposit of any instrument of ratification, acceptance, approval or accession;

c. any date of entry into force of this Charter in accordance with Articles 19 and 20;

d. any notification received in application of the provisions of Article 3, paragraph 2;

e. any other act, notification or communication relating to this Charter.

---

11. CONVENTION CONCERNING INDIGENOUS AND TRIBAL PEOPLES IN INDEPENDENT COUNTRIES

Article 1

2. Self-identification as indigenous or tribal shall be regarded as a fundamental criterion for determining the groups to which the provisions of this Convention apply.

Article 2

1. Governments shall have the responsibility for developing, with the participation of the peoples concerned, co-ordinated and systematic action to protect the rights of these peoples and to guarantee respect for their integrity.

2. Such action shall include measures for:

(a) ensuring that members of these peoples benefit on an equal footing from the rights and opportunities which national laws and regulations grant to other members of the population;

(b) promoting the full realisation of the social, economic and cultural rights of these peoples with respect for their social and cultural identity, their customs and traditions and their institutions;

Article 4

1. Special measures shall be adopted as appropriate for safeguarding the persons, institutions, property, labour, cultures and environment of the peoples concerned.

Article 5

In applying the provisions of this Convention:

(a) the social, cultural, religious and spritual values and practices of these peoples shall be recognised and protected, and due account shall be taken of the nature of the problems which face them both as groups and as individuals;

(b) the integrity of the values, practices and institutions of these peoples shall be respected;

Article 6

1. In applying the provisions of this Convention, governments shall: ...

(c) establish means for the full development of these peoples' own institutions and initiatives, and in appropriate cases provide the resources necessary for this purpose.

Article 12

The peoples concerned shall be safeguarded against the abuse of their rights and shall be able to take legal proceedings, either individually or through their representative bodies, for the effective protection of these rights. Measures shall be taken to ensure that members of these peoples can understand and be understood in legal proceedings, where necessary through the provision of interpretation or by other effective means.

Article 28

1. Children belonging to the peoples concerned shall, wherever practicable, be taught to read and write in their own indigenous language or in the language most commonly used by the group to which they belong. When this is not practicable, the competent authorities shall undertake consultations with these peoples with a view to the adoption of measures to achieve this objective.

2. Adequate measures shall be taken to ensure that these peoples have the opportunity to attain fluence in the national language or in one of the official languages of the country.

3. Measures shall be taken to preserve and promote the development and practice of the indigneous languages of the peoples concerned.

Article 29

The imparting of general knowledge and skills that will help children belonging to the peoples concerned to participate fully and on an equal footing in their own community and in the national community shall be an aim of education for these peoples.

Article 30

1. Governments shall adopt measures appropriate to the traditions and cultures of the peoples concerned to make known to them their rights and duties, especially in regard to labour, economic opportunities, education and helth matters, social welfare and their rights deriving from this Convention.

2. If necessary, this shall be done by means of written translations and through the use of mass communications in the languages of these peoples.

12. UNITED NATIONS UNIVERSAL DECLARATION ON RIGHTS OF INDIGENOUS PEOPLES

II. First revised part of the draft (1991)

4. The (collective) right to maintain and develop their ethnic, and cultural characteristics and distinct identity, including the right of peoples and individuals to call themselves by their proper names.

5. The individual and collective right to protection against ethnocide. This protection shall include, in particular, prevention of any act which has the aim or effect of depriving them of their ethnic characteristics or cultural identity, of any form of forced assimilation or integration, of imposition of foreign life-styles and of any propaganda derogating their dignity and diversity.

6. The right to preserve their cultural identity and traditions and to pursue their own cultural development. The rights to the manifestations of their cultures, including archaeological sites, artefacts, designs, technology and works of art, lie with the indigenous peoples or their members.

7. The right to require that States grant — within the resources available — the necessary assistance for the maintenance of their identity and their development.

8. The right to manifest, teach, practise and observe their own religious traditions and ceremonies, and to maintain, protect and have access to sacred sites and burial-grounds for these purposes. 9. The right to develop and promote their own languages, including an own literary language, and to use them for administrative, juridical, cultural and other purposes.

10. The right to all forms of education, including in particular the right of children to have access to education in their own Ianguages, and to establish, structure, conduct and control their own educational systems and institutions.

23. The (collective) right to autonomy in matters relating to their own internal and local affairs, including education, information, culture, religion, health, housing, social welfare, traditional and other economic activities, land and resources administration and the environment, as well as internal taxation for financing these autonomous functions.

---

13. Resolutions from the First Continental Conference on 500 Years of Indian Resistance

July 17—21, 1990

Education, Culture and Religion Commission

Just as a plant needs the earth, water, air, sun and fertilization for its integral development, culture is a whole which needs all aspects necessary for lives of dignity. Education is the exchange of knowledge and cultural values that are in constant harmony with nature and humanity.

Over the past 500 years we have suffered deeply from an education and a religion of European origin which have devalued the age-old knowledge of the nationalities of Abya-Yala (the American Continent).

This European education only serves to expose us to processes of acculturation, subjugation and individualism. We refer to this as "banking education." ...

4. That bilingual, intercultural education be officially recognized in the constitutions of all countries of the Continent.

8. We demand the immediate withdrawal ot the Summer Institute of Linguistics from our communities and territories.

We not only demand the withdrawal of the Summer Linguistics Institute and other organisms that embrace cultural norms which are foreign to our communities, but that the movable goods and property that these groups have appropriated should be handed over to our communities and used for our benefit and service.

10. To carry out a campaign to teach literacy to our Indigenous Peoples in our own languages.

11. To establish a university for Indigenous Peoples of America and to ensure that it is controlled by our own peoples.

15. That any research about Indigenous Peoples be undertaken only with the approval and collaboration of the community involved. A copy of the research should be left with the appropriate organization.

17. That (the teaching of) Indigenous spirituality, languages, traditional knowledge and customs be included in our education.

18. Instead of whites, mestizos or others to writing about and distorting our perspectives, and selling magazines, books and newspapers about us to other communities, there should be writers and reporters from our own Indigenous communities present at all meetings and conferences of Indigenous Peoples.

20. That history be written by our own Indigenous Peoples. ...

— To demand the creation of bilingual vocational schools to train Indigenous teachers.

— To demand (access to) popular channels of communication to spread knowledge of our cultures among Indigenous Peoples and Nations.

— That bilingual education be extended to the mestizo population, and that the teaching of English be replaced with the teaching of autochthonous languages, given the fact that one of the reasons why bilingual education is rendering our own languages obsolete is due to the failure to educate the mestizo population in these languages.

— That our education become a source of strength for our culture, rather than as a source of destruction which has been the case for the last 500 years.

— That as Indigenous Peoples we do not become the objects of research, and that we evaluate what intellectuals and research centers are doing. We should train ourselves to become the primary researchers of our own culture.

Distributed by the South & Meso American Indian Information Center (SAIIC) PO Box 28703, Oakland CA 94604 (415) 834—4263 26

---

14. DOCUMENT OF THE COPENHAGEN MEETING OF THE CONFERENCE ON THE HUMAN DIMENSION OF THE CSCE

(22) The participating States reaffirm that the protection and promotion of the rights of migrant workers have their human dimension. In this context, they
...

(22.4) – express their readiness to examine, at future CSCE meetings, the relevant aspects of the further promotion of the rights of migrant workers and their families.

(31) Persons belonging to national minorities have the right to exercise fully and effectively their human rights and fundamental freedoms without any discrimination and in full equality before the law.

The participating States will adopt, where necessary, special measures for the purpose of ensuring to persons belonging to national minorities full equality with the other citizens in the exercise and enjoyment of human rights and fundamental freedoms.

(32) To belong to a national minority is a matter of a person's individual choice and no disadvantage may arise from the exercise of such choice.

Persons belonging to national minorities have the right freely to express, preserve and develop their ethnic, cultural, linguistic or religious identity and to maintain and develop their culture in all its aspects, free of any attempts at assimilation against their will. In particular, they have the right

(32.1) – to use freely their mother tongue in private as well as in public;

(32.2) – to establish and maintain their own educational, cultural and religious institutions, organizations or associations, which can seek voluntary financial and other contributions as well as public assistance, in conformity with national legislation;

(32.3) – to profess and practise their religion, including the acquisition, possession and use of religious materials, and to conduct religious educational activities in their mother tongue;

(32.5) – to disseminate, have access to and exchange information in their mother tongue;

Persons belonging to national minorities can exercise and enjoy their rights individually as well as in community with other members of their group. No disadvantage may arise for a person belonging to a national minority on account of the exercise or non-exercise of any such rights.

(33) The participating States will protect the ethnic, cultural, linguistic and religious identity of national minorities on their territory and create conditions for the promotion of that identity. They will take the necessary measures to that effect after due consultations, including contacts with organizations or associations of such minorities, in accordance with the decision-making procedures of each State.

Any such measures will be in conformity with the principles of equality and non-discrimination with respect to the other citizens of the participating State concerned.

(34) The participating States will endeavour to ensure that persons belonging to national minorities, notwithstanding the need to learn the official language or languages of the State concerned, have adequate oppotunities for instruction of their mother tongue or in their mother tongue, as well as, wherever possible and necessary, for its use before public authorities, in conformity with applicable national legislation.

In the context of the teaching of history and culture in educational establishments, they will also take account of the history and culture of national minorities.

(35) The participating States wil] respect the right of persons belonging to national minorities to effective participation in public affairs, including participation in the affairs relating to the protection and promotion of the identity of such minorities.

The participating States note the efforts undertaken to protect and create conditions for the promotion of the ethnic, cultural, linguistic and religious identity of certain national minorities by establishing as one of the possible means to achieve these aims, appropriate local or autonomous administrations corresponding to the specific historical and territorial circumstances of such minorities and in accordance with the policies of the State concerned.

(40) The participating States clearly and unequivocally condemn totalitarianism, racial and ethnic hatred, anti-semitism, xenophobia and discrimination against anyone as well as persecution on religious and ideological grounds. In this context, they also recognize the particular problems of Roma (gypsies). They declare their firm intention to intensify the efforts to combat these phenomena in all their forms and therefor will

(40.1) − take effective measures, including the adoption, in conformity with their constitutional systems and their international obligations, of such laws as may be necessary, to provide protection against any acts that constitute incitement to violence against persons or groups based on national racial, ethnic or religious discrimination, hostility or hatred, including anti-semitism;

(40.2) − commit themselves to take appropriate and proportionate measures to protect persons or groups who may be subject to threats or acts of discrimination, hostility or violence as a result of their racial, ethnic, cultural, linguistic or religious identity, and to protect their property.

---

15. PROPOSAL FOR A EUROPEAN CONVENTION FOR THE PROTECTION OF MINORITIES

Council of Europe/Conseil de l'Europe, CDL (91) 7, European Commission for Democracy through Law/Commission européenne pour la démocratie par le droit (adopted during the 6th meeting, on 8 February 1991)

PREAMBLE

Considering that minorities contribute to the pluriformity and cultural diversity within European States;

Considering that an adequate solution to the problem of minorities in Europe is an essential factor for democracy, justice, stability and Peace;

Being resolved to implement an effective protection of the rights of minorities and of persons belonging to those minorities,

Chapter I − General Principles

Article 1

1. The international protection of the rights of ethnic, linguistic and religious minorities, as well as the rights of individuals belonging to those minorities, as guaranteed by the present Convention, is a fundamental component of the

international protection of Human Rights, and as such falls within the scope of international co-operation.

2. It does not permit any activity which is contrary to the fundamental principles of international law and in particular of sovereignty, territorial integrity and political independence of States.

Article 2

1. For the purposes of this Convention, the term "minority" shall mean a group which is smaller in number than the rest of the population of a State, whose members, who are nationals of that State, have ethnical, religious or linguistic features different from those of the rest of the population, and are guided by the will to safeguard their culture, traditions, religion or language.

2. Any group coming within the terms of this definition shall be treated as an ethnic, religious or linguistic minority.

3. To belong to a national minority shall be a matter of individual choice and no disadvantage may arise from the exercise of such choice.

Chapter II — Rights and Obligations

Article 3

1. Minorities shall have the right to be protected against any activity capable of threatening their esistence.

2. They shall have the right to the respect, safeguard and development of their linguistic identity.

Article 6

1. Persons belonging to a minority shall have the right to freely preserve, express and develop their cultural identity in all its aspects, free of any attempts at assimilation against their will.

2. In particular, they shall have the right to espress themselves. to receive and to issue information and ideas through means of communication of their own.

Article 7

Any person belonging to a linguistic minority shall have the right to use his language freely, in public as well as in private.

Article 8

Whenever a minority reaches a substantial percentage of the population of a region or of the total population, its members shall have the right, as far as possible, to speak and write in their own language to the political, administrative and judicial authorities of this region or, where appropriate, of the State. These authorities shall have a corresponding obligation.

Article 9

Whenever the conditions of Article 8 are fulfilled, in State schools, obligatory schooling shall include, for pupils belonging to the minority, study of their mother tongue. As far as possible, all or part of the schooling shall be given in the mother tongue of pupils belonging to the minority. However, should the State not be in a position to provide such schooling, it must permit children who so wish to attend private schools. In such a case, the State shall have the right to prescribe that the official language or languages also be taught in such schools.

Article 13

States shall refrain from pursuing or encouraging policies aimed at the assimilation of minorities or aimed at intentionally modifying the proportions of the population in the regions inhabited by minorities.

---

16. Taken from the submissions of the Waitangi Tribunal (see bibliography)

5. OBJECTIONS TO THE RECOGNITION OF TE REO MAORI AS AN OFFICIAL LANGUAGE OF NEW ZEALAND

5.1 The claimants seek recognition of te reo Maori as an official language. We have decided that it would be helpful to consider now some of the commonly expressed objections to that course. We do not profess to canvass every possible objection because there may be some that have not occurred to us. We have not had the benefit of Counsel to assist us who would have been able to direct our minds to points that were not made before us. With the passing of the Treaty of Waitangi Amendment Act 1985 we will be able to have such assistance in the future.

5.2 **There is no need for recognition because Maori people can speak English anyway**.

This objection assumes that the only issue is functional — if a person can understand and be understood in speaking English nothing more is required. We think it unsound because some Maori people are more comfortable speaking Maori than in speaking English. That fact alone is important when considering this objection but we go further. It is an important part of this claim that Maori as a language is smothered by the prevalent use of English and is adversely affected as a consequence. To protect the language it must be used. Opportunities for use must be provided. Whether a speaker understands English well or not is a side issue. To protect te reo Maori and to provide opportunities for its use official recognition will give public acknowledgement of that need. Underlying our comments on this topic is our conclusion that the Maori language is worth protecting and deserves protection, quite apart from the Crown's duty under the Treaty to provide such protection.

5.3 **The Maori Language Cannot Meet the Needs of Modern Society**.

This objection usually refers to the existence in English of many words describing modern concepts — computer, helicopter, nuclear energy, television, microwave, telex, electricity, carburettor to mention but a few — which do not have an equivalent in Maori. One of the qualities of any living language is its ability to take in new words directly from other languages or to adapt such words. English is full of words taken from other languages — garage, chauffeur, telephone, television, avionics, blitzkrieg, parallel, fiord, ski, automobile — or adapted from other languages of which an exhaustive list would run into hundreds of examples. Maori is just as capable of doing the same thing. When the first Polynesian navigators came to these shores they had no words in their language for our native trees and birds, nor for things they had never experienced — ie, snow, ice, geysers, boiling pools — yet the language was adapted to meet all these new things. So also in modern times te reo Maori is well capable of adopting or adapting new words to meet modern needs and concepts.

5.4 English is an international language and therefore much more useful than Maori.

There is no question that English has become an international language and that Maori is almost unknown outside New Zealand. But official recognition of Maori will not affect the international use of English and the issue is not whether Maori is more useful or less useful than English. Usefulness depends upon circumstances. The mono-lingual New Zealander speaking nothing but English soon learns on a marae that his limited education puts him at a disadvantage. Furthermore it seems to be accepted in educational circles that to learn a second or third language is a distinct advantage in speaking and understanding the language of first preference.

5.5 Most New Zealanders cannot speak or understand Maori.

To say that most New Zealanders cannot speak Maori suggests that the only criterion for official recognition is a matter of numbers. We do not agree that official recognition should be decided on this basis. For one thing such recognition may encourage more people to acquire a knowledge of Maori and for another the fact that many of us are limited in our education to one language only does not mean that others not so disadvantaged should be deprived of the opportunity of using their skill. Official recognition will increase that opportunity of using their skill. Official recognition will increase that opportunity even though most New Zealanders find that they are not able, at the present time, to take advantage of it themselves. Because one, or some, or even a majority of us cannot take advantage of something does not seem to justify denying to others the opportunity that they are able to exploit.

5.6 Official Recognition Will Become Too Expensive.

This objection pre-supposes that by official recognition all public documents -statutes, regulations, public notices, perhaps even street-signs — should be published in both languages. We do not agree. The extent to which official recognition would require efforts of this kind will depend upon subject-matter, locality, audience and other factors as well as costs. We cover this in more detail later in this Finding but for the moment we simply observe that official recognition — the right to speak Maori on public occasions — is likely to be comparatively inexpensive when balanced against the corresponding importance of ensuring that the language does not die.

5.7 Minority Languages Always Die Out Eventually So Why Try To Save Maori By Giving It Official Recognition.

Some minority languages have died out, as in Scotland and to an extent in Ireland where Gaelic or Erse are rarely to be heard, but many countries are bilingual and show signs of remaining so. There are minority groups speaking their own language in Belgium, Sweden, Finland, Canada, Wales and elsewhere. We do not think it correct to say that minority languages *always* die out, but we agree that they are likely to do so if they are suppressed in their use and if they are not recognised which limits their usefulness and as a result, their usage.

5.8 The Maori Is Only A Minority In New Zealand And Should Not Be Allowed To Force The Majority To Adopt His Standards And Values.

Official recognition does not force Maori standards and values on to anyone. English speaking New Zealanders can continue their lives as before, but Maori New Zealanders will be able to use their language on occasions when they cannot do so now. If any New Zealanders want to use te reo Maori on a public occasion official recognition will permit them to do so. No penalty will attach to those who do not want to do so. Official recognition does not imply compulsion.

5.9 **Official Recognition Is An Empty Gesture Of No Benefit To Anyone**.

We are inclined to think that official recognition will go some distance towards eliminating the attitude that te reo Maori is of no worth or value. The fact that it cannot now be used in some public places and if not discouraged is not encouraged to be used in other places contributes to the assessment that it is of no value.

In particular among Maori New Zealanders it has been made obvious to us that official recognition will go a long way towards restoration of the mana of the language which has suffered in the past from failure to give it official status.

5.10 **There Is Not Enough Time Available Now To Meet The Educational Needs Of Our Children**.

This objection pre-supposes that official recognition means that Maori must be taught as a compulsory subject in schools. We do not see that compulsory education of this kind necessarily follows official recognition. Some subjects are recognised by society as being necessary for a sound education, others are not. We think it likely that Maori will be taught in the schools to the extent that parents want it to be taught to their children. Some will regard it as an important subject, others will take a different view, and the proportions of sectors in the community of one view or the other may vary from time to time as social circumstances change. Even geographical areas may be a factor -it may be more highly valued as a skill by parents in one district than in another. If a facility in the Maori language is regarded as more important than skill in French or in European history then those parents of that mind should be enabled to ensure that the curriculum is shaped accordingly. And more importantly, their children should be able to learn Maori if that is what their parents want.

5.11 **If Maori Is To Be Given Official Recognition, We Will Have To Recognise Other Ethnic Minority Languages As Well — Samoan, Tongan, Chinese For Example**.

We do not accept that the Maori is just another one of a number of ethnic minority groups in our community. It must be remembered that of all minority groups the Maori alone is party to a solemn treaty made with the Crown. None of the other migrant groups who have come to live in this country in recent years can claim the rights that were given to the Maori people by the Treaty of Waitangi.

Because of the Treaty Maori New Zealanders stand on a special footing reinforcing, if reinforcement be needed, their historical position as the original inhabitants, the tangata whenua of New Zealand, who agreed to allow our European forebears to come and settle here with them.

5.12 **If Maori is Given Official Recognition it will cause Divisions in the Community**.

This objection assumes that divisiveness is caused by differences. We suggest that the true cause of divisiveness in any community is a lack of respect for other (different) groups and/or a lack of understanding of other groups. New Zealand's population has different groups within it today and will continue to have such groups in the future.

There need not be divisiveness because of differences. And in other parts of the world it has been recognised that to impose one language or culture on another is more conducive to divisive hostility than to allow two languages or cultures to exist side by side.

The International Commission of Jurists made this point in submissions presented to us and it was also referred to by the Secretary for Maori Affairs Dr Reedy (see paras 8.1.5 et seq).

---

17. Declaration of the Tallinn symposium on linguistic human rights

We, participants at the Symposiun, of Linguistic Human Rights (LHRs), held in Tallinn, 13 – 15 October 1991, at the invitation of the National Language Board of the Republic of Estonia ...

3) we recognize that LHRs, both individual and collective, are an inherent part of human rights;

4) we are aware that language is a key element in many conflictual situations worldwide, and that there is an increased awareness of the significance of LHRs for autochthonous and immigrant minority groups;

5) we believe that respect for LHRs can significantly contribute to the establishment and maintenance of peace and harmony;

6) we affirm that language use in private life may not be restricted by governments, and that LHRs should be respected in key domains such as education, public administration and justice, political life, social affairs and commerce, and the mass media;

7) we note the desirability of the maintenance and development of all languages and their respective cultures, and the significant role that education through the medium of the mother tongue can play in achieving this;

8) we believe that the promotion of the LHRs of minority languages need in no way be to the detriment ot official languages;

9) we reaffirm the right of every people to ensure for its language its rightful place in the life of the nation, while respecting the LHRs of other peoples, particularly when a language has been marginalised or is threatened;

10) LHRs should be the concern of all people, and in particular of educators, intellectuals, cultural workers, and policy makers; the provision of resources for language cultivation is a matter of urgency;

11) we encourage the UN, UNESCO, ILO, and governmental and non-govermnental organisations at all levels to undertake or support research and other measures to promote LHRs;

12) we urge scholars to undertake scientific research in the area of LHRs: among the key domains are the following:
   – LHRs in relation to other rights and obligations,
   – social and linguistic constraints on, and impacts of, LHRs,

— acceptance and implementation of LHRs;
13) we encourage the relevant authorities to take vigorous steps to implement LHRs.

---

18. TESOL Resolution on language rights

TESOL, Teachers of English to Speakers of other Languages
An international professional organization for those concerned with the teaching of English as a second or foreign language and of standard English as a second dialect

WHEREAS TESOL is an organization which promotes programs that provide speakers of other languages the opportunity to learn English; and
WHEREAS TESOL supports the study of other languages for native English speakers; and
WHEREAS, in recognition of the right of all individuals to preserve and foster their linguistic and cultural origins, TESOL also supports learners of English maintaining their native tongues during and after their learning of English; and
WHEREAS these rights have been affirmed by such intemational organizations as UNESCO and the European Economic Community and in such international treaties as the Helsinki Accord; and
WHEREAS several states within the United States of America have enacted and other states and the United States Congress are considering legislative measures which could be used to deny these basic language rights; and
WHEREAS the considerable resources being spent to promote and implement English only policies in the United States of America could be allocated more effectively for language instruction, including English as a second language, at all educational levels and within all educational settings;
THEREFORE BE IT RESOLVED that TESOL support measures which proteet the right of all individuals to preserve and foster their linguistic and cultural origins;
BE IT FURTHER RESOLVED that TESOL oppose all measures declaring English the official language of the United States of America or of any legally eonstituted part thereof; and
FINALLY BE IT RESOLVED that TESOL circulate this resolution to its affiliates and interest sections, to other professional organizations and to appropriate public officials, especially those officials in localities where policies counter to the principles established in this resolution are being considered.
WE IN TESOL STRONGLY BELIEVE THAT THIS RESOLUTION RE-AFFIRMS THE HIGHEST IDEALS AND TRADITIONS OF OUR PRO-FESSION AS TEACHERS OF ENGLISH TO SPEAKERS OF OTHER LAN-GUAGES NAMELY THAT ALL INDIVIDUALS HAVE THE OPPORTU-NITY TO ACQUIRE PROFICIENCY IN ENGLISH WHILE MAINTAINING THEIR OWN LANGUAGE AND CULTURE.

19. Linguistic Society of America Resolution

WHEREAS several states have recently passed measures making English their "official state language," and

WHEREAS the "English-only" movement has begun to campaign for the passage of similar measures in other states and has declared its intention to attach an official language amendment to the U.S. Constitution, and

WHEREAS such measures have the effect of preventing the legislature and state agencies and officials from providing services or information in languages other than English,

Be it therefore resolved that the Society make known its opposition to such "English-only" measures, on the grounds that they are based on misconceptions about the role of a common language in establishing political unity, and that they are inconsistent with basic American ideals of linguistic tolerance. As scholars with a professional interest in language, we affirm that:

The English language in America is not threatened. All evidence suggests that recent immigrants are overwhelmingly aware of the social and economic advantages of becoming proficient in English, and require no additional compulsion to learn the language.

American unity has never rested primarily on unity of language, but rather on common political and social ideals.

History shows that attempts to impose a common language by force of law usually create divisiveness and disunity.

It is to the economic and cultural advantage of the nation as a whole that its citizens should be proficient in more than one language, and to this end we should encourage both foreign language study for native English speakers, and programs that enable speakers with other linguistic backgrounds to maintain proficiency in those languages along with English.

---

20. FIPLV Draft articles for A universal Charter of basic human language rights

(FIPLV Fédération Internationale des Professeurs de Langues Vivantes)

Draft Articles:
1. All persons have the right to acquire their mother tongue.
2. All persons have the right to acquire the official language (or at least one of the official languages) of the State responsible for their formal education.
3. All persons have the right to special assistance in order to overcome illiteracy or other forms of language handicap.
4. All persons have the right to learn languages of their own choosing.
5. All persons have the right to freedom of expression in any language.
6. All young persons have the right to be taught the language with which they and their family most readily identify. .
7. All persons have the right to be taught the official language (or at least one of the official languages) of the State in which they permanently reside.

8. All persons have the right to be taught at least one additional language in order to extend their social, cultural, educational and intellectual horizons and promote understanding between people from other cultures and nations.
9. The right to use a language, speak, read or write a language, to learn, teach or access a language, may not be wilfully suppressed or prohibited.

Addendum

Provision for those persons to whom these rights have so far not applied should be made through home, community, secondary, further, adult or higher education.

---

21. Towards equality and self-reliance

Resolution of the XI WFD World Congress
The Xl World Congress of the World Federation of the Deaf, which was held in Tokyo, Japan, from 5 to 11 July 1991, attracted more than 7,000 people from 69 countries. The Congress Resolution is a summary of the work carried out by 9 Scientific Commissions and 3 Non-Scientific Sections during the Congress.

In every country there are deaf persons who use sign language for communication. The foundation upon which a deaf person develops his/her abilities and makes full use of his/her human resources is sign language. With sign language human rights, self-reliance and equal opportunities can become a reality. Therefore the World Federation of the Deaf calls on national associations of the Deaf, other organizations, institutions, and individuals to join their efforts with the United Nations system, governments and other decision-makers for the recognition of indigenous Sign languages in all countries. The use of sign language in deaf education is of vital importance. Equally important is that deaf adults are involved in order to reach this goal. The WFD calls on the United Nations for the inclusion of recognition of sign language in the final document marking the end of the United Nations Decade of Disabled Persons and World Programme of Action Concerning Disabled Persons to the year 2000 and beyond.

Following the theme of the Congress, Equality and Self-Reliance, we urge that the following measures are taken:
1. Taking into account that the first three years are the most important ones for a child's language development children under school-age must have the opportunity to grow up in an environment using sign language and hearing parents must be provided counselling services and instruction in the use of sign language. All nations are reminded that the United Nations Convention on the Rights of Children also applies to deaf children.
2. Deaf children need separate schools where sign language and Deaf culture have a prominent role. They also need qualified Deaf teachers and other staff members as role models. This way it will be possible to raise the quality of deaf education. It is necessary to reach the same level as in schools for hearing children. If deaf children are given the opportunity to fully develop their learning abilities in various subjects they will have the possibility to study at university level and also have a wider choice of job opportunities. Sign language should be included in the curricula and used in teaching other subjects in order for the

children to become bilingual or multilingual. Another goal should be a working knowledge of the national written language and foreign languages.

3. Deaf persons with mental health problems, the elderly deaf, the deafblind, and deaf persons with multiple disabilities should be provided special services in sign language and be encouraged to join the Deaf community.

4. Deaf professionals, such as teachers, medical doctors, psychologists, social workers, engineers, technicians, and specialists in communication, spiritual care, deaf arts and culture as well as researchers at university level will be needed for deaf persons to make use of the services offered by society to the public. Full participation in society requires that sign language interpreting services are provided free of charge for deaf persons. For this purpose, training programmes for sign language interpreters must be created, so that deaf persons have access to all public services and can participate in politics, economics and the societal life as equals with other citizens.

5. Deaf persons have the right to get all the information available to all citizens and they have the responsibility to give information to the hearing community. The use of modern technology makes possible extensive interaction based on sign language, sub-titles, and other visual means. It also makes possible the standardization of telecommunication applications and emergency alarm systems for the use of deaf persons. Even the Universal Declaration of Human Rights calls for such technical applications: nations are responsible for providing information; no-one should be left outside society.

6. Welfare is not equally distributed on earth. About 80 percent of all deaf persons in the world still get no education. Very many deaf persons are unemployed, their human rights are violated, and their dignity not respected. More resources must be allocated to developing countries in particular. Resources are specially needed for sign language development, raising the amount and level of deaf education, and for support to national Deaf associations, and engaging Deaf experts in this work.

7. Deaf persons in countries which have officially recognized Sign Languages should help deaf persons in countries where sign language is rejected, assisting them in finding their cultural identity, i. e. their human resources, and arranging leadership training programmes so they can take full responsibility for themselves and for other people. All over the world, deaf persons should be given the opportunity to research into their own language and culture and to participate in their promotion. They should also take part in the preservation of universal cultural heritage. Given every chance to rule over their own lives — in harmony with the environment — and given the freedom to choose even deaf persons will gain Equality and Self-Reliance.

22. World Federation of the Deaf calls for recognition of sign languages

The Xl World Congress of the WFD which was held in Tokyo, Japan, in 1991 adopted the above recommendations as an official position paper of the WFD.

The WFD Commission on Sign Language puts forward the following recommendations:

1. We recommend that the WFD call for the recognition of sign languages and of the right to use sign languages around the world.

A. This calls on every government to propose (if not already implemented) official recognition of the sign language(s) used by deaf people in their country as one of the country's indigenous languages.

B. This calls on every government to abolish any remaining obstacles to the use of sign language as the primary and everyday language of deaf people.

2. We recommend that the WFD call for the right of deaf children to have full early exposure to sign language, and to be educated as bilinguals or multilinguals with regard to reading and writing.

A. A sign language should be recognized and treated as the first language of a deaf child.

a) The sign language in question must be the national sign language, that is, the natural sign language of the adult Deaf community in that region.

b) In order for deaf children to acquire their first language early and with full fluency, they must be guaranteed the right to be exposed to sign language early in life, in a environment which includes highly skilled signers.

B. Deaf children have the right to be educated, particularly with regard to reading and writing, in a bilingual (or multilingual) environment.

a) The national sign language should be the language of instruction for most academic subjects.

b) Instruction in the national spoken and written languag should occur separately but in parallel, as is common in bilingual/multilingual educational programs for other languages.

C. Sign language teaching programs should be established and further developed for parents and personnel working with deaf children.

D. Teachers of the deaf must be expected to learn and use the accepted natural sign language as the primary language of instruction.

E. In order to achieve A.-D. above, the national sign language must be included as an academic subject in the curriculum of programs for the deaf, including both the programs which deaf students attend and the programs which train teachers of the deaf.

3. We recommend that the WFD call for substantially increased government support for research on the native sign languages, with fluent deaf users of sign language prominently included at every level.

A. Research on sign language must be established at universities, research institutes, and educational institutions in every country.

B. Because deaf individuals are the primary fluent users of sign language, Deaf individuals and national Deaf associations must be closely involved with the research and its dissemination.

a) Deaf individuals who are fluent native users of their national sign language should be recognized as the legitimate arbiters in the correct usage of the indigenous sign language and should hold significant positions in research efforts.

b) Funds must be provided for advanced training of deaf individuals in sign language research, so that adequate numbers of Deaf researchers are available.

c) Deaf individuals should be encouraged to attend meetings concerning sign language in national and international settings.

C. Research findings should be disseminated to deaf people around the world, through the national Deaf associations, as well as through other means which will inform Deaf people about research on their languages.

D. Research findings on sign language should be used to guide the teaching of sign language, the training of interpreters, and the training of parents and professionals. Training and teaching programs established for these purposes should be encouraged to combine research with training and teaching.

4. We recommend that the WFD call for massive expansion of sign language instruction in every country.

A. Programs offering sign language instruction must be available to all of the following groups:

a) Relatives and friends of deaf children.

b) All professionals working with deaf children and adults.

c) Deaf people with no prior knowledge of sign language.

d) Deafened and severely hard of hearing individuals with poor lipreading skills.

B. Programs offering broader training in sign language studies must be available to the above groups, as well as to all deaf children, deaf adults, and teachers of the deaf. Sign language studies curricula should include training in the structure of natural sign languages, as well as in the culture of the Deaf communities in which these sign languages are used.

C. Training programs must be available for sign languag instructors, including both training in language instruction and broader academic training in sign language studies.

D. Specialized programs must be offered for those dealing with deaf-blind individuals.

E. All the above programs should be initially established in cooperation with the national organization of the Deaf to maximize the academic quality of the program. This cooperation and supervision should occur with governmental or non-governmental organizations according to the traditions each country.

5. We recommend that the WFD call for the right of all deaf individuals to have access to high quality interpreting between the spoken language of the hearing community and the sign language of the Deaf community. This in turn requires the establishment of qualified interpreter training programs, and the establishment of mechanisms in every country for making professional interpreters widely available to deaf individuals.

A. It must be recognized that sign language interpreters are the principal means by which deaf individuals gain access to the facilities, services, and information of the larger communities in which they live. Sign language interpreters are thus a crucial mechanism by which deaf individuals obtain equal access and opportunities as the hearing individual in any society.

B. Interpreting between sign language and spoken language must involve full translation between two different languages.

C. In order to fulfill A. and B. above, sign language interpreting must be recognized as a highly skilled profession requiring both extensive training and extensive and well-funded employment mechanisms. (See the recommendations from the Commission on Interpreting for further details.)

6. We recommend that the WFD call for Government support of widespread availability of the media through sign language.

A. Broadcasting authorities must include translation into sign language of TV news programs, programs of political interest, and to the extent possible, a selection of programs of cultural or general interest.

B. Broadcasting authorities must include sign language programs for deaf adults and children, and sign language teaching programs for the general public.

C. Written materials of the same types as described in A. and B. (e.g. newspapers, news or political documents and information) should be translated into sign language and made available in video form.

D. Support should be provided for the expansion of TV, video, film, and books which are developed in sign language (e g. sign language stories, drama, poetry) or which are about sign language (e.g. materials to inform the Deaf communities about their sign languages or materials to be used in teaching sign language).

WORLD FEDERATION OF THE DEAF
P.O.Box 65, SF-00401 HELSINKI, FINLAND
phone +358−0-58031, telefax +358−0-580 3770

---

23. "The Kurdish people — no future without human rights"

Bonn Declaration

The International Conference "The Kurdish People — No Future without Human Rights" took place from 27 to 28 September 1991 under the auspices of the Ministerpresident of Niedersachsen, Gerhard Schröder, in the Representation of the State of Niedersachsen to the Federation (Vertretung des Landes Niedersachsen beim Bund) in Bonn, Federal Republic of Germany.

The International Conference deliberated in depth on the situation of the Kurdish people. It calls on the goverments of Turkey, Iran, Iraq and Syria:

1. to recognize the existence of the Kurdish people and its right to self-determination and a life lived in freedom and dignity,

4. to recognize Kurdish as an official language and to promote its use in all areas of society, especially as a general language of instruction, in accordance with the Helsinki Documents,

11. The Conference appeals to the United Nations, the organs of the EC, and the Member States of the EC and the Council of Europe to act in solidarity with the Kurdish people and their legitimate struggle, and in the spirit of the demands of this Declaration,

12. and to make any form of political or economic cooperation with the states in which Kurds and other minorities are persecuted and oppressed dependent upon whether these states recognize fundamental human rights and the right to self-determination,

16. The Conference calls in particular on the European governments to recognize Kurdish immigrants and refugees as being a distinct people, to provide instruction in their mother tongue for Kurdish children in the schools, and to make it possible to broadcast in Kurdish on radio and television.

Consolidated bibliography

Abdoolcader, Levane
1989   *Sydney voices: a survey of languages other than English in catholic schools.*
        Sydney: Catholic Education Office.
Abou, Sélim
1989   "Fondements des politiques linguistiques", in: Pupier — Woehrling (eds.),
        21—34.
Ada, Alma Flor
1988   "The Pajaro Valley experience: Working with Spanish-speaking parents to
        develop children's reading and writing skills through the use of children's
        literature", in: Skutnabb-Kangas and Cummins (eds.), 223—238.
Adler, Max K.
1978   *Naming and addressing: A sociolinguistic study.* Hamburg: Helmut Buske
        Verlag.
Africa, Hugh
1980   *Language in education in a multilingual state: a case study of the role of English
        in the education system of Zambia.* Toronto: University of Toronto [Ph.D.
        dissertation].
Aguirre Beltrán, Gonzalo
1983   *Lenguas vernáculas.* Su uso y desuso en la enseñanza: la experiencia de México,
        Ediciones de la Casa Chata 20, México: CIESAS.
Akinnaso, F. Niyi
1991   "Toward the development of a multilingual language policy in Nigeria",
        Applied Linguistics 12:1, 29—61.
Alatis, James (ed.)
1978   *International dimensions of bilingual education.* Georgetown University Round
        Table Monograph, Washington, D. C.: Georgetown University Press.
Alatis, James E. — K. Twaddell (eds.)
1976   *English as a second language in bilingual education.* Washington, D. C.: TE-
        SOL.
Albó, Xavier
1988 a   "Bilingualism in Bolivia", in: Paulston (ed.), 85—108.
Albó, Xavier
1988 b   "El futuro de los idiomas oprimidos", in: Orlandi (ed.), 75—104.
Alderson, Charles J.
1984   "Reading in a foreign language: a reading problem or a language problem?"
        in: Alderson — Urquhart (eds.), 1—27.
Alderson, Charles J. — A. H. Urquhart (eds.)
1984   *Reading in a foreign language.* Harlow: Longman.
Alfredsson, Gudmundur
1989   "The United Nations and the rights of indigenous peoples", *Current Anthro-
        pology* 30:2, 255—259.
Alfredsson, Gudmundur
1991   "Minority rights: equality and non-discrimination", in: Krag et Yukhneva
        (eds.) 1991, 19—41.

Alisjahbana, S. Takdir
1990   "The teaching of English in Indonesia", in: Britton — Shafer — Watson
          (eds.) 1990, 315—327.
Allais, Maurice
1989   "(July 30) Europe's need to be multi-lingual", *The Guardian Weekly*, 14.
Alston, Philip
1991   "The legal framework of the Convention on the Rights of the Child", *UN
          Bulletin of Human Rights* 91/2, 1—15.
Alston, Philip (ed.)
1992   *The United Nations and human rights: a critical appraisal.* Oxford: Clarendon
          Press.
Amadio, Massimo
1987   "Caracterización de la educación bilingüe intercultural", in: Amadio — Varese
          — Picon (eds.), 19—25.
Amadio, Massimo
1987 a   "Políticas educativo-culturales en algunos países sudamericanos y México",
          in: Zúñiga et al (eds.), 21—30.
Amadio, Mássimo — Stefano Varese — César Picón (eds.)
1987 b   *Educación y pueblos indígenas en Centroamérica.* Santiago de Chile: UNESCO-
          OREALC.
Amadio, Massimo — Madeleine Zúñiga
1989   *La educación intercultural y bilingüe en Bolivia. Experiencias y propuestas.* La
          Paz: UNICEF-UNESCO.
América Indígena, México: Instituto Indigenista Interamericano.
Ammon, Ulrich (ed.)
1989   *Status and function of languages and language varieties.* Berlin: Walter de
          Gruyter.
Andreassen, Bård-Anders — Theresa Swinehart (eds.)
1993   *Human rights in developing countries.* Copenhagen, Lund, Oslo, Åbo/Turku:
          Nordic Human Rights Publications.
Andrýsek, Oldrich
1989   *Report on the definition of minorities.* Netherlands Institute of Human Rights,
          Studie-en Informatiecentrum Mensenrechten (SIM), SIM Special No 8.
An-naim, Abdullahi Ahmed — Francis M. Deng (eds.)
1990   *Human rights in Africa: Cross-cultural perspectives.* Washington, D. C.: The
          Brookings Institution.
Annamalai, E.
1986   " Comment: legal vs social", *International Journal of the Sociology of Lan-
          guage* 60, 145—151.
Annamalai, E.
1986   " A typology of language movements and their relation to language planning",
          in: Annamalai — Jernudd — Rubin (eds.) 1986, 6—17.
Annamalai, E.
1993   "Planning for language survival", *New Language Planning Newsletter* 8:1,
          1—2.
Annamalai, E. — Björn Jernudd — Joan Rubin (eds.)
1986   *Language planning, Proceedings of an Institute.* Mysore — Honolulu: Central
          Institute of Indian Languages and East-West Center.

Ansre, Gilbert
  1979   "Four rationalisations for maintaining European languages in education in
            Africa", *African Languages* 5/2, 10−17.
Appel, René
  1988   "The language education of immigrant workers' children in The Netherlands",
            in: Skutnabb-Kangas and Cummins (eds.), 57−78.
Appel, René − Pieter Muysken
  1987   *Language contact and bilingualism.* London: Edward Arnold.
Arana de Swadesh, Angelina et al
  1975   *Las lenguas de México I.* México: INAH.
Argemi, Aureli
  1991   "European recognition for Catalan", *Contact: Bulletin of the European Bureau
            for Lesser Used Languages* 8:1, 6.
Arizpe, Lourdes
  1988   "Pluralidad cultural y proyecto nacional", in: Stavenhagen (ed.), 69−74.
Asian Studies Council
  1988   *A national strategy for the study of Asia in Australia.* Canberra: Australian
            Government Publishing Service.
Ashby, Eric
  1966   *Universities: British, Indian, African, a study in the ecology of higher education.*
            Cambridge, MA.: Harvard University Press.
Aubague, Laurent et al
  1983   *Dominación y resistencia lingüística en Oaxaca.* Oaxaca: SEP-UBAJO.
Aubert, Vilhelm
  1978   *Den samiske befolkning i Nord-Norge* [The Sámi population in northern
            Norway]. Artikler fra statistisk sentralbyrå nr. 107, Oslo.
Aylwin Oyarzún, José
  1990   "Tierra mapuche: derecho consuetudinario y legislación chilena", in: Staven-
            hagen − Iturralde (eds.), 333−354.
Baetens Beardsmore, Hugo
  1990 a   "The multilingual school for mixed populations: a case study", in: Baetens
            Beardsmore 1990b, 1−51.
Baetens Beardsmore, Hugo
  1990 b   *Bilingualism in education: theory and practice.* Brussel/Bruxelles: Linguistic
            Circle og the Vrije Universiteit Brussel and the Université Libre de Bruxelles.
Baetens Beardsmore, Hugo
  1993   "The European School experience in multilingual education", Paper presented
            at 10th World Congress of Applied Linguistics, Symposium "Multilingualism
            for All" and written for the book *Multilingualism for all,* ed. by Tove
            Skutnabb-Kangas, in preparation.
Baetens Beardsmore, Hugo − J. Kohls
  1988   "Immediate pertinence in the acquisition of multilingual proficiency: the
            European Schools", *The Canadian Modern Language Review* 44, 2: 240−260.
Baetens Beardsmore, Hugo − Merrill Swain
  1985   "Designing bilingual education: aspects of immersion and "European School
            Models"", *Journal og Multilingual and Multicultural Development* 6, 1: 1−
            15.

Bain, Bruce — Agnes Yu
1978   "Towards an integration of Piaget and Vygotsky: a cross-cultural replication
            France, Germany, Canada concerning cognitive consequences of bilingual-
            ity", in: Paradis (ed.), 113—126.
Baker, Keith — Adriana De Kanter
1981   *Effectiveness of bilingual education: a review of the literature.* Washington,
            D. C.: Office of Planning and Budget, U. S. Department of Education.
Bamgbose, Ayo
1991   *Language and the nation: the language question in Sub-Saharan Africa.* Edin-
            burgh: Edinburgh Press, for the International African Institute.
Bamzsai, P. N. K.
1973   *A History of Kashmir.* New Delhi: Metropolitan Book Co.
Baran, Ute
1989   "Deportations: Tunceli Kanunlari", in: *Human rights in Kurdistan,* 110—116.
Barbiana, School of,
1970   *Letter to at teacher.* Harmondsworth: Penguin.
Barkin, Florence — Elisabeth A. Brandt — Jacob Ornstein-Galicia (eds.)
1982   *Bilingualism and languages in contact. Spanish, English, and native American
            languages.* New York: Teacher's College.
Barkowski, Hans — Gerd R. Hoff (hrsg)
1991   *Berlin Interkulturell.* Ergebnisse einer Berliner Konferenz zu Migration und
            Pädagogik. Berlin: Colloquium Verlag.
Baron, Dennis
1990   *The English-Only question: an official language for Americans?* New Haven:
            Yale University Press.
Barth, Frederik (ed.)
1969   *Ethnic groups and boundaries.* Oslo: Universitetsforlaget.
Bartolomé, Miguel Alberto
1989   "Nación y etnias en Paraguay", in: *América Indígena* XLIX, 3: 405—418.
Bastarache, Michel et al. (ed.)
1987   *Language rights in Canada.* Montréal: Yvon Blais Inc..
Bedir Khan, Emir Djeladet — Roger Lescot
1970   *Grammaire kurde (Dialecte Kurmandji).* Paris.
Besikci, Ismail
1990   "A Nation Deprived of Identity: The Kurds, Report to Minority Rights
            Conference", in: *Minority rights, policies and practice in South-East Europe.*
Bethell, Tom
1979   "Against bilingual education", *Harper's,* February.
Bettoni, C. (ed.)
1986   *Italians abroad — Altro-Polo.* Sydney: University of Sydney.
Black, Peter
1979   *Status of Australian Languages.* Canberra: Australian Institute of Aboriginal
            Studies.
Blaine, Carl P.
1974   "Breaking the language barrier: New rights for California's linguistic minor-
            ities", *Pacific Law Journal* 5: 648—674.

Boletím Jurídico 1: 5 1989.
Bonfil, Guillermo (ed.)
1981   *Utopía y revolución. El pensamiento político de los indios en América Latina.*
            México: Editorial Nueva Imagen.
Boston, Ken
1989   Address delivered at a seminar on "Future Directions of Multiculturalism
            and Ethnic Affairs in South Australia", Adelaide, October 16.
Boudoin, Jean-Claude — Claude Masse
1973   Étude comparative et évolutive des droits linguistiques en Belgique et en
            Suisse, Étude E15, la commission d'enquête sur la situation de la langue
            française et sur les droits linguistiques au Québec, Québec: l'éditeur officiel
            du Québec.
Boyd, Sally
1985   *Language survival. A study of language contact, language shift and language
            choice in Sweden.* Gothenburg Monographs in Linguistics 6, Gothenburg:
            University of Gothenburg.
Bozarslan, Mehmet Emin
1968   *Alfabe.* Istanbul [banned and burned; republished in Sweden in 1980].
Braën, André
1987   "Language rights", in: Bastarache (ed.), 3 — 63.
Bremen Declaration on the human rights in Kurdistan,
1989   in: *Human rights in Kurdistan,* 231 — 233.
Britton, James
1970   "Their language and our teaching", *English in Education* 4, 2: 5 — 13.
Britton, James — Robert E. Shafer — Ken Watson (eds.)
1990   *Teaching and learning English worldwide.* Clevedon: Multilingual Matters.
Brudnoy, D.
1990   "The scandalous obstructionism of bilingual ed." *Human Events,* July 14,
            590 — 591.
Bruner, Jerome
1976   "Language as an instrument of thought", in: Davies (ed.).
Brunot, Ferdinand
1967   Histoire de la langue française des origines à nos jours, tome IX, La révolution
            et l'empire. Paris: Armand Colin.
Bucak, Ali
1989   "The Turkish Penal Code and the Kurds", in: *Human rights in Kurdistan,*
            122 — 133.
Bucak, Sertaç
1989   "The right of self-determination and the Kurdish question", in: *Human rights
            in Kurdistan,* 167 — 179.
Bucak, Sertaç
1990   "Violations of human rights in Turkish Kurdistan, Report to Minority Rights
            Conference 1990", in: *Minority rights, policies and practice in South-East
            Europe.*
Bucak, Sertaç
1991   "The linguistic human rights of the Kurds in Turkey", Paper at the Conference
            "Linguistic rights of the minorities", University of Lapland, Rovaniemi,
            Finland, 30 May -1 June 1991.

Bucak, Sertaç (ed.)
1993   *Das Kurdische Volk — keine Zukunft ohne Menschenrechte.* Bremen: Internationaler Verein für Menschenrechte in Kurdistan.
Bull, W. E.
1955   "Review of UNESCO 1953", *International Journal of American Linguistics* 21, 288–294.
Butler, R. E. "Rusty"
1985   *On creating a Hispanic America: A nation within a nation?* Washington". D. C.: Council for Inter-American Security.
Cahn, Edgar S. — W. Hearne (eds.)
1969   *Our brother's keeper: the Indian in white America.* New York: New Community Press.
California State Department of Education
1981   *Schooling and language minority students: a theoretical framework.* Evaluation, Dissemination and Assessment Center, California State University, Los Angeles.
California State Department of Education
1983   *Basic principles for the education of language minority students. An overview.* Sacramento: California State Department of Education.
Calvet, Louis-Jean
1974   *Linguistique et colonialisme: petit traité de glottophagie.* Paris: Payot.
Calvet, Louis-Jean
1987   *La guerre des langues et les politiques linguistiques.* Paris: Payot.
Camartin, Iso
1985   [1982] Les relations entre les quatre régions linguistiques, in: Schläpfer *et alii* (eds.), 253–284.
Camartin, Iso
1989   [1985] *Rien que des mots? Plaidoyer pour les langues mineures.* Genève: Zoé.
Canada [Government of]
1988   *Loi sur le multilinguisme Canadien.* Ministère du Multiculturalisme et de la Citoyenneté, Ottawa.
Candelier, Michel
1990   "Langues et Droits de l'Homme: convergence ou divergence", *Les langues modernes* 2, 9–14.
Capotorti, Francesco
1979 a   *Étude des personnes appartenant aux minorités ethniques, religieuses et linguistiques.* New York: Nations Unies.
Capotorti, Francesco
1979 b   *Study of the rights of persons belonging to ethnic, religious and linguistic minorities.* New York: United Nations.
Carneiro da Cunha, Manuela
1987   *Os direitos do índio.* Sao Paulo: Ediçoes Loyola.
Carneiro da Cunha, Manuela
1990   "El concepto de derecho consuetudinario y los derechos indígenas en la nueva Constitución de Brasil", in: Stavenhagen — Iturralde (eds.), 299–314.
Carrasco, Robert
1981   "Expanded awareness of student performance: a case study in applied ethnographic monitoring in a bilingual classroom", in: Trueba — Guthrie — Au (eds.), 153–177.

Castellanos Guerrero, Alicia
1990   "Para una propuesta de autonomía de las regiones étnicas de México", *Alteridades. Anuario de Antropología 1990*, México: UAM 139–155.
Cathomas, Bernard
1988   "Les Grisons canton trilingue", in: Institut National Genevois (ed.).
Cavalcanti, Marilda — Rainer Enrique Hamel(eds.)
        Educación indígena en América Latina. Campinas-México: UNICAMP-UAM, forthcoming.
Cavalcanti, Marilda — Rainer Enrique Hamel — Tereza M. Maher
1989   *Projeto Guaraní Educaçao indígena bilingue bicultural (Currículum e formaçao do professor índio).* Campinas, ms.
Cazden, Courtney B. — Catherine Snow (eds.)
1990   *English plus: Issues in bilingual education.* Newbury Park, Ca: Sage.
Cawson, Frank
1975   "The international activities of the Center for Applied Linguistics", in: Fox (ed.), (volume 2), 385–434.
Census of India,
1971   CCXL: ii, Vol. 1, Part 11 C (ii).
Center for Applied Linguistics
1977   *Bilingual education: current perspectives. Volume 3. Law.* Arlington: Center for Applied Linguistics.
Centre of African Studies
1986   *Language in education in Africa*, Seminar proceedings 26, proceedings of a seminar at the Centre of African Studies. University of Edinburgh, 29–30 November, 1985, Edinburgh: Centre of African Studies.
Ceri/ecalp/83.03
1983   *Education and cultural and linguistic pluralism (ecalp) country surveys: Finland.* Paris: OECD, Centre for Educational Research and Innovation.
Cerron-Palomino, Rodolfo
1989   "Language policy in Perú a historical overview", *International Journal of the Sociology of Language* 77: 11–34.
Chaliand, Gerard (ed.)
1980   *People without a country. The Kurds and Kurdistan.* London: Zed Press.
Chavkin, Samuel
1991   "Don't whitewash Chile's '73 coup", *The New York Times*, Tuesday, March 12, p. A22.
Cheshire, Jenny (ed.)
1991   *English around the world: sociolinguistic perspectives.* Cambridge: Cambridge University Press.
Chishimba, Maurice M.
1981   "Language teaching and literacy: East Africa". *Annual Review of Applied Linguistics*, II, 168–188.
Chomsky, Noam
1987   *On power and ideology: The Managua lectures.* Boston: South End Press.
Chomsky, Noam — Edward Herman
1979   *The Washington connection and third world fascism: The political economy of human rights. Volume 1.* Montreal: Black Rose Books.

Cifuentes, Bárbara — Rainer Enrique Hamel — Luis Fernando Lara
1990   "Práctica lingüística y derechos indígenas. Propuesta de la Asociación Mexicana de Lingüística Aplicada A. C. (AMLA)", in: Marco del Pont (ed.) 1990, 63—66.
Cingranelli, David L. (ed.)
1988   *Human rights: theory and measurement.* Basingstoke: Macmillan.
Clarke, Mark — Jean Handscombe (eds.)
1983   *On TESOL '82. Pacific perspectives on language learning and teaching.* Washington, DC: TESOL.
Clason, Elin — Mahmut Baksi
1979   *Kurdistan. Om förtryck och befrielsekamp. [Kurdistan: On oppression and liberation struggle]* Stockholm: Arbetarkultur.
Clyne, Michael
1982   *Multilingual Australia.* Melbourne: River Seine.
Clyne, Michael
1985   *Australia — meeting place of languages.* Canberra: Pacific Linguistics, Australian National University.
Clyne, Michael (ed.)
1986   *An early start. Second language at primary school.* Melbourne: River Seine Publications.
Clyne, Michael
1988   "Community languages in the home: a first progress report", *Vox* 1, 22—27.
Clyne, Michael
1991   *Community languages. The Australian experience.* Cambridge, New York, Port Chester, Melbourne — Sydney: Cambridge University Press.
Cobarrubias, Juan
1983   "Ethical issues in status planning", in: Cobarrubias — Fishman (eds.), 41—85.
Cobarrubias, Juan — Joshua A. Fishman (eds.)
1983   *Progress in language planning: international perspectives.* Berlin Mouton.
Colonna, Fanny
1975   *Instituteurs algériens: 1883—1939.* Alger: Office des publications universitaires.
Comisión de Autonomía
1987   *Autonomía: rescate de la unidad nacional.* Managua: Comisión de Autonomía.
Comissão Pro-Indio
1981   *A questao da educação indígena.* Sao Paulo: Editora Brasilense.
Committee of Review of the Australian Institute of Multicultural Affairs,
1983   *Report.* Canberra: Australian Government Printing Service.
Commonwealth Advisory Committee on the Teaching of Asian Languages and Cultures (*Auchmuty Report*)
1970   Canberra: Australian Government Printing Service.
Commonwealth Department of Education,
1987   *National policy on languages* (Lo Bianco Report). Canberra: Australian Government Publishing Service.
Conversi, Daniele
1990   "Language or race? The choice of core values in the development of Catalan and Basque nationalisms", *Ethnic and Racial Studies* 13, 1: 50—70.

Corvalán, Graziella
1989   "Bilingüismo y rendimiento educativo en Paraguay", *América Indígena* XLIX, 3: 581–604.
Coulmas, Florian (ed.)
1984   *Linguistic minorities and literacy. Language policy issues in developing countries.* Berlin, New York, Amsterdam: Mouton.
Coulmas, Florian (ed.)
1991   *A language policy for the European Community: Prospects and quandaries.* Berlin: Mouton de Gruyter.
Council of Europe, Standing Conference of Local and Regional Authorities,
1989   (March 15–17), Resolution 192 (1988), (Adopted March 16 1988) Doc CPL (23), 8 Part I, presented by the Committee on Cultural and Social Affairs, Raporteur, H. Kohn).
Council of Europe
1991   *Charte Européenne des Langues Régionales ou Minoritaires,* Comité ad hoc d'experts sur les langues régionales ou minoritaires en Europe, Strasbourg [24–25. 04. 91].
Craig, John
1990   *Comparative African experiences in implementing educational policies.* (World Bank Discussion Papers, Africa Technical Department Series, 83) Washington, D. C.: World Bank.
Crandall, Susan Emlet
1992   "Speaking freely: a constitutional right to language", *The CATESOL Journal* 5, 2: 7–18.
Crawford, James
1989   *Bilingual education: History, politics, theory, and practice.* Trenton, NJ: Crane Publishing Co..
CSCE
1990   *Document of the Copenhagen meeting of the conference on the human dimension of the CSCE.* Copenhagen [no publisher].
CSCE
1990   *Charter of Paris for a New Europe,* 16 November 1990/version 2. [no place, no publisher].
Cubberly, Elwood
1909   *Changing conceptions of American education.* Boston: Houghton Mifflin Company.
Cummins, Jim
1984 a   "Wanted: A theoretical framework for relating language proficiency to academic achievement among bilingual students", in: Rivera (ed.), 2–19.
Cummins, Jim
1984 b   "Bilingualism and cognitive development and the minority language child", in: Shapson — D'oyley, 71–92.
Cummins, Jim
1984 c   *Bilingualism and special education: issues in assessment and pedagogy.* Clevedon: Multilingual Matters.
Cummins, Jim
1987   *Empowering minority students.* Toronto: Ontario Institute for Studies in Education.

Cummins, Jim
   1987   "Theory and Policy in Bilingual Education", *Multicultural Education* (Centre
             for Educational Research and Innovation (CERI)), Paris: Organization for
             Economic Cooperation and Development.
Cummins, Jim
   1988   "From multicultural to anti-racist education An analysis of programmes and
             policies in Ontario", in: Skutnabb-Kangas − Cummins (eds.), 127−157.
Cummins, Jim
   1989 a   "Language and literacy acquisition in bilingual contexts", *Journal of Multi-
             lingual and Multicultural Development* 10, 1: 17−32.
Cummins, Jim
   1989 b   *Empowering minority students*. Sacramento: California Association for Bilin-
             gual Education.
Cummins, Jim
   1991   "Forked tongue: The politics of bilingual education: a critique", *Canadian
             Modern Language Review* 47, 4: 786−793.
Cummins, Jim − Marcel Danesi
   1990   *Heritage Languages. The development and denial of Canada's linguistic re-
             sources*. Montréal: Our Schools/Our Selves Education Foundation.
Cummins, Jim − Merrill Swain
   1986   *Bilingualism in education*. Harlow: Longman.
Dalby, David
   1985   "The life and vitality of African languages: a charter for the future", in:
             Mateene − Kalema − Chomba (eds.), 29−34.
Davidson, Basil
   1992   *The black man's burden. Africa and the curse of the nation-state*. London:
             James Currey.
Davies, Alan (ed.)
   1976   *Problems of language and learning*. London: Heinemann.
Dejean, Yves
   1983   "Diglossia revisited, French and Creole in Haiti", *Word* 34, 3: 189−213.
Deloria, Vine (ed.)
   1985   *American Indian policy in the twentieth century*. Norman, OK: University of
             Oklahoma Press.
Denison, Norman
   1977   "Language death or language suicide?" *International Journal of the Sociology
             of Language* 12: 13−22.
Department of Education and Science (U. K.),
   1989   (May 19), *Education Reform Act 1988: Modern and foreign languages in the
             national curriculum*. London, Circular No.9/89.
Department of Employment, Education and Training (DEET)
   1990   *The language of Australia: discussion paper on an Australian literacy and
             language policy for the 1990s*, Vol. I. Canberra.
Department of Immigration, Local Government and Ethnic Affairs
   1991   "The changing profiles of ethnic communities", *Migration* 84, 10−11.

Desheriyev, Y. (ed.)

1982   *Jazyk v razvitom socialističeskom obščestve. Jazykove problemy razvitija sistemy massovoj kommunikacii v SSSR* [Language in developed socialist society; language problems in the development system in the mass media in the USSR]. Moscow: Nauka.

De Vreede, Erik

1991   "Education in plural societies: an attempt to develop a conceptual framework for the discussion of intercultural education", in: Barkowski — Hoff (eds.) 1991, 151–158.

De Witte, Bruno

1989   "Droits fondamentaux et protection de la diversité linguistique", in: Pupier — Woehrling (eds.), 85–101.

Díaz-Polanco, Héctor

1988   *La cuestión étnico-nacional.* México: Fontamara.

Díaz-Polanco, Héctor

1989   "Etnias y democracia nacional en América Latina", *América Indígena* XLIX, 1: 35–56.

Díaz-Polanco, Héctor

1990   "Los pueblos indios y la Constitución", *México Indígena* 15: 9–13.

Díaz Müller, Luis

1991   "Las minorías étnicas en sistemas federales ¿Autodeterminación o autonomía?", in: Instituto de investigaciones jurídicas (ed.), 47–80.

Dittmar, Norbert — Brigitte Schlieben-Lange (eds.)

1982   *Die Soziolinguistik in den romanischsprachigen Ländern — La sociolinguistique dans les pays de langue romane.* Tübingen: Narr.

Dittrich, Eckhard J. — Frank-Olaf Radtke (eds.)

1990   *Ethnizität. Wissenschaft und Minderheiten.* Opladen: Westdeutscher Verlag.

Djité, Paulin G.

1990   "Les langues africaines dans la francophonie", *Language problems and language planning* 14: 1, 20–32.

Dolson, David — Kathryn Lindholm

1993   "World class education for children in California: a comparison of the bilingual/immersion and European School Model", Paper presented at 10th World Congress of Applied Linguistics, Symposium "Multilingualism for all" and written for the book *Multilingualism for all*, ed. by Tove Skutnabb-Kangas, in preparation.

Dormon, James

1981   "Ethnicity in contemporary America", *Journal of American Studies,* 15, 325–339.

Dostal, P.

1989   *Regional interests and the national question under Gorbachev, Nationalism in the USSR. Problems of nationalities.* Amsterdam: Second World Center.

Drobizheva, L.

1984   *Nõukogude rahva vaimne ühtsus* [The mental unity of the Soviet people]. Tallinn: Perioodika.

Duff, Patricia A.
1991   "Innovations in foreign language education: an evaluation of three Hungar-
          ian-English dual-language schools", *Journal of Multilingual and Multicultural
          Development* 12, 6: 459–476.
Dunn, Lloyd
1987   *Bilingual Hispanic children on the U. S. mainland: A review of research on their
          cognitive, linguistic, and scholastic development.* Circle Pines, Minnesota:
          American Guidance Service.
Eckert, Penelope
1981   "L'imposition de la diglossie", *Lengas*, Montpéllier, 9, 1–8.
Eide, Asbjørn
1990 a   *Possible ways and means of facilitating the peaceful and constructive solution
          of problems involving minorities.* Progress report submitted to Sub-Commis-
          sion on Prevention of Discrimination and Protection of Minorities at its 42nd
          session (e/CN.4/Sub.2/1990/46).
Eide, Asbjørn
1990 b   *Preliminary report* submitted to Sub-Commission on Prevention of Discrim-
          ination and Protection of Minorities at its 43rd session (e/CN.4/Sub.2/1991/
          43).
Ekka, Francis
1984   "Status of minority languages in the schools of India", *International Education
          Journal* 1, 1: 1–19.
Erdem, Mahmut – Tove Skutnabb-Kangas
1980   "Rätten till eget språk. Kurder i Norden vill ha undervisning i kurdiska"
          [The right to one's own language. The Kurds in the Nordic countries want
          instruction in Kurdish], *Audhumla* 4, Copenhagen: Nordic Cultural Secretar-
          iat.
Escobar, Alberto
1975   "¿Qué significa la oficialización del quechua?", in: Escobar – Matos Mar –
          Alberti, 59–106.
Escobar, Alberto
1983   "Fundamentos lingüísticos y pedagógicos de la enseñanza de una segunda
          lengua en poblaciones indígenas", in: Rodriguez et al (eds.), 315–340.
Escobar, Alberto
1988   "Lingüística y política", in: Orlandi (ed.), 11–26.
Escobar, Alberto – José Matos Mar – Giorgio Alberti,
1975   *Perú ¿País bilingüe?* Lima: Instituto de Estudios Peruano.
Espinosa, Aurelio Macedonio
1911   *The Spanish language in New Mexico and Southern Colorado.* Santa Fe, NM:
          New Mexico Publishing Company.
Estrada, H. M.
1986   " 'Pajaro experience' teaches parents how to teach kids", *Santa Cruz Sentinel*,
          Friday October 31, p. A4.
European Parliament Working Documents, *Document* 1–83/84, Brussels: European Com-
          munities.
Fanon, Frantz
1952   *Peau noire, masques blancs.* Paris: Seuil.

Fesl, Eve D.
1988   "Language loss in Australian languages", Paper presented to the Conference
          on the Maintenance and Loss of Minority Languages, Institute of Applied
          Linguistics, University of Nijmegen, The Netherlands.
FIPLV
1993   *Language policies for the world of the twenty-first century: Report for
          UNESCO.* World Federation of Modern Language Associations.
Firth, J. R.
1961   "The study and teaching of English at home and abroad", in: Wayment (ed.),
          11–21.
Fishman, Joshua A.
1964   "Language maintenance and language shift as fields of inquiry", *Linguistics*
          9, 32–70.
Fishman, Joshua A.
1967   "Bilingualism with and without diglossia; diglossia with and without bilin-
          gualism", *Journal of Social Issues*, XXIII, 2: 29–38.
Fishman, Joshua A.
1976   "Bilingual education: What and why?" in: Alatis – Twaddell (eds.), 263–272.
Fishman, Joshua A.
1980   "Bilingualism and biculturalism as individual and societal phenomena", *Jour-
          nal of Multilingual and Multicultural Development* 1, 1: 3–15.
Fishman, Joshua A.
1982   "Whorfianism of the third kind: Ethnolinguistic diversity as a worldwide
          societal asset", *Language in Society* 11: 1–14.
Fishman, Joshua A.
1984   "Minority mother tongues in education", *Prospects*, 14, 1: 51–61. Paris:
          UNESCO.
Fishman, Joshua A.
1987   "Language spread and language policy for endangered languages", in: Lowen-
          berg (ed.), 1–15.
Fishman, Joshua A.
1989   *Language and ethnicity in minority sociolinguistic perspective.* Clevedon –
          Philadelphia: Multilingual Matters.
Fishman, Joshua A.
1991   *Reversing language shift.* Clevedon, Avon: Multilingual Matters.
Fishman, Joshua, A (ed.)
1972   *Advances in the sociology of language*, Vol. 2. The Hague: Mouton.
Fishman, Joshua A. (ed.)
1974   *Advances in language planning.* The Hague: Mouton.
Fishman, Joshua A. – Charles A. Ferguson – Jyotirindra Das Gupta (eds.)
1968   *Language problems of developing nations.* New York: Wiley.
Foster, Charles
1980   "The unrepresented nations", in: Foster (ed.), 1–7.
Foster, Charles (ed.)
1980   *Nations without a state: ethnic minorities in Western Europe.* New York:
          Praeger.

426   *Consolidated bibliography*

Fox, Melvyn (ed.)
1975   *Language and development: a retrospective survey of Ford Foundation projects, 1952–1974.* New York: Ford Foundation (volume 1, Report; volume 2, Case studies).
Fraser, Malcolm
1981   "Inaugural address on multiculturalism", delivered to the Institute of Multicultural Affairs, Melbourne, November 30.
Fuad, Kemal
1988   "Die Kurdische Widerstandsliteratur", in: Mönch-Bucak (ed.), 22–29.
Fuchs, Estelle — Robert J. Havinghurst
1972   *To live on this earth: American Indian education.* Garden City, NJ: Anchor Books.
Furer, Jean-Jacques
1991   *La germanisaziun en Surselva,* paper presented at the 3rd Scuntrada, Laax, Switzerland.
Gaiger, Julio M. G.
1989 a   *La conquista de las naciones indígenas en la Asamblea Nacional Constituyente del Brasil.* Lima: Centro de Investigación y Promoción Amazónica.
Gaiger, Julio M. G.
1989 b   *Direitos indígenas na Constituçao Brasileira de 1988.* Brasília: CIMI.
Galabawa, C. J.
1990   *Implementing educational policies in Tanzania.* (World Bank Discussion Papers, Africa Technical Department Series, 86) Washington, D. C.: World Bank.
Galarza, Ernesto — Hermán Gallegos — Julián Samora
1969   *Mexican-Americans in the Southwest* Santa Barbara. CA: McNally and Loftin Publishers.
Galtung, Johan
1980   *The true worlds: A transnational perspective.* New York: The Free Press.
García, Ofelia (ed.)
1991   *Bilingual education: Festschrift in honor of Joshua A. Fishman on the occasion of his 65th birthday.* Amsterdam — Philadelphia: John Benjamins.
Gaup, Johanne
1991   *Guovttegielalasvuohta Sis-Finnmarkku sami suohkaniin* [Bilingualism in Sámi councils in Inner Finnmark]. Guovdageaidnu: Sámi Instituhtta.
Gendron, Jean-Denis — Alain Pujiner — Richard Vigneault (eds.)
1982   *Identité culturelle approches méthodologiques.* Québec: CIRB-ICRB.
Genesee, Fred
1987   *Learning through two languages: studies of immersion and bilingual education.* Cambridge, MS: Newbury House.
Giles, Howard (ed.)
1977   *Language, ethnicity and intergroup relations.* London: Academic Press.
Giordan, Henri (ed.)
1992   *Les minorités en Europe: droits linguistiques et droits de l'homme.* Paris: Kimé.
Gleich, Utta von
1989   *Educación primaria bilingüe intercultural en América Latina.* Eschborn: GTZ.
Goffman, Ervin
1955   "On face-work: an analysis of ritual elements in social interaction", *Psychiatry* 18, 213–231.

Gomes de Matos, Francisco
1984 "A plea for a language rights declaration", *ALSED-FIPLV Newsletter* 34, 3.
Gonzales, Andrew (ed.)
1984 *Panagani*. Manila: Linguistic society of the Philippines.
González Gaudiano, Edgar
1988 "El desarrollo curricular de la educación básica indígena", paper presented to the *XVI Asamblea Nacional Plenaria del Consejo Nacional Técnico de la Educación*, México, ms.
Gordon, Milton M.
1964 *Assimilation of American life: the role of race, religion and national origin*. New York — Oxford: Oxford University Press.
Gordon, Milton M.
1981 "Models of pluralism", *Annals of the American Academy of Political and Social Sciences*, 454: 178—188.
Gorter, Durk — Jarich F. Hoekstra — Lammert G. Jansma — Jehannes Ytsma (eds.)
1991a *Fourth International Conference on Minority Languages, Volume 1*. Journal of Multilingual and Multicultural Development 11: 12.
Gorter, Durk — Jarich F. Hoekstra — Lammert G. Jansma — Jehannes Ytsma (eds.)
1991b *Fourth International Conference on Minority Languages*, Vol. 2: Western and Eastern European Papers. Clevedon: Multilingual Matters.
Grandguillaume, Gilbert
1990 "Language and legitimacy in the Maghreb", in: Weinsten (ed.), 150—166.
Grierson, Sir George A.
1919 *Linguistic survey of India*, Vol. 8, Part 2. Calcutte: Royal Asiatic Society.
Grin, François
1991 "The Estonian language law presentation with comments", *Language Problems and Language Planning* 15, 191—201.
Grin, François
1991 "Territorial multilingualism", *Linguistic Decisions,* 15, Washington: Center for the Humanities, University of Washington.
Grin, François
1992 "Towards a threshold theory of minority language survival", *Kyklos* 45, 69—97.
Grupo de Barbados (ed.)
1979 *Indianidad y descolonización en América Latina. Documentos de la segunda reunión de Barbados*. México: Editorial Nueva Imagen.
Guboglo, M. (ed.)
1989 *Čto delat'? V pojskax idei soveršenstvovanija mežnacional'nyx otnočenii v SSSR* [What to do? On research into ideas for optimalizing inter-ethnic relations in the USSR]. Moscow.
Guy, Gregory
1989 "International perspectives on linguistic diversity and language rights", *Language Problems and Language Planning,* 13, 45—53.
Haarmann, Harald
1991 "Monolingualism vs. selective multilingualism; On the future alternatives for Europe as it integrates in the 1990s". *Sociolinguistica* 5, 7—23.

Haberland, Hartmut — Carol Henriksen — Robert Phillipson — Tove Skutnabb-Kangas
1991   "Tak for mad! Om sprogæderi med dansk som livret" [Thanks for the meal!
        On linguistic cannibalism, with Danish as the favourite dish], in: Jørgensen
        (ed.), 111−138.
Hagman, Tom — Jouko Lahdenperä
1988   "9 years of Finnish medium education in Sweden — what happens afterwards?
        The education of immigrant and minority children in Botkyrka", in: Skut-
        nabb-Kangas — Cummins (eds.), 328−335.
Halliday, M. A. K.
1975   *Learning how to mean*. London: Edward Arnold.
Hamel, Rainer Enrique
1984   "Sociocultural conflict and bilingual education — the case of the Otomi
        Indians in Mexico", *International Social Science Journal* 99, 113−128.
Hamel, Rainer Enrique
1988 a *Sprachenkonflikt und Sprachverdrängung. Die zweisprachige Kommunikations-
        praxis der Otomi-Indianer in Mexico*. Bern, Frankfurt, Paris, New York:
        Verlag Peter Lang.
Hamel, Rainer Enrique
1988 b "Las determinantes socio-lingüísticas de la educación indígena bilingüe",
        Signos. Anuario de Humanidades 1988, UAM-I, México, 319−376.
Hamel, Rainer Enrique
1988 c "La política del lenguaje y el conflicto interétnico. Problemas de investigación
        sociolingüística", in: Orlandi (ed.), 41−73.
Hamel, Rainer Enrique
1989   "Politiques et droits linguistiques des minorités indiennes au Mexique:
        quelques aspects sociolinguistiques", in: Pupier — Woehrling (eds.), 445−456.
Hamel, Rainer Enrique
1990 a "Lenguaje y conflicto interétnico en el derecho consuetudinario y positivo",
        in: Stavenhagen — Iturralde (eds.), 205−230.
Hamel, Rainer Enrique
1990 b "Language development, literacy, and sociolinguistic acceptance in bilingual
        Indian education in Mexico", paper presented to the *IX World Congress of
        Applied Linguistics (AILA)*, Thessaloniki, 21. 4. 1990.
Hamel, Rainer Enrique
1990 c "Lengua nacional y lengua indígena en el proceso histórico de cambio. Teoría
        y metodología en el análisis sociolingüístico de los procesos de desplazamiento
        y resistencia", *Alteridades. Anuario de Antropología 1990*, México: UAM-I
        175−196.
Hamel, Rainer Enrique
1990 d "Derechos lingüísticos y reforma constitucional", in: Marco del Pont (ed.),
        81−85.
Hamel, Rainer Enrique — Yolanda Lastra de Suárez — Héctor Muñoz Cruz (eds.)
1988   *Sociolingüística latinoamericana*. Actas del 10o Congreso Mundial de Socio-
        logía. México: UNAM.
Hamel, Rainer Enrique — Héctor Muñoz Cruz
1982   "Conflit de diglossie et conscience linguistique dans des communautés in-
        diennes bilingues au Mexique", in: Dittmar — Schlieben-Lange (eds.)
        249−270.

Hamel, Rainer Enrique — Héctor Muñoz Cruz
1988   "Desplazamiento y resistencia de la lengua otomí el conflicto lingüístico en
          las prácticas discursivas y la reflexividad", in: Hamel — Lastra de Suarez —
          Muñoz Cruz (eds.), 101—146.
Hamel, Rainer Enrique — Héctor Muñoz Cruz et al
1989   *Adquisición del lenguaje y desarrollo académico de alumnos indígenas.* (Proyecto
          de investigación), México: UAM-I.
Hancock, Graham
1989   *Lords of poverty. The free-wheeling lifestyles, power, prestige and corruption
          of the multi-billion dollar aid business.* London: Macmillan.
Harley, Birgit — Patrick Allen — Jim Cummins — Merrill Swain
1990   *The development of second language proficiency.* Cambridge: Cambridge Uni-
          versity Press.
Harmstorf, Ian
1983   *Homburg, Robert, (1848—1912) and Hermann Robert (1874—1964), Austra-
          lian Dictionary of Biography, 1891—1939*, 9, 354—357.
Haselhuber, Jakob
1991   "Erste Ergebnisse einer empirischen Untersuchung zur Sprachsituation in der
          EG-Komission (Februar 1990)", *Sociolinguistica* 5, 37—50.
Hasenau, M.
1990   "Setting norms in the United Nations system: the draft Convention on the
          Protection of the Rights of All Migrant Workers and their Families in relation
          to ILO in Standards on Migrant Workers", *International Migration* XXVIII,
          2: 133—157.
Hassanpour, Amir
1989   *The language factor in national development: the standardization of the Kurdish
          language, 1918—1985.* University of Illinois at Urbana-Champaign [also 1992,
          Mellen Research University Press, CA].
Heath, Shirley Brice
1972   *Telling tongues. Language policy in Mexico. From colony to nation.* New York
          and London: Teachers College Press.
Heine, Bernd
1990   "Language policy in Africa", in: Weinstein (ed.), 167—184.
Helsinki Watch
1990   *Destroying ethnic identity. The Kurds of Turkey. An Update*, September 1990.
          New York — Washington, D. C..
Hernández Moreno, Jorge — Guzmán G. Alba
1982   "Trayectoria y proyección de la educación bilingüe y bicultural en México",
          in: Scanlon — Lezama Morfin (eds.), 83—109.
Hernández-Chávez, Eduardo
1978   "Language maintenance, bilingual education, and philosophies of bilingual-
          ism in the United States", in: Alatis (ed.), 527—50.
Hernández-Chávez, Eduardo
1979   "Meaningful bilingual bicultural education: A fairytale", in: Ortiz (ed.),
          48—57.
Hernández-Chávez, Eduardo
1988   "Language policy and language rights in the United States: Issues in bilin-
          gualism", in: Skutnabb-Kangas and Cummins (eds.) 45—56.

Hernández-Chávez, Eduardo
1990   "The role of suppressive language policies in language shift and language
          loss", *Estudios Fronterizos, Revista del Instituto de Investigaciones Sociales*,
          VII-VIII, 18–19: 123–135.
Hettne, Björn
1987   *Etniska konflikter och internationella relationer* [Ethnic conflicts and inter-
          national relations]. Stockholm: DEIFO.
Hettne, Björn
1990   *Development theory and the three worlds*. Harlow: Longman.
Hill, Jane H. – Kenneth C. Hill
1986   *Speaking Mexicano. Dynamics and syncretic language in Central Mexico*.
          Tucson: The University of Arizona Press.
Hilton, Anthony
1990   "Une perestroïka à la canadienne", *Le Devoir*, Montréal, June 8.
Hint, Mati
1990   " Vene keele mõjud eesti keelele 1383–1404" [The influence of the Russian
          language on the Estonian Language 1383–1404], *Akadeemia* 2: 7.
Hobsbawm, E. J.
1990   *Nations and nationalism since 1780: Programme, myth, reality*, Cambridge:
          Cambridge University Press.
Hodges, John
1982   "Fraser reaffirms multiculturalism", *Canberra Times*, October 25.
Hodson, J. A.
1902   *Imperialism, a study*, London: Allen and Unwin.
Hornberger, Nancy H.
1988   *Bilingual education and language maintenance. A southern Peruvian Quechua
          case*, Dordrecht: Foris Publication.
Hornberger, Nancy H.
1989   "Can Peru's rural schools be agents for Quechua language maintenance?",
          Journal of Multilingual and Multicultural Development 10, 2: 145–160.
Hornby, Peter (ed.)
1977   *Bilingualism: psychological, social and educational implications*. NY: Academic
          Press.
Horvath, Barbara
1986   *An investigation of class placement in New South Wales schools*, Sydney: Ethnic
          affairs commission. Short version available as VARBRUL Analysis in Applied
          Linguistics: a Case Study, *Australian Review of Applied Linguistics* 1987, 10,
          2: 59–67.
Horvath, Ronald – David Tait
1984   *Sydney ... a social atlas*. Canberra: Division of National Mapping and
          Australian Bureau of Statistics.
Hulstijn, Jan H. – Johan F. Matter (eds.)
1991   *Reading in two languages*. AILA Review 8, Amsterdam: Free University Press.
Human rights in Kurdistan
1989   *Documentation of the International Conference on Human rights in Kurdistan*,
          14–16 April 1989. Hochschule Bremen, Bremen: The Initiative for Human
          Rights in Kurdistan.

Human rights in Kurdistan
1990   *Silence is killing them*, Bremen: The Initiative for Human Rights in Kurdistan.
Hyltenstam, Kenneth — Åke Viberg (eds.)
    in press   *Progression and regression in language: sociocultural, neuropsychological and linguistic dimensions*. Cambridge: Cambridge University Press.
Illich, Ivan
1981   *Shadow work*. Boston and London: Marion Boyars.
Imhoff, Gary
1990   "The position of U. S. English on bilingual education", in: Cazden — Snow (eds.), 48−61, and *The Annals of the American Academy of Political and Social Science*, Vol. 508, March, 48−61.
India, Government of
1950   *The Constitution of India*. New Delhi: Ministry of Law.
Iniciativa de decreto que adiciona el artículo 4o. de la Constitución política de los Estados Unidos Mexicanos para el reconocimiento de los derechos culturales de los pueblos indígenas, México, 7. 12. 1990.
Inquiry into the Teaching of Asian Studies and Languages in Higher Education
1989   *Asia in Australian Higher Education*, (Ingelson Report), Submitted to Asian Studies Council. Canberra.
Institut National Genevois (ed.)
1988   *Majorités et minorités linguistiques en suisse*. Lausanne: L'âge d'homme.
Instituto de Investigaciones Juridicas (ed.)
1991   *Aspectos nacionales e internacionales sobre derecho indígena*. México: UNAM.
Iturralde, Diego
1989   "Movimiento indio, costumbre jurídica y usos de la ley", *América Indígena* XLIX, 2: 245−262.
IWGIA Yearbook 1989
1990   Copenhagen: IWGIA (International Workgroup for Indigenous Affairs).
Jaimes, M. Annette — Ward Churchill
1988   "Behind the rhetoric: "English Only" as counterinsurgency warfare", *Issues in Radical Therapy* 13, 1−2: 42−50.
Jansson, Jan-Magnus
1985   "Language legislation", in: Uotila (ed.), 77−89.
Jordan, Deirdre
1988   "Rights and claims of indigenous people. Education and the reclaiming of identity: the case of the Canadian natives, the Sami and Australian Aborigines", in: Skutnabb-Kangas — Cummins (eds.), 189−222.
Jupp, James
1988   *The Australian people: An encyclopedia of the nation, its people and their origins*. Sydney and London: Angus and Robertson.
Jørgensen, Jens Norman (ed.)
1991   *Det danske sprogs status år 2001. Er dansk et truet sprog?* [The status of the Danish language in the year 2001. Is Danish a threatened language?]. Copenhagen: Danmarks Lærerhøjskole.
Kachru, Braj B.
1969   "Kashmiri and other Dardic languages", in: Sebeok (ed.), 284−306.
Kachru, Braj B.
1986   *The alchemy of English: the spread, functions and models of non-native Englishes*. Oxford: Pergamon.

Kala, K.
1991   "Eesti tööstuse areng" [The development of Estonian industry], *Akadeemia*
             3: 12.
Kandimaa, R.
1981   "Rahvusliku enesetadvuse ideoloogilisest mõjutamisest 1970–1980 aastail"
             [The ideological influence of ethnic self-consciousness during the 1970s and
             1980s], *Eesti Kommunist*, 10: 64–71, 11: 33–42.
Kashoki, Mubanga E.
1989   "On the notion and implications of the concept of mother tongue in literacy
             education in a multilingual context: the case of Zambia", in: Zuanelli (ed.),
             3–14.
Kellerman, Eric – Mike Sharwood Smith(eds.)
1986   *Crosslinguistic influences in second language acquisition*. Oxford: Pergamon
             Press.
Kenyatta, Jomo
1979   *Facing Mount Kenya*, London: Heinemann.
Khanazarov, K.
1982   *Rešenie nacionalno-jazykovoj problemy v SSSR* [The solution of ethnolinguistic
             problems in the USSR]. Moscow: Nauka.
Khubchandani, Lachman M.
1963   *The acculturation of Indian Sindhi to Hindi: A study of Language in contact.*
             [Ph.D. dissertation, University of Pennsylvania]; Ann Arbor: University Mi-
             crofilm corporation (Abstract in *Linguistics; An International Review*, Vol 12,
             1965).
Khubchandani, Lachman M.
1969   "Equipping major languages for new roles", in: Poddar (ed.), 89–90.
Khubchandani, Lachman M.
1979   "A demographic typology for Hindi, Urdu, Panjabi speakers in South Asia",
             in: McCormack – Wurm (eds.), 183–194.
Khubchandani, Lachman M.
1981   Language privileges (Chapter IV); Squabbles among language-elites (Chapter
             V), in *Language, education, social justice*, Vol. 2, Pune: Centre for Commu-
             nication Studies.
Khubchandani, Lachman M.
1983   *Plural languages, plural cultures: communication, identity and sociopolitical
             change in Contemporary India.* An East-West Center Book. Honolulu: The
             University of Hawaii Press.
Khubchandani, Lachman M.
1986a   Identity and communication in plurilingual societies: a South Asian experi-
             ence, in: Lo Jacomo (ed.), 85–100.
Khubchandani, Lachman M.
1986b   Multilingual societies: Issues of identity and communication, *Sociolinguistics*
             XVI, 1: 20–34.
Khubchandani, Lachman M.
1989   "Diglossia and functional heterogenity", in: Ammon (ed.), 592–607.
Khubchandani, Lachman M.
1991   *Language, culture and nation-building: challenges of modernisation.* Shimla:
             Indian Institute of Advanced Study and Manohar Publications.

Klopčič, Vera
1992   "Le droit des langues dans l'ex-Yougoslavie", in: Giordan (ed.), 325 – 344.
Kloss, Heinz
1971   "The language rights of immigrant groups", *International Migration Review* 5, 250 – 268.
Kloss, Heinz
1977   *The American bilingual tradition.* Rowley. MA: Newbury House.
Konstantinov, Julian – Gulbrand Alhaug – Birgit Igla et al
1990   *Name behaviour of Pomaks in Bulgaria. A report of the findings of the field-study investigating the name behaviour of the Pomaks in the region of Zlataritza,* August 6 – 15, 1990. Sofia: Bulgarian Society for Regional Cultural Studies.
Koul, Maharaj K.
1986   *A sociolinguistic study of Kashmiri.* Patiala, India: Indian Institute of Language Studies.
Koul, Omkar N. – R. L. Schmidt
1983   *Kashmiri: a sociolinguistic survey.* Patiala, India: Indian Institute of Language Studies.
Kripalani, Acharya J. B.
1958   *Collected works of Mahatma Gandi: all men are brothers.* Ahmedabad: Navajivan.
Krag, H. – N. Yukhneva (eds.)
1991   *The Leningrad Minority Rights Conference. Papers.* Copenhagen: The Minority Rights Group.
Kulichenko, M.
1981   *Rascvet i sblizhenie nacii v SSSR* [The blossoming and convergence of nations in the USSR]. Moscow: Nauka.
Kummer, Werner
1985   "Probleme der Funktionserweiterung von Sprachen. Der Sprachausbau bei den Shuara in Ecuador", in: Rehbein (ed.), 121 – 149.
Kuutman, Alar
1984   *Om kurder [On Kurds].* Norrköping: Statens Invandrarverk.
Labov, William
1972 a   "Rules for ritual insults", in: Labov, 297 – 353.
Labov, William
1972 b   *Language in the Inner City.* Philadelphia: University of Pennsylvania Press.
Ladeira, María Inés
1981   *Os índios da Serra do Mar: A presença Mbya-Guaraní em São Paulo.* São Paulo: Nova Stella.
Laje, María Inés
1983   "Federación Shuar: un sistema alternativo de enseñanza", in: Rodríguez et al (ed.), 431 – 448.
Lambert, Wallace E.
1975   "Culture and language as factors in learning and education", in: Wolfgang (ed.).
Lambert, Wallace
1977   "The effects of bilingualism on the individual: cognitive and sociocultural consequences", in: Hornby (ed.), 15 – 27.

Lambert, Wallace E. — Richard G. Tucker
1972   *Bilingual education of children. The St.Lambert experiment.* Rowley, Mass.:
          Newbury House.
Lara, Luis Fernando
1987   "Une politique du langage échouée: la Comisión para la Defensa del Idioma
          Español du Mexique", in: Maurais (ed.), 317—358.
Lau, Hazel
1983   "Bases metodológicas para la educación bilingüe bicultural en Nicaragua",
          in: Rodríguez et al (eds.), 191—198.
Laurin, C.
1977   *Québec's Policy on the French Language.* Québec: L'éditeur officiel du Québec.
Lawson, Edwin D.
1987   *Personal names and naming: an annotated bibliography.* New York — London:
          Greenwood Press.
League of Nations
1929   *League of Nations Official Journal,* special supplement no. 73 of June 13th
          1929.
Legaretta, Dorothy
1979   "The effects of program models on language acquisition by Spanish-speaking
          children", *TESOL Quarterly* 13, 521—534.
Leibowitz, A. H.
1969   "English literacy: legal sanction for discrimination", *Notre Dame Lawyer* 45,
          7: 7—67.
Leitner, Gerhard
1991   "Europe 1992: a language perspective", *Language Problems and Language
          Planning* 5, 282—296.
Lindholm, Kathryn J.
1992   "Two-way bilingual/immersion education: theory, conceptual issues, and ped-
          agogical implications", in: Padilla — Benavides, 195—220.
Lo Bianco, Joseph
1990   "A hard-Nosed multiculturalism: revitalising multicultural education?", *Vox*
          4, 80—94.
Lo Jacomo, E. (ed.)
1986   *Plurilingualism et communication,* Seminar of UNESCO and Association de
          Universelle d'Esperanto. Paris: Society d'Etudes Linguistique et Anthropo-
          logique de France.
López, Luis Enrique
1988   "Balance y perspectivas de la educación bilingüe en Puno", in: López (ed.),
          79—106.
López, Luis Enrique (ed.)
1988   *Pesquisas en lingüística andina.* Lima-Puno: CONCYTEC-GTZ-Universidad
          Nacional del Altiplano.
López, Luis Enrique
1989   "Problemática sociolingüística y educativa de la población aymara-hablante
          en el Perú", *International Journal of the Sociology of Language* 77, 55—68.
López, Luis Enrique — Ruth Moya (eds.)
1990   *Pueblos indios, estados y educación.* Lima-Quito: PEP-P/EBI/ERA.

López, Luis Enrique
forthcoming "Educación bilingüe en Puno hacia un ajuste de cuentas", in: Cavalcanti
— Hamel (eds.).
Lowenberg, Peter H. (ed.)
1987   *Language Spread and Language Policy: Issues, Implications, and Case Studies,*
            GURT '87. Washington, DC: Georgetown University Press.
Mackey, William F.
1984   "Mother tongue education: problems — prospects", *Prospects* 14, 1: 37—49,
            Paris: UNESCO.
Mackey, William F.
1991   "Language diversity, language policy and the sovereign state", *History of*
            European Ideas, 13, 1—2: 51—61.
Marcó del Pont, Raúl (ed.)
1990   *Foro de discusión de la propuesta de reforma constitucional para reconocer los*
            derechos culturales de los pueblos indígenas de México. México: CEAS/CMA/
            ENAH.
Marjoribanks, Kevin
1980   *Ethnic families and children's achievements.* Sydney: George Allen and Unwin.
Mar-Molinero, Clare — Patrick Stevenson
1991   "The 'territorial imperative' debate in the European context", *Language*
            Problems and Language Planning 15: 162—176.
Marshall, David F. (ed.)
1986   "The question of an official language: language rights and the English Lan-
            guage Amendment", *International Journal of the Sociology of Language* 60,
            7—75.
Marta, Claudio
1991   "Dall'assimilazionismo al multiculturalismo. Vent'anni di politica e di ricerca
            sociale sull'immigrazione in Svezia (1966—1985)", *Studi Emigrazione/Etudes*
            Migrations 101: 59—81.
Masferrer, Elio
1983   "La situación social de los grupos indígenas en América Latina", in: Rodrí-
            guez et al (ed.), vol. 2, 589—605.
Massey, Douglas
1981   "Dimensions of the new immigration in the United States and prospects for
            assimilation", *Annual Review of Sociology* 7: 57—85.
Mateene, Kahombo — John Kalema — Bernard Chomba (eds.)
1985   *Linguistic liberation and unity of Africa.* Kampala: OAU Inter-African Bureau
            of Languages, OAU/BIL Publication 6.
Matras, Yaron
1990   *Some problems of Kurdish orthography, Summary of thesis,* University of
            Hamburg, Dept. of Linguistics.
Matsuda, Mari J.
1991   "Voices of America: accent, antidiscrimination law, and jurisprudence for the
            last reconstruction", *The Yale Law Journal* 100: 1329—1406.
Maurais, Jacques
1991   *La situation des langues autochtones d'Amérique.* Québec, ms.
Maurais, Jacques (ed.)
1987   *Politique et aménagement linguistique,* Québec: Conseil de la langue française
            — Paris: Le Robert.

Mazrui, Ali A.
1968   "Some sociopolitical functions of English literature in Africa", in: Fishman
          — Ferguson — Das Gupta (eds.), 183—1988.
McCormack, W. C. — S. A. Wurm
1979   *Language and society: anthropological issues*. The Hague: Mouton.
McLaughlin, Barry
1985   *Second language acquisition in childhood: Volume 2. School-age children*. Hills-
          dale, NJ: Laurence Erlbaum Associates.
McRae, Kenneth D.
1983   *Conflict and compromise in multilingual societies, Switzerland*. Waterloo, On-
          tario: Wilfrid Laurier University Press.
McRae, Kenneth D.
1986   *Conflict and compromise in multilingual societies, Belgium*. Waterloo, Ontario:
          Wilfrid Laurier University Press.
Meade, Philip
1983   *The educational experience of Sydney high school students: a comparative study
          of migrant students of non-English-Speaking origin and students whose parents
          were born in an English-Speaking country*. Canberra: Australian Government
          Publishing Service.
Medvedyev, V.
1986   "Osobennosti funkcionirovanija jazykov v uslovijax socializma, Materjaly
          pjatoj respublikanskoj naučnoi konferencii molodyx lingvistov" [The char-
          acteristics of the functioning of languages in the conditions of socialism.
          Materials from the 5th Republican Scientific Conference of Young Linguists],
          Yerevan, 171—172.
Melià, Bartomeu
1974   "Hacia una 'tercera lengua' en el Paraguay", *Estudios paraguayos*, 2, 2:
          31—72.
Melià, Bartomeu
1979   *Educaçao indígena e alfabetizaçao*. Sao Paulo: Ediçoes Loyola.
Melià, Bartomeu
1988   *Una nación, dos culturas*. Asunción: RP Ediciones CEPAG.
Mem och Zîn
          *Mem och Zîn. Det kurdiska nationaleposet i tolkning och översättning från
          engelska av Robert Alftan, med en inledning av Gisbert Jänicke* [Mem and
          Zîn. The Kurdish national epic, interpreted and translated from English by
          Robert Alftan, with an introduction by Gisbert Jänicke]. Helsingfors: Re-
          voltförlaget.
Menezes, Claudia
1989   "Estado y minorías étnicas indígenas en el Brasil", *América Indígena* XLIX,
          1: 153—170.
Meri, M.
1990   "Kenen kieli?" [Whose language?] *Elias* 91, 2: 13—14.
Metelitsa, L.
1982   *Edinstvo internacionalnogo i patriotičeskogo vospitanija* [The unity of inter-
          national and patriotic education], Moskva: Nauka.
Meyer-Ingwersen, Johannes
1989   "The Kurdish language and the formation of identity in Kurdish children
          and youths", in: *Human rights in Kurdistan*, 34—48.

Mihhailov, D.
1989   "Pop-politika i tabeli o rangax, ili kto grešit protiv istiny" [Populistic politics and tables about groups, or who sins against the truth?], *Soveckaja Ėstonija*, December 23, 1989.
Miles, Robert
1989   *Racism*, London: Routledge.
Minority rights, policies and practice in South-East Europe
1990   Report for the Conference at Christiansborg, Copenhagen, March 30thApril 1st 1990, Copenhagen: The Danish Helsinki Committee — The Minority Rights Group.
Mioni, Alberto M.
1989   "Problems of language growth and the preparation of schoolbooks in Africa", in: Zuanelli (ed.), 277—286.
Modiano, Nancy
1988   "Public bilingual education in Mexico", in: Paulston (ed.), 313—327.
Montoya Medinaceli, Víctor
1983   "La educación bilingüe en proyectos integrados", in: Rodríguez et al (eds.), 57—82.
Montserrat, Ruth
1987   "Para um auténtico bilingüismo", in: Projeto interaçao (ed.), 87—92.
Montserrat, Ruth
1989   "Cojuntura atual da educaçao indígena", in: Opan — Operaçao Anchieta (ed.), 245—255.
Mullard, Chris
1984a   "Anti-Racist Education: A Theoretical Basis", in: Mullard 1984b, 10—28.
Mullard, Chris
1984b   *Anti-racist education: the three O's*. Cardiff: The National Association for Multi-Racial Education.
Mullard, Chris
1988   "Racism, ethnicism, and etharcy or not? The principles of progressive control and transformative change", in: Skutnabb-Kangas — Cummins (eds.), 359—378.
Munzel, Martha C. — Pérez Gónzalez, Benjamín
1987   "México: panorama general de las lengua indígenas", *América Indígena* XLVII, 4: 571—605.
Murdoch, G. P.
1967   *Ethnographic Atlas*, Pittsburgh: University of Pittsburgh Press.
Muttersprache Kurdisch
1980   Komkar publikation 2. Frankfurt: KOMKAR (Föderation der Arbeitervereine Kurdistans in der Bundesrepublik Deutschland).
Muttersprachlicher Unterricht in der Bundesrepublik Deutschland
1985   Sprach- und bildungspolitische Argumente für eine zweisprachige Erziehung von Kindern sprachlicher Minderheiten (mit der Neubearbeitung des Memorandums zum muttersprachlichen Unterricht, BAGIV (hrsg). Hamburg: Verlag Rissen.
Mönch-Bucak, Yayla (ed.)
1988   *Kurden: Alltag und Widerstand*. Bremen: Eigenverlag (Holbeinstrasse 20, 2800 Bremen, Germany).

Mönch-Bucak, Yayla
1989   *The Kurdish language in Turkey. Repression and cultural resistance.* Bremen: Kurdish Pen Club/ University of Oldenburg, ms.
Nanda, Amulya R.
1991   *Census of India-1991*, Series I India, Paper 1 Provisional population totals, New Delhi: Registrar General.
Neustupný, Jiři V.
1974   "Basic types of treatment of language problems", in: Fishman (ed.).
Neustupný, Jiři V.
1984   "Language planning and human rights", in: Gonzales (ed.), 66—74.
Neve, Edward F.
1912   *Beyond the Pir Panjal: life among the mountains and valleys of Kashmir.* London: T. Fisher Unwin.
Ngalasso, Mwatha Musanji
1990   "Les droits linguistiques individuels et collectifs", *Les langues modernes* 1990: 2, 15—26.
Ngũgĩ, wa Thiong'o
1985   "The language of African literature", *New Left Review*, April-June, 109—127.
Nostitz, Wolfgang von
1989   "The European Parliament and the Kurdish question", in: *Human Rights in Kurdistan*, 159—161.
Nutt, M.
1989   "Homo soveticus", *Looming* 2: 221—225.
O'Barr, William M.
1982   *Linguistic evidence: language, power and strategy in the courtroom.* New York: Academic Press.
OAU Inter-African Bureau of Languages
1985   "Linguistic liberation and unity of Africa", in: Mateene — Kalema — Chomba (eds.), 7—17.
O'Brien, Sharon
1985   "Federal Indian policies and the internatinal protection of human rights", in: Deloria (ed.), 35—61.
Obura, Anna
1986   "Research issues and perspectives in language in education in Africa: an agenda for the next decade", in: Centre of African Studies, 413—444.
O'Donaghue, Lois
1990   "Immigration and Australia's Aboriginal communities", address of chair of the Aboriginal and Torres Strait Islander Commission (ATSIC) to the National Immigration Outlook Conference, Bureau of Immigration Research, Melbourne, November 14—16.
Ogbu, John
1978   *Minority education and caste.* New York: Academic Press.
Okumus, Esref
1990   "Report to Minority Rights Conference", see *Minority rights, policies and practice in South-East Europe.*
Opan — Operaçao Anchieta (ed.)
1989   *A conquista da escrita.* Sao Paulo: Iluminuras.

Orlandi, Ení Pulcinelli (ed.)
1988   *Política Lingüística na América Latina*. Campinas: Pontes.
Ortiz, Roberto (ed.)
1979   *Language development in a bilingual setting*. Pomona, CA: National Multilingual Multicultural Materials Development Center.
Padilla, Raymond V. (ed.)
1980   *Theory in bilingual education*. Ypsilanti, Mich.: Eastern Michigan University.
Padilla, Raymond V. — Benavides, Alfredo H.
1992   *Critical perspectives on bilingual education research*. Tempe, Arizona: Bilingual Press/Editorial Bilingüe.
Palley, Claire
1984   *Possible ways and means to facilitate the peaceful and constructive resolution of situations involving racial, national, religious and linguistic minorities*. Working paper submitted to Sub-Commission on Prevention of Discrimination and Protection of Minorities at its 41st session (e/CN.4/Sub.2/1984/43).
Paradis, Michel (ed.)
1978   *Aspects of bilingualism*. Columbia, SC: Hornbeam Press.
Pattanayak, Debi P.
1969   *Aspects of applied lingustics*, London: Asia Publishing House.
Pattanayak, D. P.
1981   *Multilingualism and mother-tongue education*. Delhi: Oxford University Press.
Pattanayak, Debi P.
1986   "Educational use of the mother tongue", in: Spolsky (ed.), 5—15.
Paulston, Christina Bratt
1988a   "Bilingualism and bilingual education an introduction", in: Paulston (ed.) 1988b, 1—15.
Paulston, Christina Bratt (ed.)
1988b   *International handbook of bilingualism and bilingual education*. New York: Greenwood Press.
Pawley, Andrew
1988   "On the place of Māori in New Zealand life: present and future", Paper presented to a meeting called by Te Taura Whiri I Te Reo Māori of all Pākehā who are fluent speakers of Māori, May 25.
Pedrasa, Jr. Pedro — John Attinasi — Gerard Hoffman
1980   "Rethinking diglossia", in: Padilla (ed.), 75—95.
Pellicer, Dora
1988   "Las migrantes indígenas en la Ciudad de México y el uso del español como segunda lengua", in: Hamel — Lastra de Suarez — Muñoz Cruz (eds.), 147—169.
Perkins, Kyle et al
1989   "First and second language reading comprehension", *RELC Journal* 20, 2: 1—9, Singapore: Regional Language Centre.
Person, Henry
1967   "The Swedes and their family names", *Scandinavian studies* 39, 209—248.
Phillipson, Robert
1988   "Linguicism: structures and ideologies in linguistic imperialism", in: Skutnabb-Kangas — Cummins (eds.), 339—358.

Phillipson, Robert
1992   *Linguistic imperialism.* Oxford: Oxford University Press.
Phillipson, Robert — Tove Skutnabb-Kangas
1986   *Linguicism rules in education.* 3 volumes, Roskilde: Roskilde University Centre, Institute VI.
Phillipson, Robert — Tove Skutnabb-Kangas
1989   "Linguistic human rights and the Kurdish language", in: *Human rights in Kurdistan*, 60−68.
Piatt, Bill
1990   *Only English? Law and language policy in the United States.* Albuquerque: University of New Mexico Press.
Pitarello, Adrian
1980   *Soup without salt: The Australian Catholic Church and the Italian migrant.* Sydney: Centre for Migration Studies.
Plaza, Pedro — Xavier Albó
1989   "Educación bilingüe y planificación lingüística en Bolivia", *International Journal of the Sociology of Language* 77, 69−92.
Pleij, Herman
1991   "Report on the Netherlands", *International Herald Tribune* (May 30).
Plourde, Michel
1988   *La politique linguistique du Québec,* Québec: Institut québécois de recherche sur la culture.
Poddar, A. (ed.)
1969   *Language and society in India.* Shimla: Indian Institute of Indian Studies.
Pogačnik, Bogdan
1986   *The culture of small nations as a communication bridge.* Paris: Inter-clubs, UNESCO no. 1.
Pool, Jonathan
1972   "National development and language diversity", in: Fishman (ed.), 213−230.
Pool, Jonathan
1991a   "The official language problem", *American Political Science Review* 85, 2: 495−514.
Pool, Jonathan
1991b   "The World Language problem", *Rationality and Society* 3, 1: 78−105.
Porter, Rosalie Pedalino
1990   *Forked tongue: The politics of bilingual education.* New York: Basic Books.
Pott, August Friedrich
1840   "Indogermanische Sprachstämme", in: Erscg/Gruber: *Allgemeine Encyklopädie der Wissenschaften und Kunste.* Leipzig.
Pozzi-Escot, Inés
1988   "La educación bilingüe en el Perú: una mirada retrospectiva y prospectiva", in: Lopez (ed.), 37−78.
Preiswerk, Roy (ed.)
1980   *The slant of the pen: racism in children's books.* Geneva: World Council of Churches.
Projeto interaçao (ed.)
1987   *Por uma educaçao indigena diferenciada.* Brasília: Fundaçao Nacional Pró Memória.

Psacharopoulos, George
1990   *Why educational policies can fail. An overview of selected African experiences.*
        (World Bank Discussion Papers, Africa Technical Department Series, 82)
        Washington, D. C.: World Bank.
Pueblos indígenas y educación
1990   15, 16, Quito: MEC-GTZ/ABYA-YALA.
Pupier, Paul — José Woehrling (eds.)
1989   *Langue et droit. Language and law. Proceedings of the First Conference of the
        International Institute of Comparative Linguistic Law.* Montréal: Wilson —
        Lafleur.
Py, Bernard
1986   "Native language attrition amongst migrant workers: towards an extension
        of the concept of interlanguage", in: Kellerman — Sharwood Smith (eds.),
        163 – 172.
Québec [Gouvernement du],
1977   [updated text 1989] *Loi 101, Charte de la langue française.* Québec: Editeur
        Officiel du Québec.
Ramirez, J. David — S. D. Yuen — D. R. Ramey
1991   *Executive summary: Final report: Longitudinal study of structured English
        immersion strategy, early-exit and late-exit transitional bilingual education
        programs for language-minority children,* Contract No. 300 – 87 – 0156, sub-
        mitted to the U. S. Department of Education. San Mateo: Aguirre Interna-
        tional.
Rannut, Mart
1989   "Šovinismilainetest" [Waves of chauvinism], *Looming* 5: 678 – 680.
Redard, F. — R. Jeanneret — J.-P. Métral (ed.)
1981   *Le Schwyzertutsh, 5e language nationale?.* Neuchatel: CILA.
Reedy, T. M.
1985   *Developing an official Māori Language Policy for Government.* Department
        of Māori Affairs.
Rehbein, Jochen (ed.)
1985   *Interkulturelle Kommunikation.* Tübingen: Narr.
Reid, Euan — Hans Reich (eds.)
1992   *Breaking the boundaries. migrant workers' children in the EC.* Clevedon, Avon:
        Multilingual Matters.
Renteln, Alison D.
1988   "A cross-cultural approach to validating international human rights: the case
        of retribution tied to proportionality", in: Cingranelli (ed.), 7 – 40.
Report of the Education Commission 1964 – 1966
1966   Education and national development. New Delhi: Ministry of Education,
        Government of India.
Ribeiro, Darcy
1970   *Os índios e a civilizaçao. O processo de integraçao dos índios no Brasil moderno.*
        Río de Janeiro: Ed Civilizaçao Brasileira.
Riggs, Fred W. (ed.)
1985   *Ethnicity. Intercocta Glossary. Concepts — terms used in ethnicity research.*
        International conceptual encyclopedia for the social sciences, Volume 1.
        University of Hawaii, Dept of Political Science.

Riggs, Fred
1986   "What is ethnic? What is national? Let's turn the tables", *Canadian Review of Studies in Nationalism* XIII, 1: 111–123.
Rivera, Charlene (ed.)
1984   *Language proficiency and academic achievement*. Clevedon: Multilingual Matters.
Rodney, Walter
1973   *How Europe underdeveloped Africa*. London: Bogle l'ouverture.
Rodrígues, Aryón Dall'Igna
1986   *Línguas brasileiras*. Sao Paulo: Ediçoes Loyola.
Rodrígues, Aryon Dall'Igna
1988   "As línguas indígenas e a constituinte", in: Orlandi (ed.), 105–110.
Rodríguez, Nemesio, J. – K. Elio Masferrer – Raúl Vargas Vega (eds.)
1983   *Educación, etnias y descolonización en América Latina*. Vol. III. México: UNESCO-III.
Rosaldo, Renato – Gustav L. Seligmann – Robert A. Calvert
1974   *Chicano: The beginnings of bronze power*. New York: William Morrow and Company.
Rosenthal, Robert – Lenore Jacobson
1968   *Pygmalion in the classroom: teacher expectation and pupils' intellectual development*. NY: Holt, Rinehart and Winston.
Rossinelli, Michel
1989   "La question linguistique en Suisse. Bilan critique et nouvelles perspectives juridiques", *Revue de droit suisse* 108: 163–193.
Roth Seneff, Andrés et al
1986   *Lingüística aplicada y sociolingüística del náhuatl de la Sierra de Zongolica*. Cuadernos de la Casa Chata 133. México: CIESAS.
Roth, Jürgen (ed.)
1978   *Geographie der Unterdrückten*. Hamburg: Rororo-Verlag.
Rubagumya, Casmir M. (ed.)
1990   *Language in education in Africa: a Tanzanian perspective*. Clevedon: Multilingual Matters.
Ruhlen, Merritt
1987   *A guide to the world's languages*. Volume 1 Classification. Stanford: Stanford University Press.
Ruíz, Richard
1984   "Orientations in languge planning", *NABE Journal*, 8, 2: 15–34.
Rumpf, Christian
1989   "The Turkish law prohibiting languages other than Turkish", in: *Human rights in Kurdistan*, 69–87.
Rustomji, Nari K.
1983   *Imperilled frontiers – India*. Delhi: Northeastern Borderlands.
Saado, Hussein
1989   "Document on the United Nations and the Kurdish question", in: *Human rights in Kurdistan*, 171–179.
Said, Abdul A. – L. R. Simmons
1976   "Introduction" and "Ethnic factor in world politics", in: *Ethnicity in an International context: The Polities of Dissociation*, New Brunswick NJ: Transaction Books.

Salt, John
   1989   "A comparative overview of international trends and types, 1950–80", *International Migration Review* 23: 431–456.
Sampaio Grizzi — Carmelina Dalva — Arcy Lopes Da Silva
   1981   "A filosofia e a pedagogia da educaçao indígena um resumo dos debates", in: Comissao pro-indio (ed.), 15–29.
Samuda, Ronald
   1979   "How are the schools of Ontario coping with a New Canadian population: a report of recent research findings", *TESL Talk* 11: 44–51.
Sánchez Cámara, Florencio — Felipe Ayala (eds.)
   1979   *Concepts for communication and development in bilingual-bicultural communities.* The Hague: Mouton.
Sanders, Douglas
   1981   *An opinion to the Supreme Court of Norway.* Mimeo.
Sandgren, Claes (ed.)
   1987   *Nordstedts Juridiska Handbok* [Nordstedt's Legal Handbook]. (13th edition) Stockholm: Nordstedts förlag.
Sato, Charlene
   1991   "Sociolinguistic variation and language attitudes in Hawaíi", in: Cheshire (ed.), 647–663.
Sato, Charlene
   in press   "Language change in a creole continuum: Decreolization"? in: Hyltenstam — Viberg (eds.).
Scanlon, Arlene P. — Juan Lezama Morfín (eds.)
   1982   *Méxicio pluricultural: De la castellanización a la educación indígena bilingüe bicultural.* México: SEP-Porrúa.
Schegloff, E. A. — G. Jefferson — H. Sacks
   1977   "The preference for self-correction in the organization of repair in conversation", *Language* 53: 361–382.
Schermerhorn, R. A.
   1970   *Comparative ethnic relations. A framework for theory and research.* New York: Random House.
Schläpfer, R. *et alii* (eds.)
   1985   *La Suisse aux quatre langues,* Genève: Zoé.
Sebeok, T. A. (ed.)
   1969   *Current trends in linguistics,* vol. 5. The Hague: Mouton.
Selleck, Richard J. W.
   1980   "The trouble with my looking glass: a study of the attitude of Australians to Germans during the Great War", *Journal of Australian Studies* 6: 1–25.
Senate Standing Committee on Education and Arts
   1984   *A National Language Policy.* Canberra: Australian Government Printing Service.
SEP (= Secretaría de Educación Pública)
   1990   *Programa para la modernización de la educación indígena.* México: SEP.
Seton-Watson, Hugh
   1977   *Nations and states.* London: Methuen.
Sfs
             Svensk författningssamling [Collection of Swedish laws, annual volumes]. Stockholm: Nordstedts tryckeri.

Shakely, Ferhad
1989   "Classic and modern Kurdish poetry", in: *Human rights in Kurdistan*, 49–59.
Shapson, S. – V. D'Oyley (eds.)
1984   *Bilingual and multicultural education: Canadian perspectives.* Clevedon: Multilingual Matters.
Shelton, Dinah
1987   "An International Treaty on Abolition of the Death Penalty", *Nordic Journal on Human Rights* 5, 3: 58–60.
Sieghart, Paul
1983   *The international law of human rights.* Oxford: Oxford University Press.
Sierra, María Teresa
1990   "Lenguaje, prácticas jurídicas y derecho consuetudinario indígena", in: Stavenhagen – Iturralde (eds.), 231–258.
Sierra, María Teresa
1992   *Discurso, cultura y poder. El ejercicio de la autoridad en pueblos hñan'hñus del Valle del Mezquital,* Pachuca: CIESAS-Gobierno del Estado de Hidalgo.
Sierra, María Teresa
1993 a   "Usos y desusos del derecho consuetudinario indígena", in: *Nueva Antropología* 44: 17–26.
Sierra, María Teresa
1993 b   *La lucha por los derechos indígenas en el Brasil actual.* México: CIESAS.
Silence is killing them. Annual report 1993
1994   On the situation of human rights in Northern Kurdistan and the Kurds in Turkey. Bremen: International Association for Human Rights in Kurdistan.
Skutnabb-Kangas, Tove
1984a   *Bilingualism or Not – the education of minorities.* Clevedon: Multilingual Matters.
Skutnabb-Kangas, Tove
1984b   "Barns mänskliga språkliga rättigheter. Om finsk frigörelsekamp på den svenska skolfronten", [Children's linguistic human rights. On Finnish Liberation Struggle on the Swedish School Front] *Kritisk Psykologi* 1–2: 38–46.
Skutnabb-Kangas, Tove
1986   "Who wants to change what and why – conflicting paradigms in minority education research", in: Spolsky (ed.), 153–181.
Skutnabb-Kangas, Tove
1987   *Are the Finns in Sweden an ethnic minority – Finnish parents talk about Finland and Sweden,* Research project The education of the Finnish minority. Working Paper Nr 1, Roskilde: Roskilde University Centre, Institute VI, August 1987.
Skutnabb-Kangas, Tove
1988a   "Multilingualism and the education of minority children", in: Skutnabb-Kangas – Cummins (eds.), 9–44.
Skutnabb-Kangas, Tove
1988b   "Resource power and autonomy through discourse in conflict – a Finnish migrant school strike in Sweden", in: Skutnabb-Kangas and Cummins (eds.), 251–277.

Skutnabb-Kangas, Tove
1988c   *Minority research between social technology and self-determination.* Working
          Paper no 2, Research Project The Education of the Finnish Minority in
          Sweden, Roskilde: Roskilde University.
Skutnabb-Kangas, Tove
1990a   *Language, literacy and minorities.* London: Minority Rights Group.
Skutnabb-Kangas, Tove
1990b   "Wer entscheidet, ob meine Sprache wichtig für mich ist?" Minderheitenfor-
          schung zwischen Sozialtechnologie und Selbstbestimmung, in: Dittrich —
          Radtke (hrsg), 329 — 351.
Skutnabb-Kangas, Tove
1991a   Interview for the Kurdish magazine "*Survival*".
Skutnabb-Kangas, Tove
1991b   "Vem kostar? [Who causes the costs?] in: Gaup, 92 — 100.
Skutnabb-Kangas, Tove
1991c   "Swedish strategies to prevent integration and national ethnic minorities",
          in: García (ed.), 25 — 42.
Skutnabb-Kangas, Tove
1991d   "Legitimating or delegitimating new forms of racism the role of researchers",
          in: Gorter et al (eds.), 77 — 100.
Skutnabb-Kangas, Tove
1993a   "A synthesis: principles for education leading towards high levels of multilin-
          gualism", Paper presented at 10th World Congress of Applied Linguistics,
          Symposium "Multilingualism for all" and written for the book *Multilingual-
          ism for all*, ed. Tove Skutnabb-Kangas, in preparation.
Skutnabb-Kangas, Tove
1993b   "Hvad kræver Danmark af andre — og af sig selv?" *[What does Denmark
          demand of others — and of itself?]*, *Information*, 22. 7. 1993.
Skutnabb-Kangas, Tove
in press "Language and (demands for) self-determination", in: *Self-determination:
          International Perspectives*, ed. Don Clark et al, London: The Macmillan Press
Skutnabb-Kangas, Tove (ed.) in preparation, *Multilingualism for All*.
Skutnabb-Kangas, Tove — Jim Cummins (eds.)
1988   *Minority education. From shame to struggle.* Clevedon: Multilingual Matters.
Skutnabb-Kangas, Tove — Robert Phillipson
1986a   "Denial of linguistic rights: the new mental slavery", in: Phillipson — Skut-
          nabb-Kangas, 416 — 465.
Skutnabb-Kangas, Tove — Robert Phillipson
1986b   "The legitimacy of the arguments for the spread of English", in: Phillipson
          — Skutnabb-Kangas, 378 — 415.
Skutnabb-Kangas, Tove — Robert Phillipson
1989a   *Wanted! Linguistic human rights.* ROLIG-papir 44. Roskilde: Roskilde Uni-
          versity Centre.
Skutnabb-Kangas, Tove — Robert Phillipson
1989b   ",Mother tongue': the theoretical and sociopolitical construction of a con-
          cept", in: Ammon (ed.), 450 — 477.
Skutnabb-Kangas Tove — Robert Phillipson
1990   "Kurdish — a prohibited language. On how the Kurds are deprived of
          linguistic human rights", Plenary paper at CSCE/CDH Parallel Activities on

"Human Rights", "Kurdish — a prohibited language", organised by KOMKAR and "Initiative for Human rights in Kurdistan", June 13 1990 [published as "Kurdisch — eine verbotene Sprache. Wie die Kurden in der Türkei sprachlicher Menschenrechte beraubt werden", *Informationsbulletin Kurdistan* 30—31, September 1990, 3—8].

Skutnabb-Kangas Tove — Robert Phillipson
1991   "The Kurdish language and literature", plenary paper given at the hearing The Kurdish People, The Louisiana Museum, May 11 1991, organized by The Danish Helsinki Committee — "Politiken".

Skutnabb-Kangas Tove — Robert Phillipson
1993   "Sprachliche Menschenrechte für die Kurden", in: Bucak (ed.), 127—142.

Skutnabb-Kangas, Tove — Pertti Toukomaa
1976   *Teaching migrant children's mother tongue and learning the language of the host country in the context of the socio-cultural situation of the migrant family*, A report prepared for UNESCO. Tampere: Department of Sociology and Social Psychology, University of Tampere, Research Reports 15.

Slade, Diana — John Gibbons
1987   "Testing bilingual proficiency in Australia: issues, methods, findings", *Evaluation and Research in Education* 1, 2: 95—106.

Smith, Eldson C.
1965   *Personal names: a bibliography*. Detroit: Gale Research [originally published in 1952 in New York by the New York Public Library].

Smith, R. F.
1991   "Fear and defiance in a land of silent dawns", *Globe and Mail*, Tuesday, March 12, p. A21.

Smitherman, Geneva
1992   "African Americans and 'English Only'", *Language Problems and Language Planning* 16, 3: 235—247.

Smolicz, Jerzy J.
1979   *Culture and education in a plural society*. Canberra: Curriculum Development Centre.

Smolicz, Jerzy J.
1981   "Core values and cultural identity", *Ethnic and Racial Studies* 4, 1: 75—90.

Smolicz, Jerzy J.
1984   "Multiculturalism and an over-arching framework of values: some educational responses for ethnically plural societies", *European Journal of Education* 19, 2: 22—24, Reprinted in: Poole M. E., de Lacey, P. R. and Randhawa, B. S. (eds.), 1985, *Australia in Transition: Culture and Life Possiblities*, Sydney and London: Harcourt, Brace, Jovanovich, 76—90.

Smolicz, Jerzy J.
1985   "Greek Australians: a question of survival in multicultural Australia", *Journal of Multilingual and Multicultural Development* 6, 1: 17—29.

Smolicz, Jerzy J.
1986a   "National Policy on Languages", *Australian Journal of Education* 30, 1: 45—65.

Smolicz, J. J.
1986b   "National Language Policy in the Philippines", in: Spolsky (ed.), 96—116.

Smolicz, Jerzy J.
1988   *Ethnicity and multiculturalism in the Australian Catholic Church*. New York: Centre for Migration Studies.
Smolicz, Jerzy J. — Lilian Lee — Malathi Murugaian — Margaret J. Secombe
1990   "Language as a core value of culture among tertiary students of Chinese and Indian origin in Australia", *Journal of Asian Pacific Communication* 1, 1: 229—246.
Smolicz, Jerzy J. — Margaret J. Secombe
1986   "Italian language and culture in Australia", in: Bettoni (ed.), 27—60.
Smolicz, Jerzy J. — Margaret J. Secombe
1989   "Types of language activation and evaluation in an ethnically plural society", in: Ammon (ed.), 478—514.
Solé, Yolanda
1990   "Bilingualism stable or transitional? The case of Spanish in the United States", *International Journal of the Sociology of Language,* 84, 35—80.
South Australian Education, September 1990
1990   *Antiracism: Policy Statement*. Adelaide: South Australian Government Printer.
South Australian Institute of Languages
1990   *The language challenge — tertiary languages planning: a policy for South Australia*. Adelaide: South Australian Institute of Languages.
South Australian ministerial taskforce on multiculturalism and education
1984   *Education for a cultural democracy* and *Education for a cultural democracy: a summary*, Adelaide: South Australian Government Printers.
Spires, Roberta Lee
1987   "Uma esperiência de educaçao bi-lingue na regiao de Oiapoque (AP)", *América Indígena* XLVII, 3: 481—488.
Spolsky, Bernard (ed.)
1986   *Language and education in multilingual settings*. Clevedon: Multilingual Matters.
Spolsky, Bernard — Patricia Irvine
1982   "Sociolinguistic aspects of the acceptance of literacy in the vernacular", in: Barkin et al (eds.), 73—79.
Stairs, Arlene
1988   "Beyond cultural inclusion. An Inuit example of indigenous education development", in: Skutnabb-Kangas — Cummins (eds.), 308—327.
Stairs, Arlene — Robert M. Leavitt
1988   *On language teaching as a cultural activity. Messages from native education to TESL Canada*. Montréal, ms.
State of California
1879   *Debates and proceedings of the constitutional convention*. Sacramento.
Stauf, Renate
1991   *Justus Mosers Konzept einer deutschen Nationalität*. Tübingen: Niemeyer.
Stavenhagen, Rodolfo
1984   "Linguistic minorities and language policy in Latin America. The case of Mexico", in: Coulmas (ed.), 56—62.
Stavenhagen, Rodolfo
1985   "Aspects socio-culturels de l'inégalité et de l'équité au Mexique", *Amérique Latine* 22: 42—49.

Stavenhagen, Rodolfo
1987   "Human rights and peoples' rights — the question of minorities", *Nordic Journal on Human Rights* 5, 3: 16 — 26.
Stavenhagen, Rodolfo
1988 a   *Derechos indígenas y derechos humanos en América Latina.* México: IIDH-El Colegio de México.
Stavenhagen, Rodolfo
1988 b   "Universal human rights and the cultures of indigenous peoples and other ethnic groups", paper presented to the Nobel Symposium on Human Rights, Oslo, June 20 — 23, 1988.
Stavenhagen, Rodolfo
1988 c   "Cultura y sociedad en América Latina", in: Stavenhagen (ed.) 1988d, 21 — 36.
Stavenhagen, Rodolfo (ed.)
1988 d   *Política cultural para un país multiétnico.* México: SEP.
Stavenhagen, Rodolfo
1989 a   "Comunidades étnicas en estados modernos", *América Indígena* XLIX, 1: 11 — 34.
Stavenhagen, Rodolfo
1989 b   "Derecho consuetudinario indígena en América Latina", *América Indígena* XLIX, 2: 223 — 244.
Stavenhagen, Rodolfo
1990 a   *The ethnic question. Conflicts, development, and human rights.* Tokyo: United Nations University Press.
Stavenhagen, Rodolfo — Diego Iturralde (eds.)
1990 b   *Entre la ley y la costumbre. El derecho consuetudinario indígena en América Latina.* México: III-IIDH.
Steiner, George
1975   *After Babel: aspects of language and translation.* New York: Oxford University Press.
Steiner-Khamsi, Gita
1989   "Ausländische sprachliche Minderheiten in der Schweiz", Materialienband zum Schlussbericht der Arbeitsgruppe zur Revision von Artikel 116 der Bundesverfassung, Bern: Bundeskanzlei, 89 — 100.
Stretton, Pamela — Christine Finnimore
1988   "Votes for Aborigines", *The Adelaide Review* 46: 10 — 11.
Suárez, Jorge A.
1983   *The Mesoamerican Indian languages.* Cambridge: Cambridge University Press.
Swain, Merrill
1979   "Bilingual education: research and its implications", in: Yorio et al. (eds.), 23 — 33.
Swain, Merrill
1986   "Bilingualism without tears", in: Cummins — Swain, 99 — 110. Previously published in: Clarke — Handscombe (eds.) 1983, 35 — 46.
Swain, Merril — Sharon Lapkin
1982   *Evaluating bilingual education: a Canadian case study.* Clevedon: Multilingual Matters.

Swain, Merrill — Sharon Lapkin — Norman Rowen — Doug Hart
1990   "The role of mother tongue literacy in third language learning", *VOX, The Journal of the Australian Advisory Council on Languages and Multicultural Education* 4: 111–121.
Switzerland [département fédéral de l'intérieur]
1989   *Le quadrilinguisme en suisse — présent et futur*. Bern: Chancellerie fédérale.
Szasz, Margaret
1974   *Education and the American Indian: the road to self-determination, 1928 – 1973*. Albuquerque: University of New Mexico Press.
Tadadjeu, Maurice
1980   *A model for functional trilingual education planning in Africa*. Paris: UNESCO.
Taylor, Andrew
1989   "A champion of the Ukrainian Language: Dmytro Pavlychko", *Lumen* (The University of Adelaide Magazine), 18, 13: 6 – 7.
Taylor, Donald — Roch Meynard — Elizabeth Rheault
1977   "Threat to ethnic identity and second language learning", in: Giles (ed.), 99 – 118.
Thompson, Vincent Bakepet
1987   *The making of the African diaspora in the Americas, 1441 – 1900*. London: Longman.
Thoolen, Hans (ed.)
1987   *Indonesia and the rule of law*, International Commission of Jurists. London: Pinter.
Tomaševski, Katarina
1993   "Aid to Eastern Europe", in: Andreassen — Swinehart (eds.), 21 – 50.
Tomaševski, Katarina
1993   *Development aid and human rights revisited*. London: Pinter.
Tosi, Arturo
1984   *Immigration and bilingual education*. Oxford: Pergamon.
Toukomaa, Pertti — Tove Skutnabb-Kangas
1977   *The intensive teaching of the mother tongue to migrant children at pre-school age*. Tampere: Department of Sociology and Social Psychology, University of Tampere Research Reports 26.
Trent, John
1991   "Language policy in tomorrow's Canada", *Langue et Société/Language and Society* 35: 8 – 10.
Trueba, Henry — Grace Guthrie — Kathryn Hu-Pei Au (eds.)
1981   *Culture and the bilingual classroom. Studies in classroom ethnography*. Rowley: Newbury House.
T'sou, Benjamin K.
1988   *Language planning issues on English in Hong Kong: pre and post 1997*, Presented at the 1988 Regional Seminar on Language Planning in a Multilingual Setting: the Role of English, 6 – 8 September 1988, Singapore.
Tsuda, Yukio
1986   *Language inequality and distortion in intercultural communication*, Amsterdam — Philadelphia: John Benjamin.
Turi, Joseph-G.
1977   *Les dispositions juridico-constitutionnelles de 147 Etats en matière de politique linguistique*. Québec: CIRB, Université Laval.

Turi, Joseph-G.
1989   "Introduction au droit linguistique", in: Pupier — Woehrling (eds.), 55—84.
Turi, Joseph-G.
1990   "Le droit linguistique et les droits linguistiques", *Les Cahiers de Droit*, Montréal, 31: 641—650.
Türk, Danilo
1990   "Minority protection in human rights conventions", Paper presented at the conference on *Minority rights policies and practice in South-East Europe*, Copenhagen, March 30-April 1, 1990, Copenhagen — London: The Danish Helsinki Committee and the Minority Rights Group.
United Nations General Assembly
1948   *Convention on the Prevention and Punishment of the Crime of Genocide*, Adopted December 9, 1948.
United Nations General Assembly
1948   *Universal Declaration of Human Rights*, Adopted December 10, 1948.
United Nations General Assembly
1966   *International Covenant on Economic, Social and Cultural Rights*, Adopted December 16, 1966.
UN
1990   *The African Charter on Human and Peoples' Rights*, hr/pub/90/1, Geneva: United Nations, Centre for Human Rights.
UN
1991   *Second Decade to Combat Racism and Racial Discrimination. Global compilation of national legislation against racial discrimination*, hr/pub/90/8, May 1991. Geneva: United Nations, Centre for Human Rights.
UN
1991   *Report of the Seminar on the political, historical, economic, social and cultural factors contributing to racism, racial discrimination and apartheid*, hr/pub/91/ 3, November 1991. Geneva: United Nations, Centre for Human Rights.
Unesco
1953   *The use of the vernacular languages in education*. Paris: UNESCO.
Unesco
1991   *Access to human rights documentation: documentation, databases and bibliographies on human rights*. Paris: UNESCO.
UNIN
1981   (Chamberlain, Richard — Amenita Diallo — E. J. John) *Toward a language policy for Namibia. English as the official language: perspectives and strategies*. Lusaka: United Nations Institute for Namibia.
United Nations
1991—92   *Human Rights Fact Sheets*, No 12 (May 1991), No 15 (May 1991), No 16 (October 1991), No 18 (March 1992). Geneva: United Nations.
Uotila, J. (ed.)
1985   *The Finnish legal system*. Helsinki: Finnish Lawyers Publishing Company.
U. S. Government Printing Office
1886   *Annual Report of the Commissioner of Indian Affairs to the Secretary of the Interior*, Washington D. C.
Valdés, Luz María
1988   *El perfil demográfico de los indios mexicanos*. México: Siglo XXI.

Valdez, Luis — Stan Steiner
1972   *Aztlán: An anthology of Mexican American literature.* New York: Alfred
          A. Knopf.
van Bruinessen, M. M.
1978   *Agha, shaikh and state. On the social and political organization of Kurdistan.*
          Utrecht: University of Utrecht.
Varese, Stefano
1983   *Indígenas y educación en México.* México: CEE-GEFE.
Varese, Stefano
1987   "La cultura como recurso el desafío de la educación indígena en el marco de
          un desarrollo nacional autónomo", in: Zuñiga et al (eds.), 169—192.
Varese, Stefano — Nemesio Rodríguez
1983   "Etnias indígenas y educación en América Latina diagnóstico y perspectivas",
          in: Rodríguez et al (eds.), 3—56.
Veltman, Calvin
1983   *Language shift in the United States.* Berlin: Mouton.
Veltman, Calvin
1988   "Modelling the language shift process of Hispanic immigrants", *International
          Migration Review,* 22: 545—562.
Verdoodt, Albert
1985   *Les droits linguistiques des immigrants,* Dossiers du Conseil de la Langue
          Française. Québec: Editeur officiel du Québec.
Verdoodt, Albert
1991   "Writing and schooling in the regional languages of the member states of the
          Council of Europe", in: García (ed.), 61—71.
Verhoeven, Ludo
1991   "Acquisition of biliteracy", in: Hulstijn — Matter (eds.), 61—74.
Viikberg, Jüri
1990   "The Siberian Estonians and language policy", in: Gorter et al (eds.),
          175—180.
Villoro, Luis
1950   *Los grandes momentos del indigenismo en México.* México: El Colegio de
          México (2nd ed. 1979, México: CIESAS).
Voigt, Pelle
1989   "The Human Rights Provisions of the 1975 Helsinki Accords and the Kurds",
          in: *Human rights in Kurdistan,* 162—166.
Waitangi Tribunal
1986   *Finding of the Waitangi Tribunal relating to Te Reo Maori and a claim lodged
          by Huirangi Waikarapuru and Nga Kaiwhakapumau i Te Reo Incorporated
          Society (the Wellington Board of Maori Language),* issued April 29, 1986.
          Wellington: New Zealand Government Printer.
Wakefield, W.
1975   *History of Kashmir: the Happy Valley,* Seema Publications [first published in
          the 1880s].
Wald, Paul — Philippe Poutignat
1982   "L'identité est-elle signifiable?", in: Gendron et al (eds.), 32—38.
Wayment, Hilary G. (ed.)
1961   *English teaching abroad and the British universities.* London: Methuen.

Weinstein, Brian (ed.)
  1990   *Language policy and political development.* Norwood, NJ: Ablex.
West, Michael P.
  1926   *Bilingualism* (with special reference to Bengal). Calcutta: Bureau of Education.
Whorf, Benjamin Lee
  1956   *Language, thought, and reality: selected writings of Benjamin Lee Whorf,* edited
          by J. B. Carrol. New York: Wiley.
Widdowson, Henry G.
  1983   *Learning purpose and language use.* London: Oxford University Press.
Wildhaber, Luzius
  1989   "Le droit à l'autodétermination et les droits des minorités linguistiques en
          droit international", in: Pupier — Woehrling (eds.), 117–132.
Wilkinson, Louise Cherry (ed.)
  1982   *Communicating in the classroom.* New York: Academic Press.
Williams, Colin — John Ambrose
  1988   "On measuring language border areas", in: Williams (ed.), 93–135.
Williams, Colin (ed.)
  1988   *Language in geographic context.* Clevedon, Avon: Multilingual Matters.
Williams, Glyn
  1980   "Review of E. Allardt's Implications of the ethnic revival in modern industrial
          society", *Journal of Multilingual and Multicultural Development,* 1: 363–370.
Wittrock, M. C. (ed.)
  1986   *Handbook of research on teaching.* (3rd ed.) New York: Macmillan.
Woehrling, Jean-Marie
  1992   "Institutions européennes et droits linguistiques des minorités", in: Giordan
          (ed.), 509–522.
Wolfgang, A. (ed.)
  1975   *Education of immigrant students.* Toronto: Ontario Institute for Studies in
          Education.
Wong Fillmore, Lily
  1982   "Instructional language as linguistic input: second-language learning in class-
          rooms", in: Wilkinson (ed.), 283–294.
Wong Fillmore, Lily
  1991   "When learning a second language means losing the first", *Early Childhood
          Research Quarterly* 6: 323–346.
Wong Fillmore, Lily — Paul Ammon
  1984   *Language learning in bilingual instruction.* Berkeley: University of California.
Wong Fillmore, Lily — Concepcion Valdez
  1986   "Teaching bilingual learners", in: Wittrock (ed.), 648–685.
World Bank
  1988   *Education in sub-Saharan Africa: policies for adjustment, revitalization and
          expansion.* Washington, D. C.: World Bank (summarized in *Comparative
          Education Review,* February 1989).
Wright, R.
  1987   "Escape to Canada". *Saturday Night,* May 1987, 44–52.
Yorio, C. A. — K. Perkins — J. Schachter (eds.)
  1979   *On TESOL '79: The learner in focus,* Washington, D. C.: TESOL.

Young, Christabel — Michael Petty — Arthur Faulkner
1980   *Education and employment of Turkish and Lebanese youth.* Canberra: Austra-
          lian Government Publishing Service.
Young, C M.
1935   *Speeches of Lord Macaulay.* London: Oxford University Press.
Zuanelli Sonino, Elisabeta (ed.)
1989   *Literacy in school and society: multidisciplinary perspectives.* New York: Ple-
          num.
Zúñiga, Madeleine — Juan Ansion — Luis Ceva (eds.)
1987   *Educación en poblaciones indigenas. Políticas y estrategias en América Latina.*
          Santiago de Chile: III-UNESCO/OREALC.

Notes on contributors

Sertaç Bucak is a Kurdish engineer and political refugee. He organized international conferences in Bremen in 1989 and Bonn in 1991 on human rights issues in Kurdistan, the proceedings of both of which have been published in German and English. He chairs the International Association for Human Rights in Kurdistan, PO Box 104551, D-2800 Bremen 1, Germany.

Jim Cummins, born in Ireland, has lived in Canada since 1971, where his writings have been influential in the bilingual education field. He has for many years been attached to the Modern Language Centre of the Ontario Institute for Studies in Education, Toronto, from 1991 to 1993 as its Director, and as head of the Heritage Language Centre.

Joshua A. Fishman is the author of more than 700 professional articles, reviews and books, general editor and founder of the *International Journal of the Sociology of Language*, and was honoured with four Festschriften for his 65th birthday in 1991. He is Emeritus Professor at Yeshiva University, New York. In his family life he is also practically concerned with counteracting language shift.

John Gibbons has been involved in language education in Spain, UK, Kenya, Poland, Hong Kong, China, Indonesia and Australia. For the last ten years he has run the MA in Applied Linguistics at the University of Sydney, where he teaches, among others, a course on bilingualism and bilingual education.

Pauline Gibbons has been involved in language education in the Solomon Islands, Iran, Germany, UK, Poland, Hong Kong, the Marshall Islands and Australia, and is author of *Learning to learn a second language*. When this article was written she was a Multicultural Adviser with the Catholic Education Office, and worked with St Mel's School in the development of the curriculum. She is a Lecturer in Language and Literacy (TESOL) at the University of Technology, Sydney.

François Grin (Ph.D., economics, Geneva) specializes in the economic analysis of language use and language policy, with particular emphasis on minority language protection, language rights, and language use in multicultural settings. After attachments to the Universities of Seattle and Montréal, he returned to Université de Genève, Département d'économie politique, in 1993.

Rainer Enrique Hamel is of Chilean and German origin, has a doctorate in Romance linguistics from the University of Frankfurt, and has lived in Mexico since 1978. He is Professor of Linguistics in the Anthropology Department of the Universidad Autónoma Metropolitana in Mexico City. His main research interests are sociolinguistics, discourse analysis, applied linguistics and anthropology.

Eduardo Hernández-Chávez is Associate Professor of Linguistics at the University of New Mexico in Albuquerque, where he teaches courses on bilingualism annd sociolinguistics. He has worked for many years with migrant farmworkers and other community groups on issues of educational and linguistic rights. He is currently researching into language shift and loss within the Chicano community.

Björn H. Jernudd is Reader in the Department of English Language and Literature, Hong Kong Baptist College. Formerly associated with the East-West Center, Honolulu, his main interests are language planning and international communication, see *The politics of language purism* (de Gruyter, 1989, edited with M. Shapiro) and *Lectures on language problems* (Bahri Publications, Delhi, 1990).

Tīmoti S. Kāretu was brought up bilingually in Māori and English. Since 1987 he has been alternately the Māori Language Commissioner for Rotearoa/New Zealand, the first to occupy the post, and Professor of Māori at Waikato University.

Lachman M. Khubchandani has a doctorate from the University of Pennsylvania and has taught in India, USA, UK, Yugoslavia, Singapore and Sudan. He has worked as a language planning consultant for UNESCO, at the East-West Center, Honolulu, and is currently director of the Centre for Communication Studies, Pune, India. His most recent book is *Tribal identity: a language and communication perspective* (Indus, 1992).

Alexei A. Leontiev has doctorates in philology and psychology, directs the Moscow Language Centre, and is a Professor of Psychology at the Academy of Sciences, Moscow. He has served as an adviser on language policy to the Russian Federation.

Robert Phillipson is British, and has taught English in Algeria, Yugoslavia and, since 1973, Denmark. He has a doctorate from the University of Amsterdam. He is currently Head of the Department of Languages and Culture, University of Roskilde. His main publications are on linguistic imperialism and the role of English worldwide, and language pedagogy.

Ole Henrik Magga has a doctorate in Finno-Ugric languages from the University of Oslo and is a Professor of Sámi at the Sámi University in Guovdageaidnu. He is chair of the Sámi Parliament, Norway, a member of the Norwegian Academy of Sciences and of UNESCO's World Commission on Culture and Development.

Mart Rannut was one of the authors of the Estonian language law of 1989. He is Director-General of the National Language Board, Republic of Estonia, and adviser to the Estonian President on human rights matters. Since 1993 he has also been Secretary-General of the Estonian Institute of Human Rights.

Tove Skutnabb-Kangas is a Finnish-Swedish bilingual Finn with doctorates from Helsinki and Roskilde. She has lived in Denmark since 1979. She has written extensively on bilingualism, minority education, linguistic rights and countering linguistic imperialism through empowerment. She is Reader in Minority Education and Linguistic Human Rights at the University of Ostrobothnia, Vasa, Finland.

Jerzy Smolicz, born in Poland, educated in Britain, holds the Chair of Education at the University of Adelaide, where he directs the Centre for Intercultural Studies and Multicultural Education. He has advised the State and Federal Governments on policy on linguistic and cultural pluralism and its implementation in Australian education, and authored books and government reports on this subject.

Makhan L. Tickoo has a Ph.D. from the University of London. He has had a long career in language education and materials development for English in India and Singapore, where he is currently at the Regional Language Centre (RELC).

Joseph-G. Turi, of French and Italian origin, has a doctorate in law from the University of Naples. He has specialized in the study of how constitutional laws express language rights. Since 1979 head of the law department of the Commission de protection de la langue française, Montréal, and Secretary General of the International Academy of Language Law.

William White has been involved in language education for more than thirty years in Papua New Guinea and Australia, and has been Coordinator, ESL and Multicultural Education for the Catholic Archdiocese of Sydney. As Principal of St Mel's School where the study described in this book was carried out, he applies the principles he formerly propounded.

Languages Index (languages, dialects/variants/ varieties, language families)

Person Index

Subject Index

ethnic/ethnocultural 7, 58, 93, 95, 104,
121, 147, 192, 278, 284–285, 295, 350, 353,
358, 369
linguistic 2, 10, 93, 95, 192, 237, 311, 350,
356, 361
loyalty (to) 13, 125, 237, 305, 314, 364
multiple 59, 305–315, 361
primordial 7, 306, 314, 362
right to, see right
"illiterate", see orate
ILO 16
ILO Convention 169 on Indigenous and
Tribal Peoples 231, 371, 395–395
immersion, see education/al programmes
immigrant rights, see rights
immigrants, see minorities, im/migrant
imperialism, see linguistic imperialism
imprisonment 2, 20, 73, 110, 199, 225, 227,
347–348, 350–351, 355, 357–358, 364,
368–370
inclusion 38
India 13, 71
India-Pakistan partition 305
indigeneous language/s, see language/s
indigenous   movements/organizing,   see
movements/organizing
indigenous peoples 13, 78, 83, 98, 189, 209–
233, 271–303
Indonesia 122, 328
Ingrians 182, 198
Ingushetia 66, 182
integration 100, 106, 158, 193, 206, 273, 276,
289, 291, 295
inter-ethnic communication, see language/s
in inter-ethnic communication
international language 184
International   Association   for   Human
Rights in Kurdistan 370
International Court of Justice 76
interpretation/translation 15, 85, 142, 150–
153, 210, 222, 227
Iran 168, 349, 369
Iraq 170, 349, 355, 369
Ireland 109
Islam/muslims 122, 131, 328, 354
islamization 350
Italy 109

Japan 123, 149
Japanese, in U.S.A. 149
Jew/ish 123, 131, 195
Jin 350–351
Judenfrei 196

Kabylia 337
Kalmyk 182
Karabakh 180
Karaganov doctrine 193
Kashmir 317–333
Kazakhstan 190, 192
killing of language/s, see linguicide
Kirgizia/Kirgizstan 182, 190
Kōhanga Reo 213–214, 217
Koran 337
Kosova Albanians, see Albanians
Kuijpers Resolution 90–91, 359
Kurd, Bonn Declaration 371, 412
Kurd, Bremen Declaration 353
Kurdistan (country) 347–370
Kurdistan (newspaper) 350–351
Kurds 3, 11, 65, 71, 81, 108, 347–370
Kuwait 170

L1 as medium, see also mother tongue; 71,
76, 90, 94, 97, 109–110, 329, 335, 347–370
L1 as subject 63–64, 68, 71, 90, 92–94, 97,
109–110, 162, 355
L2 as medium, see also immersion; 106, 159,
213, 280, 323–325, 343
L2 as medium, Swahili 343
L2 as subject 68, 70, 110, 243, 243, 355, 364
labour migrant(s)/migration, see migrant(s)/
migration
Ladins 54
language as defining characteristic 10, 105,
107, 237, 307
as subject 216–217
chauvinism 183, 305
consciousness of –, see awareness
death, risk of –, see linguicide
deprivation of – 1–24, 71, 104, 246, 293,
347–370
development 2, 72, 350–351, 356, 367
law/legislation, see law/s
maintenance of –, see maintenance